Teen Health

Course 1

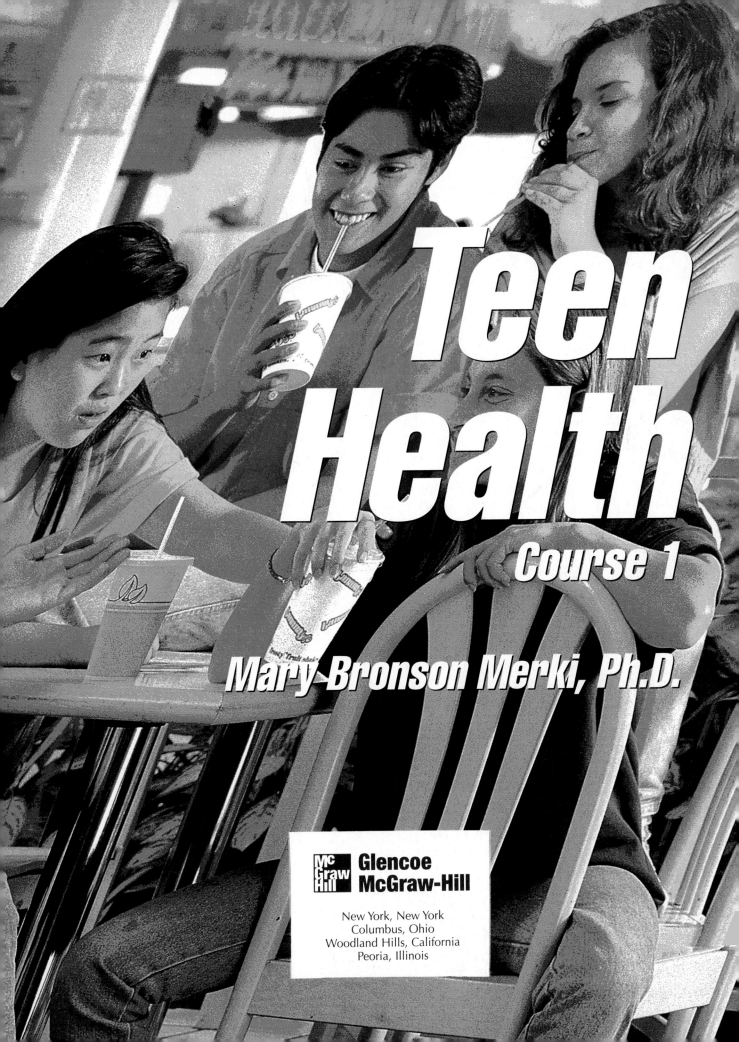

Teen Health

Course 1

Mary Bronson Merki, Ph.D.

Glencoe McGraw-Hill

New York, New York
Columbus, Ohio
Woodland Hills, California
Peoria, Illinois

Meet the Author

Mary Bronson Merki has taught health education in grades K–12, as well as health education methods classes at the undergraduate and graduate levels. As Health Education Specialist for the Dallas School District, Dr. Merki developed and implemented a district-wide health education program, *Skills for Living,* which was used as a model by the state education agency. She also helped develop and implement the district's Human Growth, Development and Sexuality program, which won the National PTA's Excellence in Education Award and earned her an honorary lifetime membership in the state PTA. Dr. Merki has assisted school districts throughout the country in developing local health education programs. In 1988, she was named the Texas Health Educator of the Year by the Texas Association for Health, Physical Education, Recreation, and Dance. Dr. Merki is also the author of *Glencoe Health,* a high school textbook adopted in school districts throughout the country. She currently teaches in a Texas public school where she was recently honored as Teacher of the Year. Dr. Merki completed her undergraduate work at Colorado State University in Fort Collins, Colorado. She earned her masters and doctoral degrees in health education at Texas Woman's University in Denton, Texas.

Editorial and production services
provided by Visual Education Corporation, Princeton, NJ.

Design by Bill Smith Studio, New York, NY.

Glencoe/McGraw-Hill
A Division of The McGraw-Hill Companies

Printed in the United States of America.

Send all inquiries to:
Glencoe/McGraw-Hill
21600 Oxnard Street, Suite 500
Woodland Hills, CA 91367

ISBN 0-02-651774-4 (Course 1 Student Text)
ISBN 0-02-651775-2 (Course 1 Teacher's Wraparound Edition)

4 5 6 7 8 9 10 11 12   004/043   04 03 02 01 00 99 98

Health Consultants

Unit 1
A Healthy You

Alice B. Pappas, Ph.D., R.N.
Assistant Professor
Baylor University School of Nursing
Dallas, Texas

E. Laurette Taylor, Ph.D.
Associate Professor
Department of Health and Sport Sciences
University of Oklahoma
Norman, Oklahoma

Unit 2
The Healthy Body

Peter D. Wood, Ph.D., D.Sc.
Professor of Medicine, Emeritus
Stanford University School of Medicine
Palo Alto, California

Kathleen M. Speer, Ph.D., P.N.P., R.N.
Joint appointment: University of Texas at
    Arlington and Children's Medical Center
    of Dallas
Dallas, Texas

David M. Allen, M.D.
Infectious Diseases Consultants of North
    Dallas
Dallas, Texas

Unit 3
Protecting Your Health

Mark Dignan, Ph.D.
Associate Professor
Department of Family and Community
    Medicine
Bowman-Gray School of Medicine
Winston-Salem, North Carolina

Prevention Materials Review Unit
National Clearinghouse for Alcohol and
    Drug Information
Rockville, Maryland

David Sleet, Ph.D.
Professor
San Diego State University
San Diego, California

Teacher Reviewers

Unit 1
A Healthy You

Randall F. Nitchie
Health Specialist
Osseo Public Schools, District #279
Maple Grove, Minnesota

Laura Williams
Health and Science Teacher
Memphis City Schools
Memphis, Tennessee

Unit 2
The Healthy Body

Raynette Evans
Director of Health, Physical Education, and
    Athletics
Bibb County Public Schools
Macon, Georgia

Ann Orman
Science/Health Teacher
West End Middle School
Nashville, Tennessee

Unit 3
Protecting Your Health

JoCyel Rodgers
Health Teacher
Glencrest Middle School
Fort Worth, Texas

Brenda C. Wilson
Director of Health Education
Iredell Statesville Schools
Statesville, North Carolina

Brief Contents

Contents

Unit 1
A Healthy You

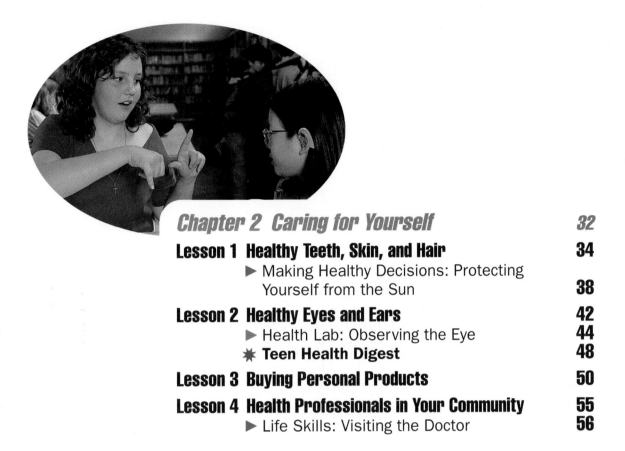

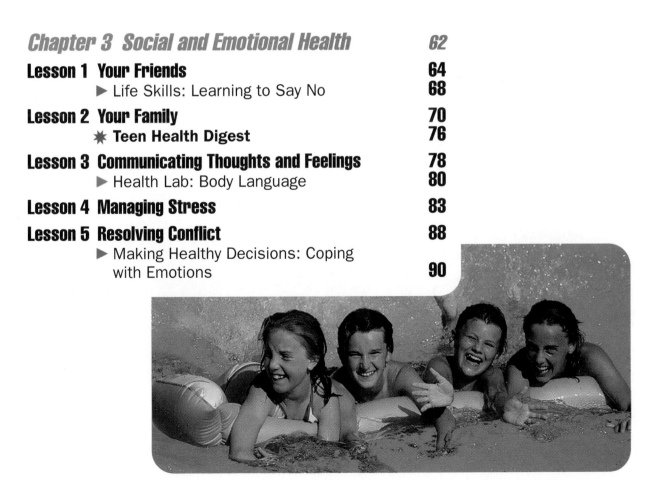

Unit 2
The Healthy Body

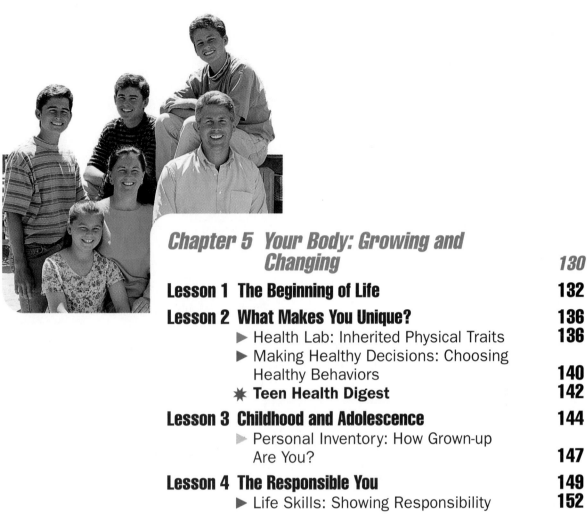

Unit 3
Protecting Your Health

Features

Health Lab

Life Skills

Making Healthy Decisions

Personal Inventory

Teen HEALTH DIGEST

Unit 1
A Healthy You

1

Chapter 1
Planning for a Healthy Lifetime

2

I can't decide what to do. Next month the county soccer league is having team tryouts. I've always enjoyed playing soccer, and my dad likes to come watch me play. My problem is that I want to try out for the school band too. My music teacher's been encouraging me, and my best friend's in the band. I can't play soccer *and* be in the band because practices are held at the same time.

I decided to ask my older cousin William for his opinion. To me, he's always seemed to know what he wanted and how to get it. He was a star of the track team and got good grades. Last month he got a great job.

When I asked him, he said he wasn't always sure what to do when faced with a problem like mine. He suggested that I do what he's learned to do when making important choices. He thinks about what is most important to him. Once he figures that out, he makes a plan for achieving his goal.

I must have had a puzzled look on my face, because he said he'd be glad to help me make a plan. I feel better already.

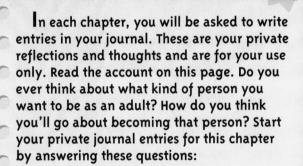

in your journal

In each chapter, you will be asked to write entries in your journal. These are your private reflections and thoughts and are for your use only. Read the account on this page. Do you ever think about what kind of person you want to be as an adult? How do you think you'll go about becoming that person? Start your private journal entries for this chapter by answering these questions:

► Do you feel that you are healthy?
► What is your view of yourself?
► Do you feel that the decisions you make are good for your health and well-being?
► What goals do you have?

When you reach the end of the chapter, you will use your journal entries to make an action plan.

The Health Triangle

This lesson will help you find answers to questions that teens often ask about health. For example:

▶ **How do I know if I'm healthy?**
▶ **What do I need to do to be healthy?**
▶ **What level of health should I aim for?**

Words to Know

health
wellness
prevention

The Three Sides of Health

"Hi, how are you?" is a greeting you hear often. How would you answer? If you're not sick, you'll probably answer, "Fine." However, there's a lot more to being healthy than just feeling good physically. For example, would you say that someone who often seems depressed or someone who is very shy is healthy?

Health is a *combination of physical, mental, and social well-being.* It might help you to think of health as a triangle. One side of the triangle is your physical health—the condition of your body. The second side is your mental/emotional health—your thoughts, feelings, and emotions. The third side of the triangle is your social health—the way you relate to others.

Figure 1.1 shows the triangle of a healthy person. Notice that the three sides are of equal length. A healthy person pays equal attention to physical, mental/emotional, and social health.

Which sides of the health triangle are these teens working on?

Elements of Physical Health

You can look after your body in a number of ways:

- Keep fit by getting regular exercise.

- Eat a well-balanced diet.

- Maintain your ideal weight.

- Practice good grooming habits.

- Avoid tobacco, alcohol, and drugs.

- Get plenty of rest.

Elements of Mental/Emotional Health

Just as you need to exercise and care for your body, you need to exercise and care for your mind too. Here are some ways you can stay mentally and emotionally healthy:

- Accept yourself and like who you are.

- Express your feelings in a healthy way.

- Develop your thinking and decision-making skills.

- Strive to learn new information.

- Learn ways of dealing with life's problems.

- Learn how to handle stress.

in your journal

Review the elements of physical health in this lesson. In your journal, make a list of the elements you think you practice. Make a second list of the elements you think you need to work on.

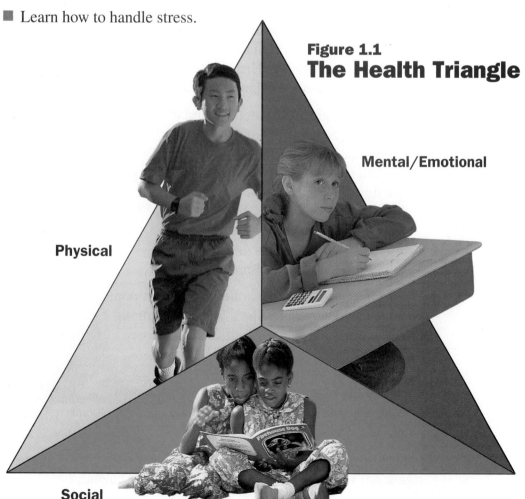

Figure 1.1
The Health Triangle

Mental/Emotional

Physical

Social

Teen Issues

Elements of Social Health

Your social health relates to the way you get along with other people. If you have good social health, you will be able to

■ get along with family members.

■ make and keep friends.

■ work well in a group.

■ disagree with others without fighting.

■ give and get support when it is needed.

Making Health Connections

Like the sides of a triangle, the three sides of your health are connected. Each side affects the other two. When you are healthy, your health triangle is balanced. When you neglect one part of your health, the other parts are affected and your health triangle becomes unbalanced. Here are some examples to show this:

■ **Dan's triangle.** Dan enjoys sports. He's on the swim team and the track team. When he's not at practice or competing, he likes to read sports magazines. He never seems to have enough time for his family and friends and is often too tired to do his schoolwork. His grades are low, and he's worried he'll have to repeat a year.

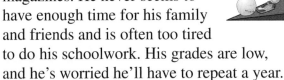

■ **Zoe's triangle.** Zoe is determined to get good grades—perhaps too determined. She studies hard most evenings and often spends time in the library on weekends. She takes little time out to see her friends. Lately, it seems, she doesn't have any friends. She sometimes goes hiking with her family, but she gets no other exercise.

■ **Kim's triangle.** Kim is one of the most popular girls in her class. She's always arranging sleepovers and spends hours on the phone talking with her friends. She likes getting all the attention but notices that she's often tired and grumpy. She always has to rely on last-minute studying before a test.

Dan, Zoe, and Kim all have unbalanced triangles. Can you figure out what they need to do to get a better balance?

Maintaining Your Health Balance

To be truly healthy, you need to work to keep your health triangle balanced. On the social side, you should spend time with both family and friends. You also need to find time to exercise regularly, eat right, and get enough rest. The social and physical sides then need to be carefully balanced with your mental/emotional side. You need to take time to study, to learn, and to think.

Nobody's health triangle is perfectly balanced all the time. However, a healthy person is aware enough to know that he or she must make a change when one side starts to get out of balance.

Spending time with your family helps to balance the social side of your triangle.

Personal Inventory

HOW HEALTHY ARE YOU?

To find out if your health triangle is balanced, write yes or no for each statement below. Use a separate sheet of paper.

Physical Health

1. I eat a well-balanced diet.

2. I snack on healthful foods.

3. I sleep eight or nine hours a night.

4. I exercise regularly.

5. I do not use tobacco, alcohol, or drugs.

6. I am within 5 pounds of my ideal weight.

7. I am usually energetic and feel good.

Mental/Emotional Health

1. I like to learn new subjects.

2. I can laugh easily.

3. I like to be alone sometimes.

4. I can name several things I do well.

5. I can tell others what I'm feeling.

6. I ask for help when I need it.

7. I take responsibility for my actions.

Social Health

1. I meet people easily.

2. I have several close friends.

3. When I have a problem with someone, I try to work it out.

4. I work well in a group.

5. I can say no to my friends.

6. I do not talk behind people's backs.

7. I get along with several different groups.

Give yourself 1 point for each yes. In any area, a score of 6–7 is very good. If you score 0–2 in any area, that side of your triangle needs work.

Wellness

As you strive each day to maintain your health balance, you are working for wellness. **Wellness** is *the achievement of a high level of overall health.* If you work at it, this high level of health can last for many years. Of course, you must take care of health problems as they come up. Even more importantly, you should look for ways to protect and improve your health.

One of the keys to wellness is the prevention of illness. **Prevention** is *keeping something from happening.* You can help prevent illness and injury in these ways:

■ Don't take unnecessary chances or risks. Avoid thinking that nothing can happen to you.

■ Know the weaknesses in your physical, mental/emotional, and social health and work on them.

■ Keep informed about health-related issues.

■ Be responsible. Do not leave your health to chance.

Degrees of Wellness

Many people, especially young people, think little about their health. As long as they don't have an illness, they think they are healthy. That is not true. There are several levels of health, as shown in **Figure 1.2.** It takes effort to stay at a high level of health and wellness.

Your Total Health

Avoid Smoking

One way to keep physically healthy is to avoid unhealthful activities such as smoking. People who smoke for many years increase their risk of lung cancer, stroke, and heart disease. Teenagers who smoke are also likely to have health problems such as decreased stamina, a fast heart rate, and coughing.

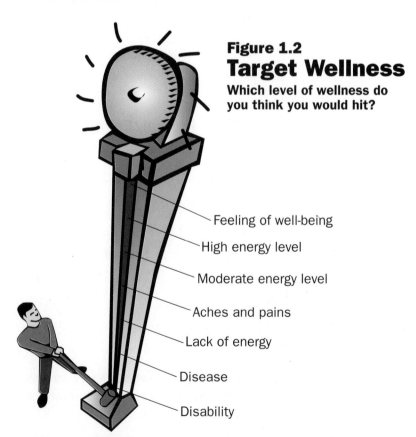

Figure 1.2
Target Wellness
Which level of wellness do you think you would hit?

Feeling of well-being

High energy level

Moderate energy level

Aches and pains

Lack of energy

Disease

Disability

Good Health Habits to Achieve Wellness

One of the first ways to achieve a high level of physical, mental/emotional, and social health is to take a look at your present health habits in each of those areas. Ignoring your health or practicing harmful habits may lead to illness or injury. Use the checklist in **Figure 1.3** to see whether you are on the road to wellness. Now is the time to start learning healthful habits. It is much easier to start a good habit now than to have to change a bad habit later.

Figure 1.3
Good Health Checklist

✔ Eat three meals a day at regular times.
✔ Eat nutritious foods low in fat, sugar, and cholesterol.
✔ Get eight to nine hours of sleep a night.
✔ Exercise at least moderately three to four times a week.
✔ Have regular medical and dental checkups.
✔ To prevent injury, think before you act.
✔ Use car seat belts and sports safety equipment.
✔ Avoid alcohol, drugs, and tobacco.
✔ Take time to relax when you are feeling stress.
✔ Try to get along with family and friends.
✔ Think positively and try to have an upbeat outlook.

Review

Lesson 1

Using complete sentences, answer the following questions on a separate sheet of paper.

Reviewing Terms and Facts

1. **Vocabulary**   Define the terms *health* and *wellness*. Use these words in a sentence that shows how health and wellness are related.

2. **Give Examples**   Name three examples of how the level of your health in one area can affect your health in another area.

3. **Identify**   What are two ways you can prevent illness and injury?

4. **List**   Name three health habits you can practice to reach a high degree of wellness. Choose one from each area of health.

Thinking Critically

5. **Explain**   Why do you think many young people take unnecessary risks with their health?

6. **Generalize**   How can positive social relationships promote good health?

Applying Health Concepts

7. **Personal Health**   Make a time line of your activities for a full 24-hour period. Next to each activity, state which side of the health triangle you are working on. Are your activities balanced to take equal care of your physical, mental, and social health?

8. **Health of Others**   Using pictures cut from magazines, make a poster that shows people who are working to promote their physical health.

Your Self-Concept

This lesson will help you find answers to questions that teens often ask about how they see themselves and how others see them. For example:

▶ How do I find out who I am?

▶ How do I know how others feel about me?

▶ How does my view of myself affect my health?

Words to Know

self-concept
reinforce
self-esteem

 in your journal

How do you see yourself? In your journal, write five words or phrases that you would use to describe yourself. Briefly tell why you think each word or phrase applies to you.

Self-Concept and Your Health

As you grow and develop, you find out a lot about yourself. You learn

■ what you think about different issues.

■ what is important to you.

■ what you like and don't like.

■ who you like to be with.

■ what you do well.

■ what you need to improve.

In other words, you get a picture of who you are. *This view that you have of yourself* is your **self-concept,** or self-image. Part of your self-concept is how you think others see you.

It is important to your overall health to have a clear view of yourself. Then you will be able to focus on your good points and improve your weaknesses. If you know yourself well, you will know what you need to do to stay physically, mentally, emotionally, and socially healthy.

Bringing your self-concept into focus is one of the tasks of your teen years.

Who Influences Your Self-Concept?

The way you see yourself is influenced by many people. When you're young, your parents are your greatest influence. You are affected by how they treat you and what they say to you. Other relatives—grandparents, brothers, and sisters—also affect how you see yourself. When you start school, friends and teachers start to have an impact on you.

People send messages through words and actions. These messages can be positive or negative. They help to **reinforce,** or *support,* the way you view yourself. Each message has an impact on your self-concept. **Figure 1.4** illustrates how one teen's self-concept was positively affected by those around him.

Literature Connection

Important Influences ACTIVITY!

Read the life story of a famous person you admire. Take note of who influenced the person to become great. Did the person overcome negative influences or benefit from positive ones?

Figure 1.4
Building a Good Self-Concept

This teen has received positive messages that are helping him reinforce his belief that he has a talent for growing beautiful flowers.

Q: I act differently when I'm with different people. Am I a phony?

A: Stop worrying. It's natural to relate to different people in different ways. With some friends, you may be quiet and serious. With others, you may joke a lot. All that means is that you have many sides to your personality.

How to Develop a Positive Self-Concept

Here are some ways you can develop a good self-concept:

■ Concentrate on what you do well. If you aren't athletic but you like music, try out for the band, not the soccer team.

■ Don't be too hard on yourself. If you put yourself down all the time, others may start to see you that way too.

■ When you need help, ask people you trust. Their help is likely to build rather than break down your self-image.

■ As you grow during your teens, your self-concept will change. You may want to try out different roles during this time to see which ones you are most comfortable with. It is better to do this with people you trust.

■ Don't read too much into each look or word. People may not mean to be hurtful, or they may offer criticism to help you.

Effects of a Good Self-Concept

When you feel good about yourself, you can do the following:

■ Build high **self-esteem,** which is *the ability to like and respect yourself.*

■ Have confidence in yourself.

■ Feel valued, loved, and secure.

■ Care about yourself and want to take care of your health.

HEALTH LAB
Reinforcement and Self-Concept

*I*ntroduction: The way you are treated by other people affects your self-concept. You are likely to feel good when people say positive things about you or are nice to you. However, when people say negative things or treat you poorly, you may start to feel bad about yourself. Your words and actions can also have the same effect on others.

Objective: Using role-playing, examine the effect that your treatment of others can have on their self-concept.

Materials and Method: With your classmates, develop one of the following role-playing situations to show ways you can help others to develop a good self-concept.

► Over the summer, one of your classmates has grown much taller than everyone else in the class. She feels very self-conscious.

► A student who is new in school comes into your computer club meeting and asks to join.

► One of your classmates isn't doing well in math and is worried about an upcoming test.

- Care about others and get along well with others.

- Bounce back after a disappointment.

You will be able to concentrate on your good points and not focus too much on your faults. You'll be able to stand up for what is important to you. You'll be able to make good choices as you face the many decisions of your teen years.

Review

Lesson 2

Using complete sentences, answer the following questions on a separate sheet of paper.

Reviewing Terms and Facts

1. **Vocabulary** Define the terms *self-concept* and *self-esteem.* Use these terms in a sentence.

2. **Identify** Name three people who have had a positive influence on your self-concept.

3. **Give Examples** Name three ways to develop a positive self-concept.

Thinking Critically

4. **Explain** Why is having a good self-concept important to overall health?

5. **Describe** Write a short biography of someone who you think has a good self-concept. You can create a person or use a real person.

Applying Health Concepts

6. **Personal Health** Write a paragraph starting with the phrase "I can feel good about myself because . . ."

Nice pass!

Have one member of the group assume the role of the person with the problem. Others can be friends or classmates who might be able to help. Have them role-play ways that they could show interest and provide support and encouragement.

Observation and Analysis: Discuss the outcome of the role-playing situations. How would the actions of those who helped affect the self-concept of the person with the problem? What might have been the outcome if these people did not support the person? What are some other situations in which your treatment of another person might help him or her build a good self-concept?

Teen HEALTH DIGEST

People at Work

School Counselor

Kevin Huang is a school counselor at the Griffith Middle School. He helps students who are having problems in the classroom. He also helps students work on family and personal problems.

One of the parts of his job that Kevin really enjoys is working with students whose troubles at home are affecting their classroom behavior. He works one-on-one with the student to find out what the problem is. He then tries to get the parents or guardians involved and to work out a solution that will help the student. His degrees in psychology and counseling have prepared Kevin well for handling these often sensitive issues.

Another part of his job that Kevin enjoys is holding informal group sessions. Students choose topics that concern them. Through these sessions, teachers and administrators learn what issues are on the students' minds, and the students get a chance to discuss problems that they may need help solving.

Myths and Realities

Is Thin Really In?

An old saying states, "You can never be too thin." Actually, being too thin can be very dangerous to your health.

A person who is seriously underweight is likely to lack energy and may be subject to many common illnesses and infections.

For some people, being thin becomes an illness. These people suffer from an eating disorder called anorexia nervosa. Many people with this disease are girls in their teens. They starve themselves because of their extreme fear of becoming overweight. Often, they must be hospitalized as their bodies are weakened to a near-death condition.

People with anorexia nervosa have an unrealistic self-concept. Even though they are so thin as to harm their health, they see themselves as being fat. To overcome this disorder, these people must change both their eating habits and their self-concept.

Teens Making a Difference

Sharing a Love of Reading

Tony Wynans is in the sixth grade. On his way home from school, he often stops by his local public library. Tony has always enjoyed going to the library to check out books. However, now he goes to the library to work.

Tony's library started a program to help get young children interested in reading. Two days a week, Tony spends an hour reading stories to small groups of three-year-olds. Sometimes he even gets the kids to act out the parts of the characters in the stories.

Tony doesn't get paid for his work at the library. He's a volunteer. According to Tony, seeing the smiling faces of the children is payment enough. Tony has gotten one other benefit. He always thought he wanted to be a teacher, and this experience has convinced him he does.

Sports
and
Recreation

Dedicated Quadrathlete

Andrea Spitzer has always been determined to reach her goals. When she was 13, she saved her baby-sitting money to pay for a trip to England she wanted to take.

Since then, she has traveled extensively and has become a professional model. Her desire to stay physically fit has led her to a new goal. She has now become a world champion at the quadrathlon sports event. This race includes four events: kayaking, running, swimming, and cycling.

Andrea spends five hours a day training to meet her new goal of winning the women's world championship for the third time. Her secret for doing what she sets out to do is "to set little goals and achieve them."

CON$UMER FOCU$

Seat Belts vs. Air Bags

Part of total wellness is practicing safe habits, including car safety. Many new cars are equipped with air bags, which inflate at the time of an accident. They are described as a safety feature that can save many lives. Do they?

Air bags do save lives. However, they are effective only when used with seat belts. You should always fasten your lap and shoulder seat belts when you ride in a car. You will increase your safety in a crash by 42 percent with seat belts. With air bags alone, you will be only 18 percent safer than if you had no protection. Also, most air bags inflate only when the front of the car is hit.

Air bags should be considered as an added protection but not as a replacement for seat belts.

Decision Making

This lesson will help you find answers to questions that teens often ask about making decisions. For example:

▶ **What kinds of decisions will I be making?**

▶ **How can I make wise decisions?**

▶ **How do the decisions I make affect my health?**

Words to Know

decision
consequence
risk
value

Types of Decisions

You face many decisions every day. **Decisions** are *choices you make.* Some decisions are minor, such as deciding what color shirt to wear. Other decisions are important. For example, as you go through adolescence and adulthood, you'll make decisions about school, job, and marriage. Making them carefully will help you be a happy and healthy person.

You are starting now to make many decisions that will affect your health and wellness. Some of the areas in which you have choices are mentioned here.

■ What foods to eat, when to eat, how much to eat

■ How to stay fit

■ Whether to try alcohol, tobacco, or drugs

■ How to stay safe

■ How to handle relationships with family and friends

■ How to organize your time to meet your obligations

During your teenage years, you will have many choices to make about the direction your life will take.

Making Everyday Decisions

How do you usually make the choices that you face each day? Do you

- just let things happen without thinking?
- do what you think will please others?
- act on impulse, or do what you feel like at that moment?
- act out of habit—do what you have always done?

These methods are quick shortcuts. They don't require much time or effort. After all, you don't need to give too much thought to deciding what to wear each day or whether to ride your bike or walk to tennis practice. These shortcuts may be harmless ways to make many everyday choices. However, important choices require more thought and planning.

Decision-Making Steps

When you have a serious problem or important choice to make, how do you deal with it? Do you worry a lot about the situation but not do anything to change it? Do you just ignore the problem, hoping it will go away? Perhaps you even use one of the methods that you use for minor choices. None of these ways will help you make a wise choice. In fact, using methods in which you don't think the problem through can hurt you.

The best approach to solving problems is to face the problem and work to find a solution. This task becomes easier if you approach the problem in the steps shown in **Figure 1.5.** Breaking a problem into steps allows you to deal with the problem in small, manageable parts.

Your Total Health

Decisions and Stress

If you have a serious problem to solve, you may become tense and not be able to sleep. These are some of the signs of stress. If you feel you have no control over the problem, the stress will get worse. All parts of your health will suffer. That is why it is so important to learn to practice the step-by-step decision-making process. You will solve your problem and help your level of health.

Figure 1.5
The Six Steps of Decision Making
Use this six-step process to make important decisions.

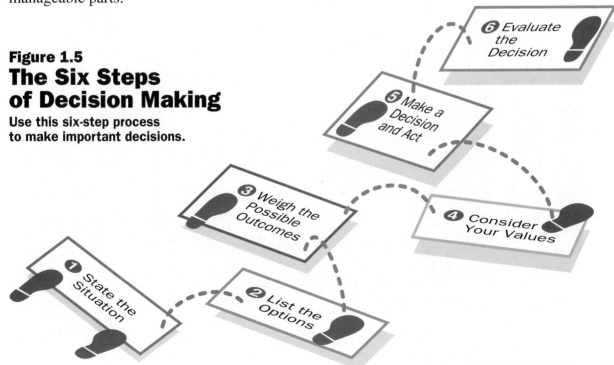

Step 1. State the Situation

The first step to solving any problem is to decide what the problem is. This may sound easy, but it is the most difficult step in solving a problem. You may find it helpful to ask yourself how the problem developed, who besides you is involved in the problem, and how much time you have to make your decision.

Look at Hannah's situation. Her family is moving to another state in the spring. Hannah is upset because she has a big part in a dance recital in June. Hannah's parents have offered her the chance to stay with her aunt to finish out the school year. Hannah's problem is that she wants to stay to perform in the recital, but she has never been away from her family before.

Step 2. List the Options

Think of as many ways as possible to solve the problem. Write down your choices. Ask for some suggestions from family, teachers, or friends. It is good to have as much information as possible as you weigh your options.

The obvious choices for Hannah are to move in the spring with her family or to stay with her aunt. Another option might be to move with the family and then return for the recital. Can you think of any other choices for Hannah?

Before making an important choice, it's a good idea to discuss your options with parents or other adults whose opinion you value.

Hannah should certainly talk to her parents and to her dance teacher. She should also talk to her aunt about what living with her will be like.

Step 3. Weigh the Possible Outcomes

Look at your list of options. Carefully think about the **consequences,** or *results,* of each option. Ask yourself, "What will happen if I carry out this option?" Be sure to think about what effects your decision will have on others besides yourself. Very few choices will make a difference to you alone.

Think about the following considerations:

- **The positive and negative parts of each option.** Every decision has some good points and some drawbacks. When you are making a decision, you should consider both.

- **The risks of each option.** A **risk** is *the chance of danger or loss.* Acting on many decisions involves some risks. If you face physical risks, you could become injured or sick. If you do something that affects another person, you may lose a friend or you may upset or disappoint your parents. Part of your choice should be whether the risk you take is reasonable or unreasonable. Is it necessary or unnecessary?

Literature Connection

Making Choices

The twentieth-century American poet Robert Frost wrote about choices: "Two roads diverged in a wood, and I—/I took the one less traveled by,/And that has made all the difference." If you think through your options and make your choices carefully, you'll be able to make a decision that's right for you—even if it isn't what everyone else is doing.

When deciding about a sport, you need to think about the risks of injury and weigh them against your skills and needs.

Think about what is important to you. What are your beliefs? In your journal, list these ideas. Write a brief description of why they are important to you.

■ **The short-term and long-term effects of each option.** Think about how your choice will affect you now and later. Some decisions may make you feel bad at first but be good for you in the long run. On the other hand, a choice that will make you happy now may make you unhappy later.

Again, consider Hannah's problem. The good point of staying behind is that Hannah will be able to practice and perform. She will see the results of her practicing. A drawback will be that her family will not be able to see her perform.

Step 4. Consider Your Values

Beliefs you feel strongly about that help guide the way you live are your **values.** Your values are based on what is important to you. They are also based on your beliefs about right and wrong. Examples of values would be the decision to always be truthful and the commitment to be dependable. Making a decision that goes against your values may make you uncomfortable.

Hannah values her talent as a dancer. Performing in the recital will give her valuable experience. On the other hand, Hannah is very close to her family and values that relationship.

Step 5. Make a Decision and Act

Review your options and the possible consequences of each. Decide which option is best for you and for people you care about. Then act on your choice.

If no option seems right, you may not make a decision. You may start the process again. You may look for new options.

MAKING HEALTHY DECISIONS
Decisions That Affect Others

*A*nita and her best friend, Gillian, have done everything together. They have studied together and played together. They even went with each other's families on vacation trips.

A month ago, when a new girl, Marie, started school, the teacher asked Anita to show her around and make her feel welcome. To Anita's surprise, she found that she and Marie had a lot in common. They enjoyed each other's company.

Gillian, on the other hand, seemed cold toward Marie. She never wanted to go along when Marie was with Anita. Yesterday, Gillian told Anita that she had to choose between her and Marie.

Hannah decides to stay with her aunt. She feels that the time will go quickly because she will be busy with practice and studying and because she and her aunt get along well. Also, it will give her a little more time to get used to the idea of leaving her old school and friends.

Step 6. Evaluate the Decision

After making and acting on a decision, evaluate your choice. Decide whether the solution worked and if the outcome was what you expected. If the problem still exists, review your list of options. Choose a different option and, using the six-step decision-making process, try to solve the problem again.

Once Hannah has rejoined her family, she tells her mother that she is happy with her decision. She is glad she got to dance in the recital. Because of that experience, she has been able to join a dance group in her new town at the advanced level. There have been drawbacks, though. She is finding it difficult to adjust to the new area because everyone else in the family is already settled in and familiar. Her sister has already made a few new friends. Hannah also missed out on the chance to get the bedroom she wanted—that went to her older brother. All in all, however, Hannah feels that her choice was the right one for her.

| **Do you think that Hannah made the right decision?**

Now Anita doesn't know what to do. She still considers Gillian her best friend, but she likes spending time with Marie. How should Anita handle the situation? Should she stop spending time with Marie? How can she solve the problem so that she can be friends with both girls? Anita decides to use the six-step decision-making process to help her solve her problem.

❶ **State the situation**
❷ **List the options**
❸ **Weigh the possible outcomes**
❹ **Consider your values**
❺ **Make a decision and act**
❻ **Evaluate the decision**

Follow-up Activities

1. Apply the six steps of the decision-making process to Anita's problem.
2. Role-playing the part of Anita, write a diary entry in which you discuss reasons to do what Gillian wants and reasons not to do it.
3. With a classmate, role-play a talk between Gillian and Anita in which they work out a compromise so that Anita can be friends with both girls.

Practicing Decision Making

You won't need to use the six-step decision-making process for every choice you make. However, it is not a good idea to wait until you are faced with a major decision to learn the steps. You may not have time then. Now is a good time to practice.

You can start by following the process for some minor decisions. For example, use the steps to choose which restaurant to go to with your family. You can consider the cost of different restaurants, which foods you like, which foods others in the family like, and what effect the foods will have on your health. You might even look at the option of staying home to eat.

By becoming familiar with the six-step process, you will become comfortable using the steps. Then, when you are faced with a difficult problem, you will be more likely to use the process to make a healthy decision.

The decisions that you make as a consumer help you practice your decision-making skills.

The Benefits of Good Decisions

You will gain many benefits from taking the time to think through your decisions carefully and making choices you are comfortable with.

■ Your self-concept and your self-esteem improve. When you face problems and decide how to solve them, you feel good about yourself.

■ You gain control of all parts of your health, including your physical health, mental/emotional health, and social health.

■ You increase your independence. You become responsible for yourself and your actions.

■ You gain control of your future. You can be sure your life is taking the direction you want it to take.

■ When you make good decisions, your relationships with family and friends improve. You learn to respect the opinions and feelings of others and they learn to respect you.

Review

Lesson 3

Using complete sentences, answer the following questions on a separate sheet of paper.

Reviewing Terms and Facts

1. **Vocabulary**   Define the terms *decision* and *risk*. Use these terms in one sentence in which you show the relationship between the terms.

2. **Recall**   Name three areas of your life in which you will have to make choices that will affect your health and wellness.

3. **List**   What are the six steps of the decision-making process?

4. **List**   Name three ways learning to make wise decisions can benefit you.

Thinking Critically

5. **Explain**   Why is it important that you consider your values when making a decision?

6. **Select**   Choose one of the six steps in the decision-making process and describe its importance to the process.

Applying Health Concepts

7. **Health of Others**   Make a chart that illustrates how the steps in the decision-making process could be followed by a person who was trying to decide whether to stay home and study for a test or go to a party at a friend's house.

Setting Goals

This lesson will help you find answers to questions that teens often ask about setting goals. For example:

▶ Why is it important to have goals?
▶ How do I set my goals?
▶ How can I achieve my goals?

Words to Know

goal
long-term goal
short-term goal

in your journal

What do you see yourself doing in ten years? In your journal, describe what you imagine. Also write about how you plan to achieve your goal.

Types of Goals

All the decisions you make are influenced by *your aims, or what you hope to accomplish.* These are your **goals.** Like Hannah in Lesson 3, who wants to become a professional dancer, you have hopes and dreams for your future. Your goals may be as broad as wanting to be happy or well liked. You may also have very specific aims, such as getting the lead in the school play.

Many of the goals you set are **long-term goals.** These *you plan to reach months or years in the future.* They include goals about your education, what job you want to do, getting married, and raising a family.

To reach a long-term goal, it is a good idea to set some **short-term goals.** *You can accomplish these goals right away.* For example, if you hope to be a doctor, you may set short-term goals of doing well in your science classes and of volunteering at a local hospital or clinic.

Short-term goals often give people the means to reach their long-term goals.

Why Set Goals?

Having and setting goals can benefit your life in many ways. For example, setting goals can help you do the following:

- ■ Gain control of your life.
- ■ Focus your energy.
- ■ Shape your life in a positive way.
- ■ Build your self-esteem.
- ■ Improve your health.

Without goals, you may feel that you are just wandering aimlessly through life. You may believe you are too young to think about these issues, but you're not. Starting now to decide what you want to accomplish will help you plan the steps you need to take to be a happy, healthy, and productive adult.

Achieving the goals you set can help you gain a feeling of accomplishment.

How Do You Select Your Goals?

When trying to decide what you want to accomplish in your life, you should consider the following:

- **What are your needs?** You have basic needs such as for food, clothing, shelter, love, and belonging.

- **What do you want or have an interest in?** You may want to wear a certain style of jacket or to eat a certain type of food. In other words, you want your needs to be met in a certain way. These are your desires. Your dreams for the future may also involve desires or preferences. You may long to hold the world record in your sport or to own a business.

- **What do you do well?** Most people select goals based on what they like to do and what they are good at. Of course, if you are determined to do something you do not have the skill for, you can set short-term goals to learn that skill.

- **What are your values?** You learned in Lesson 3 that your values are beliefs you feel strongly about. You should look at them when you are setting goals. If you value being physically fit, you may set a goal to run three times a week.

Making an Action Plan

To achieve your goals, you need to set realistic goals. By following the seven steps described on the following pages, you can learn how to set and reach goals. Once you learn this process, you can use it in almost all areas of your life.

Health Goals for the Year 2000

Healthy People 2000 is a report put out by the U.S. Department of Health and Human Services. It sets health goals for Americans to reach by the year 2000. These goals are related to preventing disease and to protecting and promoting health. For adolescents, the focus is to prevent injuries and violence that hurt and kill teens and to help teens develop lifelong good attitudes and behaviors about their health.

LIFE SKILLS
Balancing Conflicting Goals

*Y*ou probably have several goals that you want to meet. For instance, you may want to go hiking with your friends. You may also want to get an A on your next English test. If the trip and the test happen in the same week, you may have a decision to make. You may have to choose one goal over another.

Any time your goals conflict, it will be helpful to place your goals in order of their importance to you. Then you will be able to decide what to do.

1. Select one goal to work on. Work on only one goal at a time. Be realistic about how much time and energy you can use to reach your goal. If you want to become a better gymnast, you may not be able to join the swimming club too. Both activities require time and energy.

2. Make your goal specific. Don't just say, "I want to be a better gymnast." Wanting to improve as a gymnast is not a very specific goal. A clearer goal may be to improve your performance on the pommel horse.

Reaching a goal usually requires concentration and effort.

3. List things you need to do to reach your goal. Try to break your goal down into a few smaller tasks. One way to do better might be to practice your routines on the pommel horse for a set number of hours a week.

4. Get help from others. Identify other people who can help you reach your goal. You can ask your coach for special help. Perhaps a friend on the team can help.

5. Set a time period for reaching your goal. Decide on a realistic period of time for you to reach your goal. A good time period for improving might be by the next competition.

To help you decide which goal is more important, ask yourself these questions about each goal:

▶ Which of my needs and wants does the goal satisfy? Which needs and wants are most important to me?

▶ Does the goal match my values? If both goals are in line with my values, which do I place more value on?

▶ What resources do I need to accomplish the goal? Do I have or can I get those resources?

Once you have examined these points, you can decide whether to drop one goal or find another way to do both.

Follow-up Activity

Do you have two goals that conflict? What problems would arise if you tried to meet both goals? Use the questions listed above to decide which goal you want to meet. What advantages and disadvantages do you see to giving up one goal?

6. Set checkpoints to evaluate your progress. Identify checkpoints for evaluating your progress between the time you start work on your goal and the time you hope to complete your goal. Evaluate your progress at each checkpoint. For example, you might check for signs of improvement every week or two.

7. Reward yourself for reaching your goal. Perhaps you can treat yourself to a cassette or compact disc you've been wanting. You might put up a sign on your bedroom door announcing your achievement and ask your parents to have your favorite meal that night.

Other Guidelines for Setting Goals

As you are setting up your action plan, you should consider these points:

- **Be positive.** Set your goal higher than just not failing. Focus your energies on succeeding.

- **Choose goals that are good for you.** Select those that meet your own values and interests. If you let someone talk you into doing something that doesn't feel right, you could cause yourself or others harm. Of course, that does not mean that you shouldn't ask for advice from your parents, teachers, friends, and others whose opinion you respect.

If you break your goals down into manageable parts, you will have a good chance of success.

■ **Don't be too hard on yourself.** If you do not accomplish your entire goal when you want to, reschedule. Set up a new action plan and work toward that. Perhaps you weren't realistic enough about how much time you would need. These experiences can help you to set effective goals in the future.

Altering Your Goals

As you set goals, the most important thing you need to remember is to be flexible. Your goals may change. You may abandon some goals completely and revise others. Perhaps you have already changed your mind several times about what you want to do for a living. You will probably change again.

During your teens, you may find that your needs, interests, skills, and values are changing. These changes can occur as you meet new people and have new experiences. For instance, when you were eight years old and started to take piano lessons, playing well may have been an important goal for you. However, when you started junior high, a friend convinced you to try out for a part in the school play. Now you find that you enjoy acting. You are spending a lot of time doing theater club activities. Playing the piano well is not as important to you.

Goal setting is a skill you will use throughout your life. You should not be afraid to alter your goals. However, you should follow the same steps you used to set your original goal.

in your journal

Can you think of a goal that you set for yourself when you were younger that you no longer want to reach? In your journal, tell why you changed your mind.

Review — Lesson 4

Using complete sentences, answer the following questions on a separate sheet of paper.

Reviewing Terms and Facts

1. **Vocabulary** Explain the difference between *long-term goals* and *short-term goals.*
2. **List** Name two of the benefits of setting goals.
3. **Identify** What four factors should you consider when you select your goals?

Thinking Critically

4. **Explain** Why do you need to consider your values when setting goals?

5. **Hypothesize** Suggest several reasons why goals may sometimes need to be changed.

Applying Health Concepts

6. **Personal Health** Make a poster that illustrates the steps a person can follow to set and reach his or her goals.
7. **Personal Health** Think about one of your goals. Outline a plan that shows the steps you will take to reach your goal. Include a description of how long it will take to reach the goal and the checkpoints you will use to evaluate your progress.

Chapter

1 Review

Chapter Summary

▶ Health is the combination of physical, mental, and social well-being. (Lesson 1)

▶ When you neglect one part of your health, the other parts will be affected. (Lesson 1)

▶ To achieve a high level of wellness, you need to pay equal attention to your physical, mental, and social health. (Lesson 1)

▶ If you know yourself well, you will know what you need to do to maintain your overall health and well-being. (Lesson 2)

▶ Developing a positive self-concept helps you build high self-esteem and self-confidence. (Lesson 2)

▶ Decisions you make about your health and wellness should be made with thought and planning. (Lesson 3)

▶ When faced with a big decision, you should follow these steps: state the situation, list the options, weigh the possible outcomes, consider your values, make a decision and act, and evaluate the decision. (Lesson 3)

▶ Facing problems and making wise choices improves your self-concept and your self-esteem and helps you gain control of your health. (Lesson 3)

▶ Setting goals can help you gain control of your life and give your life positive direction. (Lesson 4)

▶ When you set goals, you should consider your needs, wants, skills, and values. (Lesson 4)

▶ To achieve the goals you set, follow a plan: select a specific goal, break it down into small tasks, set a time limit, check your progress as you work toward the goal, and reward yourself when you reach the goal. (Lesson 4)

Using Health Terms

On a separate sheet of paper, write the vocabulary term that best matches each definition given below.

1. The achievement of a high level of overall health (Lesson 1)

2. The view that you have of yourself (Lesson 2)

3. The ability to like and respect yourself (Lesson 2)

4. The chance of danger or loss (Lesson 3)

5. The results of an action (Lesson 3)

6. Your aims, or what you hope to accomplish (Lesson 4)

Reviewing Main Ideas

Using complete sentences, answer the following questions on a separate sheet of paper.

1. What are the three sides of the health triangle? (Lesson 1)

2. What does it mean to have a balanced health triangle? (Lesson 1)

3. What are three of the things you learn about yourself that form your self-concept? (Lesson 2)

4. What are two of the questions you should ask yourself when you start the first step of the decision-making process? (Lesson 3)

5. When making a decision, what three considerations should you think about as you weigh each of your options? (Lesson 3)

6. What are the seven steps in the action plan for achieving goals? (Lesson 4)

Thinking Critically

Using complete sentences, answer the following questions on a separate sheet of paper.

1. **Analyze** How might poor mental health affect your physical or social health? (Lesson 1)

2. **Explain** Why is it good to examine your level of wellness even if you don't feel sick? (Lesson 1)

3. **Analyze** Why do some people send negative messages to others? (Lesson 2)

4. **Interpret** How can a good self-concept affect your mental health? (Lesson 2)

5. **Deduce** Why is it a good idea to ask for help when making an important decision? (Lesson 3)

6. **Analyze** Why should you consider both long-term and short-term effects of your decisions? (Lesson 3)

7. **Contrast** To show the difference between long-term goals and short-term goals, give an example of each. (Lesson 4)

8. **Synthesize** Break down the long-term goal of achieving physical fitness into several short-term goals that can be reached one at a time. (Lesson 4)

Your Action Plan

To maintain a high level of health, you must try to keep the parts of your health balanced. Look through your private journal entries for this chapter. Does a part of your health need work? An action plan can help you decide what you want to improve and how to go about making changes.

Write down a long-term goal. It should be realistic and specific. For example, you may want to improve your social health. Then set up short-term goals to help you meet that long-term goal. A short-term goal may be to try to get along better with your sister or brother.

Make a realistic schedule for reaching each short-term goal. Keep checking your schedule to keep on track. When you reach your long-term goal, reward yourself. You might go to a movie with your sister or brother to celebrate.

Building Your Portfolio

1. It is a good idea to consider your values every time you make a decision or set a goal. On a sheet of paper, list your values. Add the list to your portfolio. Refer to it when you are making important decisions or setting goals during the year.

2. When you set goals for yourself, it is helpful to consider how other people have achieved those same goals. Choose a person who has a job that interests you. Arrange to interview the person about why she or he chose that career and how to prepare for it. Ask the person for permission to tape-record the conversation. Include the tape in your portfolio.

In Your Home and Community

1. Ask one or both parents to describe a major decision they made when they were your age. Ask what steps they followed to make the choice and whether they were happy with their decision.

2. Clip newspaper articles to include in a handbook that shows how people in your community have achieved their goals. Get approval from the school librarian to place the handbook in the library. Create flyers to post in the library to encourage students to use the handbook for suggestions about setting and achieving goals.

Chapter 2
Caring for Yourself

Student Expectations
After reading this chapter, you should be able to:
1. Describe how to keep your teeth, skin, and hair healthy.
2. Explain how to protect your sight and hearing.
3. Give guidelines for purchasing personal products.
4. Compare different sources of health care.

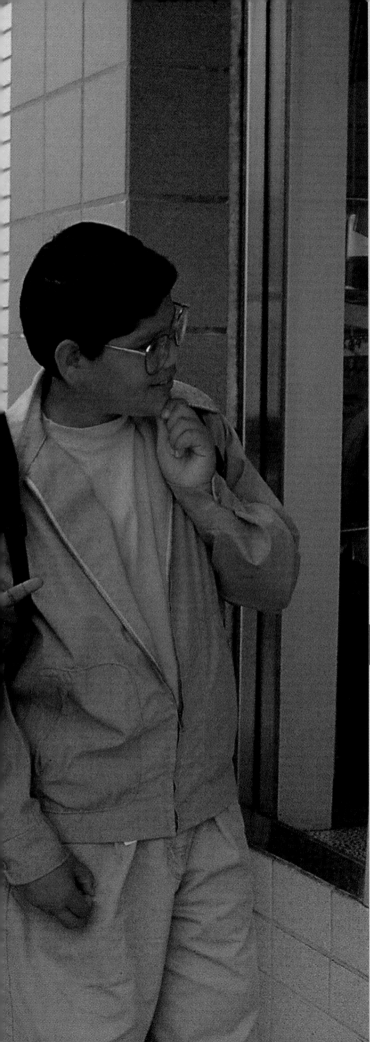

I'm almost a teenager now, so the way I look is getting more and more important. Some of my friends have done some pretty wild things to make themselves look better. Tessa has started using really thick makeup to cover up her bad skin. Jake stopped wearing his glasses because he thinks they make him look weird. He says he doesn't need glasses to hear his favorite music.

My friend Carrie spends every penny of her allowance on different kinds of shampoo and other hair stuff. Jason chews breath mints all day, but his breath still needs help.

Dyanne spends every minute she can lying in the sun. She says she doesn't need sunscreen, but I'm not so sure.

I wish I knew how to look better and still stay healthy. The stores are full of different kinds of toothpaste and shampoo and sunscreen. Every label and every ad says its product is best. How can they all be right?

Now I have this rash on my back again. Mom wants to take me to a specialist. Do I really need to go?

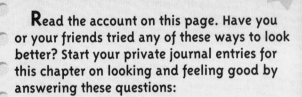

in your journal

Read the account on this page. Have you or your friends tried any of these ways to look better? Start your private journal entries for this chapter on looking and feeling good by answering these questions:

► How do you feel about the way your teeth, skin, and hair look?
► How are your sight and hearing?
► What would you like to know about buying personal products?
► What questions do you have about going to a doctor?

When you reach the end of the chapter, you will use your journal entries to make an action plan.

Healthy Teeth, Skin, and Hair

This lesson will help you find answers to questions that teens often ask about their teeth, skin, and hair. For example:

▶ **How can I keep my teeth healthy and looking their best?**
▶ **What is the best way to care for my skin?**
▶ **What do I need to know about hair care?**

Words to Know

plaque
tartar
cavity
fluoride
epidermis
dermis
melanin
acne
dermatologist
dandruff
head lice

Healthy Teeth

You know that your teeth help you chew food, but did you realize they also help you talk? In addition, they shape your mouth and your smile. Your teeth affect your health and your appearance, so you need to know how to take care of them. Good dental care helps prevent tooth decay. **Figure 2.1** shows the parts of a tooth and the stages of decay.

Figure 2.1
Tooth Structure and Tooth Decay

Your teeth have a strong built-in defense mechanism, but they need your help to keep them clean. Decay usually occurs because people fail to practice good dental care.

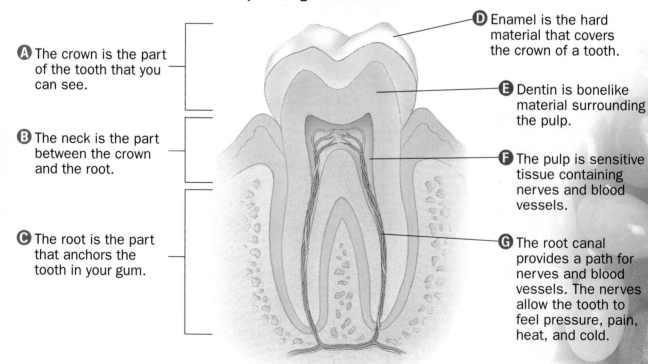

A The crown is the part of the tooth that you can see.

B The neck is the part between the crown and the root.

C The root is the part that anchors the tooth in your gum.

D Enamel is the hard material that covers the crown of a tooth.

E Dentin is bonelike material surrounding the pulp.

F The pulp is sensitive tissue containing nerves and blood vessels.

G The root canal provides a path for nerves and blood vessels. The nerves allow the tooth to feel pressure, pain, heat, and cold.

What Harms Teeth?

Teeth are always being exposed to food and bacteria. These substances can cause tooth decay. The best way to avoid decay is to keep your teeth clean.

Decay starts when a substance called plaque is left on the teeth too long. **Plaque** (PLAK) is *a soft sticky film created by the bacteria that live in your mouth.* Plaque forms constantly on your teeth, even when you are not eating. It can then combine with the sugar in the foods that you eat to form an acid. This acid can harm the enamel on your teeth. Look at **Figure 2.1** again to see what happens when the acid forms.

If you do not remove plaque from your teeth every day, it may harden into a *hard material* called **tartar** (TAR·ter). Tartar threatens gum health. Brushing and flossing cannot remove tartar. Only the special skills and instruments of a dentist or a dental hygienist can remove tartar.

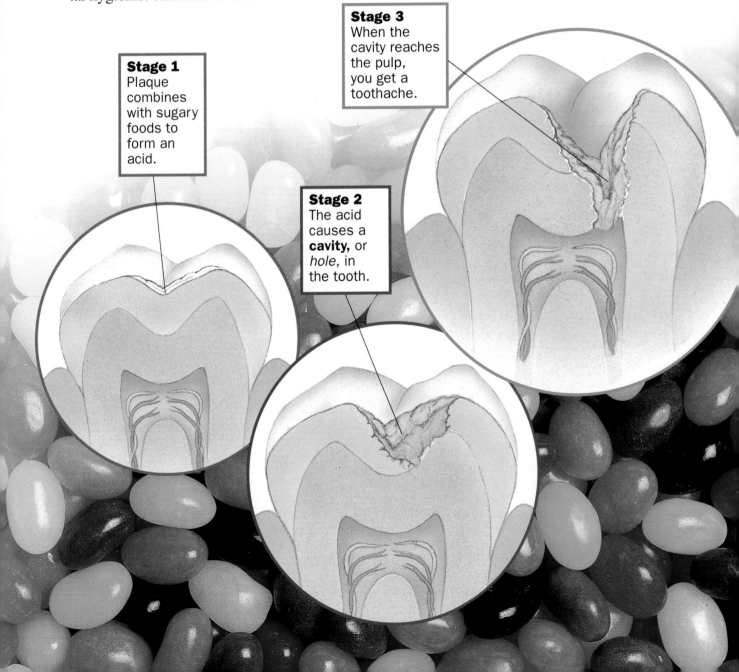

Stage 1
Plaque combines with sugary foods to form an acid.

Stage 2
The acid causes a **cavity,** or *hole,* in the tooth.

Stage 3
When the cavity reaches the pulp, you get a toothache.

Taking Care of Your Teeth

Taking care of your teeth means attending to them every day. It means regular brushing and flossing. It also means eating the right kinds of foods and having your teeth checked regularly by a dentist. **Figure 2.2** tells you what you need to know about brushing and flossing.

Eating Right

You can help keep your teeth strong and healthy by eating fresh fruit and vegetables, as well as foods high in calcium (such as milk, cottage cheese, and yogurt). You should avoid candy or other sugary foods.

Visiting the Dentist

A dentist can look for signs of tooth decay and gum disease and treat them before they become problems. A dental hygienist cleans teeth thoroughly to prevent decay and disease. You should see a dentist at least once a year.

Figure 2.2
Brushing and Flossing

Regular brushing and flossing, using the correct techniques, will help ensure healthy teeth and an attractive smile.

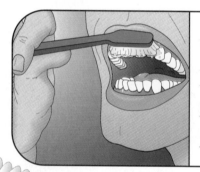

Brushing Whenever you can, brush after eating. Use toothpaste that contains **fluoride** (FLAWR·eyed), a *substance that fights tooth decay*. Start brushing by tilting the top of your toothbrush toward your gum. Brush downward on the upper teeth and upward on the lower teeth. Move the brush in short circular strokes across the outside of your teeth. Then brush the inside and chewing surfaces. It is especially important to brush your teeth regularly if you have braces on them because the braces can trap food particles.

Flossing Floss at least once a day to remove food particles the toothbrush cannot reach. Take about 18 inches of dental floss and wrap the ends around the middle finger of each hand. Hold the floss tight between your thumbs and forefingers and slide it gently between your teeth. Move it down to the gum line with a gentle sawing motion to remove any plaque that has formed there. Repeat the process between all teeth.

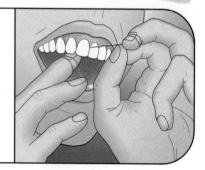

Healthy Skin

Your skin is the largest of your body organs. Like the other organs in your body, it performs a number of important functions. **Figure 2.3** explains what your skin does for you.

The Parts of the Skin

As you might imagine, the skin is complex. It is made up of several kinds of tissues. They work together to perform the skin's many functions. Your skin has two main layers. The *outer layer of skin* is called the **epidermis** (e·puh·DER·mis). The *inner layer of skin* is called the **dermis** (DER·mis). **Figure 2.4** on the next page shows the work that these different layers of skin do.

Figure 2.3
Functions of the Skin

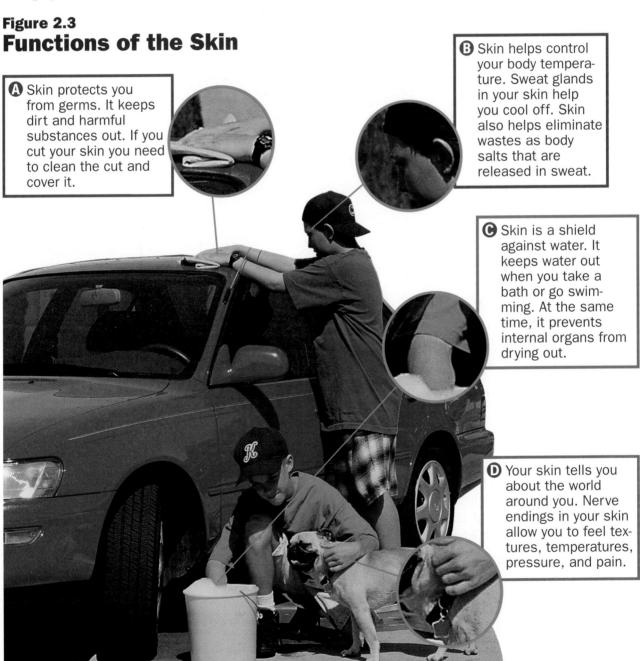

A Skin protects you from germs. It keeps dirt and harmful substances out. If you cut your skin you need to clean the cut and cover it.

B Skin helps control your body temperature. Sweat glands in your skin help you cool off. Skin also helps eliminate wastes as body salts that are released in sweat.

C Skin is a shield against water. It keeps water out when you take a bath or go swimming. At the same time, it prevents internal organs from drying out.

D Your skin tells you about the world around you. Nerve endings in your skin allow you to feel textures, temperatures, pressure, and pain.

Taking Care of Your Skin

The most important thing you can do for your skin is to keep it clean. You also need to protect it from the sun, eat sensibly, and get plenty of exercise and sleep.

Figure 2.4
The Skin

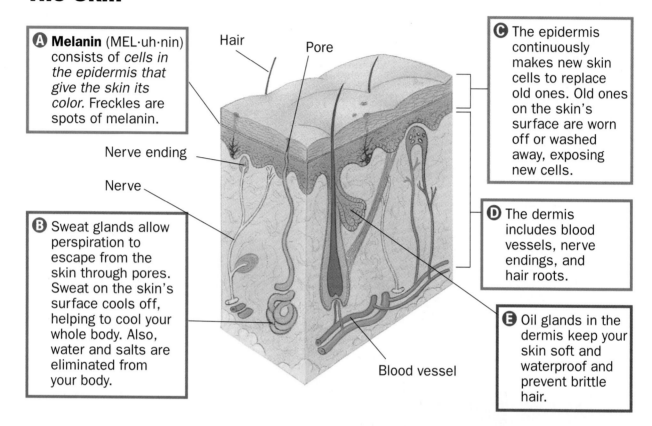

A **Melanin** (MEL·uh·nin) consists of *cells in the epidermis that give the skin its color.* Freckles are spots of melanin.

Hair

Pore

C The epidermis continuously makes new skin cells to replace old ones. Old ones on the skin's surface are worn off or washed away, exposing new cells.

Nerve ending

Nerve

B Sweat glands allow perspiration to escape from the skin through pores. Sweat on the skin's surface cools off, helping to cool your whole body. Also, water and salts are eliminated from your body.

D The dermis includes blood vessels, nerve endings, and hair roots.

E Oil glands in the dermis keep your skin soft and waterproof and prevent brittle hair.

Blood vessel

MAKING HEALTHY DECISIONS
Protecting Yourself from the Sun

*K*en's friends are going to the beach. They plan to spend the whole afternoon in the sun, working on their tans. Ken's skin burns easily, and he knows the sun can damage his skin, possibly causing skin cancer later in life.

His mom already had a small cancer removed from her forehead. She told him she spent a lot of time in the sun when she was younger. Back then, she said, no one knew you could get cancer from the sun. Now she uses a sunblock whenever she cannot avoid being in the sun.

"Come on, Ken," his friend Alison begs. "We have plenty of suntan lotion. Everyone will be there. You will look great with a tan!"

Ken has a problem. He does not want to miss the fun. Still, he wonders if he and his friends will be sorry later, like his mom. Maybe he will be okay if he uses lots of sunblock.

To make up his mind, Ken uses the step-by-step decision-making process.

❶ **State the situation**

❷ **List the options**

- **Keep your skin clean.** Regular washing with soap and water is especially important in the early teen years. At that stage of life the sweat glands increase their activity. Because sweat feeds the bacteria on your skin, they reproduce rapidly. When the bacteria have increased, they begin to smell, especially those under your arms and on your feet. If you are not already using a deodorant, this may be a good time to start.

- **Protect your skin from the sun.** The sun's ultraviolet rays damage your skin. Try to stay out of the sun between 10:00 a.m. and 2:00 p.m., when these rays are strongest. Whenever you are in the sun, use sunblocking agents or sunscreens with a sun protection factor (SPF) of at least 15. An SPF of 15 gives your skin 15 times its natural protection from the sun. Read the label on the sunscreen bottle so that you will know how often to apply it.

- **Eat a balanced diet.** Eat foods that contain vitamin A (such as milk, egg yolks, liver, green and yellow vegetables).

- **Get enough exercise and sleep.** Exercise gives your skin a healthy glow. Skin cells are replaced during sleep.

Skin Problems

As you become a teenager, the oil glands in your skin begin to work harder. The extra oil they produce can clog pores and cause whiteheads, blackheads, and pimples.

Science Connection

Ozone and You

In 1935, only one person in 1,500 was diagnosed with melanoma, a type of skin cancer. By the year 2000, the number may be 1 in 75. Scientists think one reason is the gradual destruction of the ozone layer that protects us from ultraviolet rays.

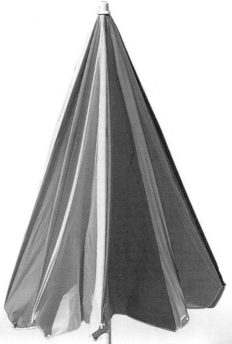

③ **Weigh the possible outcomes**
④ **Consider your values**
⑤ **Make a decision and act**
⑥ **Evaluate the decision**

Follow-up Activities

1. Apply the decision-making process to Ken's dilemma.
2. Imagine that you are Ken. Explain your decision to your friends.
3. Use the library to find out how a cloudy day affects the sun's rays, how tanning beds affect the skin, and how suntan lotions work.

Acne (AK·nee) is the *skin condition caused by overly active oil glands.* Most teens experience acne at some time. Usually, it is mild and can be treated at home. For serious cases, you may want to see a **dermatologist** (DER·muh·TAHL·uh·jist), *a doctor who treats skin disorders.*

If you have acne, wash your skin at least twice a day with mild soap and warm water. Then blot it dry with a clean towel. Don't squeeze or pick at pimples. Avoid greasy creams and heavy makeup. Use only skin preparations that your doctor recommends.

Healthy Hair

Do you wear your hair long or short? Straight or curly? Teens often experiment with hairstyles, but the best-looking styles always begin with clean, healthy hair.

No part of you grows faster than your hair. The hair shaft, the part that you can see, is made of dead cells that overlap each other, like shingles on a roof. It is the shape of the hair shaft that determines the overall appearance of your hair (see **Figure 2.5**).

Hair color comes from the melanin cells, the same cells that give your skin its color. The color of your hair is passed along to you through your parents' genes.

Taking Care of Your Hair

Caring for your hair is simple. All you need to do is wash it often and brush it regularly.

Figure 2.5
Hair Shapes

It is the shape of each hair shaft that determines whether your hair is straight, wavy, or curly.

Oval shaft, wavy hair

Round shaft, straight hair

Flat shaft, curly hair

- **Washing.** Use a gentle shampoo. If possible, let your hair dry by itself. Blow dryers and curling irons can over-dry hair and cause split ends. Many people use conditioners after shampooing. Conditioners are supposed to make the hair feel thicker and smoother. However, they may make the hair look greasy.

- **Brushing.** Brushing once a day helps spread the natural oils down the hair shaft. This makes your hair shine. However, too much brushing can break the hair shaft or pull hair out.

Hair and Scalp Problems

Have you ever noticed white flakes on your shoulders? They may have been **dandruff.** This is a *flaking of the outer layer of dead skin cells.* It is a very common scalp problem, usually caused by a dry scalp. You can usually control dandruff by washing your hair regularly. Special dandruff shampoos are also available to control the problem.

At times an itchy scalp is caused by **head lice.** These are *tiny insects that live in the hair.* Head lice are very common and easy to catch from someone else. If you get head lice you will need to use a special medicated shampoo. You will also need to wash all bedding, towels, combs and brushes, and clothing that have been in contact with your head. Everyone else who lives in your house will need to take these special precautions, too.

Review

Lesson 1

Using complete sentences, answer the following questions on a separate sheet of paper.

Reviewing Terms and Facts

1. **Vocabulary** Explain the difference between plaque and tartar. How is each removed?

2. **Summarize** What are three things you can do to take care of your teeth?

3. **Vocabulary** What is dandruff? How do you get rid of it?

Thinking Critically

4. **Explain** What can you do to avoid damage to your skin by the sun?

5. **Hypothesize** Why do you think most teens are concerned about the way their hair looks?

Applying Health Concepts

6. **Health of Others** Make a videotape that demonstrates how to floss teeth. Be sure to explain why flossing is important. Show the tape to younger health classes.

7. **Consumer Health** Write a radio advertisement urging young people to use gentle soap and warm water to treat their acne. Make your ad sound as convincing as those for creams and lotions that claim to "cure" acne.

8. **Growth and Development** Work with other students to make a poster showing all the different colors and textures of hair in your school. Think of a title for the poster that encourages people to appreciate all kinds of hair. Display your poster in the library or hallway.

Healthy Eyes and Ears

This lesson will help you find answers to questions that teens often ask about their eyes and ears. For example:

▶ Why do some people have to wear glasses or contacts?
▶ Can loud music really hurt my ears?

Words to Know

farsightedness
nearsightedness
astigmatism
sound wave
decibel

Healthy Eyes

Your eyes allow you to recognize your friends, shoot baskets, check out the latest fashions, read your favorite magazines, and do a lot more. In fact, people with full vision gather about 80 percent of their knowledge through their eyes. Taking care of your eyes will help you look and feel good. To be able to take care of your eyes, you first need to understand how the eye works (see **Figure 2.6**).

Figure 2.6
The Eye

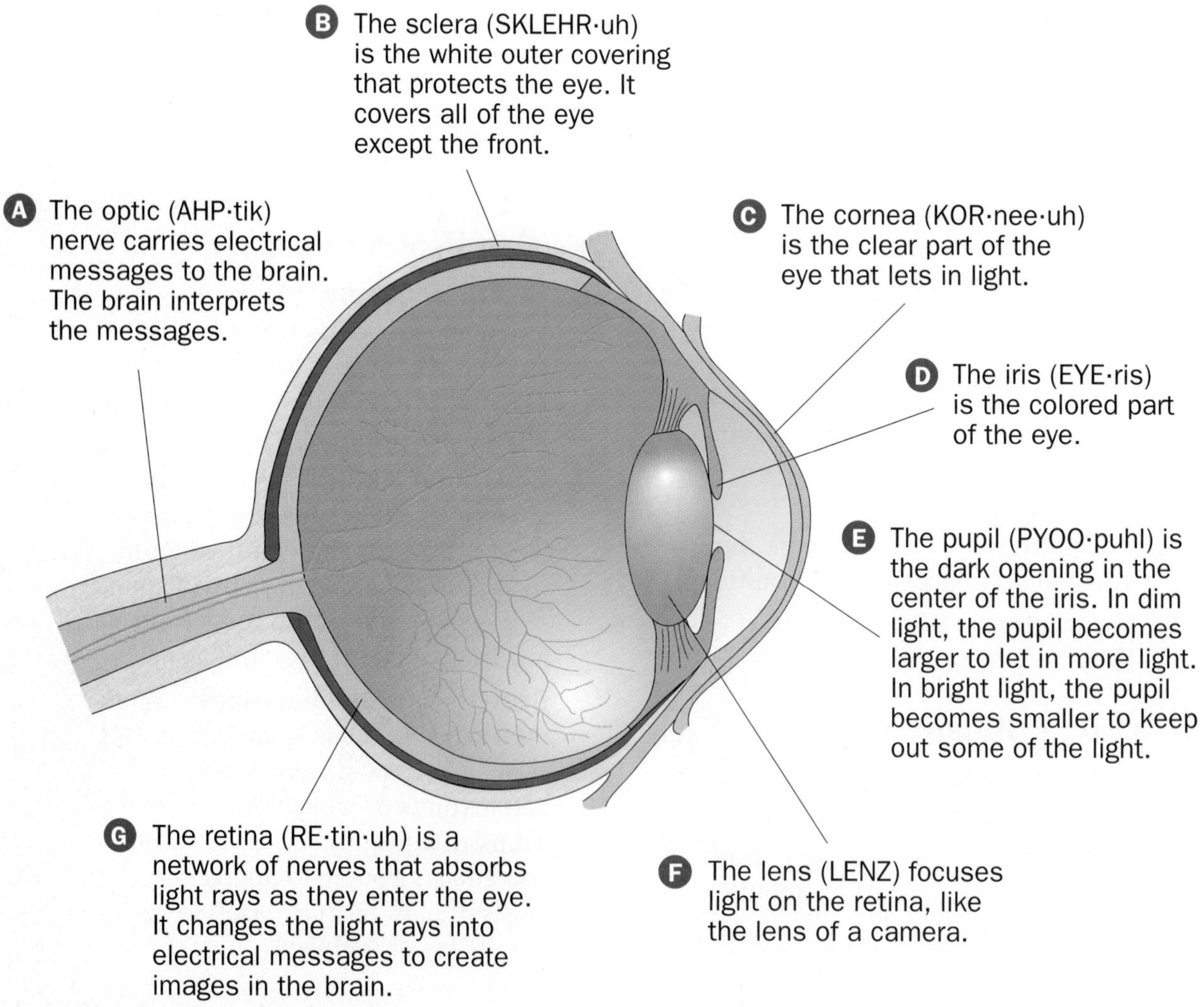

B The sclera (SKLEHR·uh) is the white outer covering that protects the eye. It covers all of the eye except the front.

A The optic (AHP·tik) nerve carries electrical messages to the brain. The brain interprets the messages.

C The cornea (KOR·nee·uh) is the clear part of the eye that lets in light.

D The iris (EYE·ris) is the colored part of the eye.

E The pupil (PYOO·puhl) is the dark opening in the center of the iris. In dim light, the pupil becomes larger to let in more light. In bright light, the pupil becomes smaller to keep out some of the light.

G The retina (RE·tin·uh) is a network of nerves that absorbs light rays as they enter the eye. It changes the light rays into electrical messages to create images in the brain.

F The lens (LENZ) focuses light on the retina, like the lens of a camera.

Taking Care of Your Eyes

Like your teeth, skin, and hair, your eyes need care to stay healthy. Listed below are some important ways to protect and care for your eyes.

- **Protect your eyes from eyestrain.** Read and watch television in a well-lighted room. Place your reading lamp so that it shines on what you are reading. Sit a comfortable distance (at least 6 feet) from the television. When writing, avoid working in your own shadow.

- **Protect your eyes from injury.** Certain sports, such as softball and hockey, carry a risk of eye injury. Wear safety glasses or a visor when playing such sports. Use safety eyewear, too, when using power tools. Avoid rubbing your eye if you get something in it. Doing so may scratch the cornea. If you get something in your eye, you should rinse it out by splashing cool water in the eye.

- **Protect your eyes from infection.** Do not rub your eyes if they hurt or itch. You may have an infection known as "pinkeye." This infection spreads easily but can be treated with medication from your doctor.

- **Get regular checkups.** Get your vision checked by a trained health care professional every year if you wear glasses or contacts. Get a checkup every two years if you don't.

Vision Problems

When the doctor examines your eyes, he or she will look for these problems:

- **Farsightedness.** *You can see far objects clearly, but closer objects appear blurry.*

- **Nearsightedness.** *You can see close objects, but distant objects appear blurry.*

- **Astigmatism** (uh·STIG·muh·tiz·uhm). *The shape of your cornea or lens causes a wavy or blurred image.*

Correcting Vision Problems

Farsightedness, nearsightedness, and astigmatism can all be corrected with eyeglasses or contact lenses. These devices help the lens of the eye focus light on the retina. The type of lenses that the doctor suggests will depend on the vision problem.

Glasses are easy to wear and come in many attractive styles. Some people dislike wearing them, however. They prefer contact lenses. These tiny lenses cling to the cornea and are nearly

Q&A ❓

I See Spots!

Q: Sometimes I see spots in front of my eyes. Is this serious?

A: These "floaters" are cells that have broken off from your retina. They float in the fluid in your eye. Unless you suddenly see a lot of them, they are normal.

Hockey is an example of a sport that carries a high risk of eye injury. What are some other examples?

invisible. A hard contact lens may irritate some eyes. A soft contact lens is more comfortable, but it may not be suitable for correcting astigmatism.

It is important to keep contacts clean. Dirt or germs on a contact lens can infect or injure your cornea. Depending on the type of lenses you have, you may need to clean them with a special solution. Your doctor will tell you how to care for your lenses. Make sure you follow the instructions carefully to avoid infection or injury to your eyes.

Healthy Ears

You know that your ears allow you to hear people talking and to listen to your favorite music. Did you know that your ears also help you keep your balance? Your ears include much more than the parts you can see. The ear is a complex body part that goes deep into your skull. Each ear has three main parts: the outer ear, the middle ear, and the inner ear. Study **Figure 2.7** to learn more about the ear.

in your journal

If you could choose between eyeglasses or contact lenses, which would you choose? Why? If you have already made that choice, explain how you made it. Use your journal to record your thoughts.

HEALTH LAB
Observing the Eye

*I*ntroduction: Your eyes are amazing. They can adjust to different light levels and see not only what is in front of you, but objects off to the side, too. Your eyes also tell you about color.

Objective: Work with a partner to observe the eye's reaction to light, measure side vision, and test for color blindness.

Materials and Method:
Checking reactions to light: Sit in a dark room with your partner for five minutes. Then turn on the lights. Quickly notice the size of each other's

Figure 2.7
The Ear

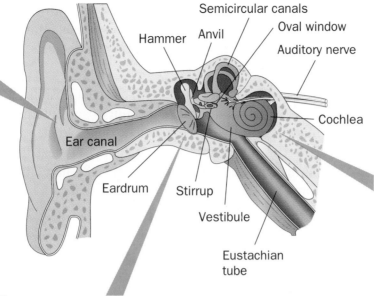

Outer Ear
The outer ear is shaped like a cup to collect sound waves.
Sound waves are *vibrations or movements in the air*.

Semicircular canals
Oval window
Hammer
Anvil
Auditory nerve
Ear canal
Cochlea
Eardrum
Stirrup
Vestibule
Eustachian tube

Inner Ear
As the oval window in the vestibule moves, it causes fluid in the curled-up cochlea (KOK·lee·uh) to move. The thousands of tiny hairs inside the cochlea feel this vibration. They send electrical messages along the auditory nerve to the brain. The brain identifies the electrical messages as speech, music, or other sounds. The semicircular canals are also filled with fluid and hairs connected to nerve endings. When your body moves, these hairs send messages to the brain that help you keep your balance.

Middle Ear
Sound waves push against the eardrum and cause it to vibrate. As the eardrum vibrates, it moves three tiny bones called the hammer, anvil, and stirrup. These three bones carry the sound vibration from the eardrum to the oval window. The eustachian tube leads from behind the eardrum to the throat. The tube helps keep the air pressure on either side of the drum equal.

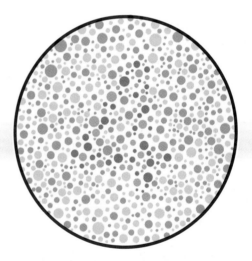

pupils. Watch your partner's pupils shrink to block out some of the light.

Measuring side vision: With string, form a semicircle on the floor about 8 feet out from the front of a chair. One partner will sit in the chair and look straight ahead. The other one will move around the semicircle, holding up objects such as a shoe or a book. The partner in the chair will try to identify the objects without turning his or her head. Take turns sitting in the chair. See how far to each side you both can see.

Testing for color blindness: About 1 in 12 men and 1 in 200 women are color-blind. Can you and your partner see a number in the circle above? If not, you may be red/green color-blind.

Observation and Analysis:
After you and your partner have completed your observations, discuss your findings with the class. What are some advantages of having pupils that change when the light changes? What are some advantages of being able to see what is beside you? What are some disadvantages of color blindness?

Taking Care of Your Ears

One important way to take care of your ears is to protect them from loud sounds. The *loudness of sound waves* is measured in **decibels.** Normal conversation is about 60 decibels. The noise from a power mower can reach 100 decibels. Rock music often exceeds 110 decibels.

A sudden loud sound, such as an explosion, can injure the tiny hairs in your inner ear. This injury can cause a temporary or permanent hearing loss. Repeated sounds louder than 80 or 90 decibels can also damage these hairs and lead to a temporary or permanent hearing loss. **Figure 2.8** shows the noise levels of some familiar objects.

You should protect your ears from the cold, too. When it's cold, wear earmuffs or a hat that covers your ears. This will prevent cold air from irritating your middle ear and causing pain.

Music Connection

A Master of Music

The great German composer Ludwig van Beethoven gradually lost his hearing. In the end, he could not even hear the audience applaud his work. Find out how this gifted man could compose symphonies when he could not hear the music.

Figure 2.8
How Noise Level Affects Hearing

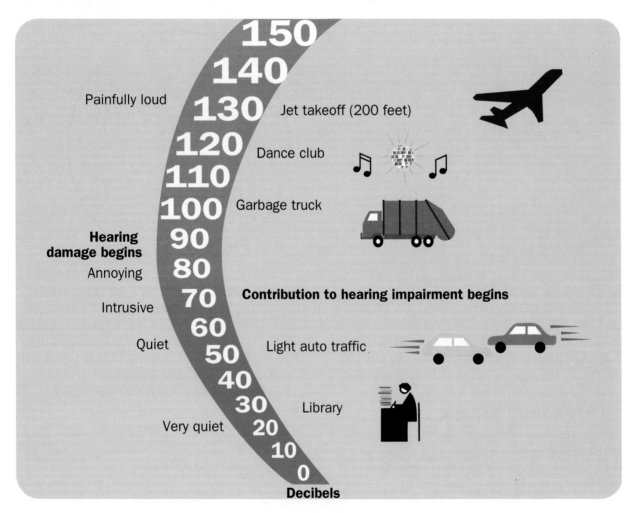

Ear Problems

The most common ear problems are infections of the middle ear. An infection of the nose or throat can lead to pain in the ear. Sometimes infections move up the eustachian tube from the throat to the ear. These infections must be treated by a doctor.

The most serious ear problems are hearing loss and deafness. A partial hearing loss can be caused by too much wax in the ear canal, an ear infection, or nerve damage. A total hearing loss can result from ear injury, disease, or birth defects.

Teen Issues

Speak Up!

Grandpa is losing his hearing, but he tells you to stop mumbling! Try facing him when you speak. Talk slowly and loudly without shouting. Do not cover your mouth.

Ask a parent to encourage Grandpa to get his hearing tested. He may need a hearing aid.

People with a hearing loss often communicate using lipreading and sign language. Some may wear hearing aids that increase the loudness of the sound waves.

Review Lesson 2

Using complete sentences, answer the following questions on a separate sheet of paper.

Reviewing Terms and Facts

1. **Vocabulary** What is the difference between farsightedness and nearsightedness?
2. **Recall** Can loud noises really damage your hearing?

Thinking Critically

3. **Compare and Contrast** Do you get more information from your eyes or your ears? Explain your answer.
4. **List** What are some things teens sometimes do that could injure their sight or their hearing? What protection could they use for each activity?

5. **Analyze** What changes could you make in your life that would give greater protection to your eyes and your ears?

Applying Health Concepts

6. **Personal Health** Survey at least six people who wear contact lenses. Find out what kinds of lenses they wear, how long they have worn them, and what kinds of problems, if any, they have had with their lenses. Prepare a chart of your findings.
7. **Health of Others** Write an announcement about the damage that loud music can cause to hearing. Arrange to have the announcement read over the school's public address system (but not too loudly). Try to motivate your friends to reduce the noise levels in their lives.

Teen HEALTH DIGEST

CONSUMER FOCUS

Health Update

Don't Forget the "Shades"

Wearing sunglasses used to be a fashion statement. Now more and more people are recognizing that sunglasses actually protect the eyes from the sun's ultraviolet radiation.

According to the American Optometric Association, teens need sunglasses more than adults do because they spend more time in the sun. Also, the lenses of their eyes are more transparent and let in more radiation.

The most effective sunglasses block out 99–100 percent of UVA and UVB radiation and screen out 75–90 percent of visible light. They should have gray, green, or brown lenses.

When choosing sunglasses, check for a UV label. Then try the glasses on in front of a mirror. If you can see your eyes through the lenses they do not block enough light.

If you plan to wear sunglasses while playing a sport, look for polycarbonate lenses. They are stronger than normal lenses and less likely to break on impact.

Sorting Out Sunscreens

Which sunscreen should you choose? Sunscreen must guard against two kinds of ultraviolet rays:

- UVA rays, which do not burn skin but penetrate deeply. These rays tangle the elastin ribbons in the dermis. The ribbons begin to pull in different directions, causing wrinkles.

- UVB rays, which do burn skin and can damage cells in the epidermis that produce new skin. Over time, these cells may begin dividing uncontrollably. The result is skin cancer.

The sun protection factor (SPF) indicates a sunscreen's ability to block only UVB rays. Choose sunscreens with an SPF of 15 or higher. Two sunscreens—Photoplex and Shade UVAGUARD—also protect against UVA rays. Metallic sunblocking agents reflect both types of UV rays.

Teens Making a Difference

A Spell of Love

Jenna sits close to her "grandfather," telling him about her school day. She does not say a word out loud. He is deaf and blind so Jenna finger-spells each word against his hand. She knows how because she is deaf, too.

Once or twice a month, about 20 students from the Ohio School for the Deaf in Columbus visit the Columbus Colony Elderly Care center. Most of the young people live at the school, so they do not often see their own grandparents. Each student is matched with a deaf or deaf and blind "grandparent" at this special nursing home.

The older people look forward to these visits very much. The children know they are reaching out to touch someone in a very special way.

People at Work

The Smile Maker

Nothing makes Dr. Susanna Rivera happier than seeing one of her patients with a great big smile. Dr. Rivera is an orthodontist, a dentist who specializes in treating teeth that do not line up properly. To become an orthodontist she first trained as a dentist, then completed a two-year program.

Orthodontists treat patients of all ages, but the majority of their patients—about 75 percent—are teens. During the early teen years, the permanent teeth grow in. Then problems can be seen and corrected.

Teeth are straightened with braces. Today, there are different kinds of braces to choose from. Some are transparent. Some fit on the inside of the teeth. Dr. Rivera still recommends the traditional stainless steel braces. She points out that they are the least expensive, break less often, and straighten teeth more quickly.

Give Up Chocolate?

Does eating chocolate and fried foods cause acne? The good news is that it doesn't. The bad news is that no matter what you eat, chances are you will get acne at some stage during your teen years.

The most common cause of acne is the change in hormones that is a normal part of adolescence. While you can't avoid that, there are some steps you can take to combat acne. The best course is to keep your skin clean. This means washing your face two or three times a day. You should also avoid picking or squeezing the skin. This could cause infection or scarring.

Over-the-counter creams, lotions, and gels may help dry the skin and speed up healing. Some of the most effective products contain benzoyl peroxide or resorcinol.

For more serious acne, a dermatologist, or doctor who treats skin problems, may prescribe antibiotic creams or other medications.

When it comes to foods, eat a healthy diet. You can continue to eat (in moderation) all the foods you normally eat—including chocolate.

Lesson 3
Buying Personal Products

This lesson will help you find answers to questions that teens often ask about buying personal products. For example:

▶ **How do I choose the best personal products for my needs?**
▶ **How can I get the most for my money?**

Words to Know

consumer
quackery
advertising
warranty
discount store
coupon
generic

Many Choices, Many Influences

We are all consumers. A **consumer** is *anybody who buys goods or services.* In this lesson you will learn about your role as a health consumer.

The health goods you buy are those that you use to care for your teeth, skin, hair, nails, and so on. They are often called personal hygiene products. Such products might include toothpaste, skin cream, suntan lotion, shampoo, and deodorant. The health services you buy are the activities offered by others to help promote your health. They include the services of people such as dentists and doctors.

Buying goods and services is not always easy. **Figure 2.9** illustrates the consumer's dilemma. You need to know how to choose from a wide variety of options and to be aware of the influences that affect your choices. In short, you need to build your consumer skills. These skills will help you choose health products and services wisely.

Figure 2.9
Making a Choice

I've always used this brand. Why change?

This one costs less.

My friend Kim uses this shampoo and her hair looks great.

This one has special secret ingredients.

That TV commercial said this brand will give my hair more body.

This brand is on sale—25 percent off.

50

Spotting False Claims

Long ago, people used to travel from town to town selling bottles of "medicine." They claimed that the medicine would cure "anything that ails you." In every town, some people would believe this false claim and buy the worthless product.

Today magazines, newspapers, and television bring some of the same quackery (KWAK·uh·ree) into our homes. **Quackery** refers to *selling worthless products or services by making false claims*. Some products falsely claim to cure arthritis, cancer, high blood pressure, and other conditions. Some unfortunate people use these products instead of changing their behavior or getting the help they need from their doctors.

Look at the products in **Figure 2.10.** They all make false claims. What are some other false claims you have read or heard in advertisements?

Think Before You Buy

One of the strongest influences on your consumer choices is **advertising.** This is *sending out messages to persuade consumers to buy.* Advertisers try to convince you that their product will make you healthier or happier. If a claim in an advertisement sounds too good to be true, it probably is. Don't be persuaded by advertising alone to buy a product. Ask people who have used the product. Check with your parents or other adults.

Be especially cautious about buying products through the mail from an unfamiliar source, through cable television shows, or from people who come to your door. If the product disappoints you, you may not be able to get your money back.

in Your Journal

Think of a personal product you purchased recently, such as toothpaste or shampoo. In your journal, list two or three reasons why you bought that brand. List two or three reasons why you did not buy a competing brand.

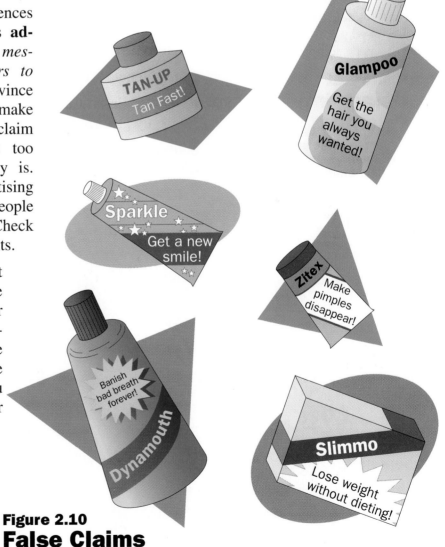

TAN-UP
Tan Fast!

Glampoo
Get the hair you always wanted!

Sparkle
Get a new smile!

Zitex
Make pimples disappear!

Dynamouth
Banish bad breath forever!

Slimmo
Lose weight without dieting!

Figure 2.10
False Claims

According to law, a famous person must actually use a product before he or she can recommend it in an advertisement. However, the law does not require that the famous person like the product. Why would a famous person help sell a product he or she does not like?

Have you ever bought a product because a famous person recommended it? Were you satisfied? Explain why or why not.

Figure 2.11
Using Unit Pricing

Figuring out the unit price will enable you to choose the best product for you—and to understand how much you might spend on packaging.

Smart Shopping

You see something you really like in a store and you buy it immediately. Later that week you see the same item in another store, for a much lower price. Does this sound familiar? You can be a smarter consumer if you comparison shop, read and understand product labels, and know ways to save money.

Looking Around

When comparing brands, consider the following:

■ **Price.** How much can you afford to spend on this product?

■ **Unit price.** How much does the product cost per ounce or per gram? (See **Figure 2.11.**)

■ **Benefits.** Does one brand have more features than another?

■ **Reputation.** Do people you know use and like this brand?

■ **Warranty.** Does this brand have a **warranty,** which is *a promise to make repairs or refund money if the product does not work as claimed?*

When comparing stores, think about the following:

■ **Convenience.** Will travel time waste your time and money?

■ **Return policies.** Can you get your money back, or will the store only give credit?

■ **Sales and discounts.** Does one store regularly have sales or offer discounted prices?

■ **Sales staff.** Are the clerks helpful and knowledgeable?

$233

Price: $2.33
Size: 7 oz.

Price per oz.:
$2.33 divided by 7
Unit price: $0.33

$269

Price: $2.69
Size: 4.4 oz.

Price per oz.:
$2.69 divided by 4.4
Unit price: $0.61

Understanding Product Labels

Before you decide which product to buy, read the labels of each brand carefully. **Figure 2.12** shows the kinds of information you should look for when examining labels. Don't be put off by the small print. Reading it and understanding what you are buying will help you become an informed consumer.

Figure 2.12
What the Labels Can Tell You

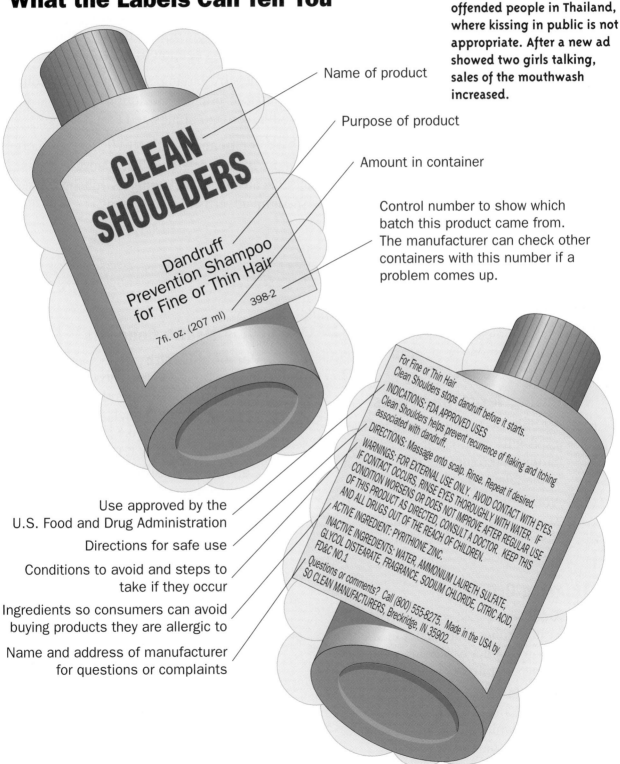

Name of product

Purpose of product

Amount in container

Control number to show which batch this product came from. The manufacturer can check other containers with this number if a problem comes up.

CLEAN SHOULDERS

Dandruff Prevention Shampoo for Fine or Thin Hair

398-2

7 fi. oz. (207 ml)

For Fine or Thin Hair Clean Shoulders stops dandruff before it starts.

INDICATIONS: FDA APPROVED USES Clean Shoulders helps prevent recurrence of flaking and itching associated with dandruff.

DIRECTIONS: Massage onto scalp. Rinse. Repeat if desired.

WARNINGS: FOR EXTERNAL USE ONLY. AVOID CONTACT WITH EYES. IF CONTACT OCCURS, RINSE EYES THOROUGHLY WITH WATER. IF CONDITION WORSENS OR DOES NOT IMPROVE AFTER REGULAR USE OF THIS PRODUCT AS DIRECTED, CONSULT A DOCTOR. KEEP THIS AND ALL DRUGS OUT OF THE REACH OF CHILDREN.

ACTIVE INGREDIENT: PYRITHIONE ZINC.

INACTIVE INGREDIENTS: WATER, AMMONIUM LAURETH SULFATE, GLYCOL DISTEARATE, FRAGRANCE, SODIUM CHLORIDE, CITRIC ACID, FD&C NO.1

Questions or comments? Call (800) 555-8275. Made in the USA by SO CLEAN MANUFACTURERS, Breckridge, IN 35902.

Use approved by the U.S. Food and Drug Administration

Directions for safe use

Conditions to avoid and steps to take if they occur

Ingredients so consumers can avoid buying products they are allergic to

Name and address of manufacturer for questions or complaints

Saving Money

Smart shoppers know how to save money. They learn where to get the best prices and how to pay less for certain goods.

You can start by shopping at **discount stores** for personal products. These are *stores that offer lower prices, but fewer salespeople and services.* Many shoppers don't mind giving up service for the benefit of lower prices.

Another way to save money is to clip and use **coupons** (KOO·pahnz) for the brands you like. *These slips of paper save money on certain brands.* However, don't buy something you don't need just because you have a coupon for it.

You can often save money by buying store brands of some products. For example, a store brand hand lotion may have the same ingredients as well-advertised brands and cost a lot less.

Finally, you can look for **generic** (juh·NEHR·ik) products. These are *goods sold in plain packages.* They cost less than brand name products because the packaging is much cheaper and little money is spent on advertising such goods.

Lesson 3 Review

Using complete sentences, answer the following questions on a separate sheet of paper.

Reviewing Terms and Facts

1. **Recall**   Why should you be especially cautious about buying products through the mail or through cable television?

2. **Vocabulary**   What is a discount store? What advantages and disadvantages does it have over a regular store?

Thinking Critically

3. **Describe**   List some ads or TV commercials that encourage people to buy a product based on the endorsement, or "pitch," of a famous person.

4. **Explain**   Give examples of ways you can use the shopping tips in this lesson while purchasing a service, such as a haircut.

Applying Health Concepts

5. **Personal Health**   Select a personal product that you use and that you would recommend to others. Prepare a presentation in which you explain to the class why you like it, where you bought it, and why it is worth its cost.

6. **Consumer Health**   Write to the manufacturer of a product that you tried and that did not fulfill its claim. Politely describe your experience with the product and ask for a refund. Share any response from the manufacturer with the class.

7. **Consumer Health**   Develop a class coupon exchange. Set up a coupon bank that everyone contributes to and can select from. Divide the bank into categories, such as shampoo, face soap, and toothpaste.

Health Professionals in Your Community

This lesson will help you find answers to questions that teens often ask about health care. For example:

▶ **How do I decide which doctor to see when I am ill?**

▶ **How does health insurance work?**

▶ **What is the government's role in health care?**

Options for Health Care

Health care involves both preventing problems and treating them. Many health workers are involved in preventing problems. These people include dietitians, dental hygienists, health teachers, nurses, and counselors. Part of their job is to help you develop healthy habits that prevent health problems. Remember that practicing good health habits is a lot easier and less expensive than treating problems. If a problem arises, doctors, dentists, nurses, pharmacists, and others can identify and treat whatever is wrong.

When you feel ill, you probably visit your family doctor first. A family doctor provides basic health care for people of all ages. In some cases, your family doctor will refer you to a **specialist** (SPE·she·list). A specialist is *a doctor who is trained to handle a particular health problem.*

Many doctors work both to prevent and treat problems. A regular checkup helps a doctor spot problems and treat them before they become serious.

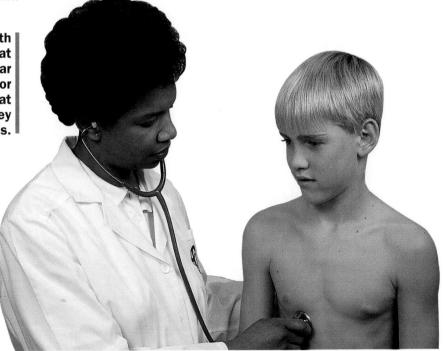

55

Specialists receive extra training after they complete medical school. The extra training enables them to focus on a particular part of the body, or on a particular illness. Because of their extra training they are able to offer more expert help in their specialty. **Figure 2.13** shows some of the specialists who work in our health care system.

Figure 2.13
The Specialists

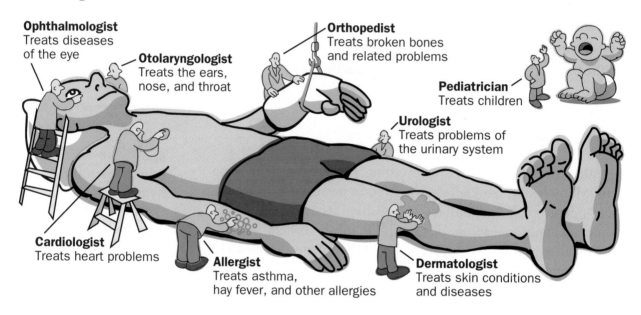

Ophthalmologist
Treats diseases of the eye

Otolaryngologist
Treats the ears, nose, and throat

Orthopedist
Treats broken bones and related problems

Pediatrician
Treats children

Urologist
Treats problems of the urinary system

Cardiologist
Treats heart problems

Allergist
Treats asthma, hay fever, and other allergies

Dermatologist
Treats skin conditions and diseases

LIFE SKILLS
Visiting the Doctor

Growing up means taking more responsibility for your health—and your health care. It is better to go to the doctor regularly for preventive care than to wait until you are ill. However, whether you need a checkup or are ill, you can take an active role when you visit the doctor's office or a clinic.

▶ **Prepare yourself.** If you are ill, write down your symptoms. State when they started and how they have changed. Jot down any questions or worries you have. For example, you might worry that your illness is contagious, especially if you have a special event coming up.

▶ **Ask questions.** The doctor or nurse may use words that you do not understand. Ask questions until you understand what he or she is telling you. If you think of more questions after you get home, see if your parents know the answers. If not, ask them to call the doctor and find out.

▶ **Take notes.** Write down the name of any prescription or over-the-counter medicines you are supposed to take and how often you must take them. List other instructions, such as whether you should apply ice or heat to an injury.

Paying for Health Care

Many people buy **health insurance** (in·SHUR·uhns) to help pay for health care. They pay *a monthly or yearly fee to an insurance company that agrees to pay for some or most costs of medical care.* Many employers pay part of the cost of health insurance for their employees. The employee pays the rest.

People who do not receive health insurance where they work can buy it on their own. The U.S. government, the insurance industry, and many health care providers are studying ways to control the costs of health care and make it more affordable.

One type of health care is called a **health maintenance** (MAYN·tuh·nuhns) **organization (HMO).** This is *a group of health care providers who give health care to members of the HMO.* The members pay a monthly or yearly fee instead of paying for treatment each time they visit the doctor.

Sources of Health Care

You can receive health care in doctors' offices, clinics, and hospitals. Your school is another source. There you learn good health practices from your teachers. The school nurse gives advice and medical care.

Some places provide health care for certain kinds of patients. Drug treatment centers give care to people who are recovering from drug abuse. Nursing homes care for older and disabled people who cannot care for themselves. Hospices care for dying people.

Health care is provided in a variety of settings—including your own school.

▶ **Do what the doctor says.** If you are supposed to rest, stay in bed or lie quietly on the couch. Do any exercises the doctor suggests. If the medicine label says to take it all, finish the bottle even if you start to feel better. Many medicines must be taken for a certain number of days. If you stop too soon, the germs will be weakened by the medicine, but may still be alive. This could cause you to become ill again. The germs may develop resistance to the medicine and be harder to kill next time.

Follow-up Activity

Think about your last visit to a doctor's office. How did you prepare? What questions do you wish you had asked the doctor or nurse? What else could you have done to follow the doctor's advice?

Math Connection

Medicare Facts

Look in almanacs from the past several years. Collect facts about the number of people helped by Medicare or the cost of the program. Make a bar graph to show the changes from year to year. Display the graph in class.

Government Health Services

Many government agencies and departments offer health care, information on health care, and payment for health care. Some of these agencies set standards that help protect our health.

Local and State Governments

All states and most cities and counties have health departments. It is the job of these departments to help prevent disease. Some departments are responsible for providing care for poor and elderly people.

Local and state health departments may be responsible for

■ making sure restaurant and hotel kitchens are clean.

■ collecting and disposing of garbage.

■ making sure your water is safe to drink.

■ teaching people how to take care of their health.

■ helping to stop the spread of disease.

■ keeping records of births, deaths, and diseases.

Federal Government

The U.S. Department of Health and Human Services provides health care and protects our health by

■ providing *Medicaid* and *Medicare.* These two programs fund health care for people who are poor or over 65 years of age.

■ helping to support people who cannot work because of chronic illness or injury.

■ helping to prevent and treat problems involving alcohol, other drugs, and mental health.

■ doing research in areas such as cancer and the health of the elderly and children.

■ identifying and stopping the spread of disease.

Government workers at both the local and federal level protect our health by keeping the environment clean.

58

Voluntary Health Groups

Voluntary health groups work to treat and eliminate certain diseases. They do not get money from the government or make money by selling a product. Instead, they ask people to donate money. The groups use some of the money to pay for research on the disease. They also teach people how to avoid the disease and help people who have the disease. **Figure 2.14** shows some logos of the many voluntary health groups in America.

You or your family members may have helped raise money for some of these organizations. Many people also give their time to help these groups do their jobs.

Figure 2.14
Health Organizations

Review

Using complete sentences, answer the following questions on a separate sheet of paper.

Reviewing Terms and Facts

1. **Vocabulary** What is a specialist? Why do people go to specialists?

2. **Recall** List four places where you can receive health care.

Thinking Critically

3. **Explain** Why do you think many health care providers are emphasizing prevention of disease?

4. **Compare** What is the difference between having health insurance and belonging to an HMO?

5. **Summarize** What are the main areas of health care for which governments take responsibility?

Applying Health Concepts

6. **Consumer Health** Find out more about health insurance by speaking to an adult who has insurance. Ask what services the policy covers, as well as those it does not cover. Find out what the "deductible" is. Ask about the person's experiences in dealing with the insurance company. Discuss what you learned with a small group of classmates.

7. **Health of Others** Some people cannot afford to buy health insurance, but they still need health care. Find out where these people can go to obtain free or reduced-cost health care.

8. **Health of Others** Work in teams to learn about the voluntary health organizations that operate in your community. Share what you learn with the class. Select one organization and raise money for it. (You might make healthful muffins and sell them during lunch.) Tell your customers how the health organization will use the money you raise.

Chapter Summary

▶ Tooth decay begins with a buildup of plaque and tartar. (Lesson 1)

▶ Protect your teeth by brushing, flossing, eating right, and visiting a dentist regularly. (Lesson 1)

▶ The skin's epidermis and dermis layers help protect our bodies. (Lesson 1)

▶ Keep your skin clean, stay out of the direct sun in the middle of the day, eat right, and get enough exercise and sleep. (Lesson 1)

▶ Keep hair healthy by keeping it clean. (Lesson 1)

▶ To protect your eyes, read and watch TV in a well-lighted room, wear protective gear, and do not rub your eyes. (Lesson 2)

▶ Common vision problems include farsightedness, nearsightedness, and astigmatism. (Lesson 2)

▶ Eyeglasses and contact lenses correct how light focuses on the retina of the eye. (Lesson 2)

▶ Sound waves travel to the brain through the eardrum, tiny bones, fluid, and tiny hairs. (Lesson 2)

▶ Protect your ears from cold weather, avoid loud noises, and keep sharp objects away from your ears. (Lesson 2)

▶ Consumers need to know about the factors that influence their purchases. (Lesson 3)

▶ Quackery means selling worthless products by making false claims. (Lesson 3)

▶ To be a smart shopper, compare brands, read product labels, and look for bargains. (Lesson 3)

▶ Health care is available from family doctors, specialists, and many other sources at different locations. (Lesson 4)

▶ Health insurance helps pay for health care. (Lesson 4)

▶ Government agencies provide direct health care, set health standards, and fund some health care. (Lesson 4)

Using Health Terms

On a separate sheet of paper, write the vocabulary term that best matches each definition given below.

1. A soft, sticky film created by the bacteria that live in your mouth (Lesson 1)

2. A substance that fights tooth decay (Lesson 1)

3. Loudness of sound waves (Lesson 2)

4. Selling worthless products or services by making false claims (Lesson 3)

5. A group of health care providers who give health care to members (Lesson 4)

Reviewing Main Ideas

Using complete sentences, answer the following questions on a separate sheet of paper.

1. What should you do to care for your teeth? (Lesson 1)

2. How can you take care of your skin? (Lesson 1)

3. How can you protect your eyes from eyestrain and injury? (Lesson 2)

4. How can you protect your ears? (Lesson 2)

5. What should you consider when comparing brands of personal products? (Lesson 3)

6. What are four ways of saving money when you are shopping for personal products? (Lesson 3)

7. How does health insurance work? (Lesson 4)

Thinking Critically

Using complete sentences, answer the following questions on a separate sheet of paper.

1. **Explain** Give at least four reasons why taking care of your teeth, skin, and hair is important. (Lesson 1)

2. **Analyze** Why do you think many young people choose to listen to loud music even though they know it might damage their hearing? (Lesson 2)

3. **Analyze** Why are some people willing to believe the false claims that are made about products? (Lesson 3)

4. **Contrast** Discuss the good and bad points of deciding to buy a personal product because a friend uses it. (Lesson 3)

5. **Predict** In what ways might our lives change if the federal, state, and local government did not take an active role in health care? (Lesson 4)

6. **Explain** What is the importance of voluntary health groups to the health care system in the country? (Lesson 4)

Your Action Plan

Most people, especially teenagers, want to look attractive and feel healthy. Look through your private journal entries for this chapter. Do you need to take better care of your teeth? Do you need to become a smarter shopper? An action plan can help you make these changes.

First, select a long-term goal. For example, you might decide that you want to become a wise consumer of health care products. Next, think of short-term goals that will help you meet your long-term goal. Short-term goals might include learning to compare prices and to compare labels.

Plan a schedule for reaching each short-term goal. Check your schedule to help keep yourself on track. When you can shop with confidence for health care products, you have reached your long-term goal. Then reward yourself.

Building Your Portfolio

1. Create a chart on which you list the actions you should take regularly to care for your teeth, skin, and hair. Make three columns on your chart, titled *daily, weekly,* and *occasionally.* List the relevant actions in each column. Post the chart in your bedroom or bathroom to remind you of what you need to do. Place a copy of your chart in your portfolio.

2. Watch television commercials for four personal products. List each product and what the commercial claims the product will do. Analyze whether each claim is exaggerated or truthful. Include your analysis in your portfolio.

In Your Home and Community

1. Volunteer to help children at a child care center learn how to brush their teeth. You might make a large picture of teeth for them to practice on. Be sure to explain *why* they need to brush carefully.

2. Arrange a family meeting to discuss what you have learned about buying personal products. Talk about shopping for the best deal. Encourage family members to share their knowledge about local stores, prices, and generic products with you and with each other so you can all gain information.

Chapter 3
Social and Emotional Health

Student Expectations
After reading this chapter, you should be able to:

1. Explain why friendships are important to social health.
2. Describe the characteristics of a healthy family.
3. Identify communication skills for building healthy relationships.
4. Describe ways to manage stress.
5. Identify ways of resolving conflicts.

This morning my mom drove me to school. There were a lot of kids in front of the building when we pulled up. Before I could get out of the car, Mom gave me a hug. I was so embarrassed! I was sure everyone was watching. Mom just laughed and said that no one could see into the car. When she said that, I got really mad. I got out of the car and slammed the door.

Later in the day, I told my best friend, Lisa, what had happened. Lisa said she wished her mom would hug her more often. I began to feel bad about the way I had treated my mom. I decided I'd talk to her when she got home from work.

After supper, I told her I was sorry for getting mad. I said that I just wished she'd stop treating me like a baby. Mom said she was sorry she had embarrassed me. She said it was hard for her to accept the fact that I'm growing up.

Mom promised not to hug me in front of my friends again. Then she said if I wanted, she'd even drop me off a block from school. There was only one condition—I'd have to let her give me a great big hug when she got home. I have the greatest mom!

in your journal

Read the story on this page. Has something like this happened to you? Do you, too, feel as if everyone is watching you? Do you sometimes have difficulty controlling your emotions? Start your private journal entries by answering these questions:

▶ How well do you communicate?
▶ What would you like to change about the way you get along with others?
▶ How do you handle stress and conflict?

When you reach the end of the chapter, you will use your journal entries to make an action plan.

Your Friends

This lesson will help you find answers to questions that teens often ask about friendships. For example:

▶ **Why is having friends important?**

▶ **How can I make and keep friends?**

▶ **What can I do when my friends want me to do things I don't want to do?**

Your Need for Others

Imagine a photo album that contains snapshots of you. Many photos show you with people who are part of your life. These people might be relatives, such as parents, grandparents, and brothers and sisters. They might be neighbors, childhood play-mates, or other people who live nearby. As you get older, the photos in your album might show you with friends and teachers from school and with teammates, coaches, and club leaders from the community. You have a relationship with all these people. A **relationship** (ri·LAY·shuhn·ship) refers to *the connections you have with other people.*

All human beings have a need to feel loved and wanted. We need to feel safe and secure. We need to feel that our actions and ideas are valued. The relationships in your life can help you meet these needs.

When you have strong, healthy relationships, you have good social health.

We took first place that spring!

May 11th – Dad's Birthday

The Importance of Friends

A **friendship** is *a special type of relationship between people who enjoy being with each other.* Friendships are important to teens. You can do homework with a friend, talk over problems, and just have fun together.

When you were younger, your parents probably chose your friends for you. Now that you are getting older, you are choosing your own friends. Right now, your friends are probably the same age and gender as you.

Different Needs, Different Friends

People choose friends for many reasons. Molly, for example, likes Tia because Tia makes her laugh. Molly is friends with Jody because she and Jody take piano lessons from the same teacher. Molly can have fun with Tia and still be Jody's friend.

Here are some reasons why teens make and keep friends. Which of these reasons apply to you and your friends?

■ **Similar interests.** Teens become friends because they enjoy the same hobbies, sports, and other activities.

■ **Similar values.** Teens become friends because their beliefs and standards of behavior are the same. They may meet friends at their place of religious worship or at a volunteer organization where they both help out.

■ **Personal qualities.** Sometimes teens choose friends for their personal qualities such as having a good sense of humor or being a good listener.

■ **Same school or neighborhood.** Sometimes teens become friends because they live close to each other or because they are in the same class or after-school club.

Cultural Diversity

Pen Pals

Many people enjoy making friends with people from different cultures. Become a friend with a teen from a different culture. Ask your teacher or school counselor for the address of an organization that links young people from different countries who want to be pen pals. When you get a pen pal, write a letter to him or her.

Friends provide companionship and keep you from being lonely.

in your journal

You have just read about the importance of friendships. In your journal describe one of your good friends. Tell what that friend means to you.

Qualities of a Good Friend

Friendships exist on several levels. Some friends are casual acquaintances. You may eat lunch with them in the school cafeteria or sit with them at a football game, but that's all.

Other friends are closer to you. You share many experiences, and you feel comfortable telling them your innermost feelings. A sign of good social health is to have one or two good friends.

A good friend demonstrates four characteristics: loyalty, reliability, sympathy, and caring. You expect these qualities in your friend, and your friend expects them in you.

- **Loyalty.** A good friend is faithful to you. If someone says something bad about you, your friend sticks up for you.

- **Reliability.** When *you can count on your friend to do what he or she said,* your friend is **reliable.** Being able to depend on a friend is important if you're working together on a project.

- **Sympathy.** A good friend is **sympathetic** (sim·puh·THE·tik). A sympathetic person is one who is *aware of how you are feeling at a given moment.* He or she understands that you feel bad after a disappointment.

- **Caring.** A good friend wants only the best for you. A caring friend may even risk your friendship by asking you to stop doing something that is hurting you or other people.

Good friends take time to comfort a friend who has been disappointed.

Pressure from Your Peers

During your teen years, relationships with your peers become increasingly important. Your **peers** are *your friends and other people your age.* They support you and give you confidence as you move from depending on your family to being on your own. In exchange, your peers may expect you to act and think like the group. *The influence you feel to go along with the behavior and beliefs of your peer group* is called **peer pressure.**

Types of Peer Pressure

There are two types of peer pressure. Positive peer pressure is what you feel when your peers inspire you to do something worthwhile. Here are some examples.

- Challenging you to work hard as a member of a team

- Inspiring you to improve your health and appearance

- Encouraging you to do your best in school

- Getting you to work with others to improve the community

Teens who see other teens keeping fit may be encouraged to exercise also.

Negative peer pressure is what you feel when your peers challenge you to do something wrong or to try something that goes against your values. Here are some examples.

- Urging you to use tobacco, alcohol, or other drugs

- Daring you to do something dangerous or unsafe

- Coaxing you to be hurtful to someone who has a disability or who is different from you and your friends

- Persuading you to do something that is immoral or illegal such as shoplifting

Dealing with Negative Peer Pressure

It's hard to stand up against negative peer pressure. If you don't go along with the group, you may feel that no one will like you. You worry about being left out. Nevertheless, it's important to be able to resist pressure to do things that are not right for you. Developing your own personal identity, apart from the group, is another part of growing up.

Fortunately, you can learn ways to deal with negative peer pressure. **Figure 3.1** on the next page shows some of these ways. Remember, too, that you can always get help from a responsible person. A parent, an older brother or sister, or a counselor will listen to your problem and help you decide what is the best thing for you to do.

Figure 3.1

Ways to Resist Negative Peer Pressure

What to Do	Example
Avoid situations where trouble might occur. Try to prevent problems by staying away from situations in which you might be subjected to negative peer pressure.	Kim has been invited to a slumber party at Angie's house. Angie's 15-year-old sister will be in charge. Kim thinks the party might get out of control and turns down the invitation.
Do a values check. Your family has taught you certain values and beliefs. When faced with negative peer pressure, consider whether you are being asked to go against what you believe.	A cute boy Pam likes wants to copy her math homework. Although Pam likes the attention, she thinks cheating is wrong. She offers to tutor the boy instead.
Get a "buddy." Find a friend who thinks the way you do. Get support from each other when other teens put on the pressure.	Seth and his friend Joe have been invited to a party where they know some older boys are bringing beer. Seth and Joe don't want to be at a party with alcohol. They decide to have their own party without alcohol.
Say no. You have the right to refuse to give in to negative peer pressure. Oftentimes, you can say no by making an excuse or suggesting a different activity.	Ben's friends get the idea to make prank phone calls to strangers. Ben thinks this is a bad idea and suggests they play cards instead.
Walk away. If the pressure is too great, the best thing to do is leave. Don't wait for a situation to get better.	Shara is approached on her front porch by an older teen who asks her if she wants to buy drugs. Shara says no. When the boy won't leave, Shara goes inside.

LIFE SKILLS

Learning to Say No

*O*ne way to be ready to say no to negative peer pressure is to plan ahead. Think of reasons for saying no. Practice what you would say and do.

With four or five classmates, role-play the following situations. For each role-play, have one group member be the teen who must resist the pressure. Have the other group members be the teens who apply the pressure. Take turns being the teen under pressure.

Situation 1   Your friends want you to shoplift from a store at the mall.

Situation 2   Some teens at a party offer you punch spiked with alcohol.

Situation 3   Your friends want you to skip school and go to a movie.

Situation 4   Your friends want you to join them in teasing a classmate who uses a wheelchair.

As you practice saying no, remember these points.

▶ Be firm; mean what you say.

▶ Speak calmly.

Using complete sentences, answer the following questions on a separate sheet of paper.

Reviewing Terms and Facts

1. **Vocabulary** Define the word *relationship* and use it in a sentence.
2. **List** Name four reasons why teens may become friends.
3. **Identify** What are four qualities that good friends have?
4. **Vocabulary** Define the term *peer pressure*. Use it in a sentence in which you give an example of such pressure.

Thinking Critically

5. **Explain** How do good relationships help you to have good social health?

6. **Describe** Give an example of how a person could show loyalty to a friend who is being laughed at behind his or her back.

Applying Health Concepts

7. **Growth and Development** Write a paragraph in which you describe a friendship you had as a child and the ways, if any, it has changed as you have grown.
8. **Health of Others** With your classmates, create a drug-prevention play that demonstrates methods of positive peer pressure. Ask your teacher if you can present the play to other classes in your school.

C'mon, don't be **Chicken.**

- ▶ Look your peers in the eye. If you act wishy-washy, your peers will think they can change your mind.
- ▶ Don't give in, even a little.
- ▶ Offer alternatives to the negative idea.

Follow-up Activity

After each role-play, review the responses of the teen dealing with the pressure. Discuss other options for a teen in that situation.

KEEP OUT

Your Family

This lesson will help you find answers to questions that teens often ask about their relationships with their families. For example:

▶ How does my family affect the kind of person I become?
▶ What type of family do I have?
▶ What is my role within my family?
▶ What can I do if my family has a problem?

Words to Know

family
nuclear family
couple family
single-parent
   family
blended family
extended family
abuse
sexual abuse
neglect

Belonging to a Family

The first relationships you formed were with your family. The **family** is *the basic unit of society.* Families come in many varieties, some of which are shown in **Figure 3.2.**

Figure 3.2
Types of Families
Families come in many sizes and have many different types of relationships.

A A **nuclear family** is made up of *two parents and one or more children.* Although it is often thought of as the most common, only one out of three families is a nuclear family.

B A **couple family** is made up of *two people who do not have children.*

C In a **single-parent family,** *the child or children live with only one parent.* The parent may be a mother or father who is divorced, single, or widowed.

Your family helps you in many ways. When you were a baby, your family provided you with everything you needed, including food, clothing, and a place to live. Your family was also responsible for giving you love and attention.

As you grow, you learn from your family the skills you need to become an independent adult. Within your family, you first start to learn who you are. Family members help you develop your personality and your attitudes. They teach you values, beliefs, and how to make good choices. They also teach you how to get along with others and to be responsible for your actions.

Other Types of Families

Families with children may also be adoptive families or foster families. These are families who have children who are not related by birth. In an adoptive family, the children have become a permanent part of the family through a legal process. In a foster family, the children cannot live with their birth families for some reason. They are placed by government agencies with foster families for a certain period of time. Sometimes the foster parents adopt the foster child.

in your journal

What type of family do you belong to? In your journal, write two positive outcomes of being in this type of family. You can also write about any challenges you may feel belonging to this type of family.

E An **extended family** is made up of *a nuclear or single-parent family plus other relatives.* Sometimes grandparents, aunts, uncles, cousins, or adult children may live together with the smaller family.

D A **blended family** forms when *people who have been married before marry each other. One or both may have children from a previous marriage.*

The Ideal Family

ACTIVITY!

Do you ever wish that your family was like your friend's because his or hers seems to be ideal? You should remember that even families that look "ideal" may have problems. You can work to make your family the best it can be by being helpful and thoughtful. Start today by offering to take on an additional household chore.

The family is much different today than it was early in the twentieth century. However, the function of the family remains the same—to provide love, care, and emotional support for the family members.

Changing Families

The way the family unit is organized and how it functions have changed dramatically in the past 50 to 100 years.

- **Single-parent families.** One out of four families today is a single-parent family, up from one in ten in 1960. The increase in this number is due largely to the increased divorce rate. In some cases of divorce, parents share custody of the children, and the children may spend time living with each parent.

- **Mothers working outside the home.** Today, more than half of mothers with children under six years old have jobs outside the home. In many cases, the money they earn is needed to support the family.

- **Smaller families.** In the past, couples often had many children. Fathers worked to support the family, and mothers stayed home to raise the children. They were often helped by grandparents or other relatives who lived with the family. Today families are usually much smaller. Reasons include the parents' concern about the costs of child care and education. Also, mothers work outside the home. Grandparents often live too far away to help. By having smaller families, parents may feel that they can do a better job raising each child.

- **Mobile families.** Families move much more often than in the past. People often move for job opportunities. Many families now live far away from their relatives.

Healthy Families

The changes that the family unit has undergone over the years present many challenges. To be healthy, families must care about, respect, and love each other. Here are some other ways families can be healthy.

- **Communicate.** Family members should talk openly and honestly to build trust.

- **Spend time together.** Families should share work and play.

- **Keep traditions.** Ethnic and religious traditions may be handed down for generations. Families may also start their own traditions.

- **Be flexible.** Families should be able to adapt to changes when they are needed.

Keeping traditions and spending time together are important ways to have a healthy family.

Dealing with Family Problems

All families have problems. Parents may divorce. A parent may lose a job. A family member may get sick. A child might have problems at school or with friends. Sometimes brothers and sisters have trouble getting along.

When a problem occurs, one of the first steps is to talk openly. Adults and children must feel free to share information and feelings. All family members need to find what they can do to help out. When a problem is too serious for the family to solve, the family should seek outside help. Many types of counseling are available.

Pattern of Abuse

Children who are abused often become abusers themselves as adults. It is the only way they know to be a parent. That is one reason why it is so important to stop a child from being abused.

Abuse in the Family

Abuse (uh·BYOOS) is a *pattern of mistreatment of another person.* Usually people who abuse another family member have low self-esteem and want to control every situation. They take out their feelings and their problems on a weaker family member. For instance, one spouse, often a husband, abuses the other spouse; parents and other relatives abuse children; and adults abuse elderly parents and relatives.

Mistreatment comes in several forms: physical, emotional, and sexual abuse, as well as neglect.

■ **Physical abuse.** Physical abuse involves the excessive use of force. There are usually signs of physical abuse—bruises, burns, bite marks, or broken bones.

■ **Emotional abuse.** Often signs of emotional abuse are not easy to spot. One sign is that a person may constantly yell at or put down another, making the other person feel worthless.

■ **Sexual abuse. Sexual abuse** is *any sexual activity between anyone and a child.*

■ **Neglect.** *The failure of parents to provide basic physical and emotional care for their children* is called **neglect.** Physical neglect involves not providing food, clothing, shelter, or medical care. Emotional neglect involves withholding love, affection, and other forms of emotional support.

Whether abuse or neglect is physical or emotional, it is harmful. Effects are long-lasting. No one has the right to abuse others, and no one should be required to accept abuse.

Getting Help

When someone is being abused, outside help is needed right away. First, someone must be told so that the person being abused can be kept safe from further harm. If a person is in immediate danger, call the police. Second, the person who is abusing others needs help in order to stop. There are many types of help for families and children in need.

■ **Family counseling.** When a family has serious trouble, professional family counselors can help. They teach family members to listen to each other and to work together to find solutions. Counseling is also provided by social service agencies, school counselors, and hospital social workers.

■ **Crisis hot lines.** There are toll-free phone numbers you can call for help. They may be listed in your telephone directory under "hot lines" or "crisis intervention." You can also dial "0" (zero) for an operator to ask for hot line numbers.

- **Youth services.** All cases of suspected child abuse must be reported to government social service agencies. These agencies take a child in immediate danger out of the home and look into the case. The easiest way to get help from these services is to call the police.

- **Shelters.** Special shelters offer a safe home for women and children who need to be protected from danger. People who are experienced in dealing with abusive situations help the family locate safe living arrangements and may provide counseling.

- **Support and self-help groups.** Some support groups are made up of victims of abuse. Others, such as Parents Anonymous, are made up of parents who have been abusive to their children. They help each other change their behavior.

Review

Lesson 2

Using complete sentences, answer the following questions on a separate sheet of paper.

Reviewing Terms and Facts

1. **Vocabulary** Define the following types of families: *nuclear family, extended family, blended family.*

2. **Give Examples** Name three needs a family provides for the children.

3. **Recall** Name four ways families have changed.

4. **List** What are four qualities that healthy families have?

5. **Vocabulary** What is the difference between *abuse* and *neglect?*

Thinking Critically

6. **Suggest** What are some problems that might occur for a child when divorced parents share custody?

7. **Explain** Why might one family member abuse another?

Applying Health Concepts

8. **Personal Health** Write a skit about a situation in which a family is practicing healthy behavior. Assign roles to your classmates, and perform the skit.

9. **Health of Others** Make a poster showing places in your community where a person who is being abused can get help. You can use the Yellow Pages of your local telephone book to find names of government agencies and private organizations. Be sure to include phone numbers on your poster.

Teens Making a Difference

Grandparents' Day

The first Friday of every month is Grandparents' Day at Jefferson Middle School. Residents of a nearby senior citizens' apartment complex spend the day at the school. They help the students with their schoolwork. They also demonstrate crafts, share their hobbies, and tell stories.

Grandparents' Day was created by Tony Cardoza, a sixth grader at the school. He got the idea after inviting his own grandfather, a retired fire fighter, to speak about safety to the sixth-grade class.

Miss Evans, the school counselor, helped Tony set up the program. Since many of the students' grandparents live far away, they decided to invite "substitute" grandparents from the apartment complex.

Grandparents' Day has been a great success. Both the children and the senior citizens benefit from the program and have developed greater respect and appreciation for one another.

High-tech Greeting Cards

Sending greeting cards is one way that people maintain their relationships. Greeting cards let others know that you're thinking about them.

Card shops offer consumers a wide assortment of cards. However, if consumers want a more personalized card, they can create one using special computer-equipped booths. These booths are installed in card stores by greeting card companies.

If you're tempted to create a high-tech greeting card, think about whether you're spending your money wisely. High-tech cards cost more than regular cards. They also are only as creative as the computer program allows.

If you want to save money and be truly original, try sending homemade cards. Friends and family members will appreciate the effort you put into creating the card.

Sports
and
Recreation

Pass It On

NFL quarterback Warren Moon grew up in a troubled neighborhood in West Los Angeles. He might have turned to gangs and violence, except for some important relationships.

Warren's father died when Warren was seven years old. His mother raised Warren and his six sisters. She taught the children many values, including the importance of sharing.

As a boy, Warren played on a police-club football team. Warren's coaches were like fathers to him. They encouraged him to work hard in school.

Now, as an adult, Warren passes that advice on to kids. While playing for the Houston Oilers, Warren started the Crescent Moon Foundation. This organization helps high school students pay for their college education.

People at Work

The Professional Mediator

Suzanne Foster knows that sometimes people cannot settle their differences. That's when Suzanne gets involved. Suzanne is a professional mediator, an expert in helping people solve their problems.

Unlike a judge, a mediator doesn't decide who is right or wrong. A mediator acts as a neutral party and helps people work out a solution together. A mediator must be a good listener and a good communicator.

Mediators often have a background in another field, such as social work or law. They must have about 40 hours of special mediation training.

Some mediators work in schools. They train teachers to resolve conflicts. Sometimes mediators train students, who then become peer mediators. These students learn how to help other students solve their disagreements.

"I teach people that disagreements can be settled peacefully," says Suzanne. "They don't have to lead to violence."

Health Update

Staying Relaxed

Stress management was once thought to be something that only adults needed. Now, stress management is being taught in many middle and elementary schools.

In one sixth-grade classroom in New York, students start every Monday morning with a one-hour "stressbuster." The principal and teachers lead discussion groups of 8 to 12 students. They talk about situations in common that cause stress in their lives: friends, homework, tests, divorce, the economy, violence, and substance abuse.

By sharing experiences, students help identify what causes them stress. They also don't feel so alone. As one student explains, they learn that "most kids are going through the same things."

3 Communicating Thoughts and Feelings

This lesson will help you find answers to questions that teens often ask about communicating thoughts and feelings. For example:

► Why do I sometimes feel angry or sad for no reason?
► What's the best way to communicate my thoughts and feelings?
► How can I be a better listener?

Words to Know

emotion
hormone
communication

Your Emotions

Are you happy right now? Maybe you're sad or even angry. Happiness, sadness, and anger are **emotions,** or *feelings.* **Figure 3.3** shows some common emotions. Can you think of others?

During your teen years, **hormones** (HOR·mohnz) cause rapid physical changes in your body. Hormones are *special chemicals, produced by glands, that regulate many body functions.* Hormones also cause emotional shifts. One minute you feel on top of the world. The next minute you are down in the dumps.

Figure 3.3
The Emotional Pendulum of Adolescence
Emotional shifts are common for young people.

Expressing Your Emotions

Learning how to deal with your emotions may take some practice. The first step is to be aware of your feelings and to accept them. You should also try to learn why you feel as you do.

It is important to know that emotions themselves are neither good nor bad. The way you express, or release, your emotions is what matters. For instance, it's natural to feel angry from time to time. However, yelling at another person is a poor way to express anger. Here are some healthy ways to express emotions such as anger, sadness, and disappointment.

- Talking to others can help you understand your feelings.
- Being alone lets you think about why you feel as you do.
- Creating something helps you express your feelings.
- Exercising helps you work out your feelings.

What Is Communication?

When you're sad or when you're happy, you might tell a friend about your feelings. Your friend might respond by giving you advice or encouragement. Your friend might also tell you about a time that he or she felt sad or happy. At times like these, you and your friend are communicating.

Communication is *the exchange of thoughts and feelings between two or more people.* As **Figure 3.4** shows, the communication process requires a message, a sender, and a receiver. Communication is a two-way process. It involves not only giving messages but also receiving them.

Your Total Health

Escape Hatch

Releasing your emotions in healthy ways benefits all sides of the health triangle.

Physical Health You will be less likely to get upset stomachs or headaches from holding in your feelings.

Mental Health You will not waste time thinking over and over about what makes you sad or angry.

Social Health You will not let your emotions upset your relationships with other people.

Figure 3.4
The Communication Process

When you send a message and another person receives it, you are communicating.

Types of Communication

People communicate with one another in many ways. Communication is more than just speaking and listening. In fact, when expressing feelings, people sometimes show more through their body movements than through their words. Your friend may say that she's fine, but the look on her face tells you that she's worried about something. People communicate through all of the following methods.

- **Words.** People communicate through speaking and listening. In addition to words, a person's tone of voice reveals his or her feelings. Sometimes people send mixed messages—their words don't match their tone of voice. Mixed messages are confusing for listeners.

- **Facial expressions.** People communicate by the expressions, or looks, on their faces. A smile suggests that a person is happy. A raised eyebrow might mean that someone is doubtful or suspicious.

- **Gestures.** People communicate by gestures, or movements of their hands and arms. A clenched fist suggests that a person is angry. People sometimes tap their fingers when they're nervous. Arms crossed tightly across the chest may mean that a person feels uncertain.

- **Posture.** People communicate with their posture, or the way they hold their bodies. Standing or sitting erect with the head held high suggests that a person feels good. People who feel sad or depressed often slouch or walk with their heads down and shoulders drooping.

HEALTH LAB
Body Language

Introduction: Facial expressions, gestures, and posture are called *body language.* They are a "language" because they communicate a person's thoughts and feelings just as words do. In fact, body language sometimes communicates thoughts and feelings more accurately than words.

Objective: Identify types of body language that people use in communication.

Materials and Method: Watch a 30-minute show on television. Observe people's facial expressions, gestures, and posture as they speak or listen.

Building Blocks of Communication

Learning to communicate well takes practice. You need to be willing to share your thoughts and feelings so that people can get to know you. In turn, you need to be willing to listen to other people's thoughts and feelings. **Figure 3.5** shows rules for developing good speaking and listening skills. Using these rules will help you improve your communication skills and build healthy relationships.

Figure 3.5
Rules of Good Communication

Following these communication rules will help you become a better speaker and listener.

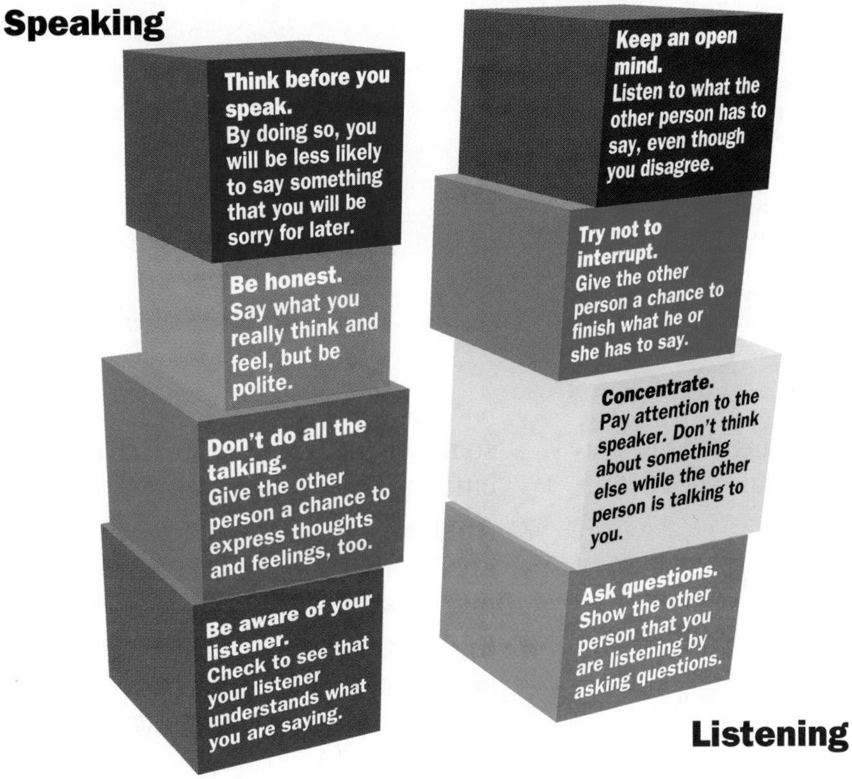

Speaking

Think before you speak.
By doing so, you will be less likely to say something that you will be sorry for later.

Be honest.
Say what you really think and feel, but be polite.

Don't do all the talking.
Give the other person a chance to express thoughts and feelings, too.

Be aware of your listener.
Check to see that your listener understands what you are saying.

Keep an open mind.
Listen to what the other person has to say, even though you disagree.

Try not to interrupt.
Give the other person a chance to finish what he or she has to say.

Concentrate.
Pay attention to the speaker. Don't think about something else while the other person is talking to you.

Ask questions.
Show the other person that you are listening by asking questions.

Listening

Cultural Diversity

Best Face Forward
ACTIVITY!

Traditional Japanese culture teaches that a person's facial expression should remain serene, even in the worst situations. Showing inner thoughts and feelings is considered rude and a sign of weakness. See if you can find other examples of cultural differences in facial expressions, gestures, and posture.

Divide a sheet of paper into two columns. In the first column, describe each type of body language that you observed. In the second column, describe what you think the body language shows about the person's thoughts and feelings.

Observation and Analysis:
Share your observations with a small group of classmates. See how many different examples of body language the group identified. In what ways might an awareness of your own body language improve your communication skills? How is communication different when body language is not used (for example, during a telephone conversation)?

Think of a person with whom you like to talk. In your journal, explain why you like to talk to that person. Does he or she feel the same way about you? Why or why not?

Developing Good Communication Skills

Developing good communication skills is important. Effective communication helps you meet your needs. No one can help you with a problem unless you say what is bothering you. Effective communication helps build healthy relationships. Misunderstandings arise when people do not say what they think or when they speak in negative ways. People who talk openly and honestly with each other will find it easier to settle conflicts.

I always feel better when I talk to you.

Good communication skills are essential to building healthy relationships.

Review

Using complete sentences, answer the following questions on a separate sheet of paper.

Reviewing Terms and Facts

1. **Give Examples** List five common emotions.
2. **List** Name three healthy ways to express your emotions.
3. **Vocabulary** Define the term *communication*. Use it in an original sentence.
4. **Recall** Name three ways in which people communicate with one another.
5. **Identify** List four rules for good speaking.

Thinking Critically

6. **Explain** Write a paragraph describing a situation in which you or someone you know expressed an emotion in a healthy way.

7. **Analyze** How might developing good communication skills help you in the future?
8. **Suggest** What actions might you take to make sure that a listener understands what you are saying?

Applying Health Concepts

9. **Growth and Development** Work with a partner to find magazine and newspaper pictures of people showing emotions through facial expressions, gestures, or posture. Use your pictures to create a collage.

10. **Health of Others** Write a short story about a teen with a communication problem. Explain how he or she solved the problem. Share your story with a classmate.

Managing Stress

This lesson will help you find answers to questions that teens often ask about stress. For example:

▶ **Is it normal for me to feel stress?**
▶ **What happens if I feel too much stress?**
▶ **What can I do when I feel stressed-out?**

What Is Stress?

Katie has to give a book report in front of the class. Her throat is dry and her stomach feels like it is twisted in knots. Why does she feel this way? Darla asks Paul to be her partner on the science project. Paul's eyes light up and his heart seems to skip a beat. What's happening?

Both Katie and Paul feel **stress.** Stress is *your body's response to changes around you.* The stress may be caused by everyday changes such as taking a math test or playing in a band concert. The stress may be caused by major life changes such as moving to a new house or the death of a pet. Stress can be caused by good situations as well as by bad situations. Whatever the situation, remember that stress is a natural part of life. Everyone feels stress.

Words to Know

stress
distress
stressor
adrenaline
fatigue

Language Arts Connection

What Is Stress? ACTIVITY!

The word stress can have several different meanings. This lesson tells you what stress means in the area of health. Do research to find out what stress means in music, in language, and in science. Write a one-page report on your findings.

Katie is feeling stress. Can you think of other examples of stressful situations?

Types of Stress

There are two types of stress. Positive stress helps you accomplish tasks and reach goals. It also helps you escape danger. Your body needs positive stress to function properly. *Negative stress,* or **distress,** holds you back. When people say they are "under a lot of stress," they are talking about negative stress. Too much negative stress can be unhealthy. **Figure 3.6** shows examples of positive and negative stress.

Environmental Stress

Negative stress can be caused by personal problems like those illustrated above. Negative stress can also be caused by your surroundings. Living in noisy, crowded conditions, for example, can produce negative stress. People who have experienced a natural disaster also experience negative stress.

Figure 3.6
Two Types of Stress

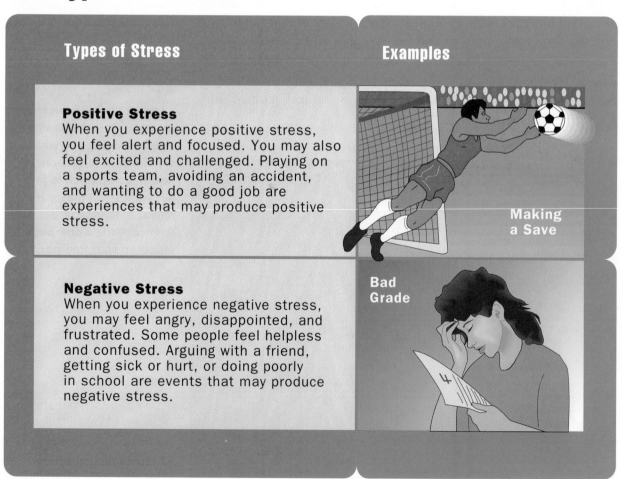

Types of Stress

Positive Stress
When you experience positive stress, you feel alert and focused. You may also feel excited and challenged. Playing on a sports team, avoiding an accident, and wanting to do a good job are experiences that may produce positive stress.

Negative Stress
When you experience negative stress, you may feel angry, disappointed, and frustrated. Some people feel helpless and confused. Arguing with a friend, getting sick or hurt, or doing poorly in school are events that may produce negative stress.

Examples

Making a Save

Bad Grade

How the Body Responds

You're waiting in line to get on the Egg Beater, an amusement park ride. As you watch the Egg Beater turn people upside down and you hear them screaming, your hands become sweaty and your muscles tighten. The ride itself and the thought of being turned upside down are **stressors.** Stressors are *objects, people, places, and events that trigger stress.* **Figure 3.7** shows how the body responds to stressors. Although the body responds to stressors in predictable ways, it isn't easy to predict what will be a stressor for a particular person. You may tense up at the thought of getting on the Egg Beater, but your friends may think nothing of it and be completely relaxed.

In Your Journal

You have just read about stressors. In your journal, make a list of the things that are stressors for you. Include situations that cause positive stress as well as those that cause negative stress.

Figure 3.7
The Body's Response to a Stressor

Physical changes occur when you experience stress. This illustration shows some of them.

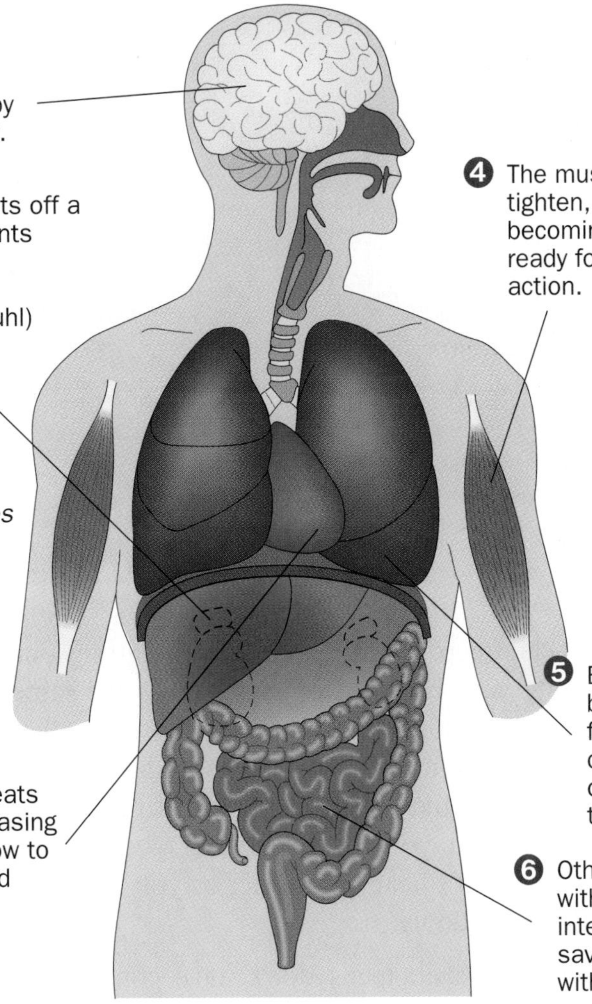

❶ The brain is stimulated by the stressor.

❷ The brain sets off a chain of events that signals the adrenal (uh·DREEN·uhl) glands to send out **adrenaline** (uh·DRE·nuhl·in), *a hormone that prepares the body to respond to a stressor.*

❸ The heart beats faster, increasing the blood flow to the brain and muscles.

❹ The muscles tighten, becoming ready for action.

❺ Breathing becomes faster and deeper. More oxygen enters the body.

❻ Other organs also help the body deal with the stressor. The stomach and intestines slow down their activities to save energy. Once the stressor is dealt with, the body returns to normal.

Q&A

Dry Mouth

Q: Why does my mouth get dry when I'm scared or upset?

A: This is another way your body reacts to a stressor. The presence of a stressor causes natural moisture in your mouth and air passages to dry up. This makes these passages bigger, allowing you to take in more oxygen.

Stress and Wellness

Emotional stress makes you more susceptible to colds, flu, and other infectious illnesses. When you catch an illness, you are likely to stay sick longer if you are experiencing emotional stress than if you are not.

Stress and Tiredness

The body operates at a high energy level to deal with stress. When a stressor continues over a long period of time or when too many stressors act at the same time, the body becomes tired. **Fatigue** (fuh·TEEG), or *extreme tiredness,* sets in. There are two types of fatigue.

■ Physical fatigue occurs after vigorous activity such as running a race or raking the yard. The muscles feel overworked and sore. The solution for this type of fatigue is rest.

■ Emotional fatigue results from too much negative stress. Worry, feelings of sadness, and boredom bring on this type of fatigue. Dealing with it involves removing the source of stress or learning how to manage it.

You will experience physical fatigue after strenuous exercise. Getting proper rest helps you deal with physical fatigue.

Managing Stress

You can keep negative stress from getting out of control and damaging your health. Doing this takes the same kinds of planning and decision making that you use in other areas of your life. First of all, identify what causes you stress. Avoid that stressor or try to remove it. Loud music from your brother's sound system may jar your nerves. Either you can go to some place where you can't hear the music, or you can ask your brother to turn the radio down.

Often, however, teens don't have control over the cause of their stress. They can't stop their teachers from giving tests. They can't stop their parents from arguing. Teens can, however, control how the stressor affects them.

Ways to Reduce Stress

When you can't control the source of your stress, work on controlling your own response. These strategies will help reduce negative stress in your life.

- **Plan ahead.** Set aside a regular time for doing homework and chores. Then you won't have to worry about getting them done at the last minute.

- **Set your priorities.** Realize that you can't do everything. Too many practices, club meetings, and other scheduled activities can be stressful.

- **Redirect your energy.** Whenever you are feeling angry or excited, you have extra energy. Use that energy to accomplish something positive.

- **Talk to someone.** Telling someone else how you feel when you are upset relieves pressure. A friend, parent, or counselor may have some good advice for you.

- **Relax.** Be sure to take time for yourself. Laugh with your friends or take a quiet walk. Try to empty your mind of troubling thoughts.

in your journal

Ask friends and family members what they do to relieve stress. Write their suggestions in your journal. Circle the strategies you would like to try.

Review

Lesson 4

Using complete sentences, answer the following questions on a separate sheet of paper.

Reviewing Terms and Facts

1. **Vocabulary** Explain the difference between *stress* and *distress*.

2. **Give Examples** Name one type of positive stress and one type of negative stress in your life.

3. **List** Name two ways the human body responds to stress.

4. **Identify** What are the two types of fatigue?

Thinking Critically

5. **Explain** Why do you think adrenaline is sometimes called "the emergency hormone"?

6. **Distinguish** Compare the causes of physical fatigue with the causes of emotional fatigue.

7. **Apply** Harley feels a lot of stress because his parents constantly argue. What advice would you give to Harley?

Applying Health Concepts

8. **Consumer Health** As a class, listen to a "relaxation tape." The tape may contain soothing classical music or the recorded sounds of nature. Discuss the pros and cons of such tapes and whether you would recommend that teens purchase them for reducing stress.

9. **Growth and Development** Make a chart that shows how you spend your time during a typical week. Then analyze your chart to see how you might improve your schedule to reduce stress. Try out your new schedule.

This lesson will help you find answers to questions that teens often ask about conflict. For example:

▶ Why do I sometimes argue and fight with other people?

▶ How can I keep conflicts from happening?

▶ What can I do if I'm not getting along with someone?

Words to Know

conflict
tolerance
compromise
peer mediation
neutral

Why Does Conflict Occur?

A **conflict** is *a problem in a relationship.* People experiencing a conflict might shout at each other, not speak to each other, or even hurt each other physically. **Figure 3.8** shows some issues or events that might ignite, or set off, a conflict.

Figure 3.8
Lighting the Fires of Conflict

This illustration depicts situations as matches that light the bonfire of conflict. What situations have led to conflict in your life?

Ⓐ Differing Expectations
Steve thinks he should get paid for mowing the lawn. Dad thinks mowing the lawn is part of Steve's responsibility as a family member.

Ⓑ Differing Values
Marissa keeps her side of the bedroom as neat as a pin. Her sister Samantha doesn't mind piles of books and clothes on her side.

Ⓒ Hurt Feelings
Gina's friend Jade went to the mall with some other girls and didn't invite Gina to go along.

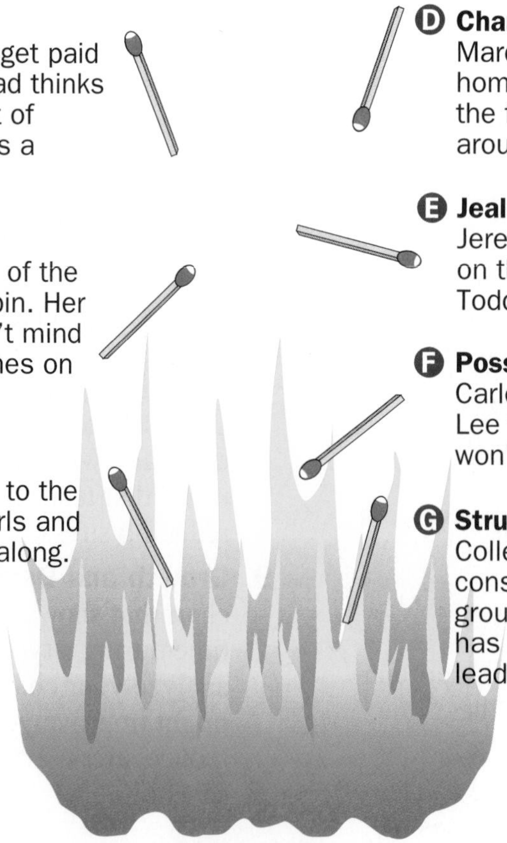

Ⓓ Changing Roles
Marc's mom got a job outside the home. Now Marc and the rest of the family have more work to do around the house.

Ⓔ Jealousy
Jeremy won the catcher's position on the softball team instead of Todd.

Ⓕ Possessions
Carlos lost his stereo headphones. Lee found the headphones and won't give them back.

Ⓖ Struggle for Power
Colleen's group of friends always considered her the leader of their group. Lately Megan, a new girl, has been challenging that leadership.

Conflict

Preventing Conflict

The best way to deal with conflict is to prevent it from occurring in the first place. Here are some things you can do.

- **Practice tolerance.** *The ability to accept other people as they are* is called **tolerance.** Remember that other people are individuals. They won't always behave as you want them to.

- **Express your thoughts and feelings.** Practicing good speaking and listening skills will keep the lines of communication open. You will be able to clear up misunderstandings early and prevent bad feelings from building up.

- **Walk away.** If you find yourself becoming angry with another person, remove yourself from the situation. Exchanging angry words and insults will only make the situation worse. Wait until you've cooled off before trying to solve the problem. Also, remember that some topics are just not worth fighting over. Know what's important to you. Save your energy for issues that really matter.

- **"Deflate" the situation.** If you feel that a conflict is about to arise, try to take the air out of it. Change the subject or turn to another activity. Telling a joke is also a way to ease tension.

Resolving Conflict

Resolving conflict peacefully is important. Fighting that goes on and on may

- permanently damage relationships.

- disturb the peace at home, school, and other places.

- cause emotional fatigue and related illnesses.

- lead to violence and serious bodily and emotional harm.

If you find yourself involved in an argument or dispute, there are several things you can do to resolve the conflict peacefully. These methods include communication, compromise, and peer mediation, which are discussed on pages 90–93.

Cultural Diversity

Learning Tolerance

Identify an event in your community or school that is designed to encourage tolerance toward people of different races, religions, and ethnic groups. Share your example with your classmates.

in Your Journal

Use your journal to describe a conflict you or someone you know had recently. What was the cause of the conflict? How could the conflict have been prevented?

You may be able to help resolve conflicts among your friends. Sometimes a person who isn't emotionally involved in the situation can see it more clearly.

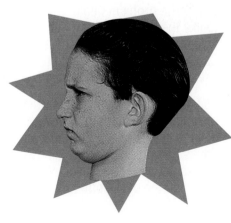

Clambake

Q: Whenever my friend is mad at me, she clams up. She doesn't say a thing. I never know why she's mad or what I've done. This makes me steamed!

A: Be patient with your friend. She may have grown up in a family where people don't express their feelings. Tell your friend how her silence makes you feel. Maybe she'll gradually open up.

Communication

One way to resolve a conflict is to talk to the other person. Try to get the person to hear your side of the argument, but also listen carefully to his or her side. Good speaking and listening skills are especially important when you are trying to settle a dispute. Here are pointers for effective communication when you are involved in a conflict.

- **Choose the right time and place.** Find a time to talk when you're not busy. Find a quiet place to talk where you know you won't be interrupted.

- **Stick to the point.** Talk only about the problem at hand. If you bring up other qualities about the person that annoy you, you'll complicate the situation.

- **Stay calm.** Try not to get angry. If you start shouting, the other person won't listen to you. If you're angry, you won't hear the other person's point of view.

- **Choose your words carefully.** Try not to say anything that will make the conflict worse. Plan ahead of time what you want to say and how to say it.

- **Show respect.** Don't judge or make fun of the other person's ideas. Avoid making threats.

- **Listen.** Make an effort to understand what the other person is saying. Think about the person's words and feelings.

MAKING HEALTHY DECISIONS
Coping with Emotions

*L*ast week Kari and Samantha were best friends. This week they can't stand each other. The problem began when both girls began to like the same boy. Kari thinks she should be able to like him because she liked him first. Samantha thinks she should be able to like him because she's in the same math class as the boy.

The girls started calling each other names and making fun of each other. Now, however, the dispute seems to be growing even worse. Kari thinks Samantha may be taking pencils and lunch tickets out of her backpack. Samantha is starting to turn some of the other girls against Kari, too.

Compromise

Resolving conflict usually requires compromise. **Compromise** (KAHM·pruh·myz) means *each person gives up something in order to reach a solution that satisfies everyone.* Compromise is sometimes called "give-and-take."

in your journal

In your journal, describe a time when you used, or could have used, compromise to resolve a conflict. What did each side give up to reach a solution?

Where do you think you're going? This is your day to mow the lawn.

The big game's today, Dad. All my friends are going. I can't miss it.

I'll make a deal with you. I'll mow the lawn today so you can go to the game, but you'll wash my car tomorrow.

That's cool, Dad, and next week, why don't we go to a game together after I mow the lawn?

Deal!

This father and son are working out a compromise. What does each one give up? What does each one gain?

Kari can't concentrate on her schoolwork, and her stomach hurts every morning. She knows she has to do something, but what? Should she turn Samantha in for stealing? Should she just forget about it and let Samantha win? Sometimes Kari wishes she and Samantha could just be friends again.

Kari can't decide what to do, so she decides to use the six-step decision-making process.

❶ **State the situation**
❷ **List the options**
❸ **Weigh the possible outcomes**
❹ **Consider your values**
❺ **Make a decision and act**
❻ **Evaluate the decision**

Follow-up Activities

1. Apply the six steps of the decision-making process to Kari's problem.
2. With a partner, role-play a scene in which Kari talks to Samantha about their conflict.
3. Role-play a scene in which a peer counselor tries to help Kari and Samantha resolve their conflict.

Did You Know?

Peer Justice

About 5,000 schools in the United States have peer mediation programs. Students like these programs because they feel they can be more open with people their age.

Peer Mediation

Another way to resolve conflict is to ask a third person, or mediator, to step in and help. This person might be a school counselor, a teacher, or another adult. Many schools now provide peer mediation programs. **Peer mediation** is *a process in which a specially trained student listens to both sides of an argument and then helps the opposing sides reach a solution.* **Figure 3.9** shows the steps a peer mediator might follow to help settle a conflict.

Figure 3.9

The Mediation Process

Peer mediators go through hours of training to help other students resolve conflicts. These are the basic steps in any mediation situation.

STEP 1

Establish neutrality.
Tell the opposing sides you will remain **neutral.** *You will not take sides or decide who is right or wrong.*

STEP 2

Set the ground rules.
Get the opposing sides to agree on rules for keeping the discussion fair and orderly. For example, you would want to prohibit name-calling and interrupting.

STEP 3

Listen to each side's story. Allow each person to tell his or her view of the situation without interruption. Ask questions if you don't understand something.

STEP 4

Search for possible solutions. Brainstorm solutions together, or ask each person to suggest a solution. Continue until you reach a solution that satisfies both sides.

STEP 5

Don't give up.
If the opposing sides can't reach an agreeable solution, ask for the help of an adult. The adult should be someone both sides trust.

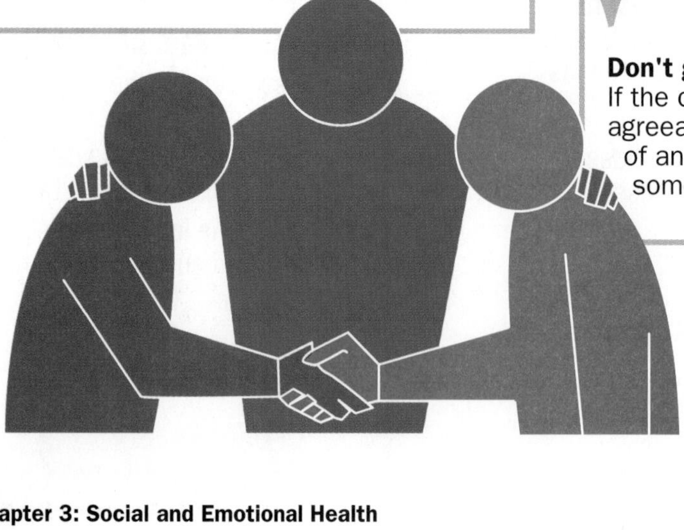

After a successful mediation, many students are asked to compose and sign an agreement. This agreement tells what each person will do—and will *not* do—to keep the fight from breaking out again. Many schools now have peer mediation programs in place. Both mediators and the other students they work with often feel better about themselves when they see that problems can be worked out without resorting to violence.

These students are working out a tough problem. In many programs, conflict-resolution mediators work in teams of two.

Review

Using complete sentences, answer the following questions on a separate sheet of paper.

Reviewing Terms and Facts

1. **Vocabulary**   Write one or two original sentences that use the terms *conflict* and *compromise* correctly.

2. **Give Examples**   Make up your own examples of each of the reasons for conflict listed on the first page of this lesson.

3. **List**   Name two ways you can prevent conflicts from occurring.

4. **Restate**   Describe each of the steps in the mediation process in your own words.

Thinking Critically

5. **Explain**   What do you think are the five most common reasons why people your age get into conflicts? Choose one of these reasons and tell what steps teens might take to keep such conflicts from getting out of hand.

6. **Apply**   Rob wants to spend Saturday afternoon playing miniature golf. His best friend, Pete, wants to go bowling. How could the boys work out this problem and still be together?

7. **Compose**   Make a list of ground rules for conducting a peer mediation session. Be ready to explain why you chose each one.

Applying Health Concepts

8. **Personal Health**   In a small group, talk about television shows or movies you have seen that feature teenagers. Discuss the conflicts between the characters. Are the conflicts ones that teens have in real life? How do the characters resolve the conflict? Do they use any of the methods in this lesson? Share your group's observations with your classmates.

9. **Health of Others**   Make a poster that promotes conflict resolution in your school. Your poster should show and explain one or more ways to avoid or resolve conflicts. Get permission to display your poster in a hallway, the cafeteria, the gymnasium, or a classroom.

Chapter Summary

▶ Friendships become increasingly important to young teens. Friends help meet many social and emotional needs. (Lesson 1)

▶ During adolescence, teens feel pressured to act and think like other people their age. Teens can learn healthy ways to deal with negative peer pressure. (Lesson 1)

▶ Many types of families exist in the United States today. All types of families can be healthy and happy. (Lesson 2)

▶ Some families are seriously troubled by various types of abuse. (Lesson 2)

▶ Most people experience a range of emotions. During adolescence, a teen's emotions may change suddenly. (Lesson 3)

▶ Emotions are neither good nor bad. The way people express emotions, however, may be healthy or unhealthy. (Lesson 3)

▶ Good communication can help people meet their needs and develop healthy relationships. (Lesson 3)

▶ Stress is your body's response to changes around you. Stress may be positive or negative. (Lesson 4)

▶ Negative stress can cause emotional fatigue. You can learn to manage negative stress. (Lesson 4)

▶ Communication, compromise, and mediation are three ways to resolve conflicts peacefully. (Lesson 5)

Using Health Terms

On a separate sheet of paper, write the vocabulary term that best matches each definition given below.

1. Friends or other people your age (Lesson 1)

2. The basic unit of society (Lesson 2)

3. Special chemicals, produced by glands, that regulate many body functions (Lesson 3)

4. A hormone that prepares the body to respond to a stressor (Lesson 4)

5. The ability to accept other people as they are (Lesson 5)

6. Not taking sides or deciding who is right or wrong (Lesson 5)

Reviewing Main Ideas

Using complete sentences, answer the following questions on a separate sheet of paper.

1. What are three examples of positive peer pressure? (Lesson 1)

2. What are five ways of dealing with negative peer pressure? (Lesson 1)

3. What are five types of families in the United States today? (Lesson 2)

4. Where can families troubled by abuse get help? (Lesson 2)

5. How do hormones affect your emotions? (Lesson 3)

6. Why is paying attention to gestures, facial expressions, and posture important in face-to-face communication? (Lesson 3)

7. Name four rules for good listening. (Lesson 3)

8. What is positive stress? What is negative stress? (Lesson 4)

9. Give two examples of environmental stress. (Lesson 4)

10. What are five ways of dealing with negative stress? (Lesson 4)

11. Name five rules for effective communication in a conflict situation. (Lesson 5)

12. What is the function of a peer mediator? (Lesson 5)

Thinking Critically

Using complete sentences, answer the following questions on a separate sheet of paper.

1. **Analyze** What are some ways your school uses positive peer pressure to help students achieve worthwhile goals? (Lesson 1)

2. **Contrast** For what types of decisions would you ask your parents' advice? For what types of decisions would you ask your peers' advice? (Lesson 1)

3. **Analyze** Why might raising children in a single-parent family be difficult? (Lesson 2)

4. **Hypothesize** Why do teens and parents sometimes have difficulty communicating with each other? (Lesson 3)

5. **Suggest** What might a teen do to open lines of communication with someone who is reluctant to talk? (Lesson 3)

6. **Contrast** What are some unhealthy ways teens might deal with stress? (Lesson 4)

7. **Analyze** In what situations might using conflict-resolution methods be inappropriate? (Lesson 5)

Your Action Plan

You have the power to improve your social and emotional health. Think of something you'd like to change about your relationships or about the way you handle stress and conflict. Make that your long-term goal. Look back at your private journal entries for this chapter for ideas.

A good way to meet your long-term goal is to set up a series of short-term goals. Perhaps your long-term goal is to make a new friend. A short-term goal might be to compliment that person's outfit or to ask the person to go to the library with you.

Make a schedule for reaching each short-term goal and check it periodically. When you reach your long-term goal, reward yourself by having fun with your new friend.

Building Your Portfolio

1. Tape-record a conversation between you and a friend. Talk about why you are friends and what you like about each other. Mention misunderstandings or conflicts you've had and what you did about them. Use good speaking and listening skills during your conversation. Add the tape to your portfolio.

2. Find a photograph or draw a picture of a quiet, peaceful scene. It could be someplace you have visited or someplace you would like to visit. Put the picture in your portfolio. When you feel under a lot of stress, take the picture out, look at it, and imagine yourself in the scene.

In Your Home and Community

1. Make an entertainment guide for your family. Using newspaper and TV ads, list fun activities for families to do in your community. For each event, include a brief description and the date, time, and cost. Try to participate in one or more events with your family.

2. With your classmates, produce a joke book that you can give to young hospital patients in your community. Assign tasks for producing the joke book, such as collecting the jokes, typing them, illustrating them, running off copies of the book, and giving out copies.

Unit 2
The Healthy Body

Student Expectations

After reading this chapter, you should be able to:

1. Identify the six main categories of nutrients, their sources, and ways they help you stay healthy.

2. Explain how to use the Food Guide Pyramid to make nutritious diet choices.

3. Describe guidelines for making healthy choices about food and weight control.

4. List and describe ways that exercise helps you stay fit.

5. Explain how to set up a realistic, effective exercise plan.

I never used to think a lot about what I ate. My parents would put something in front of me, and I'd just eat it. Lately, things have started to change around my house.

For example, it seems like a couple of times every week my mother tries out a new recipe. Everything is "light" or "low-fat." I like a lot of the new meals she makes.

We're definitely more aware of what we're eating these days. My parents even check the nutrition labels on the snacks and cereals we buy. A lot of these changes began about nine months ago, when Uncle Mike went in the hospital with a heart attack. He was only 43 at the time, and it scared everyone a little— including me. He and I do a lot together, and suddenly it looked like I was going to lose my favorite uncle.

Anyway, Uncle Mike is doing really well now. He's watching his diet and has started swimming three mornings a week at the high school pool. I've started to join him. I decided that since I'm broadening my horizons with my diet, I may as well start exercising too.

in your journal

Read the account on this page. Do any of these thoughts sound familiar to you? Start your private journal entries for this chapter on nutrition and fitness by answering these questions:

▶ Do you think the kinds of food you eat have an effect on how you look and feel? Is it a positive or negative effect? Explain your answer.

▶ Do you think you are in good shape physically? What, if anything, would you like to change?

When you reach the end of the chapter, you will use your journal entries to make an action plan.

Nutrients for Your Body

This lesson will help you find answers to questions that teens often ask about food. For example:

▶ **Why does it matter what I eat?**

▶ **What kinds of foods does my body need?**

▶ **Why are some foods better for me than others?**

Words to Know

nutrition
diet
nutrient
carbohydrate
protein
fat
vitamin
mineral
Recommended
 Dietary
 Allowance
 (RDA)

Food for Living

During the teenage years, your body will grow more rapidly than it has at any time since you were an infant. That makes it important for you to eat the foods your body needs to grow, develop, and work properly. Knowing about nutrition (noo·TRI·shuhn) can help you do this. **Nutrition** is *the science that studies how the body makes use of the substances in food and how and why people eat the way they do.* (The word *nutrition* is also used for the process of taking in food.) **Figure 4.1** shows the steps in the process of satisfying the need for food.

Figure 4.1
Food—An Energy Source

When you eat nutritious foods, you have the energy to do the activities you want to do each day.

❶ Your body needs energy.

❷ You become hungry.

❸ You eat.

❹ You feel satisfied.

❺ Your body uses more energy.

What Food Does for You

Providing energy for living each day is only one way food helps you. It also helps in these ways:

- Food gives your body the raw materials it needs to grow.

- Eating is an enjoyable activity you can share with friends and family.

- Food helps many people feel content and secure.

Meals can be important times for families to share information about their day.

A Balanced Diet

Are you following a diet? Yes, you are! Everyone follows a diet. Your **diet** is *everything you regularly eat and drink.* Although people usually think of a diet as a plan to lose weight, that is only one kind of diet.

Although everyone follows a diet, not all diets are healthy. A healthy diet provides all the nutrients you need. **Nutrients** (NOO·tree·ents) are *the substances in food that your body needs.* Most foods contain a number of different nutrients. To have a healthy, balanced diet, you must eat the right amounts of six types of nutrients. **Figure 4.2** shows some of the foods that make up a balanced diet.

Figure 4.2
A Balanced Diet

A balanced diet includes a variety of nutritious foods.

in your journal

Write down everything you remember eating for the past three days. Include the amount of each food and the time when you ate it. As you read this lesson, you will find out whether the foods you listed make up a balanced diet.

The Six Categories of Nutrients

Scientists have identified more than 40 nutrients that contribute to good health. These nutrients can be grouped into six main categories:

- Carbohydrates
- Proteins
- Fats
- Vitamins
- Minerals
- Water

Different nutrients help you in different ways. Some provide energy and others help your body work properly. **Figure 4.3** shows several good food sources for each category of nutrient.

Carbohydrates

Carbohydrates are *the main source of energy for your body.* Simple carbohydrates, or sugars, are found in fruits, milk, and table sugar. Starchy foods such as bread, rice, and pasta contain complex carbohydrates. Digestion breaks them down into simple sugars. The fiber in starchy foods helps the digestion process.

Proteins

Proteins are *essential for the growth and repair of body cells.* Proteins are made of amino (uh·MEE·noh) acids, which are chains of building blocks. Your body can produce some amino acids. Others, called essential amino acids, must come from the foods you eat. Foods that contain all the essential amino acids are called complete proteins. All of these foods come from animals. Foods that contain only some of the essential amino acids

Figure 4.3
The Six Categories of Nutrients

The nutrients your body needs are available in a variety of delicious foods.

A Good sources for carbohydrates are breads, rice, pasta, and potatoes.

B Proteins are found in meats, poultry, eggs, fish, nuts, dried beans, and milk products.

C Butter, eggs, red meat, and many cheeses are sources of fats.

are called incomplete proteins. Plant foods provide incomplete proteins. Even so, you can get complete proteins without eating meats. By combining certain plant foods with others you can obtain all the proteins you need. Eating rice along with beans, for example, supplies complete proteins.

Fats

Fats are *another source of energy.* Your body depends on fat cells for energy storage and protection against temperature changes. Fats also carry certain vitamins in your bloodstream and help keep your skin healthy. Yet eating too much fat will cause weight gain and may lead to other health problems.

Vitamins

Vitamins are *substances that help regulate body functions.* Vitamins help you in many ways. For example, they help your body use other nutrients and fight infection. Some vitamins, such as vitamin C and the B-complex vitamins, dissolve in water. Others, including vitamins A, D, E, and K, dissolve only in droplets of fat. Vitamins that dissolve in water are called water-soluble. They must be replaced every day. However, your body can store fat-soluble vitamins for longer periods.

Minerals

Minerals are *elements that help your body work properly.* Calcium and phosphorus, for example, strengthen bones, keep muscles healthy, and help your heart beat regularly. Several minerals allow the body to use the other types of nutrients.

Water

Water is essential to life. Water carries nutrients around your body. It also helps with digestion, removes wastes, and cools you off. You should drink six to eight glasses of water every day.

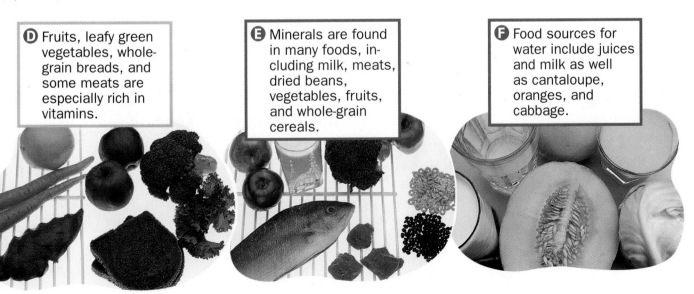

D Fruits, leafy green vegetables, whole-grain breads, and some meats are especially rich in vitamins.

E Minerals are found in many foods, including milk, meats, dried beans, vegetables, fruits, and whole-grain cereals.

F Food sources for water include juices and milk as well as cantaloupe, oranges, and cabbage.

Do your food preferences ever cause arguments at home? Sometimes parents wish their teens would eat a more varied diet.

Ask your parents to recall their favorite foods when they were teenagers. Discuss why many people eat a wider variety of foods as they grow older. Plan ways to increase the variety of foods you eat.

How Much Should You Eat?

To help people eat wisely, scientists have developed *guidelines for the amount of each nutrient to be eaten each day.* These guidelines are called the **Recommended** (re·kuh·MEN·ded) **Dietary** (DY·uh·tehr·ee) **Allowances** or RDA.

Your RDA of each nutrient depends on many things, including your gender, activity level, and age. For example, teens need extra calcium because their bones are still growing.

How can you get your RDA of important nutrients? Start by reading food package labels. They list the main nutrients and tell what percentage of the average person's RDA is in each serving. Reading the next lesson will help, too. It gives tips for achieving a balanced diet.

Wise food choices will help you get the nutrients you need for good health every day.

Lesson 1

Review

Using complete sentences, answer the following questions on a separate sheet of paper.

Reviewing Terms and Facts

1. **Vocabulary**   Define the term *nutrition.* Use it in an original sentence.

2. **Identify**   List three things that food does for you.

3. **List**   Name the six categories of nutrients.

4. **Give Examples**   List factors that might make a difference in your Recommended Dietary Allowance of a nutrient.

Thinking Critically

5. **Justify**   Describe a snack (it may include more than one food) that

contains all six categories of nutrients. Justify your choice.

6. **Predict**   Describe how you might be affected if you suddenly cut down on foods high in carbohydrates.

7. **Analyze**   Which of the six nutrients is most likely to be lacking in a meatless diet? How could someone who wanted to avoid meat make up for any missing nutrients?

Applying Health Concepts

8. **Consumer Health**   Analyze the ingredients in a recipe from a magazine or newspaper. Explain which of the six nutrients are included in the recipe and which are missing. Suggest other foods that could be served at the same meal to provide balance.

The Five Food Groups

This lesson will help you find answers to questions that teens often ask about planning a healthy diet. For example:

► **How can I plan a healthy diet?**
► **What are the five food groups?**
► **How much of the different kinds of food should I eat?**

The Food Guide Pyramid

A handy tool is available to help you plan what to eat each day. The **Food Guide Pyramid** is *a guideline to help you choose what and how much to eat to get the nutrients you need.* The pyramid was developed by the U.S. Department of Agriculture (USDA), with the help of the Department of Health and Human Services.

The foods in the pyramid are divided into five basic groups, plus a sixth group that includes fats, oils, and sweets. The foods within a particular group provide similar nutrients. If you eat enough servings from all of the five basic groups, you will get the nutrients you need to stay healthy.

Words to Know

Food Guide Pyramid

Social Studies Connection

Helpful Labels

Both the USDA and the Food and Drug Administration (FDA) have been working for several years to make food labels more helpful to consumers. The USDA handles meat and poultry labeling. The FDA handles labels for all other kinds of foods.

People enjoy nutritious foods in many different settings.

Figure 4.4 shows the Food Guide Pyramid. The size of each section in the pyramid corresponds roughly to the amount of that kind of food you should eat daily. The bread, cereal, rice, and pasta section is the largest. You should eat the most servings each day from this group. Teens and young adults should get three full servings from the milk, yogurt, and cheese group. Nutrients from this group are important for growth. The fats, oils, and sweets section is the smallest. These foods provide calories, but few nutritional benefits. Notice that there are no recommended number of servings from this group.

Figure 4.4
The Food Guide Pyramid: A Guide to Daily Food Choices

A balanced diet includes foods from the five basic groups. Each group provides some of the nutrients you should have each day.

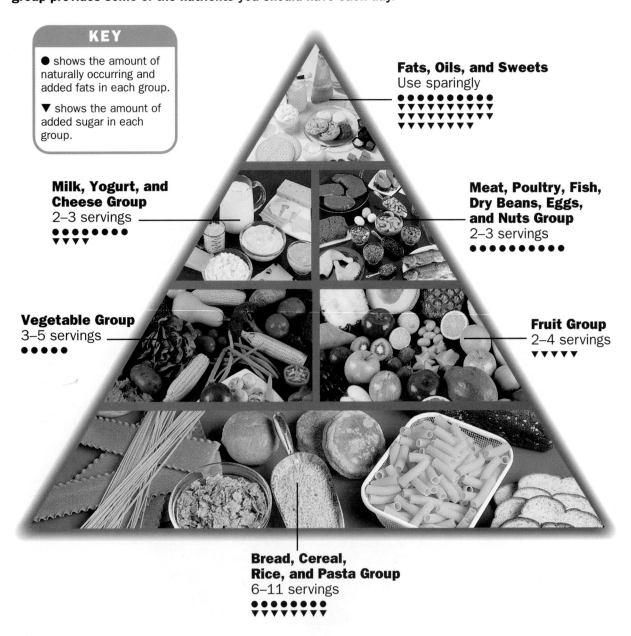

KEY

● shows the amount of naturally occurring and added fats in each group.

▼ shows the amount of added sugar in each group.

Fats, Oils, and Sweets
Use sparingly

Milk, Yogurt, and Cheese Group
2–3 servings

Meat, Poultry, Fish, Dry Beans, Eggs, and Nuts Group
2–3 servings

Vegetable Group
3–5 servings

Fruit Group
2–4 servings

Bread, Cereal, Rice, and Pasta Group
6–11 servings

The Food Groups

What kinds of nutrients do the food groups in the Food Guide Pyramid provide? **Figure 4.5** tells about the nutrients on each level of the pyramid, from the base to the top.

Figure 4.5
Nutrients in the Food Groups

Ⓐ Bread, Cereal, Rice, and Pasta Group
6–11 servings

Ⓑ Vegetable Group
3–5 servings

Ⓒ Fruit Group
2–4 servings

Ⓓ Milk, Yogurt, and Cheese Group
2–3 servings

Ⓔ Meat, Poultry, Fish, Dry Beans, Eggs, and Nuts Group
2–3 servings

Ⓕ Fats, Oils, and Sweets
Use sparingly

Ⓐ The foods at the base of the pyramid come from grains, such as wheat and corn. This group provides energy from complex carbohydrates, but adds little sugar to your diet. Foods from this group also provide proteins, vitamins, minerals, and fiber. The largest number of daily servings should come from this group.

Ⓑ Ⓒ Both groups on this level come from plants. Most people need to eat five to nine servings from these two groups to get enough vitamins, minerals, and fiber. Foods from these groups are also naturally low in fat and high in carbohydrates.

Ⓓ Milk, yogurt, and cheese are important sources of calcium. Foods in this group also provide other minerals, as well as proteins, carbohydrates, and vitamins. Milk also contains water, an essential nutrient. Teens should get three servings from this group every day.

Ⓔ All the foods in this group are high in protein. Most also include important vitamins and minerals. Two to three servings are recommended from this group daily.

Ⓕ This group includes foods such as cream, butter, sugar, gravy, salad dressing, soft drinks, and sweets. These foods should be eaten sparingly. Most Americans eat too many fatty foods. Nutritionists recommend that people limit fats to no more than 30 percent of their total calories.

in your journal

Most Americans eat too much fat. As a result, many people are overweight and have high blood pressure and heart disease. In your journal, explain two or three reasons why you think many Americans "overdose" on fatty foods.

Q & A

Make Mine Yogurt! ᴀᴄᴛɪᴠɪᴛʏ!

Q: Is yogurt as good for me as milk?

A: It may be even better than milk if you choose the right kind of yogurt! Although yogurt is made from milk, plain low-fat yogurt actually has more calcium than milk. This is because it is usually thickened with nonfat milk solids. Nonfat yogurt has even more calcium than the low-fat variety. Yogurt is also a better source of certain vitamins than milk. Compare the nutrition facts on several types of yogurt. Make a chart to show similarities and differences.

Using the Food Guide Pyramid

The Food Guide Pyramid can help you plan your diet by suggesting a number of daily servings for each type of food. The number of servings you need from each food group depends on your age, gender, size, and activity level. How much of each food makes up a serving?

What Counts as One Serving?

Figure 4.6 helps you see what makes up a serving of each type of food. Remember, though, that many foods include servings from different groups. Pizza, for example, has full or partial servings from the bread group (crust), the milk group (cheese), and the vegetable group (tomatoes).

Did You Know?

About How Much?

▶ An ounce of cheese is about the size of a walnut.

▶ One-half cup of rice or pasta is about the size of a tennis ball.

▶ Three ounces of meat or fish is about the size of a deck of cards.

Figure 4.6
Serving Sizes

These guidelines can help you make sure you get the nutrients you need each day.

Fats, Oils, and Sweets
• No recommended servings

Meat, Poultry, Fish, Dry Beans, Eggs, and Nuts Group
• 2–3 ounces of cooked lean meat, poultry, or fish
• $\frac{1}{2}$ cup of cooked dry beans
• 1 egg
• 2 tablespoons of peanut butter

Milk, Yogurt, and Cheese Group
• 1 cup of milk or yogurt
• $1\frac{1}{2}$ ounces of natural cheese
• 2 ounces of process cheese

Vegetable Group
• 1 cup of raw leafy vegetables
• $\frac{1}{2}$ cup of other cooked or chopped raw vegetables
• $\frac{3}{4}$ cup of vegetable juice

Fruit Group
• 1 medium apple, banana, or orange
• $\frac{1}{2}$ cup of chopped, cooked, or canned fruit
• $\frac{3}{4}$ cup of fruit juice

Bread, Cereal, Rice, and Pasta Group
• 1 slice of bread
• 1 ounce of ready-to-eat cereal
• $\frac{1}{2}$ cup of cooked cereal, rice, or pasta

Using complete sentences, answer the following questions on a separate sheet of paper.

Reviewing Terms and Facts

1. **Vocabulary**   What is the Food Guide Pyramid?
2. **Match**   For each food group, list the number of daily servings you need.
3. **Identify**   Name five foods that you should eat sparingly.
4. **Give Examples**   Provide an example of a single serving from each of the five food groups.

Thinking Critically

5. **Plan**   Create a low-fat meal menu that has one-third of the daily servings from all five food groups.

6. **Compose**   Write down three "rules" that summarize the guidance from the Food Guide Pyramid.
7. **Recommend**   Working in small groups, make a list of snack foods that you think would be both nutritious and enjoyable. Identify the food groups represented by your snack food choices.

Applying Health Concepts

8. **Consumer Health**   Collect food advertisements from several magazines. Make a chart categorizing the advertisements into the five food groups plus fats, oils, and sweets. (Some advertisements fit into several food groups.) Decide which group is advertised most and explain how you think this affects the American diet.

LIFE SKILLS
Reading a Food Label

*L*abels on food packages, such as this one, can help you choose nutritious foods. The information about **serving size** and **servings per container** lets you figure out the cost per serving. Knowing the **calories per serving** can help you maintain your desirable weight.

The **percentages** beside each nutrient let you compare nutrients provided by different products. The items in the **ingredients** section are listed from the largest to smallest amount.

Follow-up Activity

On a box or can of food at home, locate each of the label parts highlighted here. Write a short paragraph describing three pieces of important information you learned from this label.

Nutrition Facts		
Serving Size 1 cup (240 mL)		
Servings Per Container		About 2
Amount Per Serving		
Calories 130		Calories from Fat 30
		% Daily Value*
Total Fat 3g		**5%**
Saturated Fat 1g		**5%**
Cholesterol 5 mg		**2%**
Sodium 720 mg		**30%**
Total Carbohydrate 21g		**7%**
Dietary Fiber 3g		**12%**
Sugars 11g		
Protein 4g		
Vitamin A 40%	•	Vitamin C 2%
Calcium 6%	•	Iron 8%

*Percent Daily Values are based on a 2,000 calorie diet. Your daily values may be higher or lower depending on your calorie needs:

	Calories:	2,000	2,500
Total Fat	Less than	65g	80g
Sat Fat	Less than	20g	25g
Cholesterol	Less than	300mg	300mg
Sodium	Less than	2,400mg	2,400mg
Total Carbohydrate		300g	375g
Dietary Fiber		25g	30g

Calories per gram:
Fat 9   •   Carbohydrate 4   •   Protein 4

INGREDIENTS: TOMATO PUREE (WATER, TOMATO PASTE), CHICKEN STOCK, ZUCCHINI, CARROTS, DICED TOMATOES, CELERY, WATER, HIGH FRUCTOSE CORN SYRUP, ENRICHED MACARONI PRODUCT (WHEAT FLOUR, EGG WHITE SOLIDS, NIACIN, FERROUS SULFATE, THIAMINE MONONITRATE, RIBOFLAVIN).

CON$UMER FOCU$

Label Detectives

Thanks to the USDA and FDA, many of the claims food producers put on their labels have specific meanings. Try to find food labels that do and *do not* follow these federal regulations:

■ To be labeled "Fat Free" or "Sugar Free," the product must contain only a tiny amount of fat or sugar. For example, products labeled "fat free" must have less than 0.5 grams of fat per serving.

■ If a product is labeled "Low-Fat," you should be able to eat it fairly often without exceeding the RDA for fat.

■ A diet product labeled "Reduced, Less, Fewer" must contain at least 25 percent less of a nutrient or calories than the regular product.

■ To be labeled "Good Source of … ," one serving must contain 10 to 19 percent of the RDA for the nutrient named.

If products do not meet these regulations, write to the manufacturers.

People at Work

A Delicious Career

Colleen Nielsen is a dietician who works with a group of doctors. Colleen sees many different types of patients, but her specialty is the treatment of adolescents with diabetes. The physical changes of adolescence create new challenges, even for those patients who have lived with diabetes for a number of years. Colleen helps her teenage patients coordinate their changing dietary needs with the type of medication they are taking to control their diabetes.

Colleen earned a college degree in dietetics and passed a written test to become a Registered Dietician.

Dieticians also work in hospitals, nursing homes, school cafeterias, child-care centers, restaurants, and health clubs. Some also work for the Peace Corps or for companies that produce food and drugs.

Health Update

Eat Your Veggies!

Scientists have discovered that some plant foods contain anticancer chemicals. A substance in soybeans seems to block the growth of new blood vessels that supply cancerous tumors. This same chemical also seems to keep cancer cells from spreading.

Yellow and green vegetables, along with melons and citrus fruits, contain substances called antioxidants that act to "sop up" certain cancer-producing chemicals. A chemical found in broccoli stimulates your body to produce protective substances that make cancer-causing cells harmless and flush them out of your body.

Someday scientists may be able to separate these chemicals from vegetables and use them to prevent and treat cancer. Until then, eat more veggies!

Teens Making a Difference

Yogurt for Youngsters

At Walnut Springs Middle School, students from the Foods and Fitness class chose to use their knowledge to help others. They decided to work with preschoolers in a nearby child-care center, hoping to guide them toward healthy eating habits.

Every Friday morning the middle school students made healthful snacks and took them to the preschoolers. The snacks included celery sticks filled with peanut butter and small cups of yogurt mixed with granola.

The students drew cartoon characters on posters to represent each nutrient. Each poster featured pictures of food sources of the nutrient. Students used these posters to teach the preschooler how nutritious food could help them grow up healthy and strong. Friday was the best day of the week, thanks to the treats from the Foods and Fitness class at the middle school.

Sports and Recreation

145 Pounds of Fitness!

Dara Torres-Gowen is the only female swimmer to earn medals for the United States in three consecutive Olympic Games. By age 8, Dara was already on a swim team. At 13, she spent up to 5 hours a day training. Now, at age 27, Dara has a new career: modeling. At a height of 6 feet, she weighs 145 pounds. That's a good weight for her, she says. She has no interest in "starving herself" to achieve a pencil-thin look.

To stay in shape, she does 45 to 60 minutes of aerobic exercises (usually running) five times a week. Dara also trains with light weights twice a week. She admits to having a good appetite but watches calories. A former tomboy, Dara now likes to dress up. Watch for her on magazine covers!

Making Healthy Food Choices

This lesson will help you find answers to more questions that teens often ask about food. For example:

▶ **How can I take more control over what I eat?**

▶ **What foods are especially good for me?**

▶ **What foods should I avoid in my diet?**

▶ **How can I control my weight and stay healthy?**

Words to Know

starch
fiber
saturated fat
cholesterol
sodium
caffeine
calorie

Understanding Your Food Choices

The first step toward making healthy food choices is knowing why you choose one food over another. Many different factors affect what goes into your daily diet (see **Figure 4.7**).

Figure 4.7
Your Food Choices
Knowing why you choose to eat the foods you do can help you make wiser choices.

Watching What You Eat

Planning ahead is the key to a healthy diet. Even teens can begin to plan their diets. For example, you can find out what your family will have for the evening meal. Then you can choose foods for your breakfast and lunch that will give you the right number of servings from each food group by the end of the day. Choosing healthy snacks is another way to help balance your diet.

Remember that how foods are prepared makes a big difference in their nutritional content. For example, baked chicken will give you all the nutrients of fried chicken, but with much less fat. You can try steaming vegetables rather than boiling them. When vegetables are boiled, a lot of the vitamins are lost in the cooking water.

The next few sections include specific tips for planning your diet. You need to get enough starch and fiber but limit the fats, sodium, sugar, and caffeine you consume.

Getting Enough Starch and Fiber

You already know that carbohydrates are an important part of your diet. Complex carbohydrates are essential to good nutrition. Starch and fiber are especially important.

- **Starch** is *the complex carbohydrate stored in potatoes, rice, wheat, and other plants.* In your body, digestion turns this starch into a sugar that gives you long-lasting energy. Starchy foods are usually rich in vitamins and minerals.

- **Fiber** is *the tough, stringy part of raw fruits, raw vegetables, wheat, and other grains that you cannot digest.* Fiber is not a nutrient, but it helps carry food and wastes through your body. You should eat at least 20 grams of fiber every day to keep your digestive system healthy.

in Your Journal

When you eat at a cafeteria or restaurant, how do you decide which food to order? Explain in your journal whether you think about the food's nutritional value, its appearance, its cost, its taste, what your friends are eating, or other factors.

Many foods that are high in fiber are delicious as well.

Limiting Certain Foods

Chocolate and other rich foods tend to overload our diets with **saturated fats.** These are *fats found mostly in animal products such as milk, butter, egg yolks, and meat.* Animal fats contain **cholesterol** (kuh·LES·tuh·rawl), *a waxlike substance our bodies produce and need in small amounts.* Too much cholesterol can lead to heart disease. Unsaturated fats come from plants and do not contain cholesterol.

Try these ways to reduce saturated fats and cholesterol:

- Choose low-fat or nonfat milk and milk products.

- Avoid fried foods.

- Choose low-fat or nonfat desserts instead of baked goods.

- Eat fish, skinless chicken, or lean meat.

Salt contains **sodium,** *a mineral that helps control the amount of fluid in our bodies.* Too much sodium makes your body hold excess fluid. Too much sodium can also lead to high blood pressure and heart disease, two dangerous conditions.

Only about 15 percent of the sodium we eat comes from the saltshaker. About 10 percent occurs naturally in foods. The other 75 percent is in canned and packaged food. For example, an ear of fresh corn has only 1 milligram of sodium, but a cup of canned corn has 389 milligrams of sodium.

Try these ways to reduce the sodium in your diet:

- Cut down on salty foods, including salty snacks, ketchup, mustard, and relish.

- Eat less processed food, such as packaged sandwich meat and canned soups and vegetables.

- Read food labels and buy brands with less added sodium.

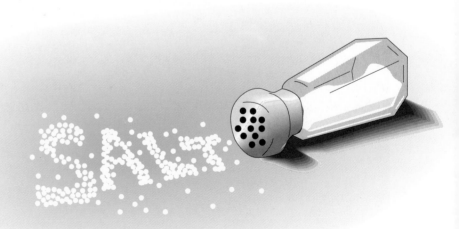

Caffeine (ka·FEEN) is *a substance, found in some foods, that can speed up body processes.* Tea, coffee, chocolate, and many cola drinks contain caffeine. The amount of caffeine in drinks ranges from about 5 milligrams in an 8-ounce glass of chocolate milk to 115 milligrams in a 5-ounce cup of brewed coffee.

Too much caffeine can cause your heart to beat rapidly or irregularly. Some people who consume too much caffeine have trouble falling asleep at night. Caffeine can also be habit forming.

If you wish to cut down on caffeine, you can

- try caffeine-free drinks.

- get enough rest so you don't need a caffeine energy boost.

- eat more carbohydrates early in the day to get energy.

Not all sugar comes from the sugar bowl. The average American eats 100 to 120 pounds of sugar a year, but 75 percent of that sugar is hidden in prepared foods. Sugar provides calories but few nutrients. It also contributes to tooth decay.

Food labels may list added sugar as brown sugar, raw sugar, honey, corn syrup, molasses, concentrated fruit juice, or corn sweeteners. Sugar is also called glucose, lactose, fructose, sucrose, galactose, dextrose, and maltose.

To reduce the amount of sugar you eat, you can cut back on foods with added sugars.

These foods include soft drinks, candy, baked goods, and fruits canned in syrup. You can also read food labels and avoid foods in which sugar is among the first ingredients listed.

Concern About Caffeine

Q: Are drinks that contain caffeine safe?

A: Caffeine affects the nervous system. Too much can make you tense and hard to get along with. People who suddenly stop using caffeine may get headaches or feel tired. However, many studies have shown that caffeine does not cause health problems if you do not "overdose" yourself.

Your Total Health

Protecting Your Sweet Tooth

Eating sweet snacks between meals does not only add unneeded calories. The sugar encourages sticky plaque to form on your teeth. If you allow plaque to build up, it leads to tartar. Tartar gives cavities and gingivitis a place to start. For your total health, limit sweet snacks.

■ in your journal

In a column in your journal, list the foods you eat that provide starch and fiber. In another column, list foods you eat that contain large amounts of fats, sodium, sugar, and caffeine. In both columns, include how often you eat each food.

Teen Issues

Exercise and Fun ACTIVITY!

Any activity is more fun if you do it with a family member or a friend. If you want to exercise more, get together with someone in your family or a few friends and make some plans. Consider starting a cycling, running, or walking club. Pick a different destination every weekend. Keep a log of where you go and how far so that you can chart your progress. The result: fun and fitness!

Swimming helps tone your muscles whether your aim is to gain or lose weight.

Maintaining a Healthy Weight

Are you concerned about your weight? The teen years are a time of rapid growth. Teens often become concerned that they are overweight or underweight. Comparing yourself with your friends isn't usually very helpful. Their body types may be very different from yours.

Your weight is probably just right for you at this time in your life. Trying to gain or lose a lot of weight can interfere with your normal growth and development. The rest of this lesson discusses healthy ways to control your weight. If you are concerned about your weight, however, ask your doctor for advice. He or she will be able to suggest the plan that is best for you.

The Role of Calories

A **calorie** (KA·luh·ree) is *a unit of heat that measures the energy available in foods.* The calories in foods provide energy for your daily activities. To maintain your weight, the calories you eat must equal those you burn as energy. If you eat food that has more calories than your body uses, the extra energy is stored as fat. About 3,500 extra calories add 1 pound of fat.

Controlling Your Weight

The amount you weigh depends on how many calories you eat and how much you exercise. The healthiest way to lose fat is to take in fewer calories and exercise more. Then you will burn the calories you do take in and they will not be stored as fat. Exercise is also important when you want to gain weight. It helps build muscle instead of fat. Muscle tissue is denser than fat and weighs more. **Figure 4.8** shows some healthy ways to gain or lose weight.

Figure 4.8
Weight Control Methods
Use these methods to gain or lose weight safely.

To Gain Weight

- Eat more food or more high-calorie foods such as milk shakes, granola, or cheese.
- Increase your carbohydrates by eating more bread, pasta, rice, beans, and vegetables. Eat healthy snacks between meals, but not too close to mealtimes. Eating too close to mealtimes may decrease your appetite.
- Use strength- and endurance-building exercises to develop and tone your muscles (see Lesson 4 of this chapter).

To Lose Weight

- Eat less food or focus on low-calorie foods such as carrot sticks, broiled skinless chicken, and nonfat yogurt.
- Drink plenty of water.
- Always eat enough to take away feelings of hunger. Eat slowly.
- Avoid shopping when you are hungry. When you are hungry, you are likely to buy high-calorie snacks.
- Always eat breakfast.
- Plan meals creatively. Learn how to prepare foods in low-calorie ways.
- Get more aerobic exercise to burn calories and to feel less hungry (see Lesson 4 of this chapter). For example, you might walk to school instead of riding the bus.

Did You Know?

What to Cut

One healthy way to cut calories is to cut fat. A gram of fat contains 9 calories. A gram of carbohydrates or protein has only 4 calories. Remember that a maximum of 30 percent of our calories should come from fat. Many Americans get 40 percent or more of their calories from fat.

Review — Lesson 3

Using complete sentences, answer the following questions on a separate sheet of paper.

Reviewing Terms and Facts

1. **List**   Name six factors that influence your food choices.

2. **Match**   Which of the following should you try to limit in your diet? Which should you increase? Items: saturated fat, fiber, starch, cholesterol, sodium.

3. **Vocabulary**   Define *calorie*. How many calories equal 1 pound of fat?

4. **Restate**   Make a list of three sensible ways either to lose or to gain weight.

Thinking Critically

5. **Infer**   Pretend you know nothing about the typical American diet. Look at the food advertisements in several magazines. Explain what the American diet might be like, based on what you see in the ads.

6. **Summarize**   Come up with four to six rules that restate the information presented in the "Watching What You Eat" section.

Applying Health Concepts

7. **Personal Health**   Plan a way to gain or lose a pound of weight in one week by making specific changes in your own diet. Make sure your additions or deletions result in a balanced and healthful diet.

The Benefits of Exercise

This lesson will help you find answers to questions that teens often ask about exercise. For example:

▶ What's the point of being physically fit?

▶ What are some ways that exercise can help me?

▶ What are aerobic exercises and why do I hear about them so often?

Words to Know

fitness
strength
endurance
heart and lung
    endurance
aerobic exercise
flexibility

in your journal

Consider your own fitness. On a scale of 1 (completely unprepared for life) to 10 (ready for anything), rate your general fitness. Explain your rating.

What Is Fitness?

Fitness means more than being physically healthy. Fitness means *being ready to handle day-to-day living,* both the fun times and the problems. Being fit

■ gives you enough energy to last the whole day.

■ helps keep your weight at the right level for you.

■ helps you deal with stress and the ups and downs of life.

■ gives you self-confidence and makes it more likely you will succeed at whatever you attempt.

■ makes your life more fun.

Fit teens are physically active teens. When you get together with your friends, *do* something. You can ride bicycles, play volleyball, or just take a walk. Try to make fitness a goal no matter where you are and what you are doing. Fitness feels great—it's worth the extra effort!

There are many fun ways to stay physically fit.

Exercise and Fitness

Exercise is an important part of being fit. It adds to your total health. Exercise helps you physically, mentally, and socially.

- **Physical benefits.** Exercise builds strong muscles, relieves stiffness, and aids coordination. It is good for your heart and lungs. Exercise also helps you maintain a desirable weight.

- **Mental benefits.** Exercise makes you feel more energetic. You'll get tired less easily. It can also help you relieve stress. In addition, you can feel proud of what you've accomplished.

- **Social benefits.** Some exercises can be done with a group. This kind of exercise allows you to meet new people and make new friends. Working out with friends also helps keep you going when you think you'd like to quit. Friends can encourage you and cheer you on.

Cultural Diversity

Getting the Kinks Out

In many Japanese offices, factories, and schools, each day begins with group exercises. Many school students may learn traditional Japanese martial arts such as judo and karate.

How do you picture the physical, mental, and social benefits of exercise?

Q: My friends say I'm a "couch potato." What's so bad about getting a little rest?

A: NASA scientists have found that for every three days of inactivity, we lose one-fifth of our maximum muscle strength. Muscles must be used to remain healthy.

How Exercise Helps You

You've just looked at some of the ways that exercise can make a difference in your life. What specific benefits will you see if you exercise regularly? Which exercises produce these benefits most effectively?

■ **Exercise can build strength.** Muscle **strength** is *the most work your muscles can do at any given time.* To develop strength, you pull or push against a force. One force you can push against is gravity. By lifting weights, for example, you can develop the strength of your arm muscles. Crunches can tighten your stomach muscles. Cycling, handball, and cross-country skiing also build strength.

■ **Exercise can build endurance.** Muscle **endurance** (en·DER·uhns) means *how well a muscle group can perform over a given time without becoming overly tired.* **Heart and lung endurance** means *how well the heart and lungs get oxygen to the body during exercise and how quickly they return to normal.* To build endurance, you must exercise several times a week for 20 minutes or more without resting. One way to do this is through **aerobic exercise,** *rhythmic, nonstop, vigorous activities, such as running or cycling, that aid the heart.* Swimming, soccer, and aerobic dancing also build endurance (see **Figure 4.9**).

Figure 4.9
Exercising for Endurance

These activities are grouped according to how effectively they build endurance.

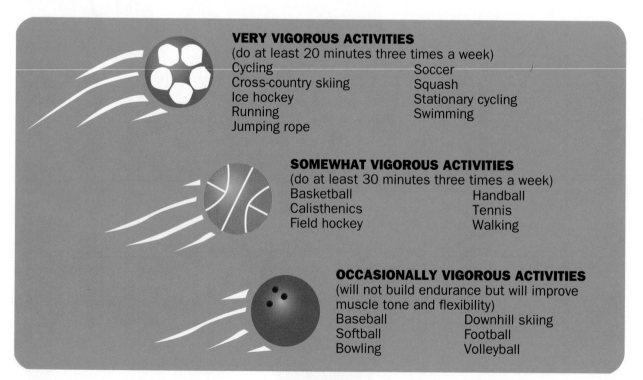

VERY VIGOROUS ACTIVITIES
(do at least 20 minutes three times a week)
Cycling   Soccer
Cross-country skiing   Squash
Ice hockey   Stationary cycling
Running   Swimming
Jumping rope

SOMEWHAT VIGOROUS ACTIVITIES
(do at least 30 minutes three times a week)
Basketball   Handball
Calisthenics   Tennis
Field hockey   Walking

OCCASIONALLY VIGOROUS ACTIVITIES
(will not build endurance but will improve muscle tone and flexibility)
Baseball   Downhill skiing
Softball   Football
Bowling   Volleyball

■ **Exercise can promote flexibility.** Your **flexibility** (flek·suh·BI·li·tee) is *the ability you have to move your body joints in certain ways.* Flexibility is important whether you are dancing or playing football. Stretching exercises develop your flexibility and make you less likely to pull a muscle while you are exercising vigorously. Activities such as ballet, tennis, swimming, and volleyball all build flexibility. Doing calisthenics (kal·uhs·THEN·iks), or repeated exercises, is an excellent means of increasing flexibility as well as strength.

■ **Exercise can relax you.** Exercise actually causes chemical changes in the brain that make you feel more relaxed. Vigorous exercise can also be a healthy outlet for anger and frustration. In addition, exercise reduces the tension in muscles, the same kind of tension that may make your leg jiggle when you are nervous. Because exercise relaxes people, it can help them sleep better.

■ **Exercise can help you control your weight.** Exercise makes your body burn calories faster. For a short time after you stop exercising, your body continues to burn calories at a higher rate. **Figure 4.10** shows the number of calories burned for different types of exercise.

■ **Exercise makes you feel and look good.** Exercise gives you more energy and helps firm up your muscles. As a result, you feel and look better.

Figure 4.10
Calories Burned in Various Activities

This graph shows how many calories are burned by a 120-pound person in an hour of each type of activity. Some exercises show a range of calories burned. The more vigorously an activity is performed, the more calories are burned.

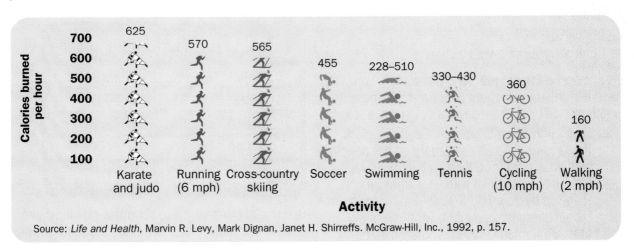

Source: *Life and Health*, Marvin R. Levy, Mark Dignan, Janet H. Shirreffs. McGraw-Hill, Inc., 1992, p. 157.

Review

Using complete sentences, answer the following questions on a separate sheet of paper.

Reviewing Terms and Facts

1. **Identify** Describe the links between exercise and your total health.
2. **Vocabulary** Contrast *strength, endurance,* and *flexibility.*
3. **Recall** To build endurance, how often should you exercise?

Thinking Critically

4. **Infer** Explain why a person with good heart and lung endurance might live longer than someone with poor endurance.

5. **Synthesize** Describe how a person could prepare through diet and exercise to play in a soccer match for several hours.

Applying Health Concepts

6. **Health of Others** Work with your class to list excuses people give for not exercising. Assign each excuse to a team. The team will write its excuse on a poster and add reasons why the excuse does not make sense. Include illustrations. Display the posters around school.

HEALTH LAB

Testing Your Heart and Lung Endurance

*I*ntroduction: During exercise, a strong heart can pump more oxygen to the muscles without beating much faster. A weak heart must beat faster. Regular exercise will strengthen your heart and lungs.

Objectives:

▶ Count your heartbeats after three minutes of exercise.

▶ Compare your rate with a chart.

Materials and Method: You will need a sturdy bench about 8 inches high and a watch or clock with a second hand. Do these steps:

1. Stand in front of the bench. Beginning with the second hand at 12, step up on the bench with your right foot, then step up with your left. Then step down with your right foot, followed by your left. Step 24 times a minute (about every two seconds) for three minutes. Straighten your leg with each step.

2. After three minutes, sit on the bench.
3. Find your pulse on your wrist or on the side of your neck. Count the number of beats in one minute and record this number.

Observation and Analysis:
Find your score in the box below. Evaluate your heart and lung endurance.

Heartbeats	Rating
70–80	Excellent
81–105	Good
106–119	Average
120–130	Fair
131+	Poor

Discuss in class why a lower pulse rate indicates good endurance. Talk about ways students your age could improve heart and lung endurance.

Planning Your Fitness Goals

This lesson will help you find answers to questions that teens often ask about setting up an exercise program. For example:

▶ **How do I plan a regular exercise program?**

▶ **How can I get the most benefit out of my exercise?**

▶ **How can I avoid injuries?**

Choosing Your Goals

Planning an exercise program is an important step. It helps you reach your goal, choose the most effective exercises, ensure that exercise is part of your life, and avoid injury. Before you start planning, answer these questions:

■ **What do you want to accomplish?** Do you hope to strengthen or tone your muscles, improve your endurance, or increase your flexibility? Maybe you want to achieve several of these goals. Think about your own abilities and needs.

■ **Where will you begin?** Start small. Entering a 5-kilometer race next month is not likely to be a realistic first goal for you. If you want to be fit enough to run in a race someday, set a goal of running several hundred yards every other day for the first week. Slowly increase your distance until you are ready for the race.

■ **What do you enjoy doing?** If you choose activities that are fun for you, you are more likely to exercise regularly.

Words to Know

warming up
target pulse rate
cooling down

Thinking carefully about your exercise program before you begin will help make it a success.

Your Total Health

Fitness up in Smoke

Do you ever wonder why you don't see athletes smoking? The tar in cigarette smoke coats the lungs, reducing the amount of oxygen they can take in. Chemicals in the smoke further reduce the oxygen in the blood. If your goal is to stay fit, do not smoke.

in your journal

Think about how much exercise you get. In one column in your journal, list the influences in your life that encourage you to exercise. In another column, list the excuses you give yourself or others for failing to exercise enough.

Setting Up an Exercise Program

Now you are ready to plan a way to meet your fitness goals. You need to consider

- which exercises to include.
- when to exercise.
- ways to avoid injury.

Selecting Exercises

Figure 4.11 shows the benefits of different sports and activities when played for 30 minutes or longer. The highest score in any category is 21. As you choose an exercise, ask yourself these questions:

- Do I want to exercise alone, with a friend, or on a team?
- What facilities are available in my community?
- What exercise equipment will I need, and how much am I willing to spend?

Figure 4.11

Fitness Ratings for Different Activities

Which exercises are strong in all three categories?

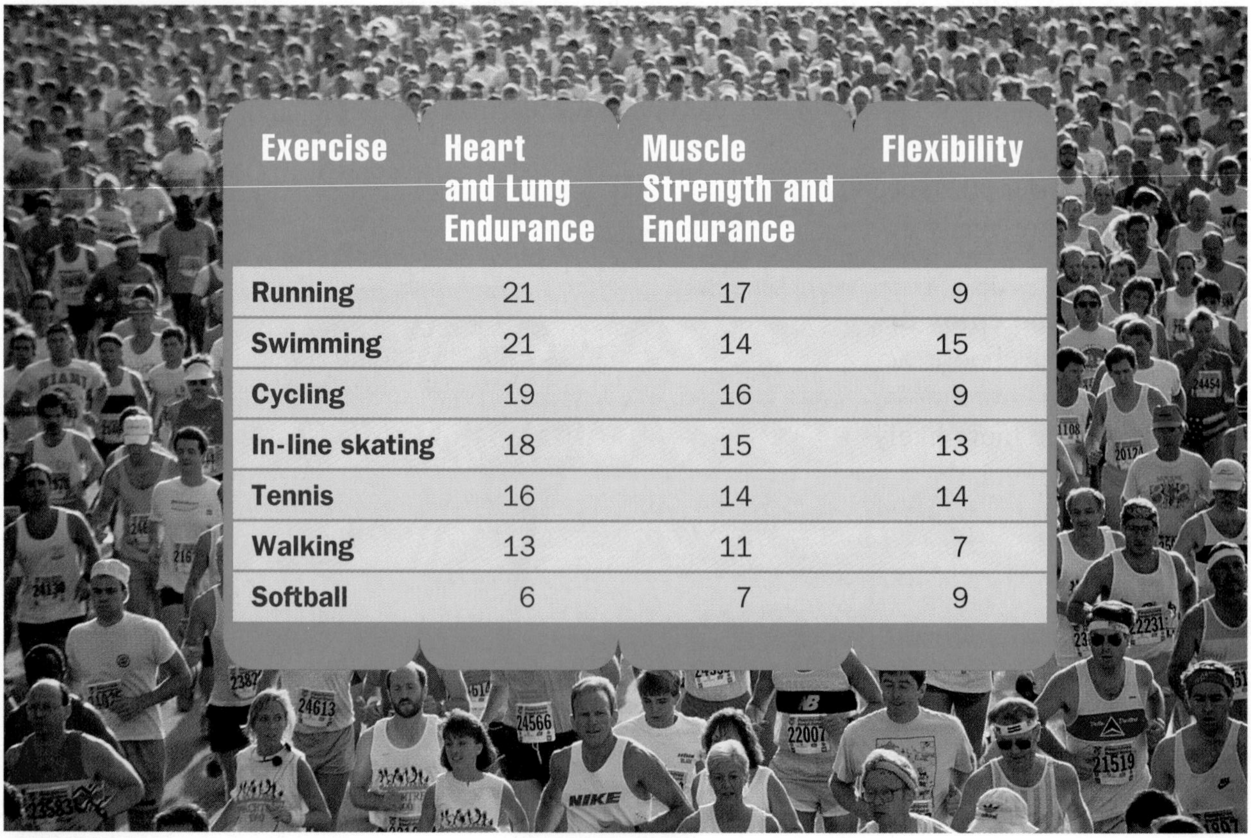

Exercise	Heart and Lung Endurance	Muscle Strength and Endurance	Flexibility
Running	21	17	9
Swimming	21	14	15
Cycling	19	16	9
In-line skating	18	15	13
Tennis	16	14	14
Walking	13	11	7
Softball	6	7	9

Making Time

Set a regular time to exercise so fitness will become part of your life. Before or after school might be best for you. If you exercise with a team, attend all the practice sessions.

You will need to adjust your activity to the time you choose. For example, you could use a stationary bike inside your house at night and save outdoor exercise for the daylight hours. Avoid exercising immediately after eating. Exercise draws oxygen to your muscles and away from your stomach. This can interfere with digestion and give you cramps or an upset stomach.

MAKING HEALTHY DECISIONS
Deciding on a Fitness Program

*M*aria and Carrie live in the same apartment building and are best friends. They want to start exercising together. Maria's family belongs to the local YMCA. Maria wants to run on the Y's indoor track three days a week.

Carrie has a problem, however. Her family does not belong to the Y, and she does not think they can afford to join right now. She knows that people who are not members can use the Y for $5 a day. Maybe she could use the money she saved from her birthdays to pay each time she goes there with Maria.

Carrie wonders if she should tell Maria she can't go to the Y with her. Then Maria might ask someone else to go with her. Would she and Carrie still be best friends?

To make up her mind, Carrie uses the decision-making process.

1. **State the situation**
2. **List the options**
3. **Weigh the possible outcomes**
4. **Consider your values**
5. **Make a decision and act**
6. **Evaluate the decision**

Follow-up Activities

1. Apply the six steps of the decision-making process to Carrie's problem.
2. With a partner, role-play a conversation in which Carrie explains her decision to Maria.
3. List at least two ways the girls could exercise together without cost.

Being Smart

Being fit is an excellent goal. You want to reach this goal safely, however. You can help avoid injuries by following these guidelines:

■ **Wear loose-fitting clothing.** Loose-fitting clothing lets your skin breathe and helps you stay cool. It also allows you to move freely.

■ **Choose good equipment.** Athletic shoes and protective clothing do not have to be expensive. They should be of good quality, however. Wear shoes that fit comfortably, support your feet, and have well-cushioned soles. Wear helmets and pads to protect yourself from possible injury.

■ **Exercise on soft, even surfaces.** Holes or ruts on a track, grass, or dirt can lead to twisted ankles and knee injuries. A soft surface will protect you in case of falls.

■ **Begin by warming up. Warming up** means *doing activities and movements that stretch your muscles.* Slowly stretching your muscles loosens them and makes them more elastic. Loose muscles are less likely to be injured as you begin to exercise more vigorously. Warming up also allows your pulse rate to begin rising slowly.

■ **Work up to your target pulse rate.** Your **target pulse rate** is *the level at which your heart and lungs receive the most benefit from a workout.* Your target pulse rate would range from about 125 to 150 heartbeats per minute. At this point, your heart and lungs are working at 60 to 75 percent of their maximum rate.

■ **Adjust for the weather.** On hot, humid days, shorten your workout. Schedule your exercise for the cooler hours of early morning or for evenings. Heat and humidity put an extra strain on your system. On cold days, wear layers of clothing so you can remove the top layer when you start to warm up.

■ **Drink plenty of fluids.** No matter what the weather or where you exercise, you will lose fluids through perspiration. Keep a water bottle with you so you can replace those fluids.

■ **Watch for pain.** If you are trying a new exercise or activity, you may feel some discomfort in your muscles. If the discomfort turns to pain, stop. Do not risk injury. If you feel pain every time you exercise, see your doctor.

■ **End by cooling down. Cooling down** means *slowly winding down an activity.* By doing an activity more slowly, you allow your heart rate to return to normal gradually. Complete your workout by stretching, just as you began.

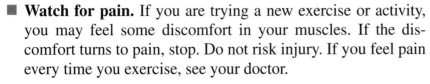

Q & A ?

Ouch!

Q: What causes muscle cramps?

A: As you exercise or play a sport, waste products build up in the muscles you are using most. These wastes can cause sharp pain. Warming up ahead of time can help loosen your muscles and avoid painful cramps.

Review

Lesson 5

Using complete sentences, answer the following questions on a separate sheet of paper.

Reviewing Terms and Facts

1. **Explain** Tell why planning is important as you begin an exercise program.

2. **List** Identify three questions you should ask yourself as you think about what exercise to include in your fitness program.

3. **Identify** What are three advantages of wearing loose-fitting clothing during exercise?

4. **Vocabulary** Use the terms *warming up, target pulse rate,* and *cooling down* in an original paragraph about planning a workout.

5. **Describe** List one way you can prepare for cold weather and one way you can prepare for hot weather.

Thinking Critically

6. **Predict** Tell what might happen if you start exercising without making a plan.

7. **Compare** Contrast an exercise program you design for yourself with an exercise program you might purchase on a videotape. What are the advantages and disadvantages of both?

8. **Deduce** Explain why it would be important to take your pulse rate every so often during exercise if you wanted to build endurance.

Applying Health Concepts

9. **Personal Health** Select an activity that will help meet one of your fitness goals. Write up a plan that shows when and where you will do this activity. Set goals for improving your performance in this activity over a four-week period.

Chapter Summary

▶ There are six essential categories of nutrients: carbohydrates, proteins, fats, vitamins, minerals, and water. (Lesson 1)

▶ A balanced diet includes the right amounts of all six categories of nutrients. (Lesson 1)

▶ The Food Guide Pyramid shows the five food groups and the number of servings people should eat from each group. (Lesson 2)

▶ Americans need to reduce the amount of fat in their diets. (Lesson 2)

▶ People should eat lots of starch and fiber but limit fats, sodium, sugar, and caffeine. (Lesson 3)

▶ Weight control can be achieved by balancing the calories consumed with energy used. (Lesson 3)

▶ Exercise is essential to fitness. (Lesson 4)

▶ Different kinds of exercise can improve strength, endurance, and flexibility. (Lesson 4)

▶ Fitness goals should be considered in planning an exercise program along with factors such as activity preference, equipment, location, and time. (Lesson 5)

▶ Exercise injuries can be minimized if proper guidelines are followed. (Lesson 5)

Using Health Terms

On a separate sheet of paper, write the vocabulary term that best matches each definition given below.

1. Nutrients that provide the main source of energy for the body (Lesson 1)

2. Nutrients that are essential for the growth and repair of body cells (Lesson 1)

3. A guideline to help you choose what and how much to eat to get the nutrients you need (Lesson 2)

4. A mineral that helps control the amount of fluid in our bodies (Lesson 3)

5. A substance, found in some foods, that can speed up certain body processes (Lesson 3)

6. How well a muscle group can perform over a given time without becoming overly tired (Lesson 4)

7. Doing activities and movements that stretch your muscles (Lesson 5)

Reviewing Main Ideas

Using complete sentences, answer the following questions on a separate sheet of paper.

1. How does each of the six types of nutrients contribute to our health? (Lesson 1)

2. What does a balanced diet include? (Lesson 1)

3. List the five food groups and two examples of foods in each group. (Lesson 2)

4. From which food group should the largest number of daily servings come? (Lesson 2)

5. How does eating foods that contain fiber help keep people healthy? (Lesson 3)

6. Why should we limit the amount of sugar in our diets? (Lesson 3)

7. What are the three specific benefits of exercise? (Lesson 4)

8. What is aerobic exercise? (Lesson 4)

9. What are three things to consider in planning an exercise program? (Lesson 5)

10. Why should you warm up before exercising? (Lesson 5)

Thinking Critically

Using complete sentences, answer the following questions on a separate sheet of paper.

1. **Explain** Why might eating what tastes good *not* necessarily lead to a healthy diet? (Lesson 1)

2. **Produce** Construct a Food Guide Pyramid that shows the relative size of each food group in the average teenager's diet. For each food group in your pyramid, explain why you chose the size you did. (Lesson 2)

3. **Explain** Why are there no servings listed in the Food Guide Pyramid for the food group that contains fats, oils, and sweets? (Lesson 2)

4. **Hypothesize** What kinds of reasons might be most effective in convincing a teen to stick to a balanced diet? (Lesson 3)

5. **Analyze** Why do so many magazines contain advertisements for exercise equipment? (Lesson 4)

6. **Predict** What three changes might occur if everyone in your community began to exercise regularly? (Lessons 4 and 5)

Your Action Plan

Most of us should eat a more balanced diet and/or improve our fitness. Look through your private journal entries for this chapter. Does your daily diet need an overhaul? Is it time to get serious about an exercise program?

Write down a realistic, long-term goal. You might set a goal to eat the correct number of servings from the Food Guide Pyramid every day. If you are concerned about fitness, you might set specific goals to improve strength, endurance, or flexibility.

Next, think of short-term goals that will help you meet your long-term goal. If you want to follow the Food Guide Pyramid, your short-term goals might be to eat the correct number of vegetables, then fruits, and so on. A short-term exercise goal might be to swim 20 laps or run 1 mile.

Plan a schedule for reaching each short-term goal. You might focus on eating your vegetables the first week and add fruits the second week. You might add 2 laps a week until you reach 20. When you reach your long-term goal, reward yourself in a healthful way!

Building Your Portfolio

1. At the grocery store, compare four brands of the same food. Make a chart showing the amounts of the main nutrients in each brand. Include a copy in your portfolio.

2. Design an advertisement for fruit and vegetables as snacks. Talk about their benefits and use pictures that make them look appetizing. Post your ad at school. Put a copy in your portfolio.

In Your Home and Community

1. Make posters for or read morning announcements to your classmates that give short, interesting nutrition facts. You could include recipes and suggestions for simple meals (for example, quick nutritious breakfasts), along with specific nutrition information.

2. Arrange to lead some simple exercises for a preschool class once a week for several weeks. Choose exercises the class can do easily. Explain why exercise is important and encourage them to exercise daily at home.

Chapter 5
Your Body: Growing and Changing

The New Ansel Adams Photog

Student Expectations

After reading this chapter, you should be able to:

❶ Describe how life starts.

❷ Explain how heredity, environment, and behavior affect who you are.

❸ Identify and describe the stages of life from infancy to adolescence.

❹ Describe how you can be responsible to yourself and to your family, friends, and community.

Carlotta, my four-year-old sister, likes to make noise. She sings. She talks. The other day, when I was trying to talk on the phone, she started banging on her drum. I had to hang up. I was so annoyed at the noise, I could have screamed.

My mother told me not to get so upset. It's just a "stage" Carlotta is going through. She claims I went through the same stage myself.

In fact, my mother claims I'm still going through stages. To prove it, she got out my school pictures. We compared this year's picture with the one from five years ago—when I was in first grade.

The difference was amazing. Five years from now, my mother says, I'll change even more. By then, I'll barely recognize myself. "How do you know all this?" I asked her.

My mother laughed. She said that when she was growing up, she went through the same changes herself. More important, she's still going through changes. "Do people ever stop changing?" I asked.

"Not really," my mother said. "As long as you live, you'll keep going through stages. You'll keep changing and growing."

in your journal

Read the story on this page. How would you describe the stage you are going through now? Start your private journal entries on growing and changing by answering these questions:

▶ In what ways have you changed in the past five years?

▶ What do you like about yourself at this stage of your life?

▶ What changes are you looking forward to as you grow toward adulthood?

When you reach the end of the chapter, you will use your journal entries to make an action plan.

1 The Beginning of Life

This lesson will help you find answers to questions that teens often ask about development before birth. For example:

▶ How does life start?

▶ How does a baby develop inside its mother's body?

▶ What are our bodies made of?

Words to Know

fertilization
egg cell
sperm cell
uterus
umbilical cord
cell
tissue
organ
system

A Single Cell

Each person starts as a single cell, or unit of matter. This single cell is formed as a result of fertilization. **Fertilization** (fer·til·i·ZAY·shuhn) is *the joining together of two special reproductive cells, one from each parent.* The *special cell in the mother's body* is called an **egg cell.** The egg cell combines with a *special cell from the father's body* called a **sperm cell.** Fertilization takes place inside the mother's body.

During the development process, the fertilized cell divides millions of times. It grows from a size smaller than that of the

Figure 5.1
Development Before Birth
After fertilization, a baby grows and develops for nine months.

in your journal

Suppose your younger sister asked you how human life begins. What would you tell her? In your journal, write your description of how human life begins.

Fertilization
A sperm cell unites with an egg cell, forming a new cell that is microscopic in size.

dot over the letter *i* to a fully developed baby (see **Figure 5.1**). Every person is made up of trillions of cells.

Development Before Birth

The baby grows inside its mother's uterus. The **uterus** (YOO·tuh·ruhs) is a *pear-shaped organ that expands as the baby grows.* To help the baby grow, it receives food and oxygen from the mother. The food and oxygen are carried to the baby through a tube called the umbilical cord. The **umbilical** (uhm·BIL·i·kuhl) **cord** *connects the lining of the uterus to the baby.* It attaches to the baby at the place where the infant's navel will form. Blood from the mother passes through the lining of the uterus and carries nourishment through the cord to the baby. The cord also carries wastes away.

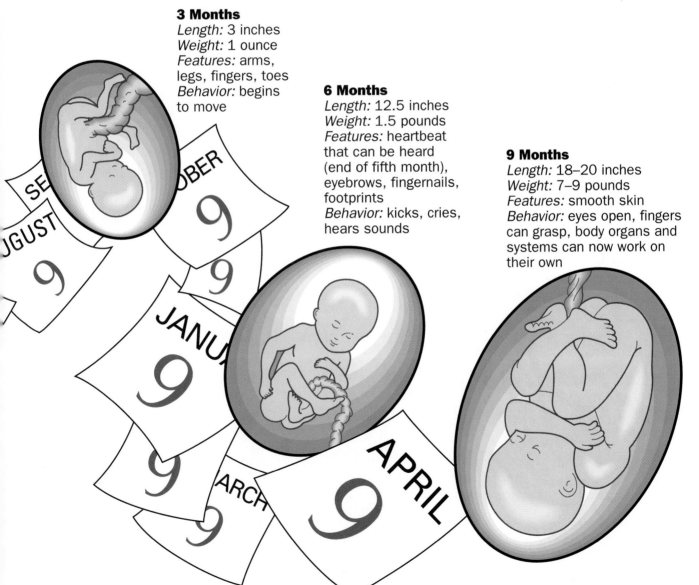

3 Months
Length: 3 inches
Weight: 1 ounce
Features: arms, legs, fingers, toes
Behavior: begins to move

6 Months
Length: 12.5 inches
Weight: 1.5 pounds
Features: heartbeat that can be heard (end of fifth month), eyebrows, fingernails, footprints
Behavior: kicks, cries, hears sounds

9 Months
Length: 18–20 inches
Weight: 7–9 pounds
Features: smooth skin
Behavior: eyes open, fingers can grasp, body organs and systems can now work on their own

The Life of a Cell

ACTIVITY!

Skin cells live for only a few days. When they die, new cells take their place. Brain cells, however, live as long as you do. If they are destroyed, brain cells are not replaced. Write a report on the risks to which people expose their brain cells by unhealthy lifestyle choices.

The Building Blocks of Life

The single cell from which a baby is formed divides into two cells, then four cells, and so on. Billions are formed eventually. These cells organize in a special way to form the tissues, organs, and systems of the developing baby (see **Figure 5.2**).

Figure 5.2
From Cell to System

❶ **Cells** are *the basic building blocks of life.* Cells work together to help your body function well. Each cell does a special job. The lung cell (shown here) helps your body get the oxygen it needs.

❹ **Systems** are formed by a *group of organs that perform a related task.* The organs of the respiratory system (shown here) bring oxygen to all cells in the body.

❸ An **organ** is a *structure that is made up of different types of tissues that do a particular job.* The various tissues in the lung (shown here) work together to provide the exchange of oxygen and carbon dioxide.

❷ **Tissues** are *groups of similar cells that do the same kind of work.* Lung tissue (shown here) is elastic and spongy because it is made up of hundreds of millions of tiny air sacs.

Care Before Birth

To be sure that the baby gets the nutrition it needs to develop properly, the mother should practice good health care while she is pregnant. She should regularly visit a health care professional who specializes in the care of pregnant women and unborn babies. The mother should also follow these steps:

- Eat nutritious foods.

- Get enough rest.

- Get the type and amount of exercise that the health care professional recommends.

- Do not use alcohol or tobacco.

- Take only the drugs that have been approved by the health care professional.

in your journal

In your journal, describe how you might eat differently if you knew that what you ate would affect the health of a person who was close to you.

When a pregnant woman takes care of herself, she increases her chances of having a healthy baby.

Review

Lesson 1

Using complete sentences, answer the following questions on a separate sheet of paper.

Reviewing Terms and Facts

1. **Identify**   What two kinds of cells are involved in fertilization?

2. **Recall**   In what organ of the mother's body does a baby grow?

3. **Vocabulary**   Define the term *tissue.*

4. **Give Examples**   Name one system in your body.

5. **List**   Give three ways a pregnant woman can take care of herself and her unborn baby.

Thinking Critically

6. **Summarize**   What happens during the process of fertilization?

7. **Describe**   How do food and oxygen reach the developing baby?

8. **Explain**   Why is it especially important for an expectant mother to practice good health care?

Applying Health Concepts

9. **Growth and Development**   Read at least two magazine articles about the experience of being pregnant. Share and discuss your reactions to the articles with a group of classmates.

10. **Health of Others**   Working with a classmate, make a poster summarizing the ways a pregnant woman should take care of her own health and the health of her baby. Use pictures about health, cut from magazines, to illustrate each point. Display your poster in a local health clinic.

Lesson

2 What Makes You Unique?

This lesson will help you find answers to questions that teens often ask about what makes each person unique. For example:

▶ **What makes children look like their parents?**

▶ **What are the main influences on my personality?**

▶ **Why do I act the way I do?**

Words to Know

heredity
chromosome
gene
personality
environment
values
behavior

Inherited Characteristics

The fact that many children look like their parents is no accident. **Heredity** (huh·RED·i·tee) is *the process by which parents pass characteristics on to their children.* Traits that are passed on include eye color, hair color, and body build. Heredity may also include the tendency a person has to get certain diseases. Every cell contains two structures that influence heredity. They are chromosomes and genes.

Role of Chromosomes

Within every cell are structures called **chromosomes** (KROH·muh·sohmz). *These tiny, threadlike pieces of matter carry the codes for inherited traits.* Chromosomes come in pairs. One-half of each chromosome pair comes from the father and one-half comes from the mother. Almost every cell in a person's body contains 46 chromosomes—23 from each parent.

HEALTH LAB
Inherited Physical Traits

*I*ntroduction: Sometimes people who are related look very much alike (for example, all are tall and blond). Relatives in other families may bear only a slight resemblance to each other. This lab will help you examine the occurrence of inherited traits within families.

Objective: Select a family to observe during the next week. You may choose your own

Special Chromosomes

The only cells in the human body that do not have 46 chromosomes are the egg cells and sperm cells. Egg and sperm cells have 23 chromosomes each. When egg and sperm cells combine during fertilization, they produce a cell with 46 chromosomes. Special chromosomes in the egg and sperm cells determine the sex of the baby (see **Figure 5.3**).

Figure 5.3
Boy or Girl?

Whether you are a boy or a girl was determined by the special chromosomes in the sperm cell and egg cell from which you developed. A sperm cell contains either an X or a Y chromosome. All egg cells contain one X chromosome.

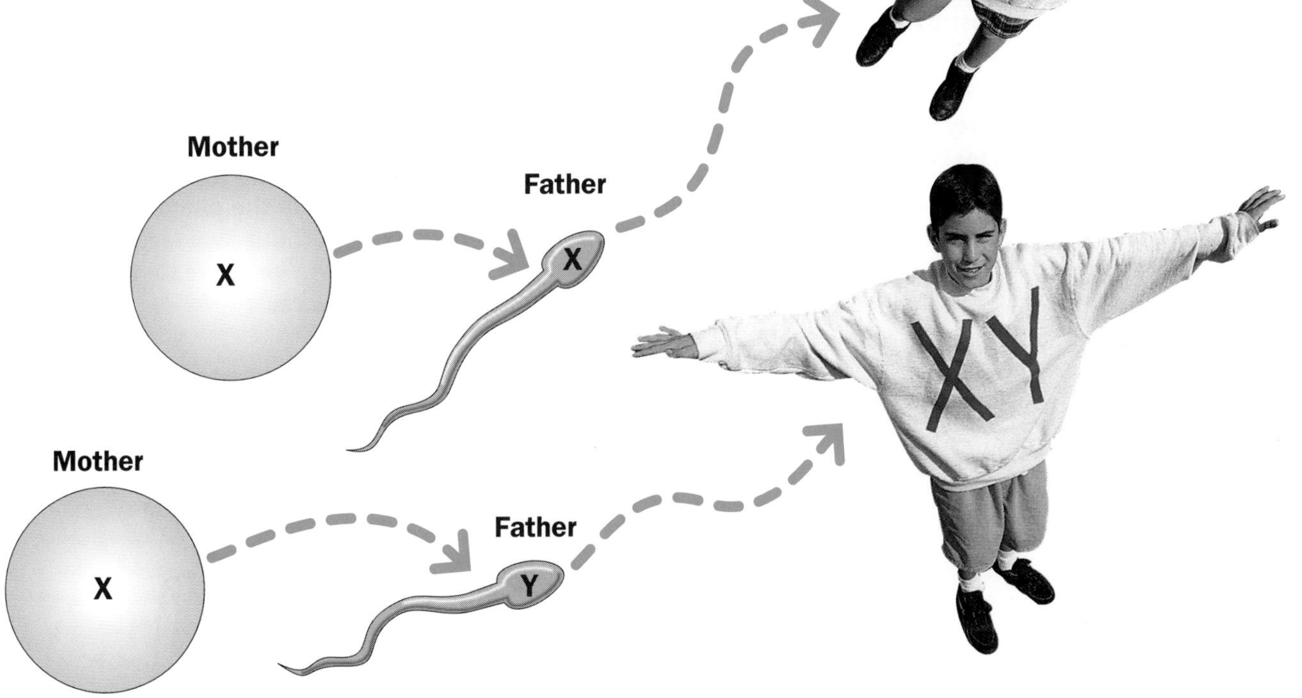

Mother

Father

X

X

Mother

Father

X

Y

family or the family of a friend or neighbor. Obtain permission to conduct your study. Observe family members and look for several inherited physical traits. You may choose from eye color, hair color, hair type (for example, curly or coarse), ears (for example, attached or free earlobe), freckles, and dimples. To make the most effective comparison, try to observe grandparents, parents, and children. Draw conclusions about how physical traits pass from generation to generation.

Materials and Method: Prepare a form that contains columns for the person's

name, the position within the family (for example, parent or child), and the traits you are going to observe. At the end of the observation, total the numbers for each trait.

Observation and Analysis:
Examine your form. Do you see any trends in your data? How frequently does each trait occur? Do some traits occur in only one or two people? Are some traits found in all the people you observed? Share your results with the class.

Faulty genes can result in health disorders. Sometimes a disorder is found almost entirely among one cultural group. For example, Jewish people whose ancestors come from one small area in Eastern Europe have the highest rates of Tay-Sachs disease. This disease destroys the nervous system. A test can tell people with this background whether they are carrying the gene for Tay-Sachs disease.

Role of Genes

Each chromosome is divided into small sections called genes. **Genes** (jeenz) are the *basic units of heredity.* They carry codes that control the individual traits that you inherit, such as height, eye color, skin color, and face shape. Except for identical twins, each person has a unique arrangement of genes.

People inherit two genes for every characteristic—one gene from each parent. Sometimes the two genes for one trait contain different codes. This arrangement affects how the trait appears in the child (see **Figure 5.4**).

Figure 5.4
Eye Color

Both of these parents have one gene for brown eyes (B) and one gene for blue eyes (b). Brown eyes are *dominant* over blue eyes. This means that each of these parents will have brown eyes. The gene for blue eyes is *recessive.* A person must have two genes for blue eyes for that person's eyes to be blue.

Four ways that these parents can pass the gene for eye color to any children they have are shown here. What is the chance that a child of these parents will have blue eyes?

Factors that Affect Your Personality

Your **personality** is the *sum total of the feelings, actions, habits, and thoughts you have.* Just as the traits you inherited are unique, so is your personality. No other person is exactly like you. The person you become is influenced by heredity. Your personality is also shaped by your surroundings and by the choices you make. Together, your heredity, environment, and behavior make you the person you are.

in your journal

Who or what do you think has most influenced the values you have? In your journal, write about how this person, place, or thing has influenced you.

Role of the Environment

Your **environment** (en·VY·ruhn·ment) is *the sum total of your surroundings.* Your environment includes people and places. Important people are your family, your teachers, and your friends. Important places include where you grew up, where you live now, where you go to school, and where you play.

■ **People.** Early in life, your family is the most important influence. Your parents teach you how to act. They help you develop your talents and skills. They also help you develop your values. **Values** are *ideas about right and wrong and about what is important in your life.* You may have learned from your parents that it is good to help others. You may have been taught to value an education or physical fitness. Other values include honesty, kindness, and respect for others.

During the teen years, you will be influenced by many people other than your family. Friends have a great influence on you. They may affect your values. For instance, from your friends you may learn to value loyalty.

Your teachers introduce you to different ways of thinking about things. You are also influenced by historical figures and by famous sports and entertainment personalities.

The people within your environment influence your growth and development and help to make you who you are.

The Right Thing ACTIVITY!

You have probably felt at some time that you were being pulled in opposite directions. You want to do what you think is right, but a friend is trying to change your mind.

This is a good time to think about what will happen if you do what your friend wants. If it has serious consequences, stand firm. A true friend will understand.

Reread Lesson 1 of Chapter 3 for ways to say no. Make an agreement with a friend, brother, or sister to help each other practice using these tips. Keep a four-week log of how many times and of the circumstances in which you assist each other.

■ **Places.** Where you live has a strong effect on your development. It also affects what is important to you. Living in a large city may offer you many opportunities outside your home. You may have museums or theme parks near you. Large cities, however, expose you to congestion and pollution.

Where you live may influence what activities you take part in.

MAKING HEALTHY DECISIONS
Choosing Healthy Behaviors

*E*ver since Rashad was small, his parents have involved him in sports. They take him to practice and cheer him on.

Rashad recently started at a new school and made some new friends. His new friends do not enjoy sports. Instead, they like to gather at the video arcade in the mall.

Rashad has a problem. He likes sports and wants to please his parents. He also wants to be with his friends. What should Rashad do? Should he ask his parents if he can drop his sports activities? Should he tell his friends he can't join them? Rashad decides to use the six-step decision-making process to make up his mind.

❶ **State the situation**
❷ **List the options**
❸ **Weigh the possible outcomes**
❹ **Consider your values**
❺ **Make a decision and act**
❻ **Evaluate the decision**

Follow-up Activities

1. Apply the six steps of the decision-making process to Rashad's situation.
2. Using role-playing, create a situation in which Rashad explains his decision to his friends.

People who live in rural areas may not have as many health care or service opportunities as those who live in a city, but they may be able to do more outdoor activities with their families.

No matter where you live, you are likely to be influenced by television, radio, newspapers, and magazines. All of these sources of information affect your values and thinking.

Role of Behavior

Behavior is *how you act in situations that occur in your life.* It is the factor in your life over which you have the most control. Your actions affect who you are and who you will become. If you act wisely, you are likely to lead a productive and healthy life.

Many factors influence how you act. You act according to your needs. Needs range from the basic need for food to the need for love. You also act according to your values. For example, if you value good health, you will practice good health habits.

Your behavior also affects other people and the place where you live. If you value loyalty, you will stand by a friend. If you value a clean environment, you may clean up your local park.

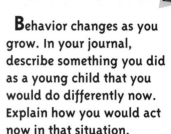

Behavior changes as you grow. In your journal, describe something you did as a young child that you would do differently now. Explain how you would act now in that situation.

Review

Lesson 2

Using complete sentences, answer the following questions on a separate sheet of paper.

Reviewing Terms and Facts

1. **Vocabulary** Define the term *heredity.* Use it in a sentence.

2. **Recall** How many chromosomes are there in most body cells? In reproductive cells?

3. **Identify** The terms *dominant* and *recessive* describe which of the following: environment, genes, or chromosomes?

4. **Vocabulary** What is the difference between *personality* and *behavior?*

5. **Give Examples** List three values that a person might have.

Thinking Critically

6. **Distinguish** List three traits that are inherited and three traits that are shaped by environment.

7. **Explain** Why is a person's behavior so important to that person's development?

8. **Analyze** Choose a person you admire. Explain what you like about that person's behavior and state why you feel that way.

Applying Health Concepts

9. **Health of Others** Sometimes babies are born with gene disorders. One gene disorder is Down syndrome. Use a reference book to read about this disorder. Find out what problem with chromosomes causes this condition.

10. **Growth and Development** Create a chart to show the relationship between the values a person has and that person's actions. In one column, list five values. In a separate column, list two actions a person might take to demonstrate each value. Display the chart in class.

Teen HEALTH DIGEST

People at Work

Pediatric Nurse

Joe DeMarco grew up in a family with six children. As an adult, Joe is still around a lot of children. He works as a pediatric nurse.

Pediatric nurses are registered nurses who specialize in helping children stay healthy. Many people think that pediatric nurses treat only babies. In fact, pediatric nurses treat children of all ages—from infancy through adolescence.

Pediatric nurses work in hospitals, doctors' offices, and health clinics. They have many responsibilities, such as taking medical histories, performing procedures, and providing care during illness and recovery. They also teach children and parents about good health and the steps they can take to stay healthy.

"No two children respond to a situation in the same way," Joe says. "They have their own personalities and backgrounds. I always keep that in mind when I'm helping my patients."

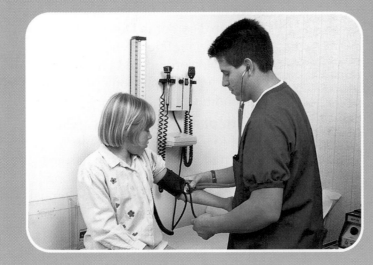

Sports and Recreation

Mighty Muggsy

Tyrone "Muggsy" Bogues is a professional basketball player. In a sport in which height is the rule, Bogues is the exception. Many of his teammates are nearly 7 feet tall. Bogues is just 5 feet, 3 inches tall. How can he compete?

Obviously, Bogues does not have the advantage of height. However, he has other skills that are just as valuable to the team.

Quickness is Bogues's secret weapon. Lightning fast, Bogues darts through the taller players. He is an expert at stealing the ball from the opposing team. With these skills, his height is never an issue.

Teens Making a Difference

Helping Hands

In the fall of 1992, students in a Montessori school in Maryland decided to reach out to the children of a tiny village in Somalia. The village children were very poor. Years of war had left them with almost nothing.

The American children began raising money to help. They started by giving their own money and going door-to-door in the town. They added $500 to their total with a bake sale. With the help of a man who had grown up in Somalia, the children decided to use the money they were raising to build a school in the village.

To get the money for such a big project, the children began asking large companies and charitable organizations for donations. They also went to other schools in the region for help. In just a few months, they had raised thousands of dollars. They showed that they care about other people in a meaningful way.

Health Update

Responsibility Grows in "Tribes"

About 20 years ago, a program called "Tribes" was started in a few California classrooms. The purpose of Tribes is to build self-esteem and responsible behavior in students.

In the Tribes program, students first agree to a set of values. They agree to listen to one another, to show each other respect, to not put anyone down, and to allow each other the right to pass (remain silent).

The class is then divided into tribes, or groups of four. Within each tribe, students are encouraged to share experiences. They work on solving problems as a team. Every four weeks, the groups change and students form new tribes.

Today, the Tribes program has spread to schools throughout the country. Teachers report that students in Tribes classes seem to show more responsibility toward their own classwork as well as the work of their "tribe."

Youth Spending Power

Did you know that kids from ages 4 to 18 earn about $70 billion each year? This figure includes the money they receive from allowances, earnings, and gifts. Young people spend much of this money on food, games, movies, clothes, and other products.

Advertisers recognize the fact that young people are big consumers. They try to create ads that will appeal to young people. For example, when one pizza company wanted to boost its sales, it did research into what kinds of advertising appealed to teens. Then it added music and a computer-animated character to its ads, hoping that more teens would buy its product.

The next time you buy something, consider how ads may affect your choices. Be a responsible consumer. Choose a product because you like the way it tastes, looks, or performs—not because you like the ad.

Childhood and Adolescence

This lesson will help you find answers to questions that teens often ask about growing up. For example:

▶ **What kind of infant and young child was I?**

▶ **Why am I changing so much now?**

▶ **When will I stop growing?**

Words to Know

infancy
toddler
preschooler
adolescence
hormone
puberty

Your Total Health

Good Nutrition

The need for good nutrition is very important during the rapid growth that takes place during infancy. It affects bone and muscle growth and coordination.

The Growth Years

The years from birth through the late teen years are a time of rapid growth and great change. During these years, people change in many ways. Their bodies grow. They go through enormous social and emotional changes. Growth follows a general pattern, but the specific times at which each person goes through these changes are unique to that individual.

Infancy

Growth is fastest during *the first year of life.* This period is called **infancy.** During this year, infants often triple their body weight and increase their height by half.

Infants learn basic movements—sitting, crawling, and standing. They begin to understand simple words that are spoken to them. They learn to say a few words.

Most important, babies form attachments to the people who take care of them, usually their parents. If their needs are met, infants feel secure and learn to trust.

An infant's needs should be met quickly and lovingly.

During early childhood, children learn to do many tasks for themselves, such as eating and dressing.

Childhood

During childhood, children learn many important physical and social skills.

- *Children ages one to three* are called **toddlers.** At this stage, children learn to walk well and to run, jump, and climb. Toddlers like to explore their surroundings. They start to want to do things on their own. If parents accept the failures and encourage the successes, the child builds confidence.

- *Children ages three to five* are often called **preschoolers.** They enjoy make-believe activities. They may even have imaginary playmates. Preschoolers ask many questions as their minds develop. If they are encouraged to be creative and curious, they will learn to start activities on their own.

- From ages six to eleven, children have many social experiences, especially through school. At this stage, children learn to get along with their peers. They begin to compare themselves with others. They learn right from wrong, and they begin to understand the reasons for rules.

Around ages three to five, children often copy what they see adults doing.

During late childhood, children enjoy creating. If they are encouraged, they develop a sense of accomplishment and pride. If not, they may feel inferior and inhibited.

Age of Puberty

In the past 100 years, the average age when puberty occurs in the United States has dropped three to four months every ten years. Do research on what factors might have influenced the change.

Adolescence

Next to infancy, adolescence is the time when you grow and change the most. **Adolescence** (a·duhl·E·suhns) marks *the period between childhood and adulthood*. At this time, changes occur in your body, in your thinking and feelings, and in your relationships with people.

The changes that happen during adolescence are related to hormones in your body. **Hormones** (HOR·mohnz) are *chemicals that control certain functions of the body.* The changes caused by these hormones are preparing you for adulthood.

Physical Changes

Adolescence begins with puberty. **Puberty** (PYOO·ber·tee) is *the time when you begin to develop certain physical traits of the adults of your sex* (see **Figure 5.5**). Girls often show the physical changes of adolescence earlier than boys. The physical changes of adolescence usually begin between the ages of 11 and 15. These changes occur over a period of several years. They usually end between the ages of 16 and 20.

Figure 5.5
Physical Changes of Adolescence

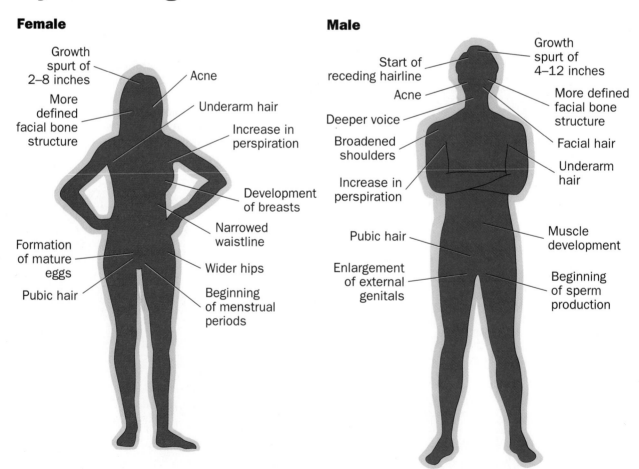

Female
- Growth spurt of 2–8 inches
- More defined facial bone structure
- Formation of mature eggs
- Pubic hair
- Acne
- Underarm hair
- Increase in perspiration
- Development of breasts
- Narrowed waistline
- Wider hips
- Beginning of menstrual periods

Male
- Start of receding hairline
- Acne
- Deeper voice
- Broadened shoulders
- Increase in perspiration
- Pubic hair
- Enlargement of external genitals
- Growth spurt of 4–12 inches
- More defined facial bone structure
- Facial hair
- Underarm hair
- Muscle development
- Beginning of sperm production

Emotional and Mental Changes

Not all changes during adolescence are physical. During adolescence, you often have mood swings. You may be very happy one minute and sad the next. You may feel like being with people one day and want to be left alone the next. These moods are often brought on by hormones.

As you mature, you begin to think about things in new ways. You consider the possible effects of your actions. You start to consider the points of view of others. You also begin to realize that some problems do not have simple solutions. During this time, you learn about who you are and you develop your own set of values.

in your journal

Choose one of the statements to which you answered no in the personal inventory. In your journal, write how you think you can improve in this area.

During adolescence, you start to make decisions about what is important to you.

Personal Inventory

HOW GROWN-UP ARE YOU?

On a separate sheet of paper, write yes or no for each statement.

1. I think about the consequences before I act.

2. I do what I think is right, even when it is hard.

3. I feel comfortable with who I am. I don't try to be something I'm not.

4. I respect other people's ideas even when they are different from my own.

5. I think about how my actions affect other people.

6. I have more adult talks with my parents than I used to.

7. I take time to listen to other people's problems.

8. I sometimes put myself in the shoes of my parents and other adults.

9. I recognize that the choices I make now will affect my future.

10. I have a good idea of the kind of adult I would like to be.

A yes answer to any of these statements indicates that you have learned to act in a grown-up way in those parts of your life. Do not worry about how many no answers you have. Each person matures at a different pace. Practice will help you grow into a healthy, responsible adult.

Social Changes

During adolescence, you begin to see yourself as separate from your parents. You see that your parents have needs and wants. At the same time, your parents begin to see that you are growing up. They may expect you to take on more responsibility.

Your friendships become very important to you. In early adolescence, you may be strongly influenced by your friends. You want their approval. As you mature, you learn to follow your own standards.

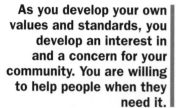

By the end of your teens, you will be able to function on your own. You will have formed your own ideas about who you are and how you fit into the world.

As you develop your own values and standards, you develop an interest in and a concern for your community. You are willing to help people when they need it.

Lesson 3 Review

Using complete sentences, answer the following questions on a separate sheet of paper.

Reviewing Terms and Facts

1. **Recall**   List two important developments that occur during infancy.

2. **Give Examples**   Name one skill that children learn as toddlers and one skill that they learn as preschoolers.

3. **Vocabulary**   What is the difference between *adolescence* and *puberty?*

4. **List**   Name five physical changes of adolescence in girls and five in boys.

5. **Recall**   Give two examples of emotional or mental changes that occur during adolescence.

Thinking Critically

6. **Summarize**   Describe briefly the skills children develop as they grow.

7. **Compare**   Think back to the things you did when you were six or seven. In what ways have you changed since then? What change is most noticeable?

8. **Analyze**   Which changes of adolescence do you think are most difficult, the physical or the emotional? Give reasons for your choice.

Applying Health Concepts

9. **Growth and Development** Interview one of your classmates. Ask your classmate to describe what he or she enjoys best about being a young teenager. Ask your classmate to state one challenge that he or she has faced during the teen years. Ask your classmate how he or she handled the challenge. Then switch roles and have your classmate interview you.

10. **Health of Others**   Create a guidebook for the teen years. In it, write your suggestions for making these years happy and productive. Share your suggestions with the class.

The Responsible You

This lesson will help you find answers to questions that teens often ask about taking responsibility. For example:

▶ **What do I gain from being responsible?**

▶ **To whom am I responsible right now?**

▶ **How can I show that I am responsible?**

What Is Responsibility?

You are probably looking forward to being more independent and to having the freedom to make your own choices. It is good to remember, however, that having freedom involves **responsibility.** When you are responsible, *you choose an action to take and you will answer for that action.*

Challenges of Responsibility

As you practice taking responsibility for what you do, you will face many challenges. Each time you successfully meet one of these challenges, you are developing life skills for the future.

■ You will have to accept the consequences of your choices.

■ You won't be able to blame other people when something goes wrong.

■ You will be expected to keep your word. When you say you will do something, you should follow through.

■ If you make an unpopular choice, you may be pressured to change your mind. You may have to defend your choice.

■ You won't be able to do everything you or others want.

■ You will have to decide how much responsibility you can handle. If you take on too much at one time, you may not be able to do everything well.

■ You will have to examine unwise decisions so that you can decide how to do better in the future.

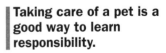

Words to Know

responsibility
initiative

Your Total Health

Stress of Responsibility

Taking responsibility may cause stress. Stress can lead to health problems.

Learning to manage stress now will help you stay healthy as you take on greater responsibility. Chapter 3 gives more information about ways to deal with stress.

| Taking care of a pet is a good way to learn responsibility.

in your journal

In your journal, describe a time recently when you practiced personal responsibility.

Rewards of Responsibility

Developing a sense of responsibility brings many rewards. Some are listed below.

■ You build self-esteem and self-respect.

■ You begin to be treated like an adult. You show that you are reliable and worthy of trust.

■ Your opinions matter.

■ You start to gain control over your life.

■ You build the life skills you will need to function as a healthy, productive adult.

Personal Responsibility

When you were younger, your parents were responsible for making all decisions about your health and well-being. Now you are starting to take on that job. You have many chances during each day to take responsibility for yourself, as shown in **Figure 5.6.** Making good choices now can help you achieve good total health as an adult.

Figure 5.6
Practicing Responsibility

Ⓐ Choosing Friends
Select friends who share your values and interests. Do not choose friends just to be part of the "in" crowd.

Ⓑ What You Eat
Eat healthful snacks and nutritious meals.

Ⓒ What You Wear
Take care of your clothes. Realize you may not be able to afford every item you want.

Ⓓ Study Habits
Set aside time to do your homework every night. Ask for help with a hard subject.

Ⓔ Choosing Activities
Select after-school activities you enjoy. Choose no more activities than you have time for.

Responsibility to Others

Part of growing up is realizing that you cannot think only of yourself. You have responsibilities toward your family members, friends, and community. Being responsible to others involves caring about their needs and feelings.

Family

As you get older and as your skills increase, you will probably have more responsibilities around the house. You may be asked to clean your room, do the dishes, take out the trash, or clean up the yard. You may also be asked to help supervise younger brothers and sisters.

You are also responsible for following the rules your parents set for you. As you develop ideas of your own, you may not always see things the way your parents do. The responsible way to behave is to respect your parents' wishes and discuss your ideas with your parents. Ask them to consider modifying their rules. You may be surprised that they are willing to change some of the rules because you are showing that you are responsible.

Part of responsibility to your family is to become more considerate of your family's feelings. This is the time when you can start taking initiative. **Initiative** (i·NI·shuh·tiv) is *doing something without being told.*

| Q & A | |

House Rules ACTIVITY!

Q: Why do I have so many responsibilities around the house?

A: The skills you learn while helping out at home will help prepare you for the time when you move away from home.

Write down the chores you do. Next to each one, describe how it will be useful to you when you begin life on your own.

When family members help each other with household responsibilities, they build respect for each other.

Teen Issues

"Ratting" on a Friend

When you know a friend is doing something dangerous, you must try to help. Talking to your friend may help. If not, convince your friend to talk to an adult. If that does not work, you should let an adult know. You are not "ratting" on a friend. You are getting your friend the help he or she needs.

You are not too young to make a difference in your community.

Friends

Friendships change during adolescence. You and your friends are more than playmates. You share dreams and listen to each other's problems.

One of the best ways to show that you are a responsible friend is to stand by a friend who is in need. You will not let a friend continue a dangerous behavior, such as using drugs or shoplifting. You will go out of your way to help if you can. Your friend may be more likely to take advice from a good friend than from parents or teachers.

LIFE SKILLS
Showing Responsibility

In most cases, you are given responsibilities when you show that you are ready for them. Here are some ways to show your parents, teachers, and friends that you are a responsible teen:

► Keep your word. If you say you are going to do something, do it. Show that you can be trusted. If you promised an elderly neighbor that you would deliver her groceries, do not go to the mall instead.

► Be reliable. If you sign up to wash cars to help raise money for the soccer team, show up on time. Stay until the job is done.

► Have a good attitude. Do not sulk when you have a chore to do.

► Do not wait to be told to do a task. If you see that a task needs to be done, do it. If your bedroom is messy, clean it.

► Take good care of what you own. This shows that you understand its value. You should be especially careful with an item you borrow. This shows that you respect the person from whom you borrowed it.

Follow-up Activity

Think about a time when you had the chance to act responsibly. What did you do? Would you act differently in the future? Why or why not?

Community

You can be a responsible member of your community in many ways. Some ideas are discussed below.

■ Respect your neighbors. For example, don't play your stereo so loud that your neighbor's baby wakes up.

■ Learn about what is going on in your community. For example, find out about a recycling program.

■ Know the rules and laws of your community and follow them. For example, be sure to wear a safety helmet when you ride your bike.

■ Tell elected officials your opinions. Even though you are too young to vote, your opinion can still be heard.

■ Do volunteer work. For example, volunteer at a soup kitchen.

Review

Lesson 4

Using complete sentences, answer the following questions on a separate sheet of paper.

Reviewing Terms and Facts

1. **Vocabulary** Define the term *responsibility*. Use it in an original sentence.

2. **Recall** What are four rewards of developing a sense of responsibility?

3. **Vocabulary** Define the term *initiative*. Use it in an original sentence.

4. **Identify** Name three ways you can show parents and friends that you are responsible.

5. **List** Give three ways you can be a responsible member of your community.

Thinking Critically

6. **Describe** Choose one freedom you do not have right now that you would like to have in the near future. Suggest a way in which you might show that you are responsible enough to earn that freedom.

7. **Name** What are two ways to show personal responsibility for what you eat?

8. **Evaluate** Which responsibilities do you think are most difficult to meet: those to yourself, to your family, or to your friends? Give reasons for your answer.

Applying Health Concepts

9. **Health of Others** With one of your classmates, prepare a report called "Givers." Evaluate the effect people have on the community they live in. Choose several examples of people in the news who have helped the community or another person. Describe the effect the givers had on their neighbors and community.

10. **Growth and Development** Choose a volunteer group in your community that you think you might like to join. (Look for listings in the newspaper or phone book.) Find out what services the group offers, how many volunteers your age work there, and what you could do to help. Prepare a report on the group for the class.

Chapter Summary

▶ Life begins when a sperm cell and an egg cell join. Inside the mother, the fertilized egg grows into a fully developed baby. (Lesson 1)

▶ All living things are made of cells, which organize into tissues, organs, and systems. (Lesson 1)

▶ Children inherit traits from their parents through a process called heredity. (Lesson 2)

▶ Genes are the basic units of heredity. They carry codes that control the traits that are passed from parent to child. (Lesson 2)

▶ Your heredity, environment, and behavior are all factors that affect the person you become. (Lesson 2)

▶ Growth occurs throughout life but is most rapid during infancy and adolescence. (Lesson 3)

▶ During the three stages of childhood, children expand their imaginations, their knowledge, and their control over their world. (Lesson 3)

▶ Adolescence marks the time when children grow into adults and begin to think about things in new ways. (Lesson 3)

▶ As children grow older, they take on more responsibilities to themselves, family, friends, and community. (Lesson 4)

▶ Responsibilities can be both rewarding and challenging. (Lesson 4)

Using Health Terms

On a separate sheet of paper, write the vocabulary term that best matches each definition given below.

1. The joining together of two special reproductive cells, one from each parent (Lesson 1)

2. The basic building block of life (Lesson 1)

3. The sum total of your surroundings (Lesson 2)

4. Ideas about right and wrong and about what is important in your life (Lesson 2)

5. The first year of life (Lesson 3)

6. Chemicals that control certain functions of the body (Lesson 3)

7. Choosing an action to take and answering for that action (Lesson 4)

8. Doing something without being told (Lesson 4)

Reviewing Main Ideas

Using complete sentences, answer the following questions on a separate sheet of paper.

1. What are the differences between an unborn baby at three months and one at nine months? (Lesson 1)

2. Explain how cells, tissues, organs, and systems in the body are related. (Lesson 1)

3. What role do genes play in heredity? (Lesson 2)

4. Of all the factors that affect who you are, which do you have the most control over? (Lesson 2)

5. During which two periods of life does the greatest amount of growth occur? (Lesson 3)

6. What role do hormones play in adolescence? (Lesson 3)

7. What are four challenges of responsibility? (Lesson 4)

8. What are four areas in which you can show personal responsibility? (Lesson 4)

Thinking Critically

Using complete sentences, answer the following questions on a separate sheet of paper.

1. **Analyze** Why is it important for a pregnant woman to regularly visit a health care professional? (Lesson 1)

2. **Deduce** Why do egg cells and sperm cells have only half the number of chromosomes that other cells in the body have? (Lesson 2)

3. **Synthesize** How do your heredity, environment, and behavior shape the person you are? (Lesson 2)

4. **Justify** Give reasons why someone might call adolescence "a time of change" in a person's life. (Lesson 3)

5. **Explain** How would you describe the changing relationship between children and their parents as the children reach adolescence? (Lessons 3 and 4)

6. **Analyze** Why might it be best for a person to take on only one new responsibility at a time? (Lesson 4)

Your Action Plan

Would you like to have more responsibilities? Make a list of the responsibilities that you would most like to have. Your short-term goals will be getting these responsibilities. Your long-term goal will be to become more responsible in general.

To get ideas for short-term goals, look through your private journal entries for this chapter. Then form a plan. Write down specific steps that will help you reach your short-term goals. For example, if you want an after-school job, write down steps you can take to get that job.

Put your plan into action. When you have reached one or two of your short-term goals, review your plan. Determine whether you are reaching your long-term goal as well as your short-term goals.

Building Your Portfolio

1. Think about how your environment affects who you are. Collect photographs or draw pictures of people and places that you feel have influenced you. Add the pictures to your portfolio. Under each one, describe what you have learned from that person or place.

2. Interview a family that has a baby. Ask the mother or father to describe the stages of the baby's development. Ask other family members about how the baby has changed their lives. What new responsibilities do they have? Summarize what you learn in your portfolio.

In Your Home and Community

1. Have a discussion in your home about values. Ask the members of your family about their values. Compare them with your own values. Are they similar or different? Write down what you learn.

2. Organize a homework chain with three or four classmates. Exchange phone numbers and addresses. If one member of the chain is absent, arrange for another member to call the absent student with the homework assignments. Take the initiative in asking your teacher for any work that you or another member of the chain has missed.

Student Expectations

After reading this chapter, you should be able to:

1. Tell what a body system is and how different systems work together.

2. Describe the function and structure of the nervous system and how you can keep it healthy.

3. Identify the function and structure of the circulatory system and how to keep it healthy.

4. Explain the function and structure of the respiratory system and how to keep it healthy.

5. Describe the function and structure of the skeletal and muscular systems and how to protect them.

6. Explain the function and structure of the digestive and excretory systems and how to protect them.

*J*ust before my baby brother, Alex, was born, my parents bought a brand new van to make room for, as my father said, "our new addition." My uncle joked that now our family has two new "babies" to take care of. My mother commented that Uncle Martin wasn't far off.

Take Alex's "engine system," for example. It doesn't even need gasoline. It runs on milk, or if you like, peanut butter.

Also, take his frame. It's very strong. Yet it can bend in many different positions. Even more amazingly, over time it grows larger.

Mother said that Alex's temperature control system is unbelievable. No matter whether it's cold or hot outside, his body stays at an even 98.6 degrees inside. Oh, and listen to this. His body can repair its own scratches and scrapes. That's even better than the new van!

Another amazing thing about Alex is his on-board computer system. He'll be able to process so much information! My mother says we'll start teaching him to talk right away. After that, he'll learn to play ball, make up songs, read—anything you like!

in Your Journal

Read the account on this page. In what ways does your body seem like a machine? Start your private journal entries on the body systems by answering these questions:

▶ What systems does your body have?
▶ Do these systems work individually or together?
▶ Are you doing everything you can to keep your "engine" in good working order?

When you reach the end of the chapter, you will use your journal entries to make an action plan.

What Are Body Systems?

This lesson will help you find answers to questions that teens often ask about their body. For example:

▶ **What are the major parts that make up my body?**

▶ **How do different parts of my body work together?**

Words to Know

body system
interrelated

Art Connection

Leonardo da Vinci   **ACTIVITY!**

Artist Leonardo da Vinci was a pioneer in the study of human body systems. In the fifteenth century, Leonardo made hundreds of drawings of the body systems. He concluded that the body was like a machine. Look in resource books to find his sketches of human body systems.

Parts of a Whole You

In many ways, your body is like a machine. If you could look inside this machine, at first you would see a tangle of parts—tissues and organs. These individual tissues and organs form body systems. Each **body system** is a *group of organs that work together to support an important body function.* The work of these body systems helps to keep you alive and healthy.

How Systems Are Organized

The systems of the body are organized by what they do, not by where they are. For example, the mouth and the small intestine are far apart. Yet they are both parts of the digestive system. **Figure 6.1** lists and explains how this system and other major body systems help you live each day.

Figure 6.1
Body Systems and Their Functions

System	Some Main Functions
Nervous system	To send and receive messages To see, hear, smell, taste, touch To control all body systems
Circulatory system	To bring food and oxygen to cells To take wastes away from cells
Respiratory system	To carry oxygen to blood To remove carbon dioxide from blood
Skeletal and muscular systems	To support and move body To protect organs
Digestive and excretory systems	To break down food for energy To get rid of wastes

How Systems Are Linked

Body systems are said to be **interrelated,** meaning that *the systems work together and are dependent on one another to keep the body functioning well.* **Figure 6.2** shows how the body systems work together to help a runner perform well.

Figure 6.2
Body Systems Working Together
Each system depends on others to do its job effectively.

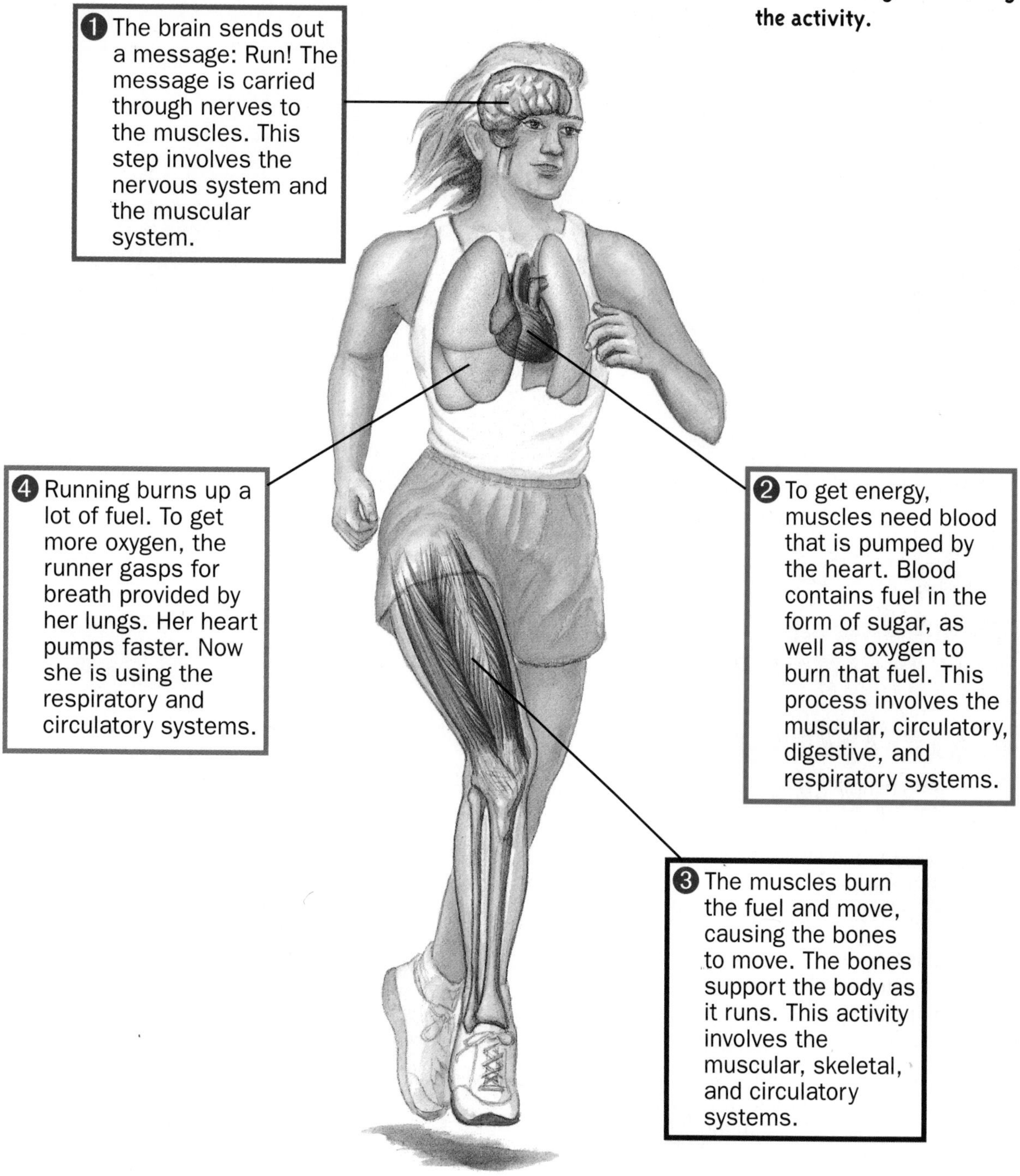

in your journal

Think of your favorite activity. Write a brief description of the body systems that are involved when you participate in this activity. Indicate how these body systems work together during the activity.

❶ The brain sends out a message: Run! The message is carried through nerves to the muscles. This step involves the nervous system and the muscular system.

❹ Running burns up a lot of fuel. To get more oxygen, the runner gasps for breath provided by her lungs. Her heart pumps faster. Now she is using the respiratory and circulatory systems.

❷ To get energy, muscles need blood that is pumped by the heart. Blood contains fuel in the form of sugar, as well as oxygen to burn that fuel. This process involves the muscular, circulatory, digestive, and respiratory systems.

❸ The muscles burn the fuel and move, causing the bones to move. The bones support the body as it runs. This activity involves the muscular, skeletal, and circulatory systems.

Keeping Body Systems Healthy

If your body were a machine, it would be the most amazing machine ever built. Your brain can solve problems that no computer could ever solve. You can move, sense, and feel things in ways that a machine could never match.

Compared to a machine, your body systems do not really need much upkeep. You do, however, need to use common sense and be responsible. In this chapter, you will learn about some of the ways to keep all of your body systems working at their best.

Nutritious foods help keep all the systems of the body's machinery healthy, including keeping bones strong, muscles functioning, and nerve impulses transmitting. Nutrients also help digestion and the elimination of wastes and maintain breathing and circulation.

MAKING HEALTHY DECISIONS
Planning for a Healthy Vacation

Scott and his family are taking a car trip to the beach for a week. They are looking forward to relaxing in the sun, swimming, and biking.

In health class, Scott has been learning about how to keep body systems healthy. He notices that his older brother and sister haven't packed some items that he thinks they should take to ensure a healthy vacation. For example, he doesn't see any sunscreen, hats, or umbrellas for the beach. They are taking their bikes, but he notices that the helmets haven't been packed yet.

He also notices some items he knows they probably should not take, such as high-fat snacks and sugary drinks. He isn't sure whether he should speak up about any of this.

To decide whether to discuss his concerns with his family, Scott uses the step-by-step decision-making process.

① **State the situation**
② **List the options**
③ **Weigh the possible outcomes**

Using complete sentences, answer the following questions on a separate sheet of paper.

Reviewing Terms and Facts

1. **Vocabulary**   Write a sentence in which you use the terms *body system* and *interrelated.*

2. **Name**   Which two body systems take in oxygen and carry it to the cells of the body?

3. **Identify**   Which two body systems support and move the body?

4. **Recall**   What are the major jobs of the digestive and excretory systems?

Thinking Critically

5. **Compare**   Think about the different body systems discussed in this lesson. Which do you seem to have control over? Which seem to work almost entirely by themselves?

6. **Explain**   Name a function of the body and tell why two or more systems sometimes need to work together to perform it.

7. **Predict**   Describe how you think an injury to one system might affect the function of another system in your body.

Applying Health Concepts

8. **Consumer Health**   With a small group, brainstorm a list of products that claim to improve the health of one or more body systems. Discuss how consumers might evaluate the truth of these claims and make healthy product choices.

④ **Consider your values**
⑤ **Make a decision and act**
⑥ **Evaluate the decision**

Follow-up Activities

1. Apply the six steps of the decision-making process to Scott's situation.

2. Role-play a scene in which Scott decides to tell his family about what he has learned in health class.

3. Discuss in class choices that Scott might make other than either telling or not telling his family about what he has learned.

Your Nervous System

This lesson will help you find answers to questions that teens often ask about their nervous system. For example:

▶ How does my brain tell my body what to do?
▶ What's happening inside me when I move my hand or blink my eye?
▶ Why are brain injuries so serious?

Words to Know

nervous system
brain
neuron
central nervous
    system (CNS)
peripheral
    nervous system
    (PNS)
spinal cord

Your Body's Control Center

The **nervous system** is *the control and communication system of the body.* Its job is to send and receive messages. Your nervous system controls all your thoughts and movements. As you read these words, cells in your eyes send electrical messages to your **brain,** *your nervous system's command center.* Your brain interprets those messages so they make sense to you. **Figure 6.3** shows how your body responds when you catch a ball.

Figure 6.3
What Happens When You Catch a Ball

Many events occur in the seconds between the striking of the ball with the bat and your successful catch.

❷ The brain sends a message to the muscles of your left hand that means "move this hand up."

❸ The hand moves up. The ball hits the glove. Touch cells in the hand send a coded message to the brain that means "the ball has arrived."

❶ As the bat hits the ball, cells in your eyes send a coded message to your brain that means "a ball is coming."

The Work of Neurons

The *cells that make up the nervous system* are called **neurons** (NOO·rahnz). Long, stringy neurons are perfect for carrying the electrical messages that are the "language" of the nervous system. In between neurons there are tiny gaps. Special chemicals carry messages between these gaps.

Three kinds of neurons do three different jobs.

- Sensory neurons, such as the ones in your skin, ears, and eyes, receive information from the outside world. Their job is to pass on this information.
- Motor neurons are responsible for sending messages to the muscles and glands.
- Connecting neurons relay messages between the sensory neurons and the motor neurons.

Let's take a look at what your neurons were doing when the ball in **Figure 6.3** hits the glove (see **Figure 6.4**).

Did You Know?

Super Cells

Neurons are thin, and some are very long. The neurons that extend from the lower part of the spine to the foot are the longest cells in the body. In a tall person these neurons may be more than 3 feet long!

Figure 6.4

A Closer Look: How Neurons Help You Catch a Ball

Your catch is not complete until you squeeze the ball in your hand. The following steps show how neurons help this happen.

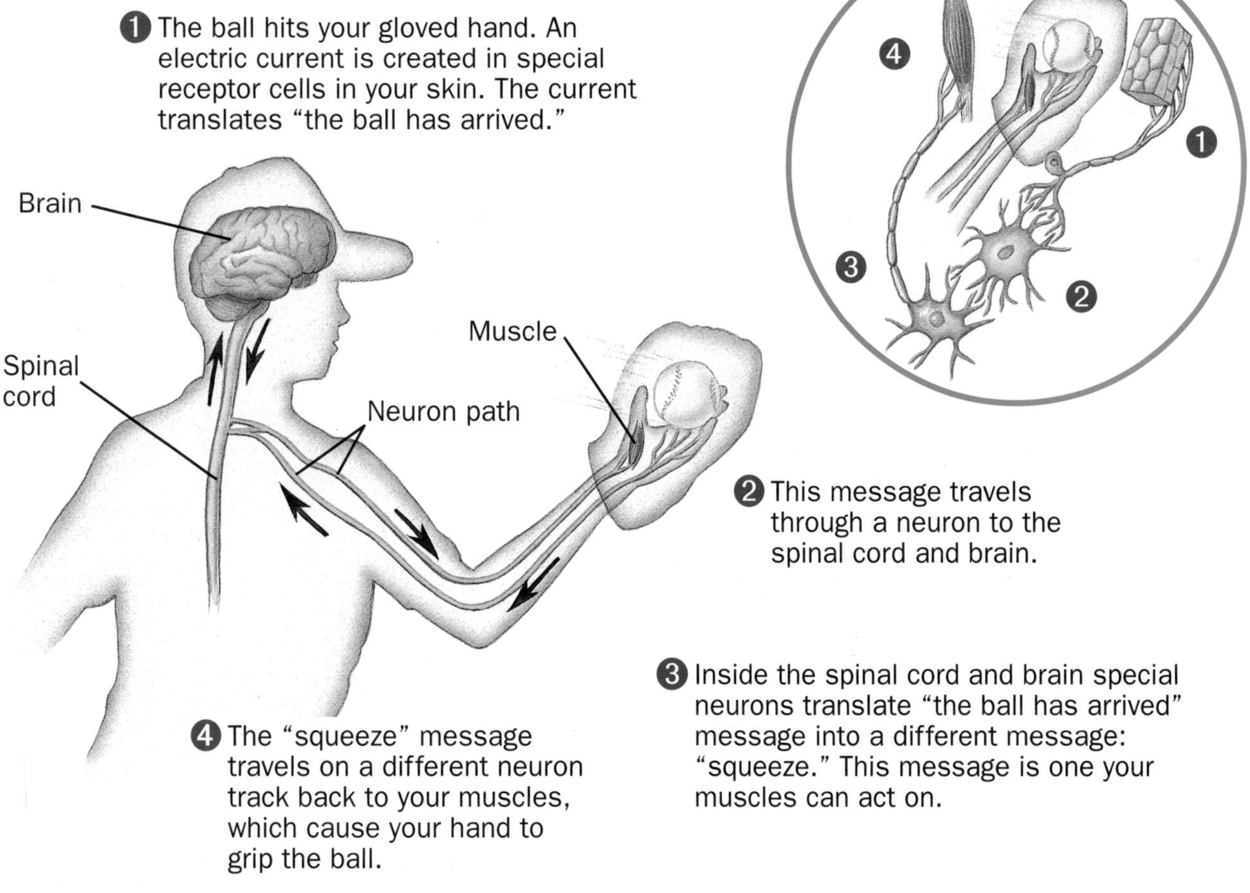

1 The ball hits your gloved hand. An electric current is created in special receptor cells in your skin. The current translates "the ball has arrived."
Brain
Spinal cord
Muscle
Neuron path
4
1
3
2
2 This message travels through a neuron to the spinal cord and brain.
3 Inside the spinal cord and brain special neurons translate "the ball has arrived" message into a different message: "squeeze." This message is one your muscles can act on.
4 The "squeeze" message travels on a different neuron track back to your muscles, which cause your hand to grip the ball.

Structure of the Nervous System

The nervous system, shown in **Figure 6.5,** is divided into the central and peripheral systems. The **central nervous system (CNS)** consists of *the brain and spinal cord.* The **peripheral** (puh·RIF·uh·ruhl) **nervous system (PNS)** is made up of *nerves that branch out from the central nervous system.*

The Spinal Cord and the Brain

The **spinal cord** is *a tube of neurons that runs up the spine.* Information from the peripheral nervous system goes to the spinal cord. Some messages are processed there. Most, however, are sent on to the brain.

The brain is the body's main information center. It is made of billions of neurons. The brain helps the body respond to the information it receives from the senses. The brain also processes thoughts. When you think, neurons in your brain are working.

Figure 6.5
Divisions of the Nervous System

The central nervous system is the body's main control center. The peripheral nervous system carries messages between the central nervous system and nerves in the rest of the body.

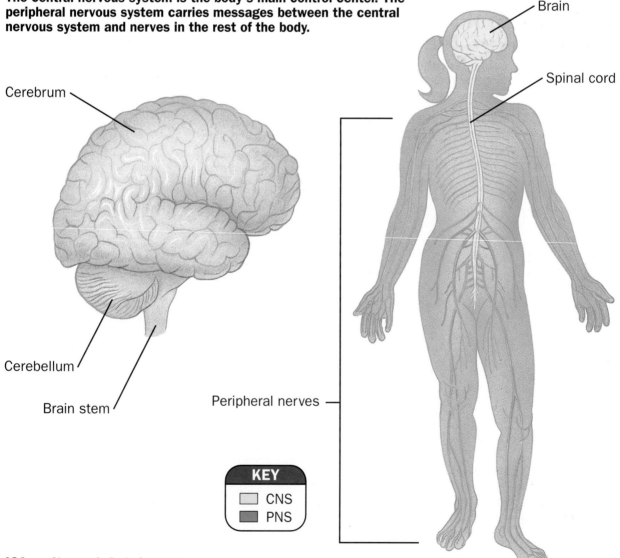

Cerebrum

Cerebellum

Brain stem

Peripheral nerves

Brain

Spinal cord

KEY

☐ CNS
■ PNS

The brain has three main parts. The largest part is the cerebrum (suh·REE·bruhm), which controls vision, touch, and other senses. It also handles movements you have control over. Thinking takes place mainly in the cerebrum. The cerebellum (ser·uh·BE·luhm) helps control balance and coordination. The brain stem is the link to the spinal cord. The brain stem controls digestion, breathing, and heartbeat.

The Peripheral Nervous System

One part of the peripheral nervous system makes possible the movements that you control, such as walking or speaking. Another part of this system handles movements that you cannot control. You think of these actions as automatic. They include such things as the beating of your heart, sweating, and digestion. Another example of an automatic action is the change in size of the pupils of your eyes as they react to light (see **Figure 6.6**).

Keeping Your Nervous System Healthy

The following are some lifestyle choices you can make to keep your nervous system healthy.

- **Get enough sleep and eat properly.** Rest and good nutrition will help you think clearly and feel calm.

- **Avoid alcohol and other drugs.** These substances can cloud your thinking. They can also kill brain cells.

- **Take care of your heart and blood vessels.** High blood pressure or a blood clot in the brain can cause a stroke. Cells near the site of the stroke die due to the lack of blood flow. Because of this destruction of cells, a person who has a stroke may be unable to talk or move certain parts of the body.

Teen Issues

Drugs and Your Brain

You probably know that it is not a good idea to take drugs that a doctor has not prescribed for you. You may not be aware of how some drugs work, however. Drugs called stimulants include cocaine, nicotine (in cigarettes), and caffeine (in coffee). These drugs cause the brain to speed up its messages. Depressant drugs such as alcohol and sleeping pills slow down brain messages. In both cases, the drugs interfere with the way the brain normally works.

Figure 6.6
The Effect of Light on Pupil Size
Control over pupil size is an example of an automatic nerve function. How does pupil size change when you go from darkness into bright light? Can you control when your pupils change size? Can you stop them from changing?

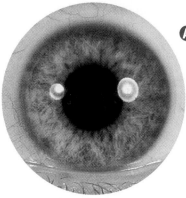

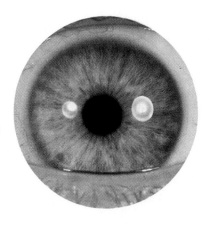

A Pupil of the eye in dim light

B Pupil of the same eye in bright light

Avoiding Head and Spinal Cord Injuries

Another very important way to keep your nervous system healthy is to prevent head and spinal cord injuries. These injuries are serious because they often damage or destroy neurons. Unlike many other cells, neurons do not grow back once they die. Head injuries can cause brain damage and even death. A blow to the spinal cord may result in paralysis, which is a loss of feeling and movement in a part of the body. How can you avoid these types of injuries?

■ **Wear a helmet.** A helmet is your most important piece of equipment for bicycling, in-line skating, skateboarding, or playing contact sports such as football.

■ **Wear safety belts.** Whenever you are riding in a car, buckle up. Be sure to use both the shoulder belt and the lap belt.

■ **Follow safety rules and use common sense.** Follow rules you already know about crossing streets and riding your bicycle. Stay out of situations in which you could receive a blow to your head or spinal cord.

■ **Lift objects properly.** Bend from the knees, not from the waist, when you lift heavy objects. Do not lift objects that are too heavy for you.

Q & A

Which Side Are You On? ACTIVITY!

Q: What do people mean when they say they are "right-brained" or "left-brained"?

A: The brain is divided into left and right halves. Experiments show that the left side of the brain controls language and logic. The right side of the brain seems to have a more creative role, playing a large part in musical and artistic abilities. Write a paragraph explaining why you think you are right- or left-brained.

Lesson 2 Review

Using complete sentences, answer the following questions on a separate sheet of paper.

Reviewing Terms and Facts

1. **Vocabulary** What are the two main parts of the nervous system?

2. **List** Name the three main parts of the brain. What is one function of each part?

3. **Recall** How does the health of the circulatory system affect the health of the nervous system?

4. **Identify** What are two ways to prevent head and spinal cord injuries?

Thinking Critically

5. **Compare** How is the nervous system similar to a telephone system?

6. **Suggest** How can drugs and alcohol be just as dangerous to your nervous system as a serious injury?

7. **Explain** How could an injury to the brain affect a muscle in a completely different part of the body?

Applying Health Concepts

8. **Health of Others** Make a paper model of the brain that shows the three major divisions. (Tape pieces of paper over a bicycle helmet, label the sections, and then take the paper off.) Use your model to demonstrate how injuries to different brain areas might affect an individual's body systems. Also use it to show how wearing a bicycle helmet helps protect the brain against injury.

Your Circulatory System

This lesson will help you find answers to questions that teens often ask about how their heart and blood vessels work. For example:

▶ **Why does the heart need to keep beating all the time?**

▶ **What is blood made of?**

▶ **How can I avoid problems with my heart and blood vessels?**

Your Body's Transportation System

The **circulatory system** is *the body's transportation system.* It allows the body to transport, or move, materials from one place to another. These materials are carried in the blood.

The *muscle that acts as the pump for the circulatory system* is the **heart.** The heart pushes blood through **blood vessels,** *tubes that carry blood throughout the body.* **Figure 6.7** shows the kinds of materials that are moved through the circulatory system to keep the body healthy.

Words to Know

circulatory
   system
heart
blood vessel
artery
vein
capillary
blood pressure

Figure 6.7
Materials Carried in the Blood
Your blood carries many different kinds of materials throughout your body.

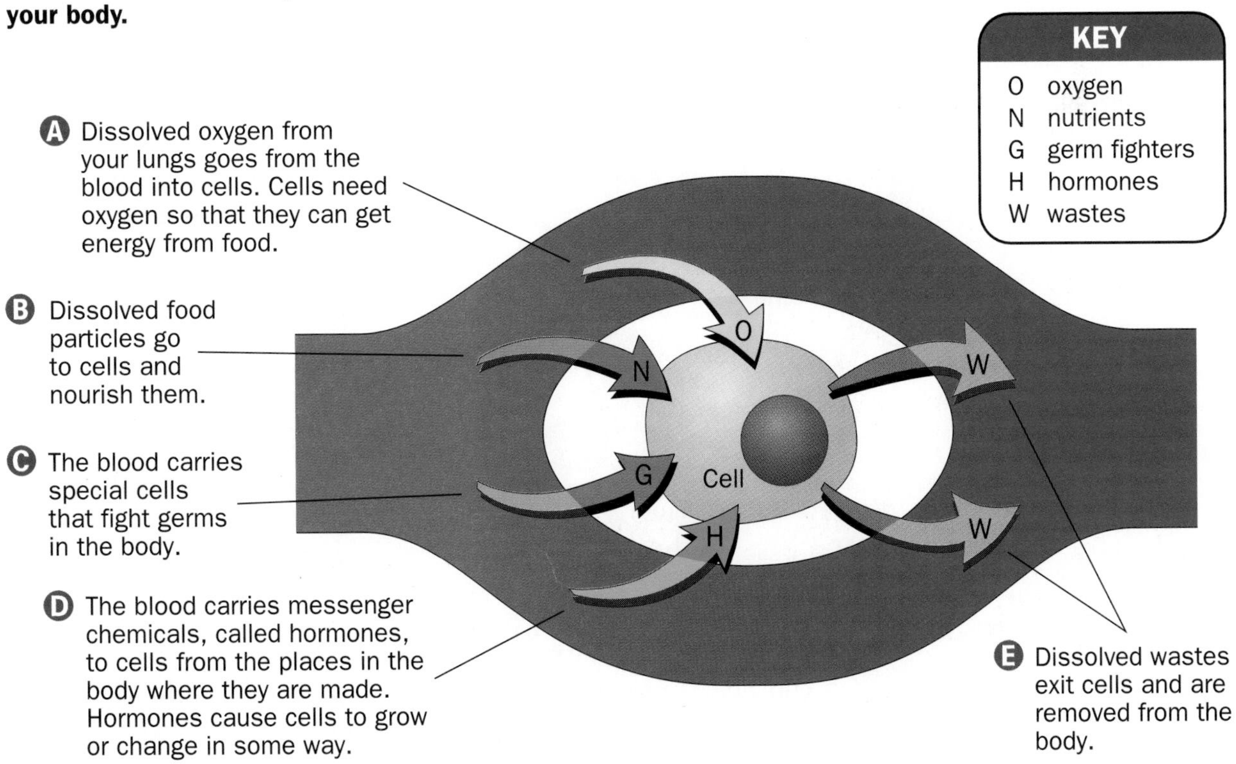

KEY	
O	oxygen
N	nutrients
G	germ fighters
H	hormones
W	wastes

A Dissolved oxygen from your lungs goes from the blood into cells. Cells need oxygen so that they can get energy from food.

B Dissolved food particles go to cells and nourish them.

C The blood carries special cells that fight germs in the body.

D The blood carries messenger chemicals, called hormones, to cells from the places in the body where they are made. Hormones cause cells to grow or change in some way.

E Dissolved wastes exit cells and are removed from the body.

Structure of the Circulatory System

In the circulatory system, blood is pumped from the heart to the body cells and back to the heart. The blood then travels to the lungs, then back to the heart to begin its journey again.

The Work of the Heart

The heart is a very strong muscle. It has four chambers, or parts. Each chamber plays a different role in the circulation of blood. **Figure 6.8** shows how the blood moves through the four chambers of the heart.

Figure 6.8
How the Heart Pumps Blood

When you look at the names of the chambers of the heart, remember that it is as if you are looking at the heart of a person standing in front of you. That person's right is on your left, and his or her left is on your right.

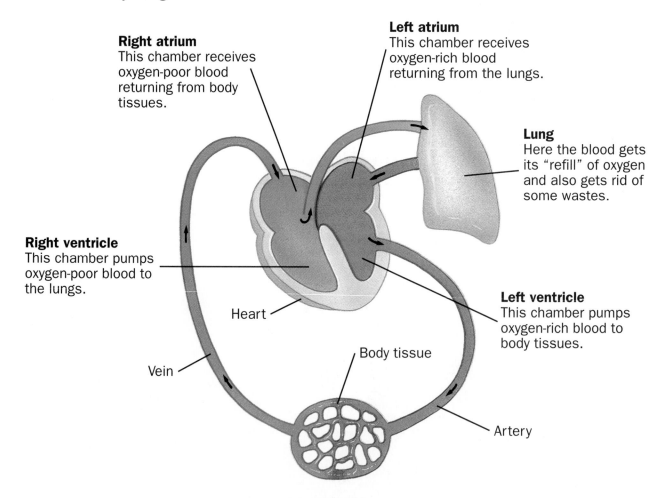

Left atrium
This chamber receives oxygen-rich blood returning from the lungs.

Right atrium
This chamber receives oxygen-poor blood returning from body tissues.

Lung
Here the blood gets its "refill" of oxygen and also gets rid of some wastes.

Right ventricle
This chamber pumps oxygen-poor blood to the lungs.

Heart

Left ventricle
This chamber pumps oxygen-rich blood to body tissues.

Vein

Body tissue

Artery

The Blood's Journey Through the Body

The heart pumps blood through a network of blood vessels that extends throughout the body. There are three main types of blood vessels: arteries, veins, and capillaries.

Arteries *carry oxygen-rich blood away from the heart.* **Veins** *carry oxygen-poor blood toward the heart.* The branches of the arteries and veins become smaller as they go away from the heart. **Capillaries** are *very tiny branches of arteries and veins.* They connect the smallest arteries with the smallest veins. Capillaries provide blood directly to cells. **Figure 6.9** shows the arrangement of arteries, veins, and capillaries in the body.

Figure 6.9
The Circulatory System

The circulatory system transports blood to and from the tissues of the body. Oxygen, food, and other materials are delivered to cells so they can grow and remain healthy. Wastes are removed from cells by the circulatory system as well.

in your journal

The circulatory system has been compared to the highway system of a big city. It has also been compared to the plumbing system of a house. In your journal, state which comparison you think is more accurate. Give at least three reasons to support the choice you made.

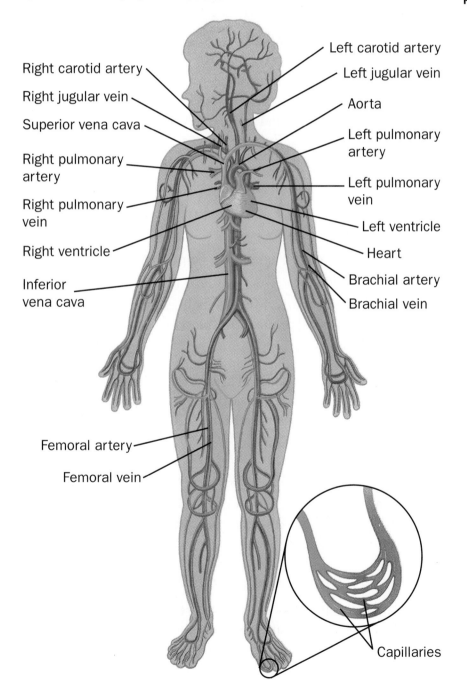

Right carotid artery
Right jugular vein
Superior vena cava
Right pulmonary artery
Right pulmonary vein
Right ventricle
Inferior vena cava
Femoral artery
Femoral vein

Left carotid artery
Left jugular vein
Aorta
Left pulmonary artery
Left pulmonary vein
Left ventricle
Heart
Brachial artery
Brachial vein

Capillaries

Blood Pressure

The force of the blood pushing against the walls of the blood vessels is called **blood pressure.** Blood pressure is greatest when the heart contracts, or pushes out blood. Blood pressure is lowest between heartbeats, or when the heart relaxes.

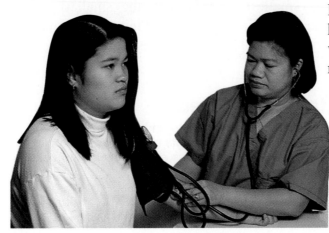

This teen is having her blood pressure measured. A measurement gives two numbers. The normal high pressure number ranges from about 100 to 140. The low pressure number ranges from 60 to 90.

Parts of the Blood

Blood contains both liquid and solid parts. Blood plasma is the liquid part of blood and makes up about half of its volume. Cells are the solid parts. Each element of blood has a purpose.

- **Plasma.** Plasma is made up of about 92 percent water. Its job is to transport dissolved food and blood cells.

- **Red blood cells.** These cells carry oxygen to all other cells of the body and carry away some waste products.

- **White blood cells.** These cells help destroy disease germs that enter the body.

- **Platelets.** These parts of cells help your blood clot. This keeps you from losing too much blood when you have a cut.

Did You Know?

Small but Mighty

Red blood cells are the smallest cells in the body. If you lined up 3,000 of them end to end, they would take up only about 1 inch of space. The body replaces these tiny cells at an incredible rate. As you read this, your body is making red blood cells at the rate of about 2.4 million every second!

Blood Types

All blood is not the same. There are four main types: A, B, AB, and O. The types are classified by the type of red blood cells a person has. Knowing a person's blood type is important when one person is receiving blood from another. Serious side effects can result when some of the types are mixed. Health officials mix only those types that can be combined safely.

Blood also contains something called an Rh factor. Blood is either Rh-positive or Rh-negative. People with Rh-positive blood can receive blood from people with either Rh-positive or Rh-negative blood. People with Rh-negative blood can receive blood only from people with the same Rh-negative factor.

When people give blood, several tests are run to make sure that their blood is safe and not contaminated with viruses such as the one that causes AIDS.

Keeping Your Circulatory System Healthy

Without your circulatory system, your cells could not receive food or oxygen or get rid of waste. Here are some ways to help you protect your circulatory system.

- **Eat a balanced diet.** A good diet can help prevent clogged blood vessels, high blood pressure, and other problems.

- **Avoid stress.** Tension strains your heart and blood vessels.

- **Exercise.** Regular activity helps the heart and circulation.

- **Try to maintain your ideal weight.** Carrying extra weight puts a strain on your circulatory system.

- **Don't smoke.** Chemicals in smoke reduce the amount of oxygen your red blood cells can carry.

This athlete has strengthened her heart through exercise. Each of her heartbeats now pumps more blood than it did before she began training.

Review

Using complete sentences, answer the following questions on a separate sheet of paper.

Reviewing Terms and Facts

1. **List** Name five materials that the blood carries into or out of cells.

2. **Vocabulary** Describe the following types of blood vessels: *capillaries, arteries, veins.*

3. **Summarize** Describe the round-trip journey of the blood around the body.

4. **Recall** Why do doctors have to be careful about blood types when people are receiving blood?

Thinking Critically

5. **Predict** Describe what might happen to your blood pressure if your blood vessels became clogged.

6. **Explain** Tell why a brother with Rh-positive blood could receive blood from his sister but might not be able to give blood to her.

Applying Health Concepts

7. **Consumer Health** Working in a group, list foods that claim in their advertisements to be good for your heart. Analyze whether the claims of two of the products are true.

Teen HEALTH DIGEST

CON$UMER FOCU$

Saying Yes to Pizza

You may want to think again if the terms *junk food* and *pizza* mean the same thing to you. Pizza can be a very nutritious food, good for your total health—as long as you choose wisely.

A typical American pizza, brimming with cheese and loaded with high-fat meats, is not the best choice. So why not make your own pizza at home? Experiment with chopped tomato instead of tomato sauce. Also try other tasty toppings, including red and green peppers, broccoli, fresh herbs such as basil, and hard cheeses such as Parmesan.

Even packaged pizzas can be a good nutritional choice. Check the nutrition label for amounts of calories, fat, and sodium. Watch the serving size, however. For some packaged pizzas, it is unrealistically small.

Sports and Recreation

Steroids

Do anabolic steroids help people become better athletes? Steroids are artificial hormones. They are chemicals that are similar to body hormones. Natural body hormones help regulate body processes, including growth.

Some studies show that steroids do increase muscle size—but at what cost? Steroids are dangerous drugs. They can damage your liver, clog blood vessels, bloat your face, and cause skin problems. Steroids can also cause mood swings and violent, unpredictable behavior.

If all this were not enough, studies done with athletes show that only a very small number of steroid users got the results they were after. In almost every case, nonusers performed better than users on the playing field. Also, use of steroids to build up muscle is illegal in organized sports. If athletes are caught using them, they are banned from competing.

Health Update

Overweight America

People in the United States are dieting more than ever. Unfortunately, they are also more overweight than ever. Experts say that rates among children are rising even faster than rates among adults.

Television is blamed for much of the problem. The average child watches three to four hours of television a day. Watching TV burns up very little energy. Even worse, high-calorie snacks many times accompany TV watching. To add to the problem, TV commercials bombard people with messages about high-fat, high-calorie foods.

Several suggestions have been made to combat this problem. One is daily physical education classes in all schools. Restricting certain kinds of advertising during children's programs and exercise campaigns in school are also recommended.

Teens Making a Difference

Alternatives

Twelve-year-old Sasha Mills looks up to Alice Cruz. Alice, 14, is a talented piano player and songwriter. Both Sasha and Alice are members of Alternatives, an antidrug program at their school.

Alternatives was formed because studies showed that fighting drugs takes more than just saying no. Younger children need role models. They need to be shown how they can have fun without drugs.

"Just being with Alice taught me a lot," Sasha says. "We do things together. I'm writing a video script. Alice is helping me with the music." What is the most important thing Sasha learned from Alice? "That cool people don't take drugs," Sasha says.

People at Work

Family Practice Doctor

Many doctors treat individual patients for illnesses such as cancer and diabetes. Some specialize in the care of the eyes, the heart, or other parts of the body. Chris Miyuzaki has a different type of medical practice—one in which he treats the whole family.

Being a family practice doctor means that Chris sees family members both separately and together. "I get to know the people," Chris says.

"As a result, they come to trust me."

Chris feels that avoiding illnesses, also called preventive medicine, is crucial. "I try to educate the whole family," he says. "Parents and children can help each other lead healthier lives. Most importantly, I stress that people should never hesitate to call. If they feel my door is open, people get their problems taken care of before they become serious."

4 Your Respiratory System

This lesson will help you find answers to questions that teens often ask about breathing and the respiratory system. For example:

▶ **What happens inside my body when I breathe?**

▶ **How do my lungs work?**

▶ **How can I avoid lung problems?**

Words to Know

respiratory
  system
lung
trachea
bronchi
diaphragm
alveoli

Oxygen helps release energy from food. The more energy you need for an activity, the more oxygen you need. Why do you think these people are out of breath?

Your Body's Air Supply

Your **respiratory** (RES·puh·ruh·tohr·ee) **system** *delivers oxygen to your body*. Each time you breathe in you take oxygen into your lungs. The **lungs** are the *main organs of the respiratory system.* Each time you breathe out you get rid of carbon dioxide.

Structure of the Respiratory System

The respiratory system has two parts (see **Figure 6.10**). In the upper part, air comes into the body through the nose or mouth and enters the **trachea** (TRAY·kee·uh), or *windpipe.* The lower part begins where the trachea divides. *The two branches of the trachea* are called **bronchi** (BRAHN·ky). The bronchi lead into the lungs. There they divide into smaller and smaller branches.

Figure 6.10
Parts of the Respiratory System
The respiratory system provides oxygen to the body.

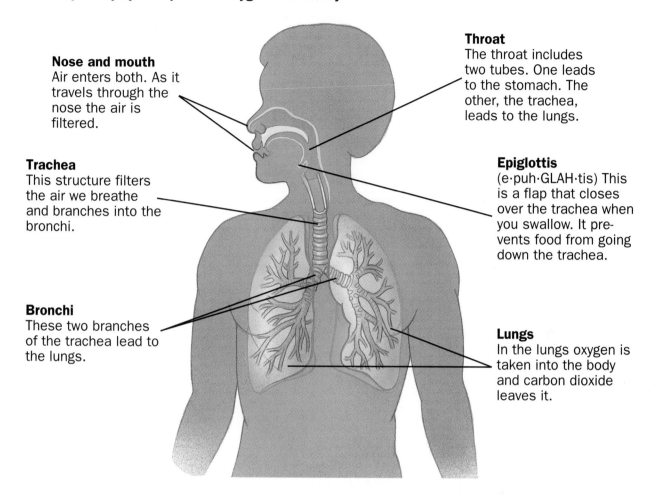

Nose and mouth
Air enters both. As it travels through the nose the air is filtered.

Trachea
This structure filters the air we breathe and branches into the bronchi.

Bronchi
These two branches of the trachea lead to the lungs.

Throat
The throat includes two tubes. One leads to the stomach. The other, the trachea, leads to the lungs.

Epiglottis
(e·puh·GLAH·tis) This is a flap that closes over the trachea when you swallow. It prevents food from going down the trachea.

Lungs
In the lungs oxygen is taken into the body and carbon dioxide leaves it.

HEALTH LAB
Breathing Rates

Introduction: Your breathing rate is a measure of how much oxygen your body is using. How do you think exercise affects your body's need for oxygen? To answer this question, you will need to compare your breathing rate both before and after exercise.

Objective: Determine how exercise affects breathing rate.

Materials and Method: You will need a clock with a second hand, paper, and pencil. At the top of your paper, write the headings "At Rest" and "After Exercise." Measure your breathing rate at rest. Record how many times

you breathe in one minute. Then run in place for one minute. Immediately afterward, measure and record your breathing rate again.

Observation and Analysis: Repeat the experiment several times. Total your results and make a graph. Show both "At Rest" and "After Exercise" breathing rates for several people in the class. Then determine how exercise affects the breathing rate. Does exercise increase or decrease breathing rate? Is the change the same for everyone? How do you think harder exercise would affect breathing rate? What does this experiment tell you about how exercise affects the amount of oxygen the body uses?

How You Breathe

Breathing starts with a *muscle at the bottom of the chest* called the **diaphragm** (DY·uh·fram). When you breathe in, the diaphragm contracts. When you breathe out, it expands. The diaphragm is the main muscle used in breathing. The breathing process is shown in **Figure 6.11.**

Figure 6.11
The Breathing Process

You breathe about 12 times every minute. This diagram shows what happens in your body each time you take a breath. The goal of breathing is to deliver oxygen to the body and to take away carbon dioxide.

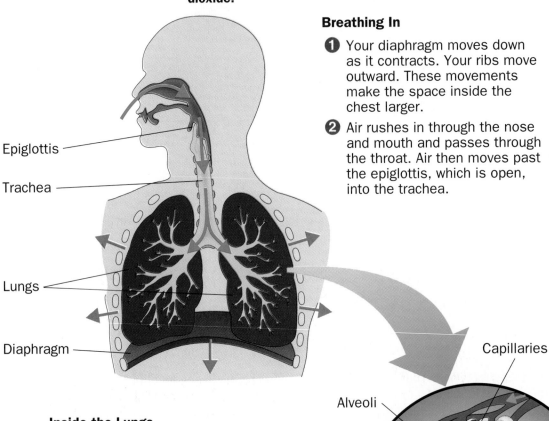

Epiglottis

Trachea

Lungs

Diaphragm

Alveoli

Capillaries

Oxygen

Carbon dioxide

Breathing In

❶ Your diaphragm moves down as it contracts. Your ribs move outward. These movements make the space inside the chest larger.

❷ Air rushes in through the nose and mouth and passes through the throat. Air then moves past the epiglottis, which is open, into the trachea.

Inside the Lungs

❸ Air moves into your bronchi. The bronchi branch out and end in *tiny air sacs*, called **alveoli** (al·vee·OH·ly).

❹ Air moves into your alveoli. Oxygen moves through the walls of alveoli and capillaries, entering the blood.

❺ Carbon dioxide moves from the blood through the walls of capillaries and alveoli in order to be expelled by the lungs.

Figure 6.12 helps you see how air moves in and out of your lungs during the breathing process.

Figure 6.12
How Your Lungs Work

Have you ever squeezed an empty plastic bottle? What happens to the air in the bottle? Your lungs work in a similar way.

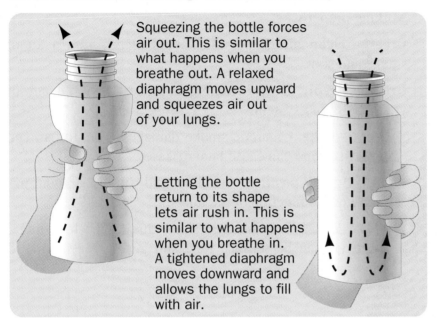

Squeezing the bottle forces air out. This is similar to what happens when you breathe out. A relaxed diaphragm moves upward and squeezes air out of your lungs.

Letting the bottle return to its shape lets air rush in. This is similar to what happens when you breathe in. A tightened diaphragm moves downward and allows the lungs to fill with air.

Cultural Diversity

Breath and Spirit [ACTIVITY!]

Many ancient cultures believed that a person's breath was closely associated with his or her spirit. The Greeks used the same word, pneuma, for both ideas. We see evidence of this ancient belief when we say "Gesundheit" when someone sneezes. It means "health." Originally people said it to protect a person whose spirit—they believed—had for a moment left the body. Look in a dictionary to find the country of origin of the word Gesundheit.

Q & A ?

Hiccups

Q: What are hiccups?

A: Hiccups are caused by a spasm of the diaphragm. A spasm is the sudden and uncontrollable tightening of a muscle. When your diaphragm tightens, air is pulled suddenly into your lungs. The "hic" sound is caused by air rushing past the vocal cords as the epiglottis closes.

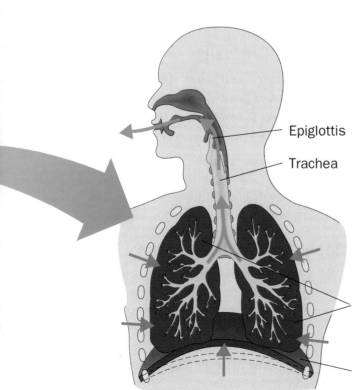

Epiglottis

Trachea

Lungs

Diaphragm

Breathing Out

6 Your diaphragm moves up as it relaxes. Your ribs move inward. These movements make the space inside the chest smaller.

7 Your lungs are squeezed and air is pushed out of the alveoli. The air travels back through your bronchi, trachea, and nose and mouth.

Keeping Your Respiratory System Healthy

You could not live for more than a few minutes without air. Your respiratory system provides it for you. Here are some rules for taking care of your respiratory system.

- **Exercise.** Regular exercise keeps your respiratory system working properly.

- **Breathe clean air.** If possible, avoid places with a lot of smoke and soot.

- **Breathe deeply.** Deep breathing improves the efficiency of your respiratory system.

- **Don't smoke.** Cigarette smoke damages nose, throat, and lung tissue and can cause fatal diseases.

- **Use good posture.** Standing and sitting straight improves the function of the lungs.

- **Take care of illnesses.** Nose, throat, and lung infections can be serious. Rest and give yourself time to recover.

These teens are getting exercise in a place where there is little pollution. Is there somewhere you can go to hike or run with your friends?

Lesson 4 Review

Using complete sentences, answer the following questions on a separate sheet of paper.

Reviewing Terms and Facts

1. **Vocabulary** Write a short paragraph that describes the passage of air from outside the body to the lungs. Use the following terms: *bronchi, lungs, trachea.*

2. **Recall** How does the position of the diaphragm change as you breathe in and out?

3. **Identify** In which organs of the body does oxygen enter the blood and carbon dioxide move out of it?

4. **List** Identify three rules for keeping your respiratory system healthy.

Thinking Critically

5. **Predict** Tell what you think might happen if your epiglottis stopped working properly.

6. **Infer** Explain how pollution could damage your respiratory system.

7. **Relate** Write a short paragraph that shows how the respiratory and circulatory systems work together.

Applying Health Concepts

8. **Consumer Health** Write an advertisement for a device that cleans the air. Explain how the device works and how it can improve the health of your respiratory system. In the ad, explain some benefits that this device will have for your health.

Your Skeletal and Muscular Systems

This lesson will help you find answers to questions that teens often ask about their bones and muscles. For example:

▶ **How many bones does my body have?**
▶ **How do I control my movements?**
▶ **What can I do to make my muscles stronger?**

How Bones and Muscles Work

The **skeletal system** is a *framework of bones and the tissues that connect to those bones.* The **muscular system** is made of *all the muscles in your body.* These systems work together to support your body and help it move. What kinds of jobs do bones and muscles do in your body?

- **Support.** Bones are the support system of your body. They work like the beams that support a building.

- **Protection.** Bones protect the soft parts of your body from injury. For example, the skull protects brain tissue.

- **Movement.** Muscles and bones move all your body's parts.

- **Internal movement.** Muscles move body organs that have no bones, such as your heart, intestines, and stomach.

- **Blood cells.** Tissue inside bones makes red and white blood cells for your circulatory system.

- **Mineral storage.** Bones store calcium and other minerals.

Words to Know

skeletal system
muscular system
joint
cartilage
ligament
tendon

in your journal

Look over the muscle and bone functions listed on this page. Then imagine you were going to build a robot. Which of the functions would your robot need? In your journal, describe or sketch how you might build these features into your robot.

How do muscles and bones work together to help this teen juggle?

Structure of the Skeletal and Muscular Systems

The skeletal and muscular systems are made up of bones, muscles, and their connectors. **Figure 6.13** shows the overall structure of the skeletal system.

The Bones

Adults have 206 separate bones in their bodies. Bones are hard on the outside and have spongy tissue inside. The spongy tissue produces blood cells for the circulatory system. Bone tissue is alive and made of cells. It is always being destroyed and remade, especially while you are still growing.

Figure 6.13
The Skeletal System
The skeletal system is your body's framework.

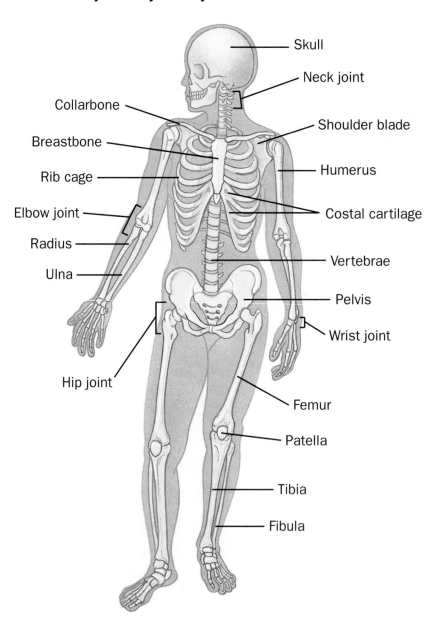

Skull
Neck joint
Collarbone
Shoulder blade
Breastbone
Humerus
Rib cage
Costal cartilage
Elbow joint
Radius
Ulna
Vertebrae
Pelvis
Wrist joint
Hip joint
Femur
Patella
Tibia
Fibula

The Joints

Joints are *places where one bone meets another.* Different joints move in different ways (see **Figure 6.14**).

The Connectors

Connecting tissues join bones to muscles and other bones. Ligaments, tendons, and cartilage are the three types of connecting tissue. Each is described below.

- **Cartilage** (KAR·tuhl·ij) is *connecting tissue that covers the ends of bones and supports certain structures.* At the ends of bones, cartilage provides a smooth surface that allows joints to move easily. In the spine, cartilage cushions individual bones. In other structures, such as the nose and ear, cartilage supports soft tissues.

- **Ligaments** (LI·guh·ments) are *connecting tissues that hold bones in place at the joints.* The knee and the ankle are held together by strong ligaments.

- **Tendons** are *connecting tissues that move bones when muscles contract.* The Achilles (uh·KI·leez) tendon above the heel is the largest tendon in your body.

Figure 6.14
Types of Joints

There are three major types of joints. Many mechanical objects you see every day work in similar ways.

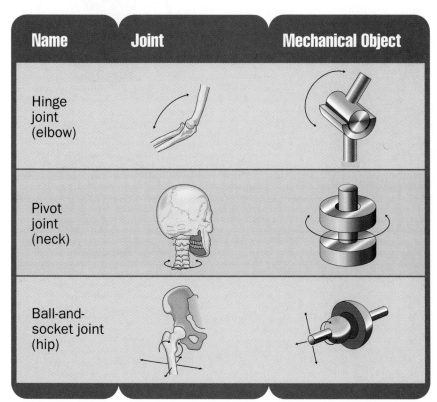

Name	Joint	Mechanical Object
Hinge joint (elbow)		
Pivot joint (neck)		
Ball-and-socket joint (hip)		

The Muscles

The body contains over 600 major muscles. Some muscles are shown in **Figure 6.15.** This figure also highlights the three types of muscle: skeletal, cardiac, and smooth. The skeletal muscles are called voluntary muscles because you control them. Locations include your arms, face, abdomen, and back. Cardiac, or heart, muscle and smooth muscles, such as those in the stomach, work without your knowing it. They are called involuntary muscles.

Figure 6.15
The Muscular System

Muscles move bones, pump blood, and move food through the stomach and intestines, among other jobs.

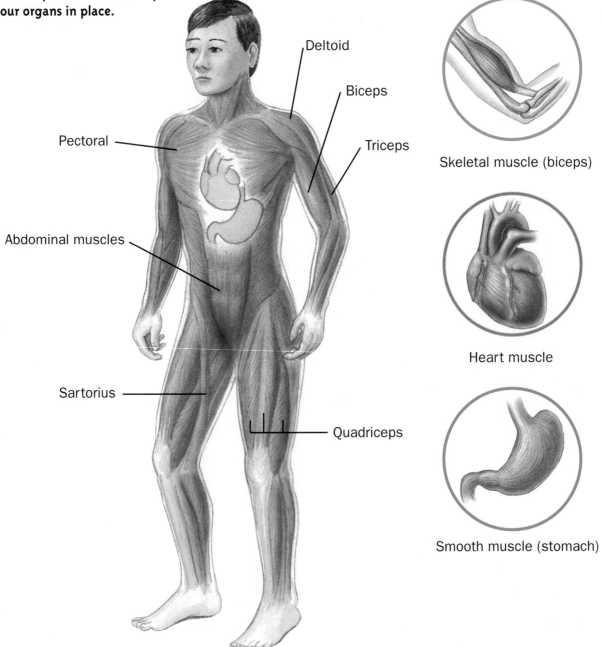

Deltoid

Biceps

Triceps

Pectoral

Abdominal muscles

Sartorius

Quadriceps

Skeletal muscle (biceps)

Heart muscle

Smooth muscle (stomach)

How You Move

Muscles work by changing length. A single muscle is made of many muscle fibers. When stimulated by a nerve, the fibers *contract,* or shorten. When the muscle fibers contract, the entire muscle tightens and shortens. If the muscle is a skeletal muscle, the contraction pulls along the bone the muscle is attached to.

Muscles can only pull bones; they cannot push them. As a result, muscles must work in pairs to move body parts. When one paired muscle contracts, the second muscle *extends,* or lengthens. To move the body part back, the second muscle must contract while the first muscle extends (see **Figure 6.16**).

Keeping Your Bones and Muscles Healthy

Your bones and muscles are still growing. To help them stay strong and healthy, follow these rules.

- **Eat a balanced diet.** Bones need foods with calcium, phosphorus, and vitamin D. Muscles need carbohydrates for energy and protein for growth.

- **Exercise safely.** Bones and muscles need regular exercise. Muscles can tear, however, if you move too fast too soon. Warm up before you exercise and cool down afterward.

- **Have good posture.** Standing and sitting straight helps bones and joints stay in place and helps muscles stay in shape.

- **Get enough rest.** Your muscles need to rest between periods of hard exercise.

in your journal

Look over the list on this page that tells how to keep your bones and muscles healthy. Record these activities in your journal. Then analyze your lifestyle. Give yourself a score of 1 (never) to 10 (always) for each item on the list. Total up your score. Finally, in your journal, write a description of how you could increase your score.

Figure 6.16
Muscles at Work

When the arm is bent at the elbow, the biceps muscle is shortened, pulling the lower arm up. The triceps is lengthened. When the arm straightens, the triceps shortens, pulling the bone of the lower arm toward the shoulder. The biceps is forced to lengthen.

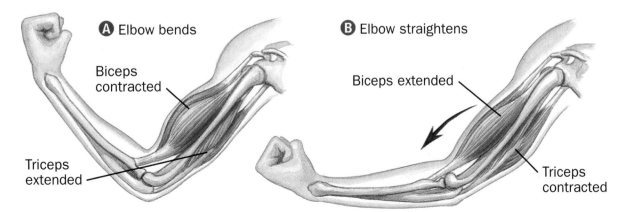

Ⓐ Elbow bends

Biceps contracted

Triceps extended

Ⓑ Elbow straightens

Biceps extended

Triceps contracted

Review

Using complete sentences, answer the following questions on a separate sheet of paper.

Reviewing Terms and Facts

1. **Vocabulary** Define the terms *skeletal system* and *muscular system.* Use them in one sentence to show the relationship between the systems.

2. **List** Identify one job that bones do and one job that muscles do.

3. **Identify** Name two connectors in the skeletal system. What does each one do?

4. **Give Examples** Name three types of joints and give an example of each.

Thinking Critically

5. **Explain** Why do muscles and bones need to work together for movement? Could you move your body without

muscles? Could you move without bones?

6. **Analyze** Examine the joint near the end of your finger. What kind of a joint do you think it is—hinge, pivot, or ball-and-socket? Explain your choice.

7. **Infer** How could a torn tendon make it impossible for a person to move his or her arm?

Applying Health Concepts

8. **Personal Health** Make a model of a joint. Use any kinds of materials you have available, including paper, soda straws, rubber bands, cardboard, plastic, paper clips, or metal. Choose a hinge joint, a pivot joint, or a ball-and-socket joint. In class, demonstrate how your joint works.

LIFE SKILLS
Warm-up Exercises

*M*uscles work best when they are warm. Warm muscles have more strength than cold muscles. Cold muscles are stiff and can tear easily.

To warm up your muscles you should have a regular routine of exercises. Here are a few basic ones.

▶ **A   Sitting toe touches.** Sit on the floor with your legs extended. Your legs should be flat on the floor. Your feet should be together. Reach for your toes. Bring your forehead as close to your knees as you can.

▶ **B   Side stretch.** Stand with your feet shoulder-width apart and your legs straight. Place one hand on your hip and curve the other arm up and over your head. Bend smoothly toward the side where your hand is on your hip. Hold for a moment. Straighten. Switch hand positions and bend to the other side.

▶ **C   Shoulder stretch.** Put your arms over your head. Hold the elbow of one arm with the hand of the other. Slowly pull the elbow behind your head. Do not strain. Hold. Repeat on the other side.

Your Digestive and Excretory Systems

This lesson will help you find answers to questions that teens often ask about how they digest food. For example:

▶ **Why do I need to eat?**

▶ **What happens to food after I eat it?**

▶ **How long does it take to digest food?**

Your Body's Engine

The engine of a car burns fuel for energy. You can think of your body as a kind of engine because your cells also get energy from burning fuel. Your **digestive** (dy·JES·tiv) **system** *breaks down the food you eat into a form that your body cells can use as fuel.* This system changes food into nutrients.

After fuel is burned in the engine of a car, it leaves waste products that come out of the exhaust system. In your body cells, the production and use of energy also leave behind wastes. Your **excretory** (EK·skruh·tohr·ee) **system** *gets rid of some of the wastes your body produces.* This system includes the kidneys and bladder.

The excretory system also controls the amount of water in your body. Your body must have the same amount of water in it at all times. So in addition to helping get rid of wastes, the kidneys are important for maintaining your body's water balance.

in your journal

This lesson compares your body to a car's engine. In your journal, make other comparisons of your body and a car. Write as many similarities as you can think of.

Car engines burn gasoline for fuel. People burn food for fuel after it has been digested. Both cars and people run on the energy released from the fuel.

Structure of the Digestive System

In the organs of the digestive system, food is broken down and is absorbed into the blood. Leftover matter that cannot be digested passes out of the body. The system responsible for receiving food, breaking it down, and getting rid of solid waste is shown in **Figure 6.17.**

Breaking Down Food

Digestion (dy·JES·chuhn) is *the process of breaking down food into a form the body can use.* Digestion begins in the mouth. Your teeth grind food into small particles that can be easily swallowed. Saliva contains chemicals called enzymes (EN·zymz) that further break down food.

The process continues in other parts of the digestive system. At the end of digestion, food has been broken down into particles small enough to be absorbed into the blood. The blood carries the digested food to all the body cells. **Figure 6.18** shows the digestive process.

Q & A

That Burning Feeling

Q: What is heartburn?

A: Heartburn is a digestive problem. There is a strong muscle at the point where the esophagus connects with the stomach. It is supposed to keep the stomach closed most of the time so that acids don't splash upward. Sometimes the muscle fails, however, and acids do enter the esophagus. This creates a burning sensation in this tube at about the level of the heart.

Figure 6.17
The Digestive System

Your digestive system extends from one end of your body to the other.

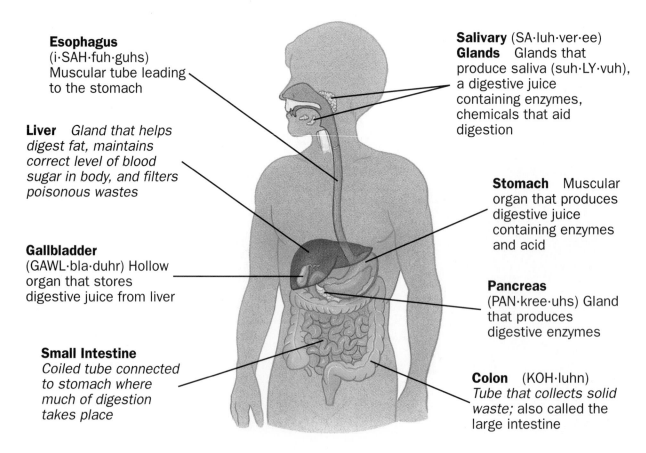

Esophagus
(i·SAH·fuh·guhs)
Muscular tube leading to the stomach

Liver   *Gland that helps digest fat, maintains correct level of blood sugar in body, and filters poisonous wastes*

Gallbladder
(GAWL·bla·duhr) Hollow organ that stores digestive juice from liver

Small Intestine
Coiled tube connected to stomach where much of digestion takes place

Salivary (SA·luh·ver·ee)
Glands   Glands that produce saliva (suh·LY·vuh), a digestive juice containing enzymes, chemicals that aid digestion

Stomach   Muscular organ that produces digestive juice containing enzymes and acid

Pancreas
(PAN·kree·uhs) Gland that produces digestive enzymes

Colon   (KOH·luhn) *Tube that collects solid waste;* also called the large intestine

The liver, gallbladder, and pancreas also aid digestion. The liver is the largest gland of the body. It does more than 500 known jobs. One of these jobs is to produce bile, a chemical that helps digest fat. The gallbladder is a storage place for bile. The pancreas makes enzymes that help break down three nutrients in food: carbohydrates, fats, and proteins.

Figure 6.18
The Digestive Process

This diagram shows what happens from the time you put food in your mouth until waste products exit from your body.

Did You Know?

Digestion Time

It takes 5 to 9 seconds to swallow a bite of food. The food spends up to 4 hours in the stomach, 5 hours in the small intestine, and 6 to 11 hours in the colon.

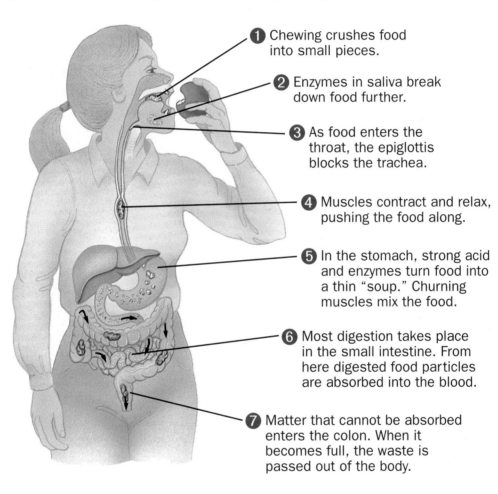

1. Chewing crushes food into small pieces.

2. Enzymes in saliva break down food further.

3. As food enters the throat, the epiglottis blocks the trachea.

4. Muscles contract and relax, pushing the food along.

5. In the stomach, strong acid and enzymes turn food into a thin "soup." Churning muscles mix the food.

6. Most digestion takes place in the small intestine. From here digested food particles are absorbed into the blood.

7. Matter that cannot be absorbed enters the colon. When it becomes full, the waste is passed out of the body.

Removing Wastes

The body gets rid of three different types of wastes. The digestive and excretory systems take care of two kinds. The respiratory system takes care of the third.

- Solid waste comes from food that cannot be digested.

- Liquid waste comes from cell activities.

- Carbon dioxide gas is a waste product made by cells when they burn food for energy. It leaves the body through the lungs when you breathe out.

The Colon

The solid part of food that cannot be absorbed in the small intestine is passed to the large intestine, or colon. In the colon, water is removed from the waste. When the colon is full, a nerve sends a message for the colon muscle to contract. By contracting, it gets rid of solid waste material.

The Kidneys and Bladder

The body needs to control its water supply at all times. To function correctly, cells need a particular balance of salt and water. The excretory system keeps this balance correct.

The **kidneys** are *a filtering system for the blood* (see **Figure 6.19**). At certain times the kidneys remove mostly water from the blood. At other times the kidneys remove mostly salts. Liquid waste material from the kidneys is stored in the bladder as urine. When the bladder is full, the urine is passed out of the body. **Excretion** (ek·SKREE·shuhn) is the name for *the process of removing liquid wastes from the body.*

Figure 6.19
The Excretory System
The excretory system helps keep your body in balance.

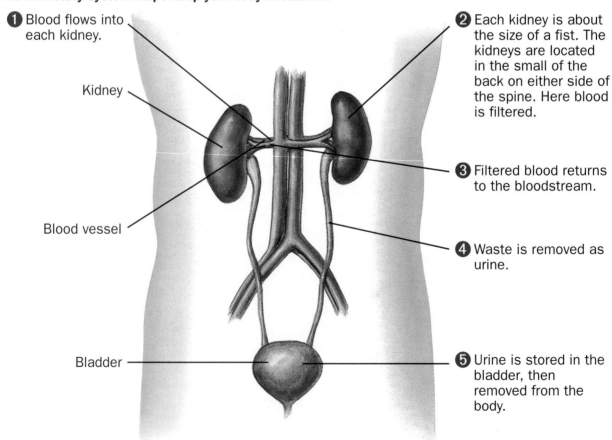

❶ Blood flows into each kidney.

Kidney

Blood vessel

Bladder

❷ Each kidney is about the size of a fist. The kidneys are located in the small of the back on either side of the spine. Here blood is filtered.

❸ Filtered blood returns to the bloodstream.

❹ Waste is removed as urine.

❺ Urine is stored in the bladder, then removed from the body.

Keeping Your Digestive and Excretory Systems Healthy

The key to healthy digestive and excretory systems is to develop good eating habits.

- **Eat a balanced diet.** Eat foods from all the food groups, especially fruits and vegetables.

- **Eat regular meals at regular times.** Don't skip meals. Try to make mealtime a relaxing experience.

- **Chew food slowly.** Don't rush. Try to stop eating before you are completely full.

- **Drink water.** Try to drink six to eight glasses of water a day.

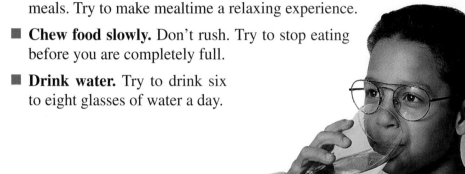

Water is important for keeping both your digestive and excretory systems working properly.

Review

Lesson 6

Using complete sentences, answer the following questions on a separate sheet of paper.

Reviewing Terms and Facts

1. **Vocabulary** Define the term *digestive system.*

2. **Identify** In what organ does the most digestion take place?

3. **Give Examples** Name two jobs the liver does.

4. **Recall** Which body system regulates the body's water balance?

Thinking Critically

5. **Explain** Why is chicken soup easier to digest than fried chicken?

6. **Contrast** Describe the difference between the jobs of the small intestine and the large intestine, or colon.

7. **Predict** Describe one result that you think might occur if your kidneys stopped working.

Applying Health Concepts

8. **Personal Health** Make a booklet that shows what happens to a piece of food as it travels from the mouth to the end of the digestive system. Design the booklet so that a person can flip through it and find out what is happening at each stage of the process.

Chapter Summary

▶ Different systems work together and are dependent on one another to keep the body functioning well. (Lesson 1)

▶ Body systems are organized by what they do. (Lesson 1)

▶ The nervous system is the body's control and communication center. (Lesson 2)

▶ The nervous system includes the brain, spinal cord, and nerves. (Lesson 2)

▶ The circulatory system transports blood, which delivers needed materials such as food and oxygen to body cells and takes away wastes. (Lesson 3)

▶ The respiratory system takes in oxygen and delivers it to cells. It also collects and removes carbon dioxide from the body. (Lesson 4)

▶ Bones form a framework that supports and protects the body. (Lesson 5)

▶ By contracting, muscles that are connected to bones move parts of the body. (Lesson 5)

▶ Smooth muscle and cardiac muscle cause movements in body organs not connected to bones. (Lesson 5)

▶ The digestive system breaks down food into particles that cells can use for energy. (Lesson 6)

▶ The excretory system controls the body's balance of water and salt in the blood and gets rid of wastes. (Lesson 6)

Using Health Terms

On a separate sheet of paper, write the vocabulary term that best matches each definition given below.

1. Groups of organs that work together to support a body function (Lesson 1)

2. Cells that make up the nervous system (Lesson 2)

3. The system that includes the heart and blood vessels (Lesson 3)

4. The main organs of the respiratory system (Lesson 4)

5. The main muscle used in breathing (Lesson 4)

6. Place where one bone meets another (Lesson 5)

7. The coiled tube connected to the stomach where much digestion takes place (Lesson 6)

Reviewing Main Ideas

Using complete sentences, answer the following questions on a separate sheet of paper.

1. Explain the relationship that exists among the body systems. (Lesson 1)

2. What are the parts of the central nervous system? (Lesson 2)

3. How are messages carried through the nervous system? (Lesson 2)

4. What happens to the oxygen in blood as it travels through the bloodstream? (Lesson 3)

5. What are the two goals of breathing? (Lesson 4)

6. What are the six main jobs of the skeletal and muscular systems? (Lesson 5)

7. What are the functions of the excretory system? (Lesson 6)

8. What eating habits can help keep the digestive and excretory systems healthy? (Lesson 6)

Thinking Critically

Using complete sentences, answer the following questions on a separate sheet of paper.

1. **Explain** Give two examples of body systems that work together. Tell how they interrelate. (Lesson 1)

2. **Decide** Josh refuses to wear his bicycle helmet when he rides. Which body system is he most likely to injure seriously? (Lesson 2)

3. **Explain** The heart pumps thousands of gallons of blood every day, yet you have only a few quarts of blood in your body. How does this happen? (Lesson 3)

4. **Compare** Suppose one balloon were blown up with a helium pump and a second balloon were blown up by a person breathing out. What would be the type of gas inside the balloon blown up by mouth? (Lesson 4)

5. **Synthesize** List a part of your muscular system that (a) allows your circulatory system to function and (b) helps you breathe. (Lessons 3, 4, 5)

6. **Explain** Tell how problems with your excretory system could affect your circulatory system. (Lessons 3, 6)

Your Action Plan

The way you live affects the health of all your body systems. Look through your private journal entries for this chapter. Is there one body system that you want to care for better?

Select a long-term goal. For example, you might want to improve your posture or eat more regular meals. Then set short-term goals to help you achieve your long-term goal. Short-term goals could include performing posture exercises every day or getting up early enough to eat a nutritious breakfast every morning.

Make a schedule that will allow you to reach your long-term goal. After a period of weeks, evaluate how you are doing. Are you beginning to reach your long-term goal? If you aren't, adjust your short-term goals. When you reach your long-term goal, reward yourself for all your hard work.

Building Your Portfolio

1. Write an "Owner's Manual for Care and Upkeep of Body Systems." It should contain facts about the body systems and how to keep them in top shape. Consult this chapter and reference books for information.

2. Make a series of posters of all the body systems. Draw in the major parts of each body system. Use reference books to make your posters as accurate as possible.

In Your Home and Community

1. Look for ways you can make changes in your home that will improve your family's health. You might encourage family members to eat regular meals together, or you could start a family exercise program. Get ideas from family members as you create your plan.

2. Contact the local office of a charity that raises money to fight a disease. Find out how the disease affects the body and how scientists are working to cure it. Then organize a plan to raise money for the charity. You might sell T-shirts or have a car wash. Donate the money you collect to the charity.

Unit 3
Protecting Your Health

Communicable and Noncommunicable Diseases

Student Expectations

After reading this chapter, you should be able to:

1. Identify the ways germs are spread and how the body defends itself against communicable diseases.

2. Describe common communicable diseases and the ways you can protect yourself against them.

3. Describe the causes, symptoms, and treatment of four common noncommunicable diseases.

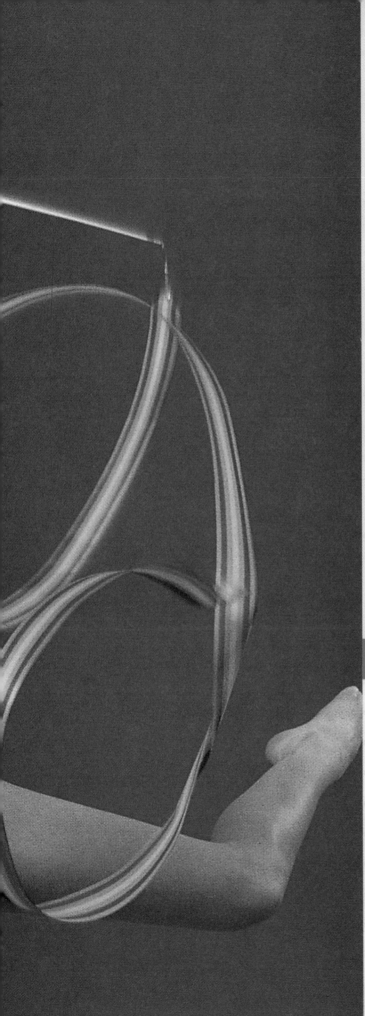

Everybody says I'm a worrier. Okay, I admit I need to lighten up a little. One thing I think I have a right to worry about, though, is getting sick. Whenever I'm around someone with an illness, I always catch it. Some of my friends never seem to get sick. Take Jody— she hasn't missed a day of school so far this year. Yet I've missed at least a day or two of school every month.

Yesterday my best friend, Tia, came home from school with me. We finished our homework and then listened to music. Tia left early. She said she felt funny, and she looked really tired.

Today Tia wasn't in school. I called her house after I got home. Her dad told me she has the flu. Now I'm worried I'll get the flu. I really don't want to get sick right now. The middle school talent show is just four days away. I've got a really great dance routine that I've been practicing for months.

If I do get sick, should I do the talent show anyway? I've been practicing for so long! I wish there were something I could do to keep from getting sick in the first place.

in Your Journal

Read the account on this page. Have you ever worried you'll get sick when you've been around someone who is ill? Do you wonder whether or not to stay home if you do get sick? Start your private journal entries for this chapter by answering these questions.

▶ How often are you sick with diseases like colds and the flu?

▶ How quickly do you bounce back to good health when you are sick?

▶ How much does being sick interfere with your life?

When you reach the end of the chapter, you will use your journal entries to make an action plan.

Causes of Communicable Diseases

This lesson will help you find answers to questions that teens often ask about the causes of communicable diseases. For example:

▶ **What are germs?**
▶ **How do I catch diseases like colds and flu?**
▶ **If germs are all around me, why don't I get sick more often?**

Words to Know

disease
communicable
   disease
noncommunicable
   disease
infection
immune system
lymphocyte
antibody
immunity

What Are Communicable Diseases?

A **disease** is *an unhealthy condition of the body or mind.* When you have a disease, your body doesn't function normally. You may not know what you have, but you probably feel sick.

There are two basic types of disease. A **communicable** (kuh·MYOO·ni·kuh·buhl) **disease,** such as a cold, is *a disease that spreads from person to person.* A **noncommunicable disease,** such as cancer, is *a disease that doesn't spread from person to person*—you can't catch it from someone else.

Causes of Communicable Diseases

Communicable diseases are caused by germs. Germs are so small they can be seen only with a microscope. An **infection** results when *germs invade the body, multiply, and cause harm to body cells.* Sometimes the body can fight off an infection. If it cannot, disease occurs.

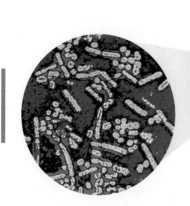

With a microscope, a scientist can see disease-causing germs that are invisible to the unaided eye.

Types of Germs

Several different types of germs cause diseases (see **Figure 7.1).** Viruses and bacteria cause the most diseases by far. Other types of germs that cause diseases include fungi and protozoa.

Figure 7.1
Most Common Disease-Causing Germs

This table describes the four most common disease-causing germs.

Viruses (VY·ruh·sez)

Description Smallest and simplest of disease-causing organisms

Typical Diseases Colds, influenza, measles, rabies, AIDS

Cultural Diversity

Bad Magic and Lost Souls

ACTIVITY!

In some cultures, the germ theory of disease is unknown. Instead, diseases are sometimes thought to be caused by magic spells, a wrong done by the sick person, or loss of the soul from the body. Even in our own culture you may hear people blame factors other than germs for the onset of a communicable disease. Make a list of some myths you have heard. Discuss in class why you think these ideas are wrong.

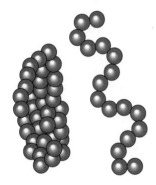

Bacteria (bak·TIR·ee·uh)

Description One-celled organisms similar to plants

Typical Diseases Strep throat, gonorrhea, tuberculosis, Lyme disease, whooping cough

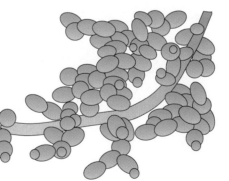

Fungi (FUHN·jy)

Description One- or many-celled primitive plants such as molds

Typical Diseases Athlete's foot, jock itch, ringworm, thrush, vaginitis

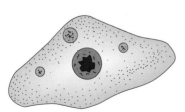

Protozoa (proh·tuh·ZOH-uh)

Description One-celled organisms similar to animals

Typical Diseases Malaria, amebic dysentery, giardiasis, toxoplasmosis

How Germs Are Spread

Germs can be spread in a number of ways. **Figure 7.2** shows the four most common ways that disease-causing germs are likely to be passed on to people.

The Body's Defenses

Even though you are exposed to millions of germs each day, you aren't sick all the time. This is because a healthy body is like a strong fortress. It has a number of barriers to keep germs out. If germs do enter, other defenses take over.

Figure 7.2
Ways Germs Spread
Knowing how germs spread can help you protect yourself against infection.

Direct Contact
Germs can be passed on to you if you touch an infected area on another person. Germs that cause skin infections and some rashes are spread this way. Some germs, such as the virus that causes AIDS, are spread through direct sexual contact.

Contact with Animals
You can get an infection from the bite of an infected insect or animal. The germ that causes rabies can be spread this way.

Indirect Contact
Germs may be passed on to you when someone who is sick sneezes or coughs near you. The sick person expels infected drops of moisture into the air and you breathe them in. Germs may also be passed on if you share cups, utensils, or other personal items with a sick person. Germs that cause colds and flu can be spread this way.

Other Contacts
You can get an infection by eating or drinking contaminated food or water. Salmonella, a type of food poisoning, can be spread this way.

HEALTH LAB
How Germs Are Spread

*I*ntroduction: One of the most common ways for germs to spread is on the hands or on objects that have been handled. Every time you shake hands or turn on a faucet, for example, you risk picking up other people's germs.

Objective: Most of us don't realize how easily germs are spread on our hands. This health lab will help convince you.

Materials and Method:
Working with a small group of classmates, place a few drops of peppermint or lemon food flavoring on a cotton ball. One member of the group should rub the cotton ball over the palm of his or her hand. After the flavoring has dried, that person should shake hands with a few others in the group. Those people, in turn, should shake hands with the rest of the people in the group.

The First Line of Defense

Your body's first line of defense includes barriers that keep germs out or trap and destroy them.

■ **Skin and mucous membranes.** Just as packaging protects foods, your skin and mucous membranes are your body's protective "wrappers." Skin covers the outside of your body. Mucous membranes line the inner parts of your body such as your nose, mouth, and throat.

■ **Saliva, tears, and gastric juices.** Some of these barriers wash germs away. Saliva, tears, and gastric juices all contain chemicals that attack and destroy certain germs.

General Reactions

If germs get through the first line of defense, your body responds with general reactions. They are called *general* because they are the same no matter what germ has entered your body.

■ Special blood cells surround germs and destroy them.

■ A chemical is released that stops viruses from reproducing.

■ Fever, or a rise in body temperature, kills some germs and makes it hard for others to reproduce.

The Immune System

If germs somehow get past the barriers and survive the general reactions, your body has another line of defense—your **immune** (i·MYOON) **system.** This is *a group of cells, tissues, and organs that fights specific germs.* **Lymphocytes** (LIM·fuh·syts), *white blood cells that attack germs,* are an important part of the immune system. When germs enter your body, some lymphocytes multiply and attack them. Other lymphocytes produce

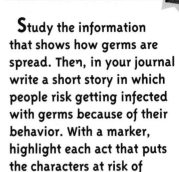

in your journal

Study the information that shows how germs are spread. Then, in your journal write a short story in which people risk getting infected with germs because of their behavior. With a marker, highlight each act that puts the characters at risk of infection.

Observation and Analysis:
Group members should smell their hands to see if any of the food flavoring was transferred to them in the process of shaking hands.

To understand the importance of frequent handwashing, answer these questions. If the food flavoring had been a mass of cold viruses, how many people in the group would have picked up germs on their hands? What might they have done later to allow germs to enter their bodies?

Helper Cells

Scientists have discovered two major types of lymphocytes: B-cells and T-cells. Both are formed in bone marrow, the soft tissue in the center of your bones. B-cells produce antibodies. T-cells do several different jobs. Some attack germs directly. Others control the activity of B-cells and other parts of the immune system.

antibodies. **Antibodies** are *chemicals produced specifically to fight a particular invading substance* (see **Figure 7.3**). If the same germ enters your body again, your immune system "remembers" how to produce the correct antibodies, giving you *resistance to infection*, or **immunity.**

Figure 7.3
The Immune System Response

When your immune system works properly, it creates substances designed specifically to attack the germs that are making you sick.

❶ Each type of germ carries unique chemicals, called antigens, on its surface. Your immune system recognizes these antigens as invaders.

❷ For each antigen, your immune system produces an antibody. This antibody is produced specifically to fight that antigen.

❸ Each antibody attaches to an antigen like a key in a lock. This kills the germ, makes it harmless, or marks it for attack by other lymphocytes.

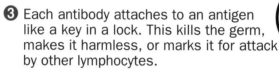

Lesson 1 Review

Using complete sentences, answer the following questions on a separate sheet of paper.

Reviewing Terms and Facts

1. **Vocabulary**   Which of the following terms are causes of disease and which are parts of the immune system response: *antibodies, infection, lymphocytes?*

2. **List**   Name the four types of germs discussed in this lesson.

3. **Summarize**   Identify four ways in which germs can be spread.

4. **Explain**   How are general reactions and immune responses different?

Thinking Critically

5. **Compare and Contrast**   What are the similarities and differences between communicable and noncommunicable diseases?

6. **Predict**   What would happen if your immune system stopped working?

Applying Health Concepts

7. **Health of Others**   With another student, present a skit that shows ways germs might be spread from person to person, such as coughing without covering the mouth or sharing eating utensils. Have the class identify each of the behaviors.

Common Communicable Diseases

This lesson will help you find answers to questions that teens often ask about the prevention and treatment of communicable diseases. For example:

▶ How can I keep from getting sick so often?

▶ What vaccines should I have?

▶ What is the best way to avoid sexually transmitted diseases?

▶ How do people get AIDS?

Preventing Communicable Diseases

In the last lesson, you looked at the ways your body works naturally to resist and destroy germs that cause communicable diseases. In this lesson, you will learn how you can work with your body's natural defenses to stay healthy.

Healthy Behaviors

When you keep germs from passing between yourself and others, you help stop the spread of communicable disease. When you have a healthy lifestyle, you increase your body's ability to fight off germs. You get sick less often, and you don't pass on diseases. **Figure 7.4** lists some practical healthy behaviors.

Words to Know

vaccine
sexually
  transmitted
  disease (STD)
abstinence
HIV
AIDS

Figure 7.4
Staying Healthy

Develop these habits to protect your health and that of others.

Protecting Yourself	Protecting Others
Wash your hands often.	Wash your hands often.
Get plenty of exercise and rest.	Stay away from others when you are sick.
Bathe or shower daily.	If you are sick, go to a doctor so you can get better faster.
Eat a balanced diet. Prepare and store food safely.	Cover your nose and mouth with a tissue when you sneeze or cough.
Don't share eating or drinking utensils.	
Avoid sexual contact.	

in your journal

In your journal, describe how you act when you are sick with a cold. Do you go to the doctor or treat the symptoms yourself? Do you stay home or do you keep going to school and to other activities? What do you do to prevent giving your germs to others?

Vaccines

Vaccines (vak·SEENZ) are *preparations of killed or weakened germs.* They are injected into the body to cause the immune system to produce antibodies. Because the germs are dead or weak, you don't get sick. The antibodies you produce, however, make you immune to the disease the next time you are exposed to it. Getting vaccines is another way to protect yourself from some communicable diseases. **Figure 7.5** shows some of the most common vaccines, the diseases they protect against, and the risks of those diseases. It also shows the ages at which most doctors recommend that children receive these vaccines.

Figure 7.5
Vaccines and the Diseases They Prevent

Vaccines have been developed to protect people from some common dangerous diseases.

Vaccine and the Diseases It Protects Against	Disease Risks	Typical Vaccination Schedule
DTP: diphtheria, tetanus, pertussis (whooping cough)	Diphtheria: blocked breathing passages, heart inflammation Tetanus: convulsions, respiratory problems, heart failure Pertussis: pneumonia All can be fatal	2, 4, 6, and 15–18 months 4–6 years, DT boosters at 14–16 and every 10 years thereafter
OPV: poliomyelitis	Permanent paralysis, possibly of muscles used to breathe Death	2, 4, and 6–18 months 4–6 years
MMR: measles, mumps, rubella (German measles)	Measles: pneumonia, brain damage Mumps: in females, inflammation of the ovaries; when contracted by adult males, sterility Rubella: when contracted by a pregnant woman, damage to the baby	12–15 months 4–6 years
HIB: diseases caused by the hemophilus influenza type B (HIB) germ	Nervous system problems that can cause brain damage Breathing problems, including inability to breathe Pneumonia	2, 4, 6, and 12–15 months
Hep B: hepatitis B	Cirrhosis of the liver Liver cancer	2, 4, and 6–18 months

Common Communicable Diseases

The most common communicable disease is the cold. Other fairly common communicable diseases include

- influenza.
- mononucleosis.
- hepatitis.
- tuberculosis.

These five diseases are discussed in **Figure 7.6** on the next page. They vary in many ways. Some can be prevented with certain vaccines, but others cannot. For those without vaccines, practicing good health behaviors and keeping yourself healthy are the best way of preventing getting the disease.

Children average four to six colds a year. Adults average about half that many.

LIFE SKILLS
Handwashing for Health

*H*andwashing may be your most important weapon against the spread of colds. It may also help prevent the spread of more serious diseases. Always wash your hands before handling or eating food. Also wash them after doing any of the following:

▶ Handling raw food, especially meat

▶ Using the bathroom or changing a diaper

▶ Handling garbage

▶ Sneezing, coughing, or blowing your nose

▶ Playing with a pet or cleaning a litter box

Read through the following instructions for proper handwashing. Then practice washing your hands using this method. Use a watch with a second hand to make sure you wash long enough.

1. Rub your hands with soap and warm water for at least ten seconds to loosen germs.
2. Wash well around fingernails and creases in your hands, where germs accumulate. A nail brush will help remove germs from under your nails.
3. Rinse away all traces of soap. Dry thoroughly.

Follow-up Activity

Make a list of times in a typical day when you should wash your hands. Post the list in several places where you will be most likely to see it when you need a handwashing reminder.

Figure 7.6
Common Communicable Diseases

Some of these diseases are quite mild. Others can cause serious health problems.

Description of Disease	How It Spreads	Treatment and Prevention
Common cold: respiratory infection caused by over 100 different viruses; symptoms include congestion, sore throat, cough	Water droplets in the air from coughs and sneezes. Direct contact with infected people. Indirect contact with objects that infected people have handled	Treat symptoms with rest, liquids, over-the-counter medicines. Handwashing and avoiding contact with infected persons reduces exposure.
Influenza (in·floo·EN·zuh), or flu: respiratory infection caused by several closely related groups of viruses; symptoms include high fever, fatigue, muscle and joint aches	Water droplets in the air from coughs and sneezes. Direct contact with infected people	Treat symptoms with rest, liquids, steam inhalations, over-the-counter medicines. Vaccine gives immunity to 60–70 percent of people immunized.
Mononucleosis (MAH·noh·noo·klee·OH·sis): viral infection common among teens and young adults; tiredness, loss of appetite, sore throat, fever	Water droplets in the air from coughs and sneezes. Direct contact with an infected person's saliva through kissing, sharing utensils	Treat symptoms with pain relievers, rest, and liquids. Avoiding contact with infected persons reduces exposure.
Hepatitis (he·puh·TY·tis): liver inflammation caused by several viruses; two major types are Type A and Type B; weakness, vomiting, fever and chills	Type A: through contaminated food or water. Type B: usually through direct contact with body fluids from an infected person	Treatment includes rest and an adequate diet. Injections provide short-term protection from Type A; vaccine is available for Type B.
Tuberculosis (tuh·ber·kyoo·LOH·sis), or TB: disease, caused by bacteria, that usually affects the lungs; cough, fatigue, night sweats, weight loss	Water droplets in the air from coughs and sneezes	Treatment consists of long-term use of antibiotics. Prevention includes giving antibiotics to persons in close contact with an infected person; vaccine available.

Teen Issues

TB Time Bomb

After years of decline, TB cases in the United States increased 20 percent from 1985 to 1992. In people 14 and younger, the increase was an alarming 35 percent. Research why TB is on the rise again in our country, especially among young people.

Sexually Transmitted Diseases (STDs)

Sexually transmitted diseases (STDs) are *communicable diseases that are spread from person to person through sexual contact.* There are no vaccines for STDs. Practicing **abstinence,** or *avoiding sexual contact,* is the only sure way to keep from getting these diseases.

Most STDs are serious diseases. They can lead to damage to reproductive organs, heart disease, and even death. Fortunately, many STDs can be cured with antibiotics.

Knowing About STDs

Teens are the age group most likely to get STDs. That is why reliable information is so important. AIDS, the most serious of the sexually transmitted diseases, is discussed later in this lesson. Here is information about four other common STDs.

■ **Chlamydia** (kluh·MI·dee·uh) is a name used for a group of infections that attack the reproductive organs. Chlamydial infections are the most common type of STD in the United States. Symptoms include pain and an unusual liquid coming from the penis or vagina. Chlamydia can be cured with the use of antibiotics.

■ **Gonorrhea** (gah·nuh·REE·uh) is an STD caused by bacteria that live in warm, moist body areas. Symptoms include a burning feeling during urination and an unusual liquid coming from the penis or vagina. Gonorrhea can be cured with the use of antibiotics.

■ **Genital herpes** (HER·peez) is a relatively common STD caused by the herpes simplex type II virus. Symptoms include fever and painful, itchy sores where the disease entered the body. Genital herpes has no cure.

It is important for teens to learn about STDs.

■ **Syphilis** (SI·fuh·lis) is an STD that attacks many parts of the body. Syphilis is fatal without treatment. Early symptoms include a reddish painless sore at the place where the disease entered the body. Syphilis can be cured with antibiotics.

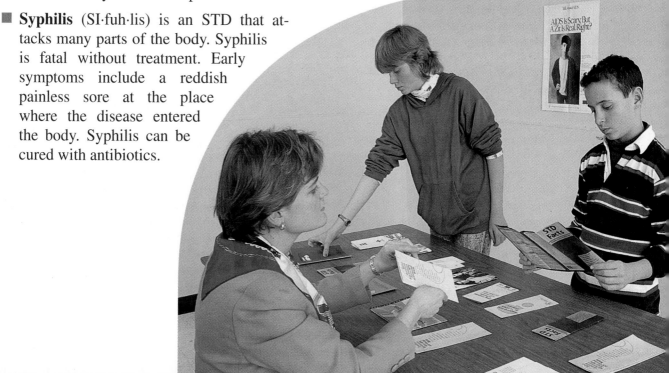

What Are HIV and AIDS?

HIV, or human immunodeficiency virus, is *the virus that causes AIDS.* HIV attacks the immune system. Early symptoms of infection with HIV may include a rash, a sore throat, fever, and tiredness. Nearly everyone infected with HIV develops AIDS. **AIDS,** or acquired immunodeficiency syndrome, is *an HIV infection combined with severe immune system problems.* People with AIDS cannot fight off diseases that healthy people could easily resist (see **Figure 7.7**). Because AIDS has no cure, people with AIDS eventually die from one of these diseases.

Figure 7.7
How HIV Attacks the Immune System
HIV keeps the immune system from responding as it should. Eventually the body is destroyed by one or more infections.

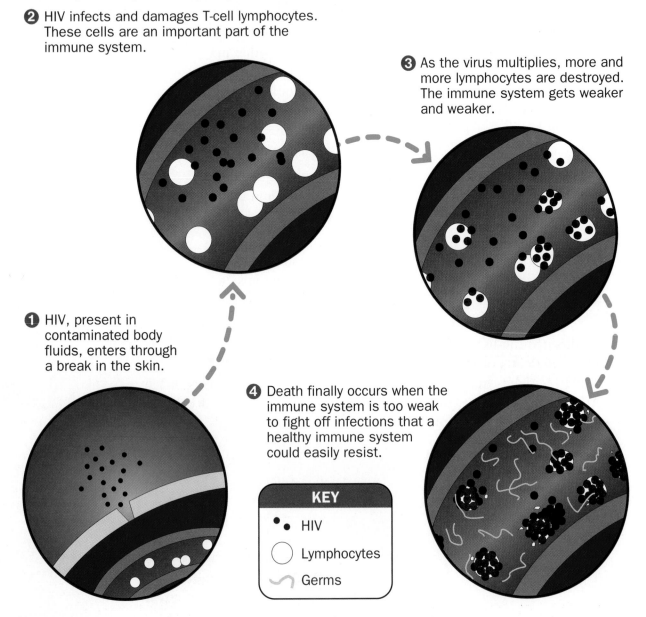

❷ HIV infects and damages T-cell lymphocytes. These cells are an important part of the immune system.

❸ As the virus multiplies, more and more lymphocytes are destroyed. The immune system gets weaker and weaker.

❶ HIV, present in contaminated body fluids, enters through a break in the skin.

❹ Death finally occurs when the immune system is too weak to fight off infections that a healthy immune system could easily resist.

KEY
- •• HIV
- ○ Lymphocytes
- ∿ Germs

Preventing the Spread of HIV

HIV is spread in these body fluids that contain the virus.

■ Infected semen

■ Infected fluid from the vagina

■ Infected blood

Any time these fluids enter the body of another person, HIV infection may occur. You can prevent the spread of HIV by practicing abstinence and never sharing with anyone else a needle or any object that breaks the skin.

Sexual activity and sharing needles are the two main ways in which HIV is spread. A pregnant woman infected with HIV can also pass the virus on to her baby. Before 1985, HIV was spread through blood transfusions with contaminated blood supplies. Today, however, donated blood is tested for HIV. Infected blood is discarded, making blood supplies much safer.

How HIV Is Not Spread

HIV is *not* spread through

■ the air.

■ sweat or tears.

■ mosquito bites.

■ donating blood.

■ touching, such as shaking hands or hugging.

■ contact with objects, such as eating utensils.

Review Lesson 2

Using complete sentences, answer the following questions on a separate sheet of paper.

Reviewing Terms and Facts

1. **Summarize** List four ways you can protect yourself and others from communicable diseases.

2. **Define** What is *abstinence?*

3. **Vocabulary** Write an original paragraph of at least three sentences that uses the terms *STD, HIV,* and *AIDS.*

4. **State** List two ways that HIV infection is transmitted.

Thinking Critically

5. **Infer** How does getting a vaccine help protect both your health and the health of those around you?

6. **Contrast** Describe the differences between the ways a person catches a cold and the ways a person gets HIV.

7. **Deduce** Why are teens one of the age groups most likely to get STDs?

Applying Health Concepts

8. **Consumer Health** Make a flyer to show the need for vaccinations. Also list required vaccines.

Teen HEALTH DIGEST

Teens Making a Difference

A Matter of Life and Breath

Brandon Gibbs is a champion wrestler. He is also a member of the track team. Most people are surprised when they learn that Brandon has asthma.

Sometimes teens with asthma get depressed because of the disease. They may feel that they miss a lot of school or that they "live on medications." Brandon used to feel this way, but he has decided not to let asthma get him down. He accepts it as a problem to be solved like any other. Brandon has learned that with teamwork he, his doctor, and his parents can keep his asthma under control.

Brandon has one other accomplishment that he is very proud of. He is a peer counselor in a support group for teens with asthma. Thanks to Brandon's inspiration, most of the teens he works with have learned to see their disease as a challenge they can overcome.

People at Work

Public Health Worker

Her name is Annie Dodge Wauneka, and she is the daughter of a Navajo tribal leader. To other Navajo, she is the "Warrior Who Scouts the Enemy"—in this case, tuberculosis. Her concern about this disease began in her childhood, when she watched TB attack and kill many of her people each year.

As chairperson of the Health and Welfare Committee on her Arizona reservation, Wauneka declared war on TB. She started a radio program about health issues. She encouraged TB patients to get prompt medical care and brought Navajo and non-Navajo doctors together to work on the disease. During her years as health director, the number of cases of TB among her people was greatly reduced. For her efforts, Annie Dodge Wauneka became the first Native American to receive the Presidential Medal of Freedom.

CON$UMER FOCU$

Antibiotics—Miracle Cures No More

Do you think of antibiotics as "wonder drugs" that can cure any infection? Actually, antibiotics have never been effective against viral infections. Antibiotics are effective only against infections caused by bacteria. However, doctors have noticed increasing numbers of bacterial infections that are not responding to antibiotics.

Disease specialists explain why. When an antibiotic is widely used against bacteria, many of the germs die. Some, however, are likely to survive. Those that do are, of course, the strongest ones. These germs then reproduce, creating over time hardier generations of germs that may at some point resist antibiotics altogether.

As a consumer, you can avoid making the antibiotic-resistance problem worse. Don't demand an antibiotic whenever you are sick. After all, your body has strong defenses against many germs. Also, question your doctor when she or he prescribes an antibiotic. The drug may not be necessary. If you do need an antibiotic, take it the way the doctor tells you. If you stop taking the antibiotic when you start to feel better, you might be allowing strong germs to survive and make you—and others—sick again.

Health Update

New Drug Hailed as Major Step in Asthma Control

Until recently, the most widely used drugs for treating asthma had a major drawback. They did not remain effective long enough to last through the night. That was unfortunate because the worst time for an asthmatic is usually about three or four o'clock in the morning. A new asthma drug, called salmeterol xinafoate, may help. A study published in 1994 showed that it helped patients breathe more freely for up to 12 hours. The new drug also helps prevent asthma attacks more effectively than previous drugs.

Myths and Realities

Gender Differences and Disease

Myth: Men are more likely to die of heart disease, but women are more likely to die of cancer.

Reality: Heart disease is the leading cause of death in women as well as men—and experts expect a continued increase among women. Although women tend to develop heart disease at a later age than men, they are more likely to die from it.

Myth: Lung cancer is the major cause of cancer deaths in men, but breast cancer causes more cancer deaths in women.

Reality: Lung cancer causes the most cancer deaths in women as well as men. In fact, about 10,000 more U.S. women die each year from lung cancer than from breast cancer.

Noncommunicable Diseases

This lesson will help you find answers to questions that teens often ask about noncommunicable diseases. For example:

▶ What can I do to help keep my heart healthy?
▶ What causes cancer?
▶ Can I catch diseases such as diabetes and asthma?

Words to Know

chronic
cancer
tumor
radiation
chemotherapy
asthma
diabetes
insulin

What Are Noncommunicable Diseases?

In this lesson you will learn about four noncommunicable diseases—heart disease, cancer, diabetes, and asthma.

Noncommunicable diseases are not caused by germs, so they aren't "catching." You can be born with a noncommunicable disease, or you can develop it later (see **Figure 7.8**). You may develop it because of your lifestyle or because of hazards around you. Many noncommunicable diseases are **chronic** (KRAH·nik), or *long-lasting*.

Figure 7.8
Causes of Noncommunicable Diseases

People develop noncommunicable diseases in one of three ways.

Diseases Present at Birth

Lifestyle Diseases

Diseases Caused by Hazards Around Us

A For some people, the problem is in their genes. Their heredity makes their bodies function abnormally. Sometimes problems occur during the development or birth of a baby, resulting in a birth defect disorder.

B Some noncommunicable diseases are more likely to occur in people whose lifestyles include unhealthy habits. Overconsumption of fatty foods, for example, or cigarette smoking may contribute to heart disease or lung cancer.

C Poisons in the air, in the water, and within buildings may contribute to lung cancer, asthma, and other noncommunicable diseases.

Heart Disease

Heart disease includes several diseases of the heart and blood vessels. It has been the number-one cause of death in the United States, causing two out of every five deaths in 1993. Many of these deaths could have been prevented if people had adopted healthy habits earlier in life. **Figure 7.9** describes the major types of heart disease. It also shows how each type of heart disease can lead to others.

Teen Issues

Chronic Frustration ACTIVITY!

A 1994 study found that teens who have continual frustration tend to show elevated blood pressure. They risk developing chronic hypertension. Look at Lesson 4 in Chapter 3 for ways to reduce stress. Start now to lower your frustration level.

Figure 7.9
Types of Heart Disease

The arrows in this illustration show how one type of disorder can lead to another.

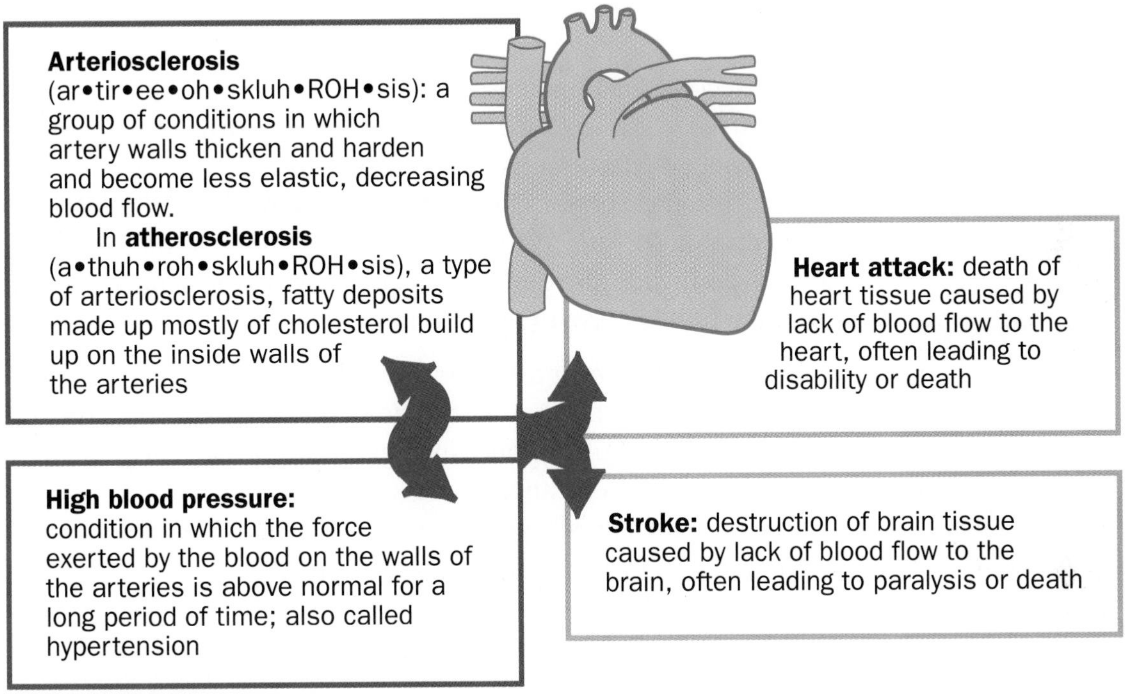

Arteriosclerosis (ar•tir•ee•oh•skluh•ROH•sis): a group of conditions in which artery walls thicken and harden and become less elastic, decreasing blood flow.

In **atherosclerosis** (a•thuh•roh•skluh•ROH•sis), a type of arteriosclerosis, fatty deposits made up mostly of cholesterol build up on the inside walls of the arteries

Heart attack: death of heart tissue caused by lack of blood flow to the heart, often leading to disability or death

High blood pressure: condition in which the force exerted by the blood on the walls of the arteries is above normal for a long period of time; also called hypertension

Stroke: destruction of brain tissue caused by lack of blood flow to the brain, often leading to paralysis or death

Preventing Heart Disease

You already know that certain lifestyle choices put you at risk for heart disease. Adopting healthy habits now, however, can reduce your risk. You can actually lessen your chances of developing heart disease later in life.

■ Exercise can strengthen the heart and lower blood pressure.

■ Losing weight can decrease the strain on the heart.

■ A diet high in fiber and low in salt, fat, and cholesterol can lower blood pressure and help keep arteries healthy.

■ Reducing stress can help lower blood pressure and decrease the risk of heart disease.

■ Not smoking can lower the risk of stroke and heart attack.

Treating Heart Disease

Although heart disease is still the leading cause of death, there have been many advances in its treatment.

- Medication can be used to dissolve blood clots, enlarge blood vessels, lower blood pressure, and control heartbeat.

- Through surgery, blocked arteries can be opened or bypassed and devices can be inserted to regulate the heartbeat. Advanced surgical techniques can even allow a new heart to be transplanted into a person's body.

- Changes in lifestyle, such as regular exercise, a healthy diet, less stress, and avoidance of alcohol and tobacco, can help lower blood pressure and prevent more heart damage.

Cancer

The second leading cause of death in the United States is **cancer,** *a disease caused by abnormal cells that grow out of control.* Many cancers start out as **tumors,** or *masses of abnormal cells,* in one tissue or organ. Noncancerous, or benign (bi·NYN), tumors do not spread. Malignant (muh·LIG·nuhnt), or cancerous, tumors do invade surrounding tissue. Eventually, cancerous cells from the tumor may spread throughout the body.

What causes cancer? A history of cancer in a family increases risk. The most important factor, however, seems to be exposure to cancer-causing substances. Cigarette smoking accounts for about 30 percent of cancer deaths. Skin cancer has been tied to exposure to the sun's rays. Exposure to certain chemicals as well as to radiation can also increase cancer risk.

As cancer cells grow, they interfere with the way normal cells function. The normal cells often die as a result.

MAKING HEALTHY DECISIONS
To Tell or Not to Tell

*E*ver since Cody's dad died when he was little, his mom has been his only family. That's one reason Cody is so worried now. When Cody's mom had her last checkup, the doctor told her she had high blood pressure. The doctor said she could easily have a heart attack or stroke. Cody's mom works two jobs and hardly has time to cook. She grabs snack foods or hamburgers and fries whenever she can. Cody recently studied about nutrition in school, so he knows more about how to have a healthy diet.

Cody realizes that his mom could reduce her risk of a heart attack or stroke by eating less fat, keeping her weight down, and exercising more. He wants to tell his mom how he feels and try to convince her to change. On the other hand, he doesn't want to upset her by seeming critical.

Cody can't make up his mind about what to do, so he decides to use the step-by-step decision-making process.

❶ **State the situation**
❷ **List the options**

Preventing Cancer

You can lower your chances of developing cancer by

- avoiding tobacco.

- protecting yourself from the sun with sun-blocking agents.

- eating a low-fat and high-fiber diet.

Treating Cancer

To be treated successfully, cancer must be discovered early. Once it spreads beyond the original tumor, it is much more difficult to treat. That is why everyone should know cancer's seven warning signs (see marginal feature).

Advances in the treatment of cancer mean that nearly half of all cancers can be completely cured.

- Surgery is used to find out whether an organ or tissue includes cancer cells. It is also used to cut out tumors and repair damaged organs.

- **Radiation** (ray·dee·AY·shuhn) is *a treatment that destroys tumors by aiming X-rays or other rays at them.* The rays kill the cancer cells.

- **Chemotherapy** (kee·moh·THEHR·uh·pee) is *a treatment that destroys cancer cells with strong chemicals.*

Surgery and radiation are better for cancers that have not yet spread. Chemotherapy can be used to fight cancers that have already spread throughout the body.

Your Total Health

Cancer's Seven Warning Signs

1. Change in bowel or bladder habits
2. A sore that does not heal
3. Unusual bleeding or discharge
4. Thickening or lump in the breast or elsewhere
5. Indigestion or difficulty swallowing
6. Change in a wart or mole
7. Nagging cough or hoarseness

③ **Weigh the possible outcomes**
④ **Consider your values**
⑤ **Make a decision and act**
⑥ **Evaluate the decision**

Follow-up Activities

1. Apply the decision-making process to Cody's dilemma.
2. Imagine you are Cody. If you decided to try to convince your mom to change her habits, what would you say to her?

Did You Know?

The Source of the Problem

People who are allergic to particular animals react to animal dander in the air. Animal dander consists of flakes of dead skin shed naturally by the animal. The reaction is not mainly to animal hair as many people believe, although dander also contains particles of hair.

Asthma

Asthma (AZ·muh) is *a chronic breathing disease caused by allergies, physical exertion, or other factors.* Untreated, it can lead to lung infections and permanent lung damage. Asthma often shows up in a child before age five. Fortunately, many children outgrow it.

People with asthma experience asthma attacks. **Figure 7.10** shows what happens during an attack and how it can be treated. The most important step in treating asthma, however, is preventing attacks from occurring. People who have asthma caused by allergies to animals, for example, can prevent attacks by avoiding the animal they are allergic to. Some people with asthma take medicine that helps reduce the chances of an attack.

Figure 7.10
An Asthma Attack
Many factors can trigger an attack, including pollen or mold, cold air, physical exercise, foods, or even a cold virus.

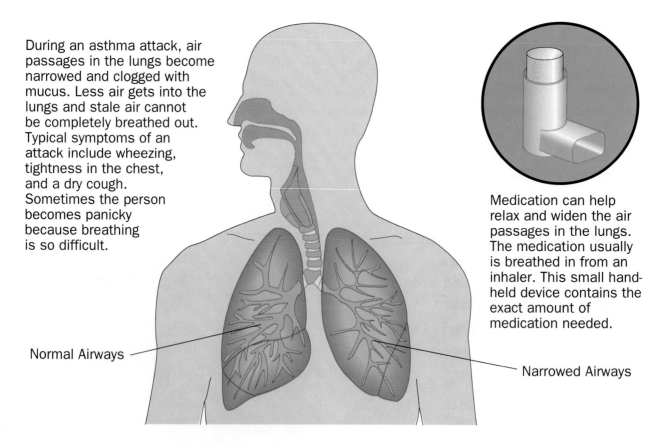

During an asthma attack, air passages in the lungs become narrowed and clogged with mucus. Less air gets into the lungs and stale air cannot be completely breathed out. Typical symptoms of an attack include wheezing, tightness in the chest, and a dry cough. Sometimes the person becomes panicky because breathing is so difficult.

Medication can help relax and widen the air passages in the lungs. The medication usually is breathed in from an inhaler. This small hand-held device contains the exact amount of medication needed.

Normal Airways

Narrowed Airways

Diabetes

Diabetes (dy·uh·BEE·teez) is *a disease that prevents the body from using the sugars and starches in food for energy.* It is caused by problems with **insulin,** *a hormone produced by the pancreas.* Normally, insulin regulates the levels of certain chemicals in the blood. When a person has diabetes, these chemicals build up and cause serious problems. The complications of diabetes include blindness, heart disease, and kidney problems.

There are two common types of diabetes. Type I, which is less common but more serious, generally develops in young people. Type II usually develops in people over 40 years of age.

Diabetes has a number of symptoms, including

- excess production of urine.
- extreme thirst.
- increased hunger.
- weight loss.
- lack of energy.
- blurred vision.

Blood or urine is tested to tell if a person has diabetes.

Diabetes cannot be cured, but it can be controlled. Many people with Type II diabetes can control the disease by regulating their diet and weight. Some also take oral medication. People with Type I diabetes usually need daily injections of insulin. They, too, should watch their diet and weight.

in your journal

Find out if any close relatives have had cancer, heart disease, diabetes, or asthma. In your journal, make a family tree that shows the diseases that different relatives have had. Then make a list of the diseases for which you have a family history.

Review Lesson 3

Using complete sentences, answer the following questions on a separate sheet of paper.

Reviewing Terms and Facts

1. **Vocabulary** Define the term *chronic.*

2. **Recall** What are three ways of getting a noncommunicable disease?

3. **List** Name two behaviors that might help reduce a person's chance of developing heart disease or cancer.

4. **Describe** Tell what happens during an asthma attack.

Thinking Critically

5. **Explain** Tell why early detection is important in the treatment of cancer.

6. **Synthesize** Why do children with asthma, diabetes, and cancer pose no risk to other children in the classroom?

7. **Compose** Choose one of the diseases discussed in this lesson. Write an original paragraph explaining what kind of treatment a person with this disease might receive.

Applying Health Concepts

8. **Health of Others** Make a poster that illustrates two good health habits that help prevent both heart disease and cancer. The poster should convince teens of the importance of adopting the two health habits.

Chapter
7 Review

Chapter Summary

▶ Communicable diseases are spread from person to person. (Lesson 1)

▶ The four major groups of germs are viruses, bacteria, fungi, and protozoa. (Lesson 1)

▶ Germs spread through direct or indirect contact with infected people, through contact with animals, or through contaminated food or water. (Lesson 1)

▶ The immune system destroys specific germs in the body and gives the body resistance to further infection from those germs if they enter the body again. (Lesson 1)

▶ Healthy behaviors help a person's own body fight off infection and keep individuals from passing infection on to others. (Lesson 2)

▶ Vaccines can give immunity to several communicable diseases. (Lesson 2)

▶ Common communicable diseases include colds, flu, mononucleosis, hepatitis, and tuberculosis. (Lesson 2)

▶ Sexually transmitted diseases (STDs) are dangerous communicable diseases that are spread through sexual contact. (Lesson 2)

▶ HIV attacks the immune system. Its spread can be limited by avoiding sexual contact and by not sharing any objects that break the skin. (Lesson 2)

▶ Noncommunicable diseases are present at birth or caused by lifestyle habits or environmental hazards. (Lesson 3)

▶ Heart disease includes a number of diseases of the heart and blood vessels. Adopting healthy habits can reduce the risk of getting heart disease. (Lesson 3)

▶ Cancer is caused by the uncontrolled growth of abnormal cells. Adopting healthy habits and avoiding certain environmental substances can reduce the risk of getting cancer. (Lesson 3)

▶ Asthma and diabetes are noncommunicable diseases that have no cure but can be treated and controlled. (Lesson 3)

Using Health Terms

On a separate sheet of paper, write the vocabulary term that best matches each definition given below.

1. Resistance to infection (Lesson 1)

2. An unhealthy condition of the body or mind (Lesson 1)

3. A preparation of killed or weakened germs (Lesson 2)

4. The virus that causes AIDS (Lesson 2)

5. Masses of abnormal cells (Lesson 3)

Reviewing Main Ideas

Using complete sentences, answer the following questions on a separate sheet of paper.

1. Explain how germs are spread by direct contact and how germs are spread by indirect contact. (Lesson 1)

2. Describe the immune system response to a germ. (Lesson 1)

3. List three diseases that can be prevented by a vaccine. (Lesson 2)

4. Name three ways that HIV is *not* spread. (Lesson 2)

5. What is a heart attack? (Lesson 3)

6. Name the three methods of treating cancer. (Lesson 3)

Thinking Critically

Using complete sentences, answer the following questions on a separate sheet of paper.

1. **Analyze** How can knowing about the ways germs are spread help you stay healthy? (Lesson 1)

2. **Describe** Explain the role of lymphocytes in producing future immunity to disease. (Lesson 1)

3. **Synthesize** Identify one healthy habit that protects both you and others from the spread of germs. (Lesson 2)

4. **Compare** How is hepatitis Type B similar to AIDS? (Lesson 2)

5. **Infer** Why do you think arteriosclerosis can lead to a heart attack? (Lesson 3)

6. **Distinguish** Describe the difference between radiation and chemotherapy in cancer treatment. (Lesson 3)

7. **Contrast** Describe the difference between Type I diabetes and Type II diabetes. (Lesson 3)

Your Action Plan

Most of us would like to avoid being sick. Look through your private journal entries for this chapter. Do you think you get sick too often? Is the way you live putting you at risk for any diseases?

Write down a realistic long-term goal. You might, for example, have a goal of reducing your risk of heart disease or cancer. You might just want to get sick less often.

Then make a list of short-term goals that will help you reach your long-term goal. You might decide, for example, to avoid certain harmful environmental conditions. You might decide to get more sleep.

Plan a schedule for reaching each of your short-term goals. Keep track of how you are doing, and reward yourself when you have reached your goal.

Building Your Portfolio

1. Obtain a copy of your vaccination record. List the diseases you are protected against. Then get a list of vaccinations that are required for attendance at your school. Compare your record with the required vaccinations. Talk with your parents or a physician about any vaccinations that you think you may be missing. Put this information in your portfolio.

2. Make an illustrated chart for one noncommunicable disease discussed in Lesson 3. List causes (if known), symptoms, treatments, and prevention techniques (if any). After displaying the chart in class, put it in your portfolio.

In Your Home and Community

1. Talk with your family about ways you can avoid spreading communicable diseases at home. Have family members consider changes they might make to keep germs from spreading. Remember that rest, a proper diet, and enough sleep will help your immune system do its job.

2. Make a list of common communicable and noncommunicable diseases. Then ask several people to identify which diseases on the list are "catching" and to tell how each can be spread. Write a summary of your survey results, listing wrong ideas people have.

Chapter 8
Drugs, Tobacco, Alcohol

Student Expectations

After reading this chapter, you should be able to:

① Explain how medicines can be used safely to help people avoid or recover from illness.

② Describe the effects of tobacco on the user and on others who breathe tobacco smoke.

③ Explain how alcohol affects the user physically and mentally.

④ Describe the consequences of abusing different types of legal and illegal drugs.

⑤ Identify ways to break an addiction to drugs, tobacco, or alcohol.

⑥ Describe ways to avoid using drugs, tobacco, and alcohol.

Drugs, tobacco, and alcohol—I've been hearing about them in school, but I have to admit I wasn't always paying attention. The only drug I really cared about was insulin. I've been taking that medicine since I got diabetes when I was four years old. So I know medicine can save your life, but I guess I should also know about drugs that can hurt you, especially after what happened to Jerry.

Jerry was thrown off our baseball team for smoking. Coach Randall said smoking is bad for us, and he doesn't want any player ruining his health. Coach also forbids drinking and all drugs.

No one has asked me to smoke or drink or anything, but I'm not sure what I'll do if it happens. I mean, I know I don't really want to smoke or drink, but how do you tell your friends that? What if they laugh or tease you? What if they stop asking you to go places with them?

I guess there's a lot I don't know. I could ask my older brother, but I'm not real sure he knows, even though he pretends to know everything. If I knew more, maybe I could have convinced Jerry to stop smoking before he was thrown off the team.

in Your journal

Read the account on this page. Do you know how drugs, tobacco, and alcohol harm your body? Do you know how to avoid these substances? Start your private journal entries on drugs, tobacco, and alcohol by answering these questions:

▶ What are two or three reasons you know for not using tobacco, alcohol, or other drugs?

▶ What are some ways you could say no to using drugs, tobacco, or alcohol?

When you reach the end of the chapter, you will use your journal entries to make an action plan that will help you stay free of drugs, tobacco, and alcohol.

1 What Are Drugs?

This lesson will help you find answers to questions that teens often ask about medicines. For example:

▶ **How do medicines help me when I'm sick?**

▶ **Why are there so many warning labels on medicines?**

▶ **What can I do to use medicines safely?**

Words to Know

drug
medicine
over-the-counter
   (OTC) medicine
prescription
   medicine
vaccine
antibiotic
penicillin
side effect
tolerance
misuse
abuse

Types of Drugs

A **drug** is *a substance other than food that changes the structure or function of your body or mind.* The word is most often used to describe cocaine, marijuana, and other illegal and harmful substances. Tobacco and alcohol are also drugs because they affect your body and mind. These drugs can also harm you.

Some drugs, however, change the structure or function of your body or mind in a good way. *Drugs that are used to cure or prevent diseases or other conditions* are called **medicines.** There are two kinds of medicines. **Over-the-counter (OTC) medicines** are *medicines that are considered safe enough to be taken without a written order from a doctor.* **Prescription** (pri·SKRIP·shuhn) **medicines** are *medicines that can be sold only with a written order from a doctor.*

Since the beginning of the twentieth century, discoveries of medicines, including antibiotics, vaccines, and pain medications, have dramatically improved people's life spans and levels of health.

How Medicines Help Your Body

People take medicines to prevent and cure disease. Medicines are also used to provide relief from symptoms while people are recovering from an illness or injury. Some of the types of medicines that are most widely used are described below.

■ **Vaccines** (vak·SEENZ) are *preparations of dead or weakened germs that cause the immune system to produce antibodies.* These antibodies keep you from getting certain diseases. You received vaccines for polio, measles, and other diseases during infancy and childhood. Vaccines are also required when you want to travel to most foreign countries.

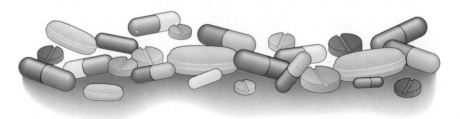

- **Antibiotics** (an·ti·by·AH·tiks) are *medicines that kill or stop the growth of certain germs.* Antibiotics can help if you have an infection caused by bacteria, but they cannot be used to treat colds, flu, or other illnesses caused by viruses. **Penicillin** (pen·uh·SI·luhn) is *a widely used antibiotic.*

- Some medicines treat heart and blood problems. They help control the heartbeat, open blocked blood vessels, and reduce high blood pressure.

- Some medicines reduce pain, such as the pain from a headache, sore muscles, a toothache, or a broken bone. Aspirin is a very common type of over-the-counter pain reliever.

Some medicines that reduce pain affect the central nervous system and may cause a change in moods and feelings.

Effects of Medicines on the Body

Both prescription and OTC medicines can have powerful effects on your body and mind. Your reaction to a medicine depends on these factors.

- The type and amount of the medicine

- The way the medicine is administered

- Your weight, age, and general health

- Any other medicines you are taking

- Any allergies you might have

Negative Reactions to Medicines

You should be aware of reactions you may experience when you take medicines. A **side effect** is *any reaction to a medicine other than the one intended.* Common side effects are drowsiness, dizziness, a rash, and an upset stomach.

Side effects may become very dangerous when you have more than one medicine in your body at the same time. The effects of one or both medicines may be greatly increased or decreased. Sometimes the result of combining medicines is unexpected.

If you have been taking a medicine for a long time, you may experience tolerance. **Tolerance** (TAHL·er·ence) develops *when the body becomes used to the effects of a medicine and needs greater amounts of the medicine to get that same effect.*

Did You Know?

Reye's Syndrome

Children under 18 years of age who have the flu, chicken pox, or other viral infections should not take aspirin. There is an association between the use of aspirin for these infections and the development of Reye's syndrome. Reye's syndrome is marked by vomiting, loss of consciousness, and seizures. It can be life threatening.

Methods of Taking Medicines

Medicines come in many forms and are taken into the body in several ways, as shown in **Figure 8.1.**

Figure 8.1
How Medicines Enter the Body

The most common ways of taking medicines are direct application to the affected area and administration through the mouth or by injection.

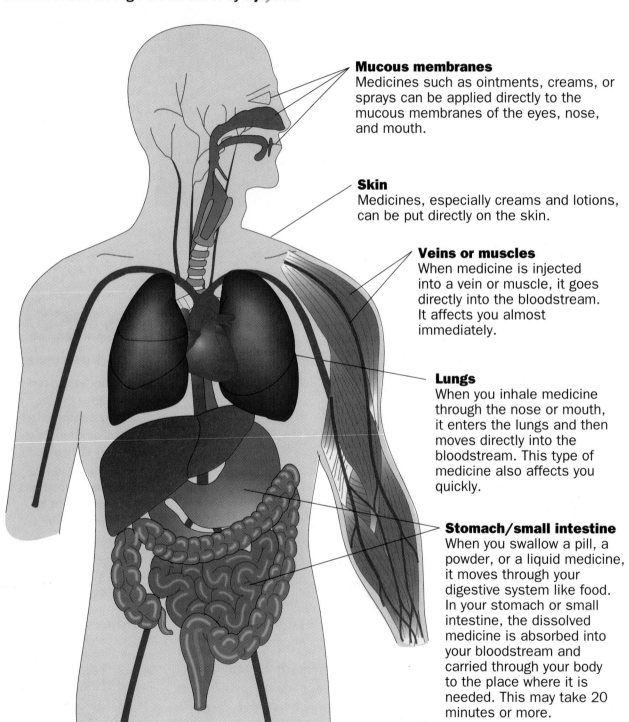

Mucous membranes
Medicines such as ointments, creams, or sprays can be applied directly to the mucous membranes of the eyes, nose, and mouth.

Skin
Medicines, especially creams and lotions, can be put directly on the skin.

Veins or muscles
When medicine is injected into a vein or muscle, it goes directly into the bloodstream. It affects you almost immediately.

Lungs
When you inhale medicine through the nose or mouth, it enters the lungs and then moves directly into the bloodstream. This type of medicine also affects you quickly.

Stomach/small intestine
When you swallow a pill, a powder, or a liquid medicine, it moves through your digestive system like food. In your stomach or small intestine, the dissolved medicine is absorbed into your bloodstream and carried through your body to the place where it is needed. This may take 20 minutes or more.

Medicine Safety

The federal government ensures that medicines are safe by strictly controlling the use of medicines and the information given to you about them. The United States Food and Drug Administration (FDA) tests all medicines before they are sold to make sure they are safe. Often it takes five or more years to determine a medicine's long-term effects, including its side effects for different groups of people.

The FDA then decides whether the medicine must be sold with a prescription or if it can be sold over the counter, without a prescription. Even if the FDA allows a medicine to be sold over the counter, the medicine is safe only when used as directed.

Labeling Rules

The FDA requires drug manufacturers to put certain information on medicine labels. Prescription labels must say how and when to take the medicine, how much to take, and special instructions for taking it. **Figure 8.2** is a sample prescription label.

Q & A ?

What's in a Name?

Q: What are generic drugs?

A: Generic drugs are approved by the FDA and are known by their chemical names. Generic drugs contain the same ingredients as brand name drugs and are often produced by the same companies. However, they cost 30 to 80 percent less.

Figure 8.2
Label on a Prescription Medicine

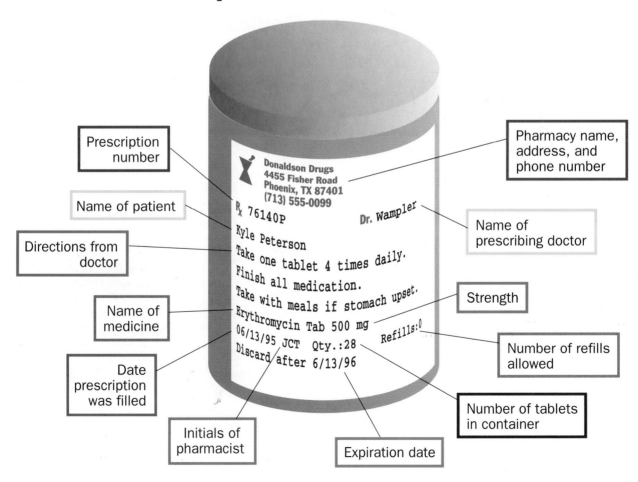

Prescription number

Name of patient

Directions from doctor

Name of medicine

Date prescription was filled

Initials of pharmacist

Pharmacy name, address, and phone number

Name of prescribing doctor

Strength

Number of refills allowed

Number of tablets in container

Expiration date

Donaldson Drugs
4455 Fisher Road
Phoenix, TX 87401
(713) 555-0099

Rx 76140P   Dr. Wampler

Kyle Peterson
Take one tablet 4 times daily.
Finish all medication.
Take with meals if stomach upset.
Erythromycin Tab 500 mg
06/13/95 JCT Qty.:28   Refills:0
Discard after 6/13/96

Explain in your journal some reasons why people may not use their medicines properly.

People are able to use over-the-counter (OTC) medicines without the advice and instruction of a doctor. Therefore, OTC medicine labels are required to have a great deal of important information on them. **Figure 8.3** is a sample OTC label.

Tips for Using Medicines Safely

When using medicines, follow these safety guidelines.

- Ask your doctor or a pharmacist if you are not sure which OTC medicine to buy or how to use an OTC medicine.

- Take medicines only as directed on the OTC medicine label or as prescribed by your doctor.

- Take medicines only for their intended purpose.

- If an OTC medicine does not help you, talk with a parent or another adult who knows about medicines. You may need to call your doctor.

- Destroy all medicines after their expiration dates pass.

- Keep medicines in child-resistant containers, and place them where children cannot reach them.

Figure 8.3
Label on an Over-the-Counter Medicine

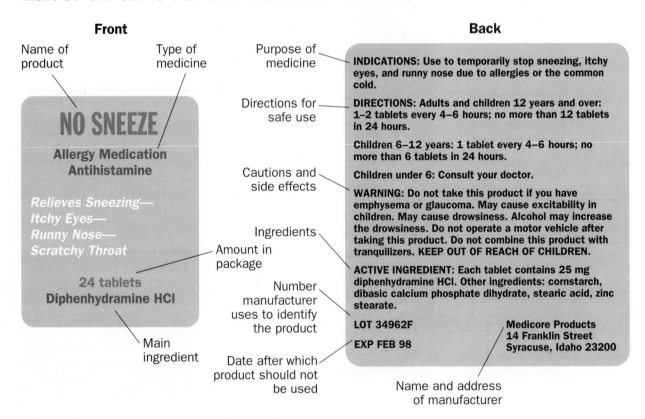

Front

Name of product

Type of medicine

NO SNEEZE

Allergy Medication
Antihistamine

Relieves Sneezing—
Itchy Eyes—
Runny Nose—
Scratchy Throat

24 tablets
Diphenhydramine HCl

Amount in package

Main ingredient

Back

Purpose of medicine

INDICATIONS: Use to temporarily stop sneezing, itchy eyes, and runny nose due to allergies or the common cold.

Directions for safe use

DIRECTIONS: Adults and children 12 years and over: 1–2 tablets every 4–6 hours; no more than 12 tablets in 24 hours.

Children 6–12 years: 1 tablet every 4–6 hours; no more than 6 tablets in 24 hours.

Children under 6: Consult your doctor.

Cautions and side effects

WARNING: Do not take this product if you have emphysema or glaucoma. May cause excitability in children. May cause drowsiness. Alcohol may increase the drowsiness. Do not operate a motor vehicle after taking this product. Do not combine this product with tranquilizers. KEEP OUT OF REACH OF CHILDREN.

Ingredients

ACTIVE INGREDIENT: Each tablet contains 25 mg diphenhydramine HCl. Other ingredients: cornstarch, dibasic calcium phosphate dihydrate, stearic acid, zinc stearate.

Number manufacturer uses to identify the product

LOT 34962F

EXP FEB 98

Date after which product should not be used

Medicore Products
14 Franklin Street
Syracuse, Idaho 23200

Name and address of manufacturer

Recognizing Misuse and Abuse of Drugs

People can harm themselves when taking medicines or other drugs. They may do this through **misuse,** which means *not taking or using medicines the way the doctor ordered.* **Abuse** (uh·BYOOS), another serious problem, is *using drugs in ways that are unhealthy or illegal.* **Figure 8.4** gives examples of misuse and abuse.

Figure 8.4
Signs of Drug Misuse and Abuse

Drug Misuse	Drug Abuse
Taking a medicine for longer than prescribed	Using a medicine for nonmedical purposes
Not taking a medicine for the full time prescribed	Swallowing or breathing a substance that was not meant to enter the body
Changing the amount of a medicine you are taking or mixing medicines without asking your doctor	Using a drug in a way that is harmful physically, mentally, or socially
Using an old prescription medicine without checking with your doctor	
Using a medicine prescribed for someone else	

Teen Issues

More Is Not Better ACTIVITY!

Suppose a sick friend is taking medicine prescribed by her doctor. She wants to get better in time for a dance Friday night, so she decides to take twice as much medicine. What would you tell her? If she insisted on taking more medicine, what could you do?

Review   Lesson 1

Using complete sentences, answer the following questions on a separate sheet of paper.

Reviewing Terms and Facts

1. **Identify**   What are the four types of medicines that are most widely used?
2. **List**   Name three factors that affect your reaction to a medicine.
3. **Vocabulary**   Define the term *side effect.* Use it in an original sentence.
4. **Give Examples**   Name four ways to use medicines safely.

Thinking Critically

5. **Infer**   Why might one doctor prescribe different medicines for two people who have the same illness?
6. **Explain**   Why do some medicines require a prescription?

Applying Health Concepts

7. **Consumer Health**   Create a collage of advertisements for over-the-counter medicines. What kinds of details do the ads provide about the products? Do they list the effects, how to use, or the cost? Do you have enough information to make a wise choice?

What Tobacco Does to Your Body

This lesson will help you find answers to questions that teens often ask about tobacco. For example:

▶ **How can smoking cigarettes affect my health?**

▶ **Why is smokeless tobacco harmful?**

Words to Know

cancer
nicotine
tar
carbon monoxide
emphysema
secondhand
   smoke
snuff

What Is in Tobacco Smoke?

Suppose the air in your school was polluted with 3,000 chemicals. What would you do? What would your teachers, parents, and others in the community do? Tobacco smoke has more than 3,000 chemicals. At least 43 of them are known to cause **cancer,** *a serious disease caused by the uncontrolled growth of cells.* Many other substances in tobacco smoke can interfere with the way your body works. Some harmful substances in tobacco smoke are listed below.

■ **Nicotine** (NI·kuh·teen) is *a stimulant drug that speeds up the heartbeat.* It causes addiction.

■ **Tar** is *a thick, dark liquid formed when tobacco burns.* Tar coats the inside of the lungs and can cause disease.

■ **Carbon monoxide** (KAR·buhn muh·NAHK·syd) is *a poisonous gas produced when tobacco burns.* This gas is also found in car exhaust.

HEALTH LAB
Finding Hidden Messages

*I*ntroduction: Companies advertise to convince people to buy their products. Cigarette advertisers, for example, frequently use selling techniques that involve hidden messages. To make wise buying choices, you need to be aware of these techniques.

Objective: Identify the hidden messages used in cigarette advertisements.

Materials and Method: Look through magazines and newspapers for cigarette advertisements. Cut out at least one example of each of these advertising techniques.

▶ Bandwagon: Everyone else buys and uses this product, so you should, too.

▶ Testimonials: People you trust and admire use this product.

Why Do Young People Smoke?

Some of the reasons young people smoke are listed below.

■ They want to fit in with their friends. However, only about one in ten teens ages 12 to 17 smokes (see **Figure 8.5**).

■ They are trying to seem older and more adult. However, the number of adults who smoke has sharply decreased, from 65.4 percent in 1974 to 28.2 percent in 1991. Many adults who once smoked quit because of concern for their health.

■ They believe that smoking won't hurt their health for many years. These young people don't realize that the harmful effects start with the first cigarette. **Figure 8.6** on pages 228 and 229 shows how smoking affects the body.

■ They are persuaded to smoke by advertising. Cigarette companies spend $4 billion a year to promote their products.

Figure 8.5
12- to 17-Year-Olds Who Smoke

Why do you think many teens are choosing not to smoke cigarettes?

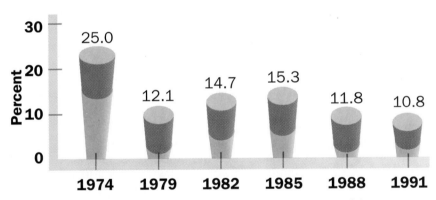

Source: U.S. Department of Commerce, *Statistical Abstract of the United States, 1993.*

▶ Popularity appeal: Using this product will make you popular with others.

▶ Lifestyle: Using this product will help you find friends and have fun.

Put the ads on a piece of posterboard or on separate sheets of paper. Under each ad, write the technique used in the ad and its specific hidden message.

Observation and Analysis:
Share your ads with your classmates. See if everyone agrees about the hidden message in each ad. Why do advertisers use hidden messages when selling cigarettes? Would these ads convince you to buy the products? Why or why not?

Cancer, heart disease, and other effects of smoking may take years to develop. Sometimes it is hard for young people to look that far into the future. Explain in your journal how you would convince a friend not to smoke because of the health risks.

Your Total Health

Smoking and Eating

A study, published in the *Journal of the American Dietetic Association,* has shown that smokers tend to consume more calories, fat, caffeine, and alcohol than nonsmokers. Women smokers also tend to eat fewer fruits and vegetables than women nonsmokers. This kind of diet, plus smoking, greatly increases the chances of heart disease and cancer.

Figure 8.6
The Harmful Effects of Smoking on the Body

Smoking cigarettes is harmful to many parts of the body.

Skin Smoking makes people look older because it causes their skin to wrinkle earlier than nonsmokers' skin.

Mouth, Teeth, and Throat Cigarette smoke causes bad breath and stains the teeth. Chemicals in the smoke can cause cancer of the mouth and throat.

Lungs The tar in cigarette smoke coats the inside of the lungs so they cannot work as well as they should. Tar is one cause of **emphysema** (em·fuh·SEE·muh), *a disease that occurs when the tiny air sacs in the lungs are damaged or destroyed.* Chemicals in the smoke can also cause lung cancer. Nearly 87 percent of lung cancer cases are caused by smoking.

Heart Nicotine increases the heart rate and causes the blood vessels to become narrower. Narrow vessels make the heart pump harder to move the blood through the body. This effort strains the heart and contributes to heart attacks.

Fingers Smoking leaves the fingers yellow and stained.

Stomach, Bladder, and Colon Harmful substances in the smoke can lead to stomach ulcers and bladder and colon cancer. Smoking makes a person ten times more likely to develop bladder cancer. Long-term smoking doubles the risk of colon cancer.

Brain   Nicotine is carried from the lungs to the brain within seven seconds. Nicotine is a stimulant that speeds up the way the body works. This drug also releases chemicals in the brain that cause the smoker to want more nicotine and to become addicted.

Blood Vessels   Carbon monoxide from the smoke reduces the amount of oxygen that the blood carries. As a result, body organs receive less oxygen from the blood.

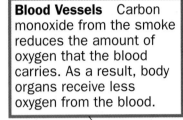

Effects of Secondhand Smoke

Secondhand smoke is *tobacco smoke in the air that is inhaled by nonsmokers.* Nonsmokers who breathe secondhand smoke are likely to develop some of the same health problems as those who smoke. For example, in 1993 the Environmental Protection Agency reported that secondhand smoke causes about 3,000 lung cancer deaths each year.

Many offices, factories, restaurants, and other places have banned smoking because of the health risks to nonsmokers. Due in part to these bans, some improvement has been made. For example, the estimated number of heart attacks due to secondhand smoke dropped from 200,000 in 1985 to 150,000 in 1994.

Secondhand smoke also causes other health problems. These problems include 150,000 to 300,000 cases of pneumonia and bronchitis every year among children under 18 months of age. You may have had burning eyes, a cough, an upset stomach, or a headache that was caused by breathing secondhand smoke.

Social Studies Connection

Smokers Need Not Apply ACTIVITY!

In 1985, 27 percent of all companies banned or restricted smoking by their employees. By 1992, the number of companies that banned smoking had more than doubled. Why would a company want employees who do not smoke? Why would employees want to work in a smoke-free building?

in your journal

Some smokers feel defensive when they are asked not to smoke. In your journal, examine the reasons why smokers might have this reaction.

Because of the dangers of secondhand smoke, many buildings—even the White House—no longer allow smoking.

Smokeless Tobacco

As its name indicates, smokeless tobacco is not smoked like a cigarette. It is chewed in coarsely ground form. It is also used as snuff. **Snuff** is *finely ground tobacco that is held in the mouth.* Because smokeless tobacco is not smoked, does this mean that it is safe? The answer is no.

This type of tobacco leads to serious health problems, especially in the mouth and stomach. When smokeless tobacco is placed in the mouth, its harmful substances mix with the saliva. The saliva comes into contact with the tissues of the mouth, which are sensitive. In addition, some of the saliva is swallowed and enters the stomach.

Smokeless tobacco is dangerous for many reasons.

- Smokeless tobacco is just as addictive as smoked tobacco.

- Tobacco juice can cause white spots on the gums and inside the cheeks. These spots can become cancerous.

- Swallowed tobacco can cause sores in the stomach.

- Smokeless tobacco causes bad breath and stains the teeth.

- Grit and sugar in the tobacco can damage gums and cause tooth decay and tooth loss.

- People who use smokeless tobacco often lose their sense of taste and sense of smell.

Did You Know?

No More Spitting

Because of the health risks, smokeless tobacco was banned in minor league baseball in 1993. Players, coaches, and managers who are caught using smokeless tobacco on or around the ball field must pay a fine.

Review — Lesson 2

Using complete sentences, answer the following questions on a separate sheet of paper.

Reviewing Terms and Facts

1. **Identify**   List three harmful substances found in tobacco smoke and describe each one.
2. **Vocabulary**   Which of the following are diseases caused by tobacco and which is a type of tobacco: *cancer, emphysema, snuff?*
3. **Vocabulary**   Define the term *secondhand smoke.* Use it in an original sentence.
4. **Recall**   Identify four of the dangers of using smokeless tobacco.

Thinking Critically

5. **Justify**   If you were a doctor, would you treat patients who insist on their right to smoke? Justify your decision.
6. **Explain**   Why could smoking be considered a social problem as well as a health problem?

Applying Health Concepts

7. **Consumer Health**   Create an advertisement against smoking. For example, the ad might show everyone avoiding a person who smokes because of his or her bad breath. Your class might post the ads in the school cafeteria.

What Alcohol Does to Your Body

This lesson will help you find answers to questions that teens often ask about alcohol. For example:

▶ Why should teenagers not drink?

▶ How does drinking alcohol affect a person's health?

Words to Know

alcohol
cirrhosis
fetal alcohol
syndrome (FAS)
blood alcohol
level (BAL)

Cultural Diversity

Approaches to Alcohol ACTIVITY!

The Hopi and some other Native American groups in the U.S. Southwest have banned alcohol. They feel that it threatens their way of life. Research other cultural groups to determine their rules about alcohol use. Write a one-page report about the culture of your choice.

Many young people who choose not to drink alcohol try to encourage their peers not to drink by teaching them about the dangers of drinking.

What Is Alcohol?

Alcohol (AL·kuh·hawl) is *a depressant drug that is produced by a chemical reaction in some foods and that has powerful effects on the body.* Some people who drink alcohol become addicted to it. When a person drinks alcohol, it enters the stomach, just as food does. However, alcohol has no nutrients—only empty calories. From the stomach and small intestine, alcohol passes quickly into the bloodstream. Because alcohol is a depressant, it causes the brain and other parts of the body to work more slowly (see **Figure 8.7**).

Why Do Some Young People Drink?

■ Some teenagers drink alcohol to fit in with their friends.

■ Some young people want to try to seem more grown up. Yet a young person who has been drinking is more likely to act immature than mature.

■ Some young people want to escape their problems. For example, they think that drinking can make the pain of a poor grade or an argument with a friend go away. Instead, drinking adds new problems.

■ Some young people see family members, and other people drink. However, drinking is against the law for anyone under the age of 21.

Figure 8.7
The Harmful Effects of Alcohol on the Body
Many parts of the body are affected by alcohol.

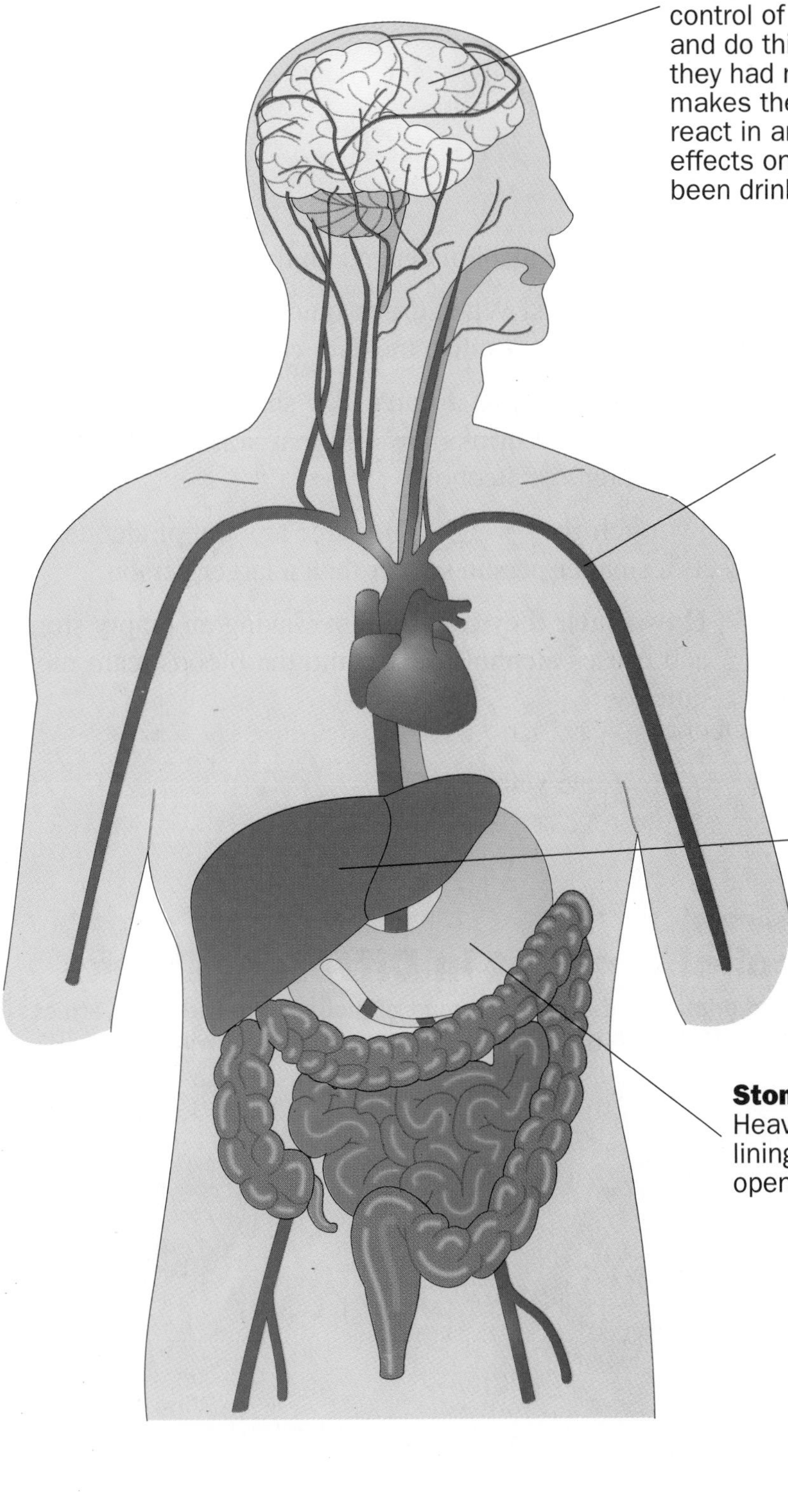

Brain
Alcohol slows down the way the brain works so the person has trouble thinking. Often drinkers do not realize that the alcohol has affected their thinking. In fact, many people who are drunk believe they are in complete control of themselves. Still, they often say and do things they would not say or do if they had not been drinking. Alcohol also makes the drinker clumsy and slower to react in an emergency. In this way, alcohol's effects on the brain make someone who has been drinking a very dangerous driver.

Blood vessels
Alcohol widens the blood vessels. More blood passes through the vessels, making the drinker feel warmer. However, as more blood flows close to the surface of the body, the body loses heat. Body temperature drops. A person who has been drinking may feel warm even in very cold weather. This may lead the person to stay outside too long, creating a dangerous situation.

Liver
Blood passes through the liver. The liver slowly changes any alcohol that is in the blood into water and carbon dioxide. However, heavy drinking over a long period can cause **cirrhosis** (suh·ROH·sis), *which is destruction and scarring of liver tissue.* Cirrhosis can lead to death.

Stomach
Heavy drinking can damage the lining of the stomach and cause open sores.

Fetal Alcohol Syndrome

The bloodstream carries alcohol throughout the body. If a pregnant woman drinks alcohol, her unborn baby will have alcohol in its bloodstream. This alcohol can cause the baby to develop **fetal** (FEE·tuhl) **alcohol syndrome** (SIN·drohm), or **FAS,** *a group of physical and mental problems caused by alcohol.* Babies with FAS often weigh less than average and may suffer from birth defects and mental retardation. Doctors are not sure how much drinking causes fetal alcohol syndrome. Pregnant women can make sure their babies do not develop this condition by not drinking any alcohol.

Factors That Influence Alcohol's Effects

People's reactions to alcohol depend on these factors:

- **How fast they drink.** When drunk quickly, alcohol builds up in the bloodstream faster than the liver can process it.

- **How much they drink. Figure 8.8** shows three types of drinks. Although the drinks are different sizes, they all contain equal amounts of alcohol.

  - **How much they weigh.** The same amount of alcohol affects a smaller person sooner than a larger person.

  - **How much they have eaten.** Having an empty stomach causes alcohol to pass into the bloodstream more quickly.

Because of the health risks, alcoholic beverages carry a warning label.

GOVERNMENT WARNING: (1) ACCORDING TO THE SURGEON GENERAL, WOMEN SHOULD NOT DRINK ALCOHOLIC BEVERAGES DURING PREGNANCY BECAUSE OF THE RISK OF BIRTH DEFECTS. (2) CONSUMPTION OF ALCOHOLIC BEVERAGES IMPAIRS YOUR ABILITY TO DRIVE A CAR OR OPERATE MACHINERY, AND MAY CAUSE HEALTH PROBLEMS.

Figure 8.8
Alcohol Content in Different Drinks

A mixed drink has the same amount of alcohol and the same effect on the brain and body as a can of beer or a glass of wine does.

Mixed drink
1.5 oz. of liquor

Beer
12 oz.

Wine
4 oz.

- **How they feel.** A person's mood before drinking affects the mood after drinking. For instance, depression may increase.

- **The use of other drugs.** Even aspirin can increase alcohol's effects. Mixing alcohol and other depressants can be fatal.

Blood alcohol level (BAL) is *a measure of the amount of alcohol in the bloodstream.* **Figure 8.9** shows various BALs and the effects on a 100-pound person.

Figure 8.9
The Effects of Alcohol

Blood Alcohol Level	Alcohol Drunk in 2 Hours	Effect on a 100-Pound Person
0.05 percent	1 mixed drink or 1–2 cans of beer	Some clumsiness and slower reactions; judgment and self-control slightly affected
0.1 percent	2–3 mixed drinks or 3–4 cans of beer	Clumsiness; problems in seeing; more loss of judgment and self-control
0.2 percent	3–4 mixed drinks or 5–6 cans of beer	Problems controlling muscles; cannot think clearly or remember; great loss of self-control, including control of emotions
0.3 percent	4–5 mixed drinks or 7–8 cans of beer	Problems moving, seeing, hearing, and judging distances
0.4 percent	6–7 mixed drinks or 9–10 cans of beer	Unable to move; brain barely working; cannot control vomiting or urination
0.5 percent	more than 7 mixed drinks or 10 cans of beer	In coma, brain unable to control breathing, which may lead to death

Review — Lesson 3

Using complete sentences, answer the following questions on a separate sheet of paper.

Reviewing Terms and Facts

1. **Vocabulary** Define the term *alcohol* and use it in a sentence.
2. **Give Examples** List three reasons some young people drink alcohol.
3. **Identify** List five factors that affect a person's reaction to alcohol.

Thinking Critically

4. **Explain** Why might a person who has been drinking think that the alcohol has not affected his or her ability to drive a car?
5. **Infer** In what ways might drinking affect a person's relationships?

Applying Health Concepts

6. **Health of Others** Work with a partner to think of a slogan that would persuade young people not to drink. Put your slogan on a button or poster.

Health Update

People at Work

Smoke-free Class of 2000

Former U.S. Surgeon General C. Everett Koop warned the public of the harmful effects of smoking in the 1980s. He called for a smoke-free society by the year 2000.

In response, three groups—the American Cancer Society, the American Heart Association, and the American Lung Association—began working together on a program in 1988. They called it the Smoke-free Class of 2000.

The program targets the 3 million students who started first grade in 1988 and who will graduate from high school in the year 2000. The goal is that all the graduating seniors that year will be nonsmokers.

The program educates students about the risks of smoking and gives them the skills they need to choose not to smoke. It also encourages these students to become antismoking advocates, or spokespersons.

Substance Abuse Counselor

Judy Philbin works at The Campus, a residential drug abuse treatment center for teenagers. Judy meets with the teens individually, as well as together with their families, to help them deal with their problems. One of her jobs is to arrange support systems for the teenagers after they leave The Campus.

Judy has a bachelor's degree in social work. She recently received certification as a counselor in her state. She is supervised by the doctors, psychologists, and social workers at the center.

Judy likes helping people. She is frustrated when a resident doesn't respond to treatment. However, she gets great satisfaction when one of the teens in her care regains control of his or her life and leaves The Campus.

CON$UMER FOCU$

"Nonalcoholic" Beverages

Nonalcoholic beers and wines are advertised as good substitutes for adults who want to limit their intake of alcohol. For example, people concerned about drinking and driving may buy these beverages.

They are not good for everyone, however. Almost all of the nonalcoholic brews on the market do contain some alcohol—usually less than ½ of 1 percent. Some experts, including those at the Center for Science in the Public Interest, fear that young people who drink nonalcoholic brews might go on to drink alcoholic beer. The experts are also concerned that these brews will have negative effects on alcoholics.

Sports
and
Recreation

TAG: You're Substance Free!

Archie Griffin won the Heisman trophy twice for being the nation's outstanding college football player. He also won hundreds of other athletic awards and was a top rusher in professional football.

Still, Griffin is aware of the needs of his community. In 1989, he helped develop a program called TAG (To Achieve Greatness) Team. The TAG Team helps fifth graders consider what they want from life and make a deliberate decision not to use drugs. Griffin and the teenagers who lead the activities stress what young people can achieve by avoiding drugs.

Griffin is now a college athletic director. There, he is a substance-free role model for hundreds of athletes who hope to follow in his footsteps.

Teens Making a Difference

It's Not Just a FAD

Students in one Pennsylvania school district are really excited about a new FAD—it's a Fight Against Drugs.

First, students in middle schools and high schools learn about the dangers of drugs in after-school programs. Then, they join FAD by signing a contract, promising that they will not take drugs.

FAD members don't stop there. They take their message to the elementary schools to teach young children about drugs through skits and puppet shows. They give out FAD T-shirts and make floats for local parades.

By serving as good role models, these FAD members hope to influence younger students to stay away from drugs.

4 What Are Illegal Drugs?

This lesson will help you find answers to questions that teens often ask about illegal drugs. For example:

▶ What are the dangers of using illegal drugs?

▶ What are the main types of illegal drugs?

Words to Know

- addiction
- stimulant
- amphetamine
- cocaine
- depressant
- narcotic
- hallucinogen
- flashback
- inhalant
- marijuana
- anabolic steroid

The Dangers of Drug Abuse

The use of illegal drugs and the abuse of legal medicines can have serious, sometimes deadly, physical effects on the user. These effects can occur even the first time the drug is used. Drug use is also harmful to social and emotional health. It causes arguments and tension in families, loss of friendships, and poor grades in school. Users may also get into trouble with the police and ruin plans they may have had for the future.

Many drug users become addicted. **Addiction** (uh·DIK·shuhn) is *a physical or mental need for a drug or other substance.* Some frequently abused addictive drugs are discussed below. **Figure 8.10** shows trends in the use of several of these drugs among young teens.

Figure 8.10
Trends in Drug Use for Eighth Graders

The use of drugs among young teens has increased from 1991 to 1993.

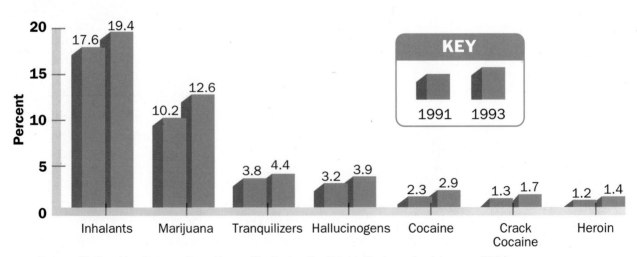

Source: National Institute on Drug Abuse, Monitoring the Future Study, revised January 1994.

Stimulants

Stimulants (STIM·yuh·luhnts) are *drugs that speed up the body's functions.* They cause blood pressure to rise, the heart to beat faster, breathing rate to increase, and the pupils of the eyes to dilate. Stimulants can be swallowed, smoked, inhaled, and injected. Two *stimulants that are very dangerous and highly addictive* are **amphetamines** (am·FE·tuh·meenz) and **cocaine** (koh·KAYN).

Amphetamines

Amphetamines may be prescribed by doctors to treat attention disorders in children, obesity, and sleep disorders. All other uses of amphetamines are illegal. Some of the street names for amphetamines are speed, uppers, ice, and crank.

Side effects of any use of amphetamines include headache, blurred vision, dizziness, restlessness, and anxiety. Use of high doses can cause loss of coordination, physical collapse, heart failure, and irregular heartbeat. Long-term use can lead to severe mental problems, including hallucinations and delusions. When amphetamines are injected or inhaled, blood pressure may rise very quickly, causing seizure and death.

Cocaine and Crack

Cocaine is *a highly addictive stimulant drug.* Although cocaine is approved for a few medical uses, it is rarely used because it is highly addictive. All other use is illegal.

The effects of cocaine are unpredictable and very dangerous. Even the first time, the user's soaring blood pressure and heart rate can cause a fatal heart attack or seizure. Here are some other dangers of cocaine use.

- Sleeplessness, loss of appetite, nervousness, and suspicion

- Infection with the human immunodeficiency virus (HIV) or hepatitis B when it is injected with an infected needle

- Death or injury from fire while preparing crack or freebase, a form of cocaine that is smoked

Depressants

Depressants (di·PRE·suhnts) are *drugs that slow down the body's functions and reactions.* They cause the heart rate and blood pressure to drop. Breathing and brain activity slow down. It is illegal to use these drugs without a prescription. Two main types of depressants are barbiturates and tranquilizers. Dangers of using depressants include poor coordination, slurred speech, drowsiness, poor judgment, confusion, and addiction.

Describe in your journal some ways that other people's drug use could affect you, directly or indirectly. Think about the physical, mental, and legal consequences of drug use.

Narcotics

Narcotics (nar·KAH·tics) are *a group of drugs that relieve pain.* This group of drugs includes morphine, codeine, and heroin. Doctors prescribe morphine to reduce severe pain, and codeine is found in some prescription cough syrups. Legal narcotics are strongly addictive and must be used very carefully.

Heroin has no legal uses. Heroin users risk unconsciousness or death. People who inject heroin also risk getting HIV from infected needles.

Hallucinogens

Hallucinogens (huh·LOO·suhn·uh·jenz) are *illegal drugs that cause the user's brain to distort real images and to see and hear things that aren't real.* In other words, these drugs cause hallucinations. They also cause the user to lose control and to behave strangely or violently. PCP, also called angel dust, and LSD, or acid, are two very dangerous hallucinogens.

Because PCP blocks the ability to feel pain, users can injure themselves seriously without feeling it. People who use PCP or LSD often think they have super strength. Many have tried dangerous acts that caused their deaths. Both drugs can cause **flashbacks,** or *delayed effects,* long after use has stopped.

Inhalants

Inhalants (in·HAY·luhnts) are *substances whose fumes are breathed in to give the effect of a hallucinogen.* These substances are household products not meant to be taken into the body. Inhaling such substances is very dangerous and illegal. Even with the first use, the fumes can fill the lungs and smother the user. The fumes can also kill brain cells, causing permanent damage or death. Other effects are nausea, balance problems, trouble thinking, and violent behavior.

On the left is a normal spider web. On the right is a web made by a spider after being given a hallucinogen.

Marijuana

Marijuana (mehr·uh·WAHN·uh), also known as pot and grass, is *an illegal drug made from the hemp plant.* Marijuana increases heartbeat and pulse rate. It may cause panic attacks.

Marijuana users lack energy and lose interest in activities they used to enjoy. Marijuana interferes with concentration and memory and makes learning new information difficult. Users lack coordination and are unable to react well in emergencies.

Steroids

Anabolic steroids (a·nuh·BAH·lik STIR·oydz) are *synthetic drugs based on the male hormone called testosterone.* When people refer to "anabolic steroids," they usually shorten the term to "steroids." Doctors sometimes prescribe steroids to treat medical conditions. Steroids are used illegally to increase body weight and muscle strength. Steroids should never be used for this purpose because of the physical and mental dangers. The user may become violent and aggressive and deeply depressed. Steroids also cause severe acne, sexual underdevelopment in both males and females, liver cancer, and heart attacks.

Using steroids can lead to more than 70 bad side effects, some of which may not surface for years after use.

Today's News
ATHLETES BANNED from games

Review

Lesson 4

Using complete sentences, answer the following questions on a separate sheet of paper.

Reviewing Terms and Facts

1. **Vocabulary** What are the differences between the physical effects of *stimulants* and *depressants?*

2. **Identify** What are five side effects of using amphetamines?

3. **Vocabulary** Define the term *hallucinogens.*

4. **List** Give two reasons why even one use of inhalants can cause death.

Thinking Critically

5. **Decide** If someone offered you cocaine, saying that just one use can't hurt, what reply would you give? Explain your answer.

6. **Predict** What do you think would happen to the grades of a person who uses marijuana? Give reasons for your answer.

Applying Health Concepts

7. **Growth and Development** Make a poster that highlights the serious dangers of one of the drugs discussed in this lesson and discourages people from using that drug. Display the poster in your classroom.

Substance Addiction

This lesson will help you find answers to questions that teens often ask about substance addiction. For example:

▶ **What are the signs of addiction?**

▶ **How can people who are addicted get help?**

Math Connection

Addiction Adds Up

Figure out how much it would cost to buy one pack of cigarettes every day for one year. Name some ways that money could be used that would not be harmful to anyone's health.

What Is Addiction?

You have learned that addiction is a physical or mental need for or dependence on a drug or other substance. People may be addicted to many substances—medicines, illegal drugs, alcohol, or tobacco. When a person has a **physical dependence** on a substance, *the body needs the substance just to function.* If a user has a **psychological,** or mental, **dependence,** *the person believes that he or she needs the drug to feel good.*

With physical dependence, the user builds a tolerance for the drug and needs larger and larger amounts of the drug to get the desired effect. If the user stops taking the drug, he or she feels **withdrawal** (with·DRAW·uhl)—*a series of painful physical and mental symptoms.* The symptoms can include shakiness, a headache, an upset stomach, a jittery feeling, and panic when the person cannot get more of the drug. Sometimes withdrawal can lead to death.

Addictive Substances

These drugs can quickly cause a strong physical addiction.

- Stimulants (nicotine in tobacco, cocaine, crack, amphetamines, and others)

- Depressants (tranquilizers, barbiturates, and others)

- Narcotics (codeine, morphine, heroin, and others)

People who use marijuana run the risk of developing a psychological addiction. Alcohol can cause a physical or psychological addiction or both.

Breaking the Tobacco Habit

To help smokers quit, offer them these tips.

- Make a list of all your reasons to quit, and read the list whenever you want to smoke.

- Set small goals, such as quitting for one hour, then increasing to one day, and so on.

- Remember that signs of withdrawal, such as nervousness and problems sleeping, are temporary.

- Change your routine to avoid times and places when you smoked and to avoid the people with whom you smoked.

- Eat healthful snacks or start exercising when you feel the desire to have a cigarette.

- Watch for improvements in the way you feel and look.

- Reward yourself in some healthy ways for not smoking.

You can also offer smokers these suggestions if they find that they cannot quit alone.

- Ask a friend to quit with you. Talk about the temptations you face and think of ways to help each other overcome them.

- Ask for support from nonsmoking friends and family members. Have them remind you how much they want you to quit.

- Enroll in a stop-smoking program, such as the one offered by the American Cancer Society or by community groups such as the YMCA or YWCA.

Q & A ?

Real Risks

Q: Can I smoke cigarettes now and then without getting addicted?

A: Probably not. In a Virginia hospital study of 99 teenagers who smoked, 75 percent thought they were addicted and almost three-fourths had tried to quit at least once.

Breaking an Addiction to Alcohol or Drugs

Alcoholism, or *addiction to alcohol,* and drug addiction are illnesses. Most addicts cannot stop drinking or using drugs without getting help. People from all backgrounds and income levels can be addicted to these substances. As shown in **Figure 8.11** on the next page, drinking and taking drugs affect the lives of the users in many ways as their addiction progresses. Their health and their relationships at home, at school, and on the job are often affected.

Exercising instead of reaching for a cigarette can help the smoker quit.

in your journal

With what you have learned about addiction, discuss in your journal why it is better not to start using a drug—even once.

Alcoholics and drug addicts can be treated, but they are never considered cured of their disease. They are considered to be always in a recovering stage. Addicts must stay away from the substances to which they are addicted.

Recovering from alcoholism and drug addiction requires people to take the following steps.

- Admit the problem.
- Stop using the drug.
- Decide to change.
- Take responsibility for their actions.

Figure 8.11
Stages of Addiction
The addiction process may be slow, taking years, or it may start with only one use.

First Use/Occasional Use
The user may be curious or may want to be accepted socially. The person may feel that using the drug just once or just occasionally can't do any harm. The user may like the relaxed feeling the drug or alcohol gives.

Regular Use
The user needs the drug more often and in greater amounts; the user tries but can't control use. The user relies on the drug to solve problems and becomes angry if other people suggest there is a drug or alcohol problem. The user may offer excuses.

LIFE SKILLS
Understanding Alcoholism

*M*any people have wrong ideas about alcoholism. Perhaps someone you know is an alcoholic, or perhaps you have a friend whose relative is an alcoholic. Knowing the truth about alcoholism may help you deal with the problem.

Myth: If an alcoholic really wanted to, he or she could control the drinking.

Reality: Alcoholism is an incurable disease; it is possible to stop drinking, but the person can never drink again.

Myth: Family members should take responsibility for making the alcoholic stop drinking.

Reality: Families cannot make the alcoholic control or stop drinking.

Sources of help include support groups such as Alcoholics Anonymous (AA) and Narcotics Anonymous. Addicts attend meetings of these groups where they help each other resist using alcohol and drugs. Other sources of help are hospitals, mental health agencies, special counselors, and drug abuse treatment centers. Some treatment programs are designed especially to help young people.

Depending on how severe an addiction is, addicts may receive long-term or short-term treatment. They may stay at the center during treatment, or they may live at home and come in for treatment each day. For severe problems, halfway houses are provided to help the addict learn to cope with everyday life.

Intensified Use
The user may mix drugs and may try to hide the problem. He or she can still function in everyday life but with difficulty.

Total Dependence
Use is uncontrolled. The user is isolated from people and has health problems. The user may have a major crisis, such as a serious accident.

Myth: If children of alcoholics would behave better, their parent would stop drinking.

Reality: The family members of an alcoholic did not cause the alcoholism and should not feel guilty.

Follow-up Activities

1. Conduct a survey to see how many people believe any of these myths. Make a poster that includes the results of the survey and the list of myths and facts.

2. Contact a support group for alcoholics or their families. Ask them to send you brochures. Ask to display them in class. Use the information in the brochures to add to the list of myths and facts.

The Road to Recovery

Q: Who or what is an enabler?

A: Enablers are people who make it easier for an alcoholic to continue to drink. Enablers might clean up messes, make excuses, or take over the alcoholic's work. Enablers must stop helping so the alcoholic will face the consequences of drinking.

Help for Families of Substance Abusers

Along with programs offered by hospitals, substance abuse treatment centers, and other agencies, special groups provide help and support for families of alcoholics and drug addicts.

- Alateen helps children of alcoholic parents learn how to cope with problems at home.

- Al-Anon helps husbands, wives, and friends of alcoholics learn more about this disease. At meetings, they also discuss ways to meet their own needs.

- Nar-Anon holds meetings for families of drug addicts.

Alateen helps teens take control of their own lives while continuing to love the alcoholic parent.

Lesson 5 Review

Using complete sentences, answer the following questions on a separate sheet of paper.

Reviewing Terms and Facts

1. **Vocabulary** What is the difference between *physical dependence* and *psychological dependence?*

2. **Vocabulary** Define the term *withdrawal.* Use it in an original sentence.

3. **Identify** Name three ways smokers can quit on their own.

4. **Recall** Name one feature of each stage of addiction.

Thinking Critically

5. **Compare** Name one similarity and one difference between addiction to smoking and addiction to alcohol and drugs.

6. **Explain** Why is an alcoholic always considered to be recovering rather than cured?

Applying Health Concepts

7. **Health of Others** Review for the class a magazine article about someone who overcame some form of drug addiction. Explain how the addiction started, the problems it caused, and how the person managed to break the addiction. Describe the person's life before, during, and after the addiction.

8. **Growth and Development** Out of every class of 25 students, four to six children live in alcoholic families. Most of them think they are the only ones at school facing these problems. Write a letter to these students and encourage them to talk to someone they trust.

Choosing to Be Substance Free

This lesson will help you find answers to questions that teens often ask about being substance free. For example:

▶ **What are some ways I can avoid using tobacco, alcohol, and drugs?**

▶ **What are the laws about substance use?**

Word to Know

alternative

Why You Should Avoid Tobacco, Alcohol, and Drugs

Staying healthy right now—looking good and feeling good—means saying no to tobacco, alcohol, and drugs. Reaching all your goals in the future also depends on staying substance free. Only you can keep your body free of harmful substances, and millions of other young people across the nation are doing it. They join you in staying substance free, healthy, and ready for life. **Figure 8.12** shows you many reasons not to use tobacco, alcohol, and drugs.

Figure 8.12
Reasons to Refuse

Reasons Not to Use Tobacco	Reasons Not to Use Alcohol	Reasons Not to Use Illegal Drugs
• Tobacco is addictive. • Smoking makes people's breath, hair, and clothes smell. It also stains their teeth and fingers. • Using tobacco can cause many serious health problems. Smoking kills 400,000 people each year. It is the leading cause of preventable death. • Smoking can make people less fit for sports and other activities. • Using tobacco is expensive.	• Alcohol can be addictive. • Drinkers have trouble controlling their bodies and emotions. They become clumsy and often do or say things they regret. • Drinking often makes people feel sick to their stomachs. • Drinking can lead to violence because alcohol causes lack of judgment and inability to control temperament. • Drinking does not solve problems. Instead, it creates them.	• Many abused drugs are addictive. • Abused drugs can cause permanent damage to a person's physical and/or mental health. They can lead to death. • Many amphetamines, narcotics, hallucinogens, and other drugs are produced in illegal laboratories by untrained people. Often chemicals—from baking powder to rat poison—are added to the drugs. The effects are completely unpredictable.

The Law Is on Your Side

Tobacco

The penalties for drug and alcohol use in some cultures are harsh. Under Islam (the major religion in Arabic countries), anyone caught drinking alcohol gets 80 lashes. In a paragraph, tell whether you think that drug use would change in the United States if we had these types of drug laws.

■ Most states have laws that permit the sale of tobacco only to people who are 18 or older.

■ The National Interagency Council on Smoking and Health has created the "Nonsmoker's Bill of Rights."
—The right to breathe clean air
—The right to speak out
—The right to act (to get smoking banned in certain places)

Alcohol

■ All states have set 21 as the minimum age for legal possession and purchase of all forms of alcohol.

Sales of tobacco in stores and vending machines is regulated by law.

This store sells tobacco products only to people who can prove they are at least 18 years of age.

When police stop a driver whom they suspect of drinking, they ask the driver to take a sobriety test, such as walking a straight line.

MAKING HEALTHY DECISIONS
Practicing Refusal Skills

Judd's first football game went all wrong. First, a pass slipped through his hands. Then the fans were yelling so loud that he couldn't hear Pete, the quarterback, make the call.

Judd ran the wrong play and ended up by himself on the wrong side of the field. He saw the disgusted look on Pete's face. He'll never want me to play again, Judd told himself.

After his team lost the game, Judd tried to hide in the locker room, but Pete found him. "Tough game tonight, but don't worry about it," Pete said. "Come to my house later. We're going to drown all our problems."

Judd couldn't believe that Pete wasn't mad. He was even more surprised when he got to Pete's house. Pete opened the door and stuck a can of beer in his hand. He smiled at Judd. "You drink a couple of those and you'll forget this whole game!"

What should Judd do? He wants to be part of the team, but he doesn't want to drink. To help him make up his mind, Judd decides to use the six-step decision-making process.

❶ **State the situation**
❷ **List the options**

In most states, a driver with a blood alcohol level (BAL) of 0.10 percent will be arrested. At least 11 states have lowered this level to 0.08 percent. Some states have even lower levels for drivers who are under the legal drinking age.

Drugs

The federal government groups drugs by their potential for abuse. Schedule I drugs, such as marijuana and LSD, are illegal. Drugs in Schedules II through V, such as stimulants and tranquilizers, have accepted, legal medical uses.

Some penalties for drug offenses are high. For example, the minimum federal jail term for possessing LSD is 10.1 years.

Penalties for selling illegal drugs are usually even higher than penalties for possessing them.

in your journal

Imagine that you are a parent. Explain in your journal what you will tell your children about using drugs, tobacco, and alcohol. Write a paragraph about each substance.

The sale and use of drugs is controlled by federal, state, and local laws.

③ **Weigh the possible outcomes**
④ **Consider your values**
⑤ **Make a decision and act**
⑥ **Evaluate the decision**

Follow-up Activities

1. Apply the six steps of the decision-making process to Judd's problem.
2. Role-play a situation in which you, as Judd, explain your decision to Pete.
3. List at least three positive actions that the team could take after a game that would not involve substance abuse.

List four reasons why you think some young people hesitate to say no to drugs. Then write what you would tell someone who offers that reason. For example, if a person accepts a cigarette because she is too shy to refuse it, what would you tell her?

Ways to Stay Substance Free

Pressure to use drugs, tobacco, and alcohol can come from many sources. It can come from others, such as "friends" who offer you these substances. Other pressure comes from advertising that tries to influence people to use tobacco and alcohol. Pressure can also come from within—from what young people tell themselves. For instance, a young person might think, if I don't smoke that cigarette, everyone will think I'm just a kid, or I have to drink this to fit in. She or he might think, I'll try this just once to prove that I'm not scared to do it.

The best way to refuse drugs, tobacco, and alcohol is to state your decision with confidence and without being insulting. Humor may help. The lists below offer some ideas to add to the ones you already know. If the person persists in offering, say, "I wish you wouldn't pressure me. I've made up my mind."

You can also say no with your actions. You can choose friends who are substance free and who know how to have fun without tobacco, alcohol, or drugs. You can avoid being around people who smoke, drink, or use other drugs. If someone starts using these substances, you can walk away.

No to Tobacco

- "I'm on the track team, and smoking would slow me down."
- "Not me! Even the smell makes me sick."
- "My grandfather died of lung cancer. He smoked all his life, but I'm not going to."
- "I don't want to smoke. It really bothers other people."
- "I have better things to do with my money than smoke."

No to Alcohol

- "I'm having a better time without drinking."
- "No, thanks. I need to keep all my brain cells working."
- "I've decided not to drink."
- "Are you kidding? My parents would ground me forever."
- "No way! I'd get thrown off the baseball team."

No to Drugs

- "No. I don't need to use drugs to have a good time."
- "There's no way that I'm going to risk destroying my brain."
- "I've got plans for my life, and I don't want to mess them up."
- "Please get that away from me. You can get arrested for just holding that stuff."

Teens who avoid using tobacco, alcohol, and drugs lead healthier lives. What healthy activities do you enjoy?

Alternatives to Drug and Alcohol Use

When you refuse drugs or alcohol, suggest a positive alternative. An **alternative** (ahl·TER·nuh·tiv) is *another way of thinking or acting*. For example, if a friend wants to sneak a beer, you might suggest playing basketball, in-line skating, or listening to music. More healthy alternatives include the following:

- **Practice something you like to do.** Practice until you are really good at it. Become a great skateboarder, a gourmet cook, a computer whiz, or the best tennis player in the school.

- **Be a volunteer.** Volunteer to work at a hospital, day-care center, or nursing home. If you like sports, help coach the Special Olympics. Volunteer to teach people how to read.

- **Start your own business.** Let friends and neighbors know that you are available for baby-sitting, yard work, and other odd jobs. Post a sign advertising your business on the bulletin board at the local supermarket.

Learning a new skill is one good alternative to using drugs and alcohol. Have you always wanted to play a musical instrument? Teach yourself, or have someone teach you.

Review

Lesson 6

Using complete sentences, answer the following questions on a separate sheet of paper.

Reviewing Terms and Facts

1. **Identify** Give two reasons not to use each of the following: tobacco, alcohol, drugs.

2. **Recall** In most states, how old must a person be to purchase tobacco legally? How old must a person be to drink alcohol?

3. **Identify** Name two ways to say no to drugs with your actions.

4. **Vocabulary** Define the term *alternative,* and use it in a sentence.

5. **Give Examples** List three healthy alternatives to using drugs or alcohol.

Thinking Critically

6. **Explain** Why do most teens who are substance free have more fun than those who use drugs or alcohol?

7. **Integrate** Write a paragraph to explain why being substance free is essential to a healthy life.

Applying Health Concepts

8. **Personal Health** Work with a partner to think of a situation in which someone might offer you alcohol or drugs. Plan a way to refuse and an alternative to offer. Put on a short skit for your classmates, demonstrating how you would say no. Ask them to suggest other ways to say no in that situation.

9. **Health of Others** Think of a new activity for young people that will provide a healthy alternative to getting involved with alcohol or drugs. Write a letter explaining your activity to the school board, city council, or other appropriate group. Give details about the activity, including suggestions on how to pay for it.

Chapter Summary

► Over-the-counter and prescription medicines can help people avoid or recover from illness if they are used correctly. (Lesson 1)

► A person's reaction to a medicine depends on many factors, including the amount and type of medicine. (Lesson 1)

► Smoking tobacco brings thousands of substances into the body, including some that cause cancer. (Lesson 2)

► Smokeless tobacco is as addictive as other tobacco and can also cause cancer. (Lesson 2)

► Alcohol is a depressant that slows down physical and mental abilities. (Lesson 3)

► Alcohol's effects depend on many factors, such as how much and how fast the person drinks and what other drugs are being taken. (Lesson 3)

► All illegal drugs can have serious physical, social, and emotional effects. (Lesson 4)

► Stimulant drugs speed up body functions, whereas depressant drugs slow them down. (Lesson 4)

► Breaking an addiction is very difficult and requires that the addict take responsibility for changing. (Lesson 5)

► It is important to your health and safety to learn to say no to using illegal drugs, tobacco, and alcohol. (Lesson 6)

Using Health Terms

On a separate sheet of paper, write the vocabulary term that best matches each definition given below.

1. Any reaction to a medicine other than the one intended (Lesson 1)

2. A stimulant drug in tobacco that speeds up the heartbeat (Lesson 2)

3. A depressant drug that is produced by a chemical reaction in some foods (Lesson 3)

4. A physical or mental need for a drug or other substance (Lesson 4)

5. A series of painful physical and mental symptoms that addicted people get when they stop taking a drug (Lesson 5)

6. Another way of thinking or acting (Lesson 6)

Reviewing Main Ideas

Using complete sentences, answer the following questions on a separate sheet of paper.

1. Why does injected medicine work faster than swallowed medicine? (Lesson 1)

2. Name four facts that must be on a prescription medicine label. (Lesson 1)

3. How does tobacco smoke contribute to heart attacks? (Lesson 2)

4. How does someone who is smoking affect people nearby? (Lesson 2)

5. Why does drinking alcohol affect a person's thinking? (Lesson 3)

6. How can a woman's drinking affect her unborn baby? (Lesson 3)

7. What are three prescription drugs that are abused? (Lesson 4)

8. How does marijuana affect the user? (Lesson 4)

9. What are three symptoms of drug withdrawal? (Lesson 5)

10. What is the first step an addict must take to recover? (Lesson 5)

11. What is the legal age for possessing or purchasing alcohol? (Lesson 6)

12. What are three ways to say no to tobacco? (Lesson 6)

Thinking Critically

Using complete sentences, answer the following questions on a separate sheet of paper.

1. **Explain** Why should medicines not be mixed without a doctor's approval? (Lesson 1)

2. **Predict** Write a paragraph or two describing the future of smoking in the United States. Will there be more or fewer smokers than now, and where and when will people smoke? Give reasons for your predictions. (Lesson 2)

3. **Justify** By giving three reasons, defend the position of nonsmokers who say they have the right not to breathe other people's smoke. (Lesson 2)

4. **Deduce** Why might someone's personality change after drinking alcohol? (Lesson 3)

5. **Explain** Why do PCP users not feel pain, which may lead to serious injury and death? (Lesson 4)

6. **Predict** What is likely to happen if an alcoholic enters a treatment program before admitting that he or she has a problem? (Lesson 5)

7. **Explain** Why is someone who offers you a drug not really a friend? (Lesson 6)

Your Action Plan

Making the decision to stay substance free is a big one. Start by looking through your private journal entries for this chapter. Review the reasons you have listed for not using drugs, tobacco, and alcohol. Have these reasons led you to decide to stay substance free? An action plan will help you achieve your goal.

First, write down a long-term goal. For example, you may decide that you will never use drugs—even once. Then list short-term goals to help you meet your long-term goal. A short-term goal might be to learn some methods of saying no to drugs.

Plan a schedule for reaching each short-term goal. You might set aside time to practice how you will respond if someone offers drugs. Your reward for having this lifelong goal will be a healthier, happier life that you control.

Building Your Portfolio

1. Think about some ways that your community would be different if people did not use tobacco, alcohol, or illegal drugs. Describe in writing or in a drawing any advantages you can think of. Add your ideas to your portfolio.

2. Interview a substance abuse counselor at a halfway house or alcohol treatment center. Find out how the counselor helps recovering addicts learn to say no to their addiction. Write a paragraph summarizing what you learn, and add it to your portfolio.

In Your Home and Community

1. Interview one or two adult members of your family. Ask them to share with you some successful ways they found to say no to people when they didn't want to do something that might harm their health. Ask your family members if you can share their methods with your classmates.

2. Gather news articles about car crashes in your community that were caused by drinking and driving. Combine the articles into a collage for a school hallway. You might also ask for permission to read a different article every day for a week during morning announcements.

Chapter 9
Personal Safety in a Healthy World

Student Expectations

After reading this chapter, you should be able to:

1. **Summarize how to act safely at home and on your way to and from home.**
2. **Explain ways to be safe in your community.**
3. **Identify ways to act safely outdoors and in weather emergencies.**
4. **Describe the basics of first aid for emergencies.**
5. **Identify ways of protecting the environment.**
6. **Describe ways to reduce the amount of garbage that is produced.**

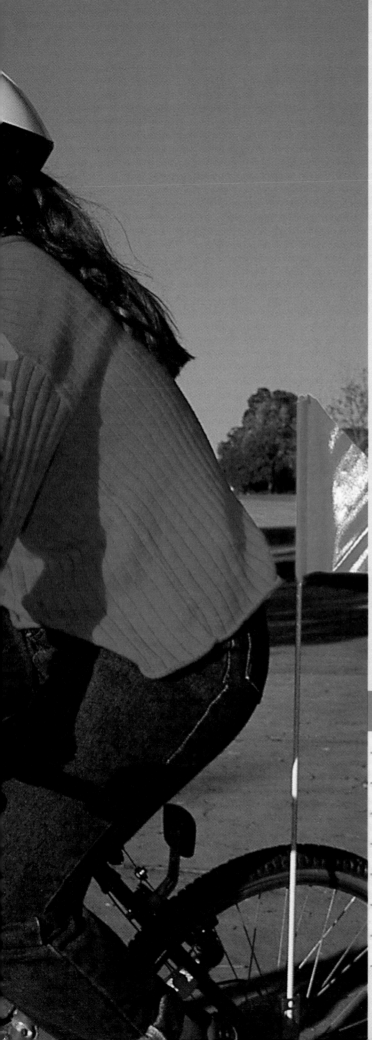

It was just another summer day, or so I thought when I started out on my usual bike ride to the pool. The next thing I can remember is opening my eyes and seeing a doctor and a nurse hovering over me. They told me that I'd been in an accident and had hit my head. I was knocked unconscious. Someone called for an ambulance, and I was taken to the hospital.

The doctor told me that I would be all right as she stitched the gash in my head. My head ached. The doctor asked me questions like "What year is it?" and "Who is president?" My mind was blank on both accounts. She told me that I had a concussion, too. I had to stay at the hospital for a few days. Even now I get tired quickly.

The other day I found out what happened from someone who had seen the accident. I was riding my bike on the wrong side of the road. A man in a car backed out of a driveway and didn't look my way to see if anything was coming. I swerved out of the way so I wouldn't get hit. Instead I bumped into a curb and fell off the bike.

The accident was my fault. My parents and I have talked about how it could have been avoided. We also talked about the bicycle rules of the road.

in your journal

Read the account on this page. Have you ever had an accident or a serious injury? Start your private journal entries for this chapter by answering these questions:

▶ What are some ways that you know of to act safely?

▶ What actions should you take in an emergency?

When you reach the end of the chapter, you will use your journal entries to make an action plan that will help you act safely.

1 Safety at Home and Away

This lesson will help you find answers to questions that teens often ask about their personal safety at home and away from home. For example:

▶ **Why is it important for me to know how to act safely?**

▶ **How can I act safely?**

▶ **What can I do to prevent accidents in my home?**

▶ **What are some safety tips for traveling to and from my home?**

Words to Know

risk
accident chain
hazard
smoke alarm
pedestrian

Building Safe Habits

An important part of being a healthy person is practicing safe habits. This means not taking unnecessary **risks,** or *potentially harmful chances.* Life is full of risks. When you ride your bicycle, you risk falling and hurting yourself. You do not have to stop riding to avoid unnecessary risks. However, you must obey the rules of the road and wear a helmet when you do ride. You can practice safe habits if you know and follow the safety rules.

Acting Safely

Safety rules are based on common sense. These rules help protect you from hurting yourself. To be safe, it is not enough to just know safety rules. You must use the rules you know and act safely. The greatest risks occur when people act carelessly. The following guidelines can help you act in a safe manner.

Figure 9.1
Example of an Accident Chain
Unnecessary risk taking led to this accident.

① The Situation
Tina wants to get a board game that is stored on the top shelf of a closet.

② The Unsafe Habit
Tina climbs on chairs or countertops to reach high shelves.

- **Don't give in to peer pressure.** Perhaps a group of your friends want to ignore a stop sign or cross a busy street before the traffic light turns green. You may be tempted to risk crossing. Remember that you are risking your health.

- **Think before you act.** When you are upset or excited, you may not concentrate on your actions. If you are feeling tired or rushed, you may not act carefully. Always keep your mind focused on what you are doing.

- **Know your own limits.** Do not take needless risks. Set limits before you start an activity. For example, if you are swimming in a lake or ocean, know how far out you can safely swim and never swim alone. If you are a nonswimmer, do not go into deep water until you learn to swim.

The Accident Chain

Many accidents do not just occur. They often happen because of a pattern of five elements known as the **accident chain.** These elements are *the combination of a situation, an unsafe habit, an unsafe act, an accident, and the results of the accident* (see **Figure 9.1**).

Breaking the Accident Chain

Most accidents can be prevented. The accident shown in **Figure 9.1** could have been avoided. The accident chain can be broken if any one of the first three elements is changed.

- **Change the situation.** If Tina had kept the game on a lower shelf, she would not have had to climb up to reach it.

- **Change the unsafe habit.** Tina should break the habit of climbing on chairs and countertops to reach high shelves.

- **Change the unsafe action.** Tina should always use a sturdy step stool when reaching for items on high shelves.

in Your Journal

Before you read this lesson, make a list of safety rules that you already know for each of the following: preventing falls in the home, electrical safety, fire safety, gun safety, highway safety, and safety on wheels. Write the lists in your journal. As you read this lesson, review your lists. Add rules that you forgot or did not know.

❸ **The Unsafe Act**
Tina stands on a chair with wheels to reach the game.

❺ **The Results of the Accident**
Tina sprains her ankle and knocks over a lamp and breaks it.

❹ **The Accident**
Tina falls off the chair.

Causes of Death

In all age groups combined, the most frequent causes of accidental death (in order from most to least common) are:

1. motor vehicle accidents
2. falls
3. poisonings
4. drownings
5. fires
6. choking
7. gunshot wounds

Safety in the Home

You probably think of your home as the comfortable place where you live. However, most homes have some **hazards** (HAZ·erdz), or *possible sources of harm.* These hazards include slippery floors, cluttered stairways, electrical outlets, ovens, and guns. Accidents and injuries caused by these hazards can be prevented by knowing and following safety rules.

Preventing Falls

- Wipe up spills right away.
- Keep steps and stairways well lit and free of objects.
- Fasten rugs firmly to the floor.
- Use nonskid mats in baths and showers.
- Do not run on wet or waxed floors.
- Use a sturdy stepladder to reach items on high shelves.

Electrical Safety

Electricity is a source of energy in homes. It has many uses, including light, heat, and entertainment. If energy is not used correctly, however, it can be very dangerous. Most injuries from electrical hazards can be prevented if you follow safety rules.

- Do not use appliances with frayed wires.
- Pull out plugs by the plug itself, *not* the cord.
- Put only two plugs in an outlet.
- Keep electrical products away from water.
- Do not use an electrical product if you are wet.

MAKING HEALTHY DECISIONS
Safety in a Friend's Home

Vincent and Pedro were friends. Both liked to play sports. They enjoyed the same kind of music. The boys spent much of their spare time together.

One Saturday afternoon, Vincent invited Pedro to come to his house to play basketball. When Pedro got there, Vincent told him that his parents were away for the day.

"I don't feel like playing basketball after all," Vincent said. "I've got a better idea. Let's borrow my dad's hunting rifle for some practice shooting. We can set up tin cans in the woods and shoot at them."

"Doesn't your dad keep the gun locked up?" Pedro asked.

"Sure," Vincent answered, "but I know where he keeps the key. He'll never even know that we borrowed it."

What should Pedro do? He doesn't want to make Vincent angry or risk losing his friendship.

Fire Safety

There are several common causes of fires in the home. They include cooking, cigarette smoking, heating devices, and problems with electrical equipment. By following the safety rules shown in **Figure 9.2,** however, most fires can be prevented. If a fire does occur, a **smoke alarm** can help you escape quickly. This *device makes a warning noise when it senses smoke.*

Figure 9.2
Fire Safety Rules in the Home

In addition to following these fire safety rules, it is a good idea to plan a fire escape route with your family.

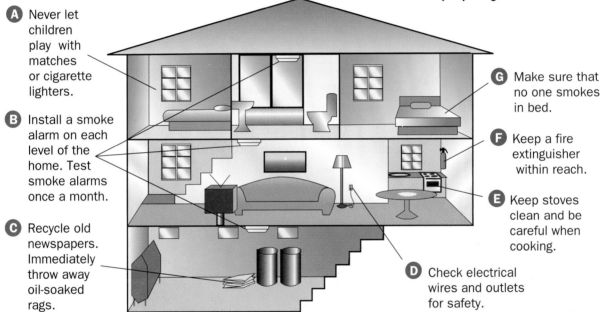

A Never let children play with matches or cigarette lighters.

B Install a smoke alarm on each level of the home. Test smoke alarms once a month.

C Recycle old newspapers. Immediately throw away oil-soaked rags.

G Make sure that no one smokes in bed.

F Keep a fire extinguisher within reach.

E Keep stoves clean and be careful when cooking.

D Check electrical wires and outlets for safety.

However, he doesn't think they should use the rifle without permission. He is also worried about someone getting hurt. To help him make up his mind, Pedro decides to use the six-step decision-making process.

❶ **State the situation**

❷ **List the options**

❸ **Weigh the possible outcomes**

❹ **Consider your values**

❺ **Make a decision and act**

❻ **Evaluate the decision**

Follow-up Activities

1. Apply the six steps of the decision-making process to Pedro's problem.

2. With a partner, role-play a situation in which Pedro explains his decision to Vincent.

3. Think about a situation in which you or someone you know felt unsafe. Write a paragraph describing the situation and how you or the other person handled it.

Gun Safety

In 1993, more than 39,000 people died from gunshot wounds. Thousands more were injured by guns. A gun is not a toy. Safety precautions must be followed when a gun is kept in the home.

■ Guns should be kept in locked cabinets.

■ Guns should be stored unloaded.

■ Children should not handle guns.

■ If guns are carried, the barrel should point downward.

■ Guns should never be pointed at anyone.

Safety on the Way

There are many hazards on your way to and from home. Awareness of them and of the safety rules that apply to them will help you prevent accidents and injuries when you travel.

Highway Safety

A **pedestrian** (puh·DES·tree·uhn), or *anyone who travels on foot,* must always be aware of possible hazards. Accidents involving pedestrians can be very serious. As with most types of accidents, however, pedestrian accidents can be avoided by acting safely and following safety rules (see **Figure 9.3**).

Figure 9.3
Highway Safety Rules

Pedestrians must follow the rules of the road just as drivers do.

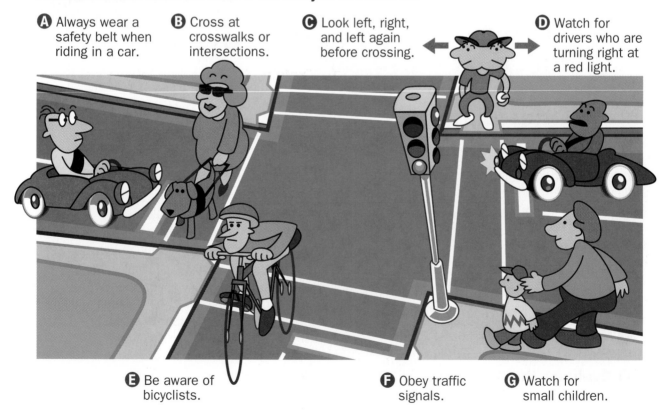

A Always wear a safety belt when riding in a car.

B Cross at crosswalks or intersections.

C Look left, right, and left again before crossing.

D Watch for drivers who are turning right at a red light.

E Be aware of bicyclists.

F Obey traffic signals.

G Watch for small children.

Safety on Wheels

There are two ways you can prevent accidents and injuries while riding a bicycle or using a skateboard or in-line skates. First, know and obey the rules of the road (see **Figure 9.4**). Second, react safely when someone else makes a mistake.

Figure 9.4

Safety Rules for Using Bicycles, Skateboards, and In-line Skates

Regularly check your bike, skateboard, or in-line skates for safety. Be sure they are in good working condition.

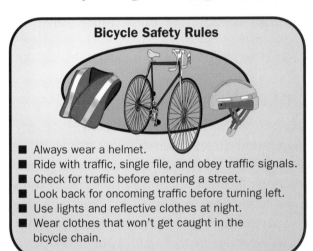

Bicycle Safety Rules

- Always wear a helmet.
- Ride with traffic, single file, and obey traffic signals.
- Check for traffic before entering a street.
- Look back for oncoming traffic before turning left.
- Use lights and reflective clothes at night.
- Wear clothes that won't get caught in the bicycle chain.

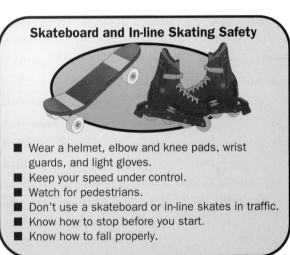

Skateboard and In-line Skating Safety

- Wear a helmet, elbow and knee pads, wrist guards, and light gloves.
- Keep your speed under control.
- Watch for pedestrians.
- Don't use a skateboard or in-line skates in traffic.
- Know how to stop before you start.
- Know how to fall properly.

Review

Lesson 1

Using complete sentences, answer the following questions on a separate sheet of paper.

Reviewing Terms and Facts

1. **Vocabulary** What is the difference between *risks* and *hazards?*
2. **Identify** Name the five parts of the accident chain.
3. **Give Examples** List three safety rules for each of the following: preventing falls, electrical safety, fire safety, and gun safety.
4. **Vocabulary** Define the term *pedestrian.* Use it in a sentence.
5. **List** Name four rules for bicycle safety and four rules for skateboard and in-line skating safety.

Thinking Critically

6. **Explain** Give examples of possible hazards in your home. Explain actions that you could take or have taken to get rid of these hazards and make your home a safer place to live.
7. **Analyze** Why do you think it is as important for bicycle riders to follow the rules of the road as it is for automobile drivers?

Applying Health Concepts

8. **Health of Others** Draw an example of an accident chain and label each part. Exchange your chain with a classmate. Analyze the chain and give three ways in which it could be broken.

Safety in Your Community

This lesson will help you find answers to questions that teens often ask about being safe from crime. For example:

▶ **What causes people to act in violent ways?**

▶ **How can I avoid becoming a victim of violent crime?**

▶ **What is being done to help make my home, school, and community safe?**

Words to Know

violence
carjacking
drive-by shooting
prejudice
hate crime
Neighborhood
    Watch program

in your journal

Have you ever been in a situation in which you were afraid of being a victim of a crime? In your journal, write how you reacted and what you learned from the experience.

Violence in Society

Violence, or *use of physical force to harm someone,* is a very serious problem in the United States. Many violent crimes such as murder and assault involve people who know each other. However, sometimes strangers attack victims at random. Certain random crimes, such as carjackings and drive-by shootings, are reported daily in newspapers and on television. A **carjacking** occurs when *a person steals a car by threatening the driver with a weapon.* **Drive-by shootings** are *shootings that occur from a moving car.* These shootings are especially frightening because very often the victims are innocent people, often children, who just happen to be nearby.

Everyone is affected by violent crime. Victims of crime and their families suffer physically and emotionally. Those who have not been victims may fear that they will be. Financial costs of crime are high, both for victims and for the community. These costs include medical care, police wages, trials, and prisons.

Causes of Violence

People do not agree about why violence is such a problem in the United States. Some people believe that crime has increased as the makeup of families has changed. Others consider changes in moral and social values and lack of respect for others as causes. Whatever the cause, many factors contribute to the occurrence of violent acts.

■ **Anger.** People who have not learned healthy ways to handle anger may act violently in a tense situation.

■ **Drugs and alcohol.** Sometimes people who use drugs or alcohol become violent. In many cases, violence results when people try to buy and sell drugs illegally.

- **Peer pressure.** Teens face pressure from other teens to be part of the group. In some cases, these groups are gangs. Gangs may ask members to commit violent acts to show loyalty. Both gang members and bystanders are killed and injured due to gang-related violence.

- **Prejudice.** *A judgment or opinion about someone that is not based on fact or knowledge of the person* is known as **prejudice** (PRE·juh·dis). This opinion is formed without careful thought. It may lead to **hate crimes,** which are *violent acts against people of a particular group.*

- **Gun possession.** Guns are easily available in the United States. People who don't know how to control their anger may use guns to solve an argument. Other reasons people, especially teens, give for using guns are to make them feel powerful and to impress peers. Guns are especially dangerous in the hands of people who do not value human life and who do not realize what death is.

Being Safe in School

School programs designed to prevent arguments from turning into violence include the following:

- Peer mediation and crisis intervention programs

- Violence prevention programs in which students are taught to respect the feelings, opinions, and values of others

- Counselors to talk with troubled students

- Student assistance programs

- Health education classes

Q & A

Avoiding Gangs ACTIVITY!

Q: I've been bothered and threatened by gang members. What should I do?

A: Ask for help and protection from your family, teachers, school counselor, or police. Talk to your teachers and other school officials about setting up a school-watch program based on the methods of Neighborhood Watch programs (see page 265).

Teens can avoid violence that stems from prejudice by learning about different ethnic groups and how to work together peacefully.

School leaders and police departments are working to keep students safe while they are in school. The following measures are being used to keep weapons and violence out of schools:

- Dress code or uniforms
- Removing lockers
- Metal detectors to search for weapons
- Security guards
- Gun- and drug-sniffing dogs
- Video cameras on school buses and on school grounds

You can help, too. Practice the methods you learned in Chapter 3 to communicate and to settle arguments nonviolently. Use the anonymous hot lines that schools set up to report crimes or people who are suspected of carrying weapons.

As a way to ban gang colors and symbols and help prevent violence, some schools require that students wear uniforms.

LIFE SKILLS
Stranger Safety

Not every stranger is dangerous, but you should learn to recognize behavior that may mean a stranger wants to harm you. Do the following to reduce your chance of being a victim.

▶ At home, do not open the door to anyone you do not know. Keep doors and windows locked.

▶ Do not tell a visitor or phone caller that you are alone.

▶ Before you go out, tell your family where you are going, what route you are taking, and when you expect to be home.

▶ Never get into a car with a stranger. If someone in a parked car speaks to you, do not go near the car.

▶ Do not hitchhike.

▶ Do not go into a building with a stranger who wants to "show you something."

▶ Do not do errands or other work for strangers.

▶ Set up a code word with your family. If a stranger tells you your family has sent for you, ask the stranger to give you the code word.

If Someone Tries to Grab You

▶ Scream and run away.

▶ Go to the nearest place where people are, and ask them to call the police and your parents.

▶ Try to remember what the person looked like and the license number of the car.

Follow-up Activity

With your classmates, create several situations that might be dangerous. For example, a stranger who is lost asks you to take him or her to an address. Brainstorm safe responses to each situation, including methods of saying no.

Being Safe on the Streets

Communities are working to keep the streets safe. Some communities have increased the number of police officers who patrol the neighborhoods. Stricter gun laws have been passed in many communities, and punishments for violent crimes have been increased.

People in many areas participate in **Neighborhood Watch programs.** In these programs, *police train residents to look for and report suspicious activity in their neighborhood.* These programs, along with curfews for teens, drug-free zones, safe-passage routes for young people going to and from school, and neighborhood cleanup programs, help reduce crime in many areas. In addition, some communities offer after-school and summer recreation programs to provide safe activities for young teenagers who may otherwise be home alone or bothered by gangs or drug dealers.

There are several steps you can take to avoid becoming a victim of crime. First, don't look like a target. Walk with a purpose and with confidence. Second, whenever possible, don't travel alone. Third, don't go into areas that are known to be dangerous or that are not familiar to you.

Teen Issues

Getting Rid of Guns

An idea being tried in some communities is a gun buy-back program. People who turn in guns to the police are given money or credit at local stores participating in the program.

Review

Lesson 2

Using complete sentences, answer the following questions on a separate sheet of paper.

Reviewing Terms and Facts

1. **Vocabulary** Define the word *violence* and use it in an original sentence.

2. **Name** What are three factors that contribute to violence?

3. **Vocabulary** What is the relationship between *prejudice* and *hate crimes?*

4. **Give Examples** What are three measures that school leaders are taking or could take to keep weapons out of schools?

Thinking Critically

5. **Analyze** Why do you think lack of respect for others can be considered a cause for the increase in violent crime?

6. **Explain** Why should you avoid going into areas with which you are not familiar?

Applying Health Concepts

7. **Consumer Health** Prepare a booklet in which you put or describe advertisements for movies and television programs that contain violent situations. Explain what effect you think these situations would have on the people watching them.

8. **Growth and Development** Think of one way students can help reduce the amount of violence in the school. Create a poster that presents your idea. Display the poster in the classroom or in the school hallway.

Teens Making a Difference

Letters End Litter

Several years ago, a civics class in a New Jersey school started a letter-writing campaign against a giant international fast-food restaurant chain. The students were concerned about the restaurant chain's use of polystyrene (pah·lee·STY·reen), which is a plastic foam used in packaging. This type of packaging is not biodegradable. It also contains gases that can harm the ozone.

The students wrote to the restaurant chain and asked the company to change the kind of packaging it used. They cited the fact that each year more than 1 billion pounds of the plastic foam were being dumped into the world's landfills.

The students' letter-writing campaign worked. In 1990 the restaurant chain started using paper wrapping materials instead of plastic foam packaging. Since then, other fast-food chains have followed the lead and have also stopped using plastic foam packaging.

Beef Burger

Health Update

UV Index

The National Weather Service recently introduced a new method of warning people about too much exposure to the sun. The Ultraviolet Potential Index rates the potential exposure on a scale of 0 to 15.

Very fair-skinned people are at the greatest risk of health problems related to sun exposure. People with dark skin have less of a risk but should still use protection against the sun.

The index's ratings are divided into five levels. The levels shown below are based on the amount of time that a fair-skinned person who is unprotected could spend in the sun before becoming sunburned.

0–2: Minimal risk of ultraviolet radiation; sunburn may occur after 30 minutes.

3–4: Low risk; sunburn may occur after 15–20 minutes.

5–6: Moderate risk; burn may occur after 10–12 minutes.

7–9: High risk; skin damage can occur after 7–8 minutes.

10 or above: Very high risk; skin damage can occur after 4 minutes.

People at Work

Helicopter Rescuer

Wayne Chang can remember the first helicopter he ever saw. He knew, even at a young age, that he wanted to be a helicopter pilot. He started taking flying lessons as soon as he was old enough.

When Wayne was in college, he developed an interest in helping emergency victims. "I took a course in first aid for emergencies," explains Wayne. "I liked the idea of being able to help someone in trouble. After I graduated from college, I decided to combine my two interests. I became a helicopter pilot for rescue missions.

"The most dangerous rescue mission I ever attempted was saving people from a burning skyscraper. I was able to land on the roof since the flames hadn't reached that far. I saved five people that day. It was a great feeling.

"My work can be dangerous," said Wayne, "but it's also very rewarding."

Myths and Realities

Buckle Up for Safety

People who don't wear safety belts often have excuses that are false.

Myth: Safety belts are necessary only for long trips or when traveling at high speeds.

Fact: About 75 percent of all traffic accidents happen within 25 miles of home and at speeds under 40 miles per hour.

Myth: Safety belts trap people in their cars. It's better to be thrown clear of the car in a crash.

Fact: Most people who are thrown clear of their cars go through the windshield or land on the pavement—and most of them die.

CON$UMER FOCU$

Get in Line to Buy Skates

Are you thinking about buying a pair of in-line skates? Here are some tips:

- Buy skate boots that fit you now. Don't buy them so big that you can still wear them a year from now. Make sure that you have the correct ankle support, which may help prevent an injury.

- The rear of the boot should have a brake made of hard rubber. Make sure that you can control a quick stop.

- The part of the skate that holds the wheels is called the frame. Make sure that the frame is hard. If you can bend it, don't buy it.

- Inside the wheels are the ball bearings. Make sure they turn smoothly when you spin the wheel.

- Buy softer wheels for skating on sidewalks, harder wheels for rinks.

- Most important, be sure to buy and use safety equipment: a helmet and elbow, wrist, and knee pads.

Lesson

3

Safety Outdoors and in Weather Emergencies

This lesson will help you find answers to questions that teens often ask about safety outdoors and in weather emergencies. For example:

▶ **Why should I have a "buddy" when I am involved in outdoor activities?**

▶ **What do I need to know about water safety to prevent drowning?**

▶ **What are some safety tips that I need to know for camping or for winter sports?**

Words to Know

hypothermia
earthquake
hurricane
tornado
tornado watch
tornado warning

Art Connection

Safety Rules

Choose a water safety rule from those discussed in this lesson. Create a poster to illustrate the rule. Write a catchy slogan and put it at the top of the poster. Display the poster in your school.

Being Safe Outdoors

Safety is just as important outdoors as it is in your home. By following basic safety rules and not taking unnecessary risks, you can have safe outdoor fun. Plan ahead and follow these guidelines for outdoor safety:

■ Use the buddy system. This is an agreement between two people to stay together and watch for each other's safety. In case of an emergency, you can help one another.

■ Know your limits. Be aware of your abilities and skills before starting an activity. For example, if you have never been hiking before, don't hike in a rugged or unmarked area.

■ Use the proper equipment for an activity.

■ Be aware of weather conditions and forecasts. Avoid electrical storms, extreme heat, and extreme cold.

■ Learn the safety rules that apply to the activity you will do.

■ Warm up before exercising, and cool down afterwards.

Water Safety

If you swim, dive, boat, or take part in other water-related activities, you need to know water safety. There are several rules to remember. The first and most important rule is to learn to swim well. You can take swimming lessons at school or at a community pool. You will be less likely to panic in a water emergency if you are a good swimmer. The second important water-safety rule to remember is not to go in or on the water alone. Go to pools or beaches that have a lifeguard on duty. You should also use the buddy system.

Another point to keep in mind is not to swim right after eating a heavy meal. Doing so might cause your muscles to tighten, making it difficult to swim easily. You should also be well rested before swimming to reduce the likelihood of problems.

If you ever feel that you are in danger of drowning, do not panic. Keep calm, call for help, and use the technique known as drowning prevention (see **Figure 9.5**). This technique uses breathing slowly and treading water to prevent drowning.

Diving is fun, but it is also a major cause of injuries. You should not try diving unless you have had lessons. To dive safely, always check to see how deep the water is before diving. If you are not sure of the depth, walk into the water first. Never dive into an aboveground pool or into shallow water. Before diving, be sure there are no people or objects in the area.

Boating is another enjoyable water activity. The most important safety rule for boating is to always wear a life jacket. You should also know the correct way to handle the boat. Before using the boat, check to make sure that it is in good condition and do not overload it. If the boat is small, try to avoid standing up and moving around so that you will not fall out. Falling into cold water puts you at risk of **hypothermia** (hy·poh·THER·mee·uh), or a *sudden drop in body temperature.* If hypothermia occurs, put on dry clothes and get warmed up quickly.

Your Total Health

Lightning Strikes

Lightning can be very dangerous. If you see lightning while you are swimming, get out of the water right away. Water conducts electricity. If you are caught outdoors during an electrical storm, try to find shelter in a building or vehicle. Do not stand under a tree, because lightning strikes the tallest object in the area.

Figure 9.5
Drowning Prevention

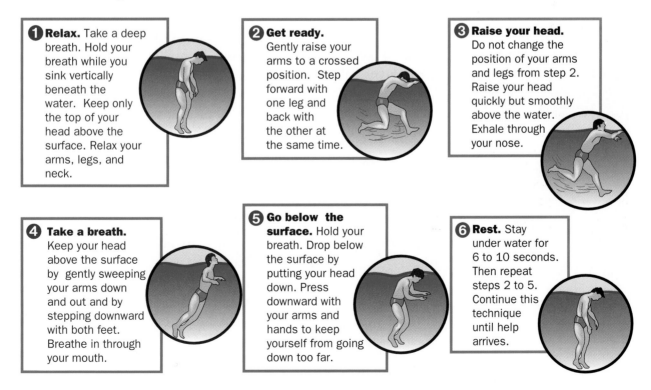

❶ **Relax.** Take a deep breath. Hold your breath while you sink vertically beneath the water. Keep only the top of your head above the surface. Relax your arms, legs, and neck.

❷ **Get ready.** Gently raise your arms to a crossed position. Step forward with one leg and back with the other at the same time.

❸ **Raise your head.** Do not change the position of your arms and legs from step 2. Raise your head quickly but smoothly above the water. Exhale through your nose.

❹ **Take a breath.** Keep your head above the surface by gently sweeping your arms down and out and by stepping downward with both feet. Breathe in through your mouth.

❺ **Go below the surface.** Hold your breath. Drop below the surface by putting your head down. Press downward with your arms and hands to keep yourself from going down too far.

❻ **Rest.** Stay under water for 6 to 10 seconds. Then repeat steps 2 to 5. Continue this technique until help arrives.

The best place to ice skate is on a supervised lake or at a public rink because the ice has already been tested.

Hiking and Camping

Hiking and camping are popular outdoor activities that require some preparation. By being prepared and following safety rules, you can help prevent injuries. When hiking and camping, follow the guidelines below.

- Wear clothing that is appropriate for the weather and the season. Wear socks and heavy shoes. If your hiking shoes are new, break them in first by wearing them for a few days in your regular routine. Wearing two pairs of socks in a double layer helps prevent blisters.

- Take the proper equipment. Include a first-aid kit, a flashlight with extra batteries, a compass, and a supply of fresh water.

- Never camp alone. Let someone know where you are going and when you plan to return.

- Stay in specified campsites or on marked trails.

- Be able to identify and avoid poisonous snakes, plants, and insects that live where you hike or camp.

- Do not cook in tents. Doing so could cause a fire or cause you to breathe poisonous gases.

- Be sure to put out all campfires. Drown them with water or smother them with dirt or sand and stir them.

Winter Sports

When taking part in winter sports, you should follow the same rules as for other outdoor activities. Winter sports, however, have added risks because of snow and cold temperatures. A good way to protect yourself from the cold is to wear the proper clothing. Lighter than wool, several newer man-made fabrics are better at keeping moisture away from the body. Dressing in many layers of clothing will trap warm air near your body and keep you warm. The outermost layer should be a windproof jacket. Wear a ski mask or scarf to protect your face.

Before starting a winter sport, check out the location. Make sure that the ice is solid before ice skating. If you are going sledding or downhill skiing, make sure that your path is clear. Get a weather report and find out the location of possible avalanche sites. Avoid skiing in those areas.

In extreme cold, it is important to avoid frostbite, or freezing of the skin. Wearing gloves, boots, and extra socks will help protect your hands and feet. If frostbite does occur, it must be treated right away. Get the person who has frostbite indoors and covered with a blanket. Then make sure that the person gets to a doctor as quickly as possible.

Weather Emergencies

As you have learned, following safety rules and being prepared will help prevent injuries during outdoor activities. It is also important to know what to do in case of unexpected outdoor events, such as weather emergencies. Being prepared will help decrease your risks if these events should occur.

Floods

The most common natural disaster is floods. All areas are at risk from floods. Some floods take days to develop, while others develop in a matter of minutes. In the event of heavy rains, listen to local radio or television stations. Be prepared to leave the area and move to higher ground.

If a flood occurs, do not walk or ride in a car through moving water because you can get trapped and swept away. Downed power lines might cause the flood waters to be electrically charged. Flood waters may have polluted the tap water, so do not drink it. Use bottled water instead.

After the flood, the parts of your home that have come in contact with flood waters need to be cleaned and disinfected. Throw out all food that came in contact with flood waters. As you help with the cleanup, wash your hands often with soap and clean water. Learn if the water supply is safe to drink.

Earthquakes

Another natural disaster is an **earthquake.** This occurs as a result of *the ground shaking as the rock below the surface moves.* If you live in an area that has earthquakes, bookcases and tall furniture should be bolted to the wall. If you are inside during an earthquake, stay inside. Brace yourself in a hallway, or crawl under a piece of sturdy furniture. Move away from objects that could fall. If you are outside during an earthquake, stand out in the open. Stay away from buildings, trees, and power lines.

Science Connection

Blizzard Dangers ACTIVITY!

Blizzards are a type of weather emergency in which heavy snow falls. Winds may reach as high as 45 miles per hour. During a blizzard, your visibility is limited to 500 feet or less. Make a list of items that would be useful to carry in a car in case you become stranded in a blizzard.

During an earthquake, most injuries occur when people are hit by falling objects.

Find out which types of weather emergencies occur in your area. Make a list of safety rules for you and your family to follow in case of each type of emergency. Write the list in your journal.

Hurricanes and Tornadoes

A **hurricane** (HER·uh·kayn) is a *strong windstorm with driving rain.* Hurricanes occur most often on the eastern and southern coasts. If you know ahead of time about a hurricane, it is best to go inland. First board up doors and windows and bring in any objects that are outside.

A **tornado** (tor·NAY·doh) is a *whirling, funnel-shaped windstorm that drops from the sky to the ground* (see **Figure 9.6**).

Figure 9.6
Tornado Facts

Tornado Watch   The National Weather Service checks weather conditions for the possibility of tornadoes. The Weather Service will issue a **tornado watch** when *the weather conditions are right for a tornado.* If this occurs, listen to local radio and television stations for further information. Prepare to take shelter.

Tornado Warning   If the Weather Service issues a **tornado warning,** it means that a *tornado is in a certain area and people are in danger.* If this happens, take shelter right away.

Tornado   In the event of a tornado, move to a storm cellar or basement. If you can't do that, go to a hallway or other place that does not have windows. If you are outdoors, lie flat in a ditch and cover yourself with something protective, such as a blanket or clothing, if you can.

Lesson 3 Review

Using complete sentences, answer the following questions on a separate sheet of paper.

Reviewing Terms and Facts

1. **Recall**   What is the buddy system?
2. **Recall**   What is the most important rule of water safety?
3. **Identify**   List four safety rules for hiking and camping.
4. **Vocabulary**   What is the difference between a *tornado watch* and a *tornado warning?*

Thinking Critically

5. **Explain**   What would you do if your "buddy" wanted to swim out farther than you think you are able to swim?
6. **Describe**   How would you protect yourself from hypothermia and frostbite if you wanted to go sledding with your friends?

Applying Health Concepts

7. **Personal Health**   Draw a layout of your home. On the sketch, indicate the best places to go for safety in the event of a tornado or an earthquake.

First Aid for Emergencies

This lesson will help you find answers to questions that teens often ask about first aid for emergencies. For example:

▶ **What do I do for someone who needs first aid?**

▶ **How can I help someone who is bleeding?**

▶ **Is there anything I can do for a person who is choking?**

▶ **What can I do to help someone who has been burned?**

What Is First Aid?

In an emergency, **first aid** is *the care first given to a person who becomes injured or ill until regular medical care can be supplied.* Knowing how to give first aid can prevent a serious and permanent injury or the death of the victim.

Knowing What to Do

The most important time in an emergency is the first five minutes. You need to remain calm and follow the first-aid steps shown below. Do the steps in the order in which they appear.

1. Rescue the victim. Move the victim only if he or she is in an unsafe location. For example, a victim should be moved if he or she is in danger of being hit by oncoming cars. Never put your own life in danger, however. If you must move the victim, do it as gently as possible.

2. Check the victim's breathing. Be sure the victim is breathing normally. Check the victim's airway. If the airway seems to be blocked, try to clear the airway. Turn the victim's head to the side to prevent him or her from choking on the tongue or mouth secretions. Later in this lesson you will learn what to do if the person is not breathing.

3. Control severe bleeding. If the victim is losing a large amount of blood, you need to stop or slow down the bleeding by applying direct pressure. Later in this lesson you will learn more about controlling severe bleeding.

4. Get medical help. Emergency Medical Services (EMS) can be called in many areas by dialing 911. If possible, stay with the victim and ask a passerby to call for help.

Q & A

Keep Them in Stitches

Q: When does a wound require stitches?

A: If you are giving first aid and you can't tell if a wound needs stitches, it probably does. If the wound is more than one inch long or if the edges of skin do not go back together, stitches are needed. When in doubt, check with a doctor.

Basic Techniques

It is important to know the basic first-aid techniques for life-threatening emergencies. Such emergencies include when a victim is not breathing, is severely bleeding, is choking, has swallowed poison, or has been burned. These victims often cannot wait for professional help. Knowing what to do when someone needs first aid helps you react quickly, carefully, and calmly.

Rescue Breathing

If you are not sure if a victim is breathing, put your ear and cheek close to the victim's nose and mouth. *Look, listen,* and *feel* for air leaving the lungs. Watch for a rise and fall of the chest. If the victim is not breathing, you can perform **rescue breathing.** This is a *substitute for normal breathing in which someone forces air into the victim's lungs* (see **Figure 9.7**). The method used in rescue breathing depends on the victim's age.

in your journal

Take a survey of family members or friends to see if they know how to perform rescue breathing. Ask them to explain the differences in rescue breathing for infants and small children and for adults and older children. Record their responses in your journal. Then compare their responses with the information in this lesson.

Figure 9.7
Rescue Breathing for Adults and Older Children

1 Lift the chin with your fingers. At the same time, place one hand on the forehead and tilt the victim's head back, pointing the chin upward. This opens the airway.

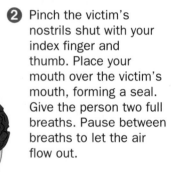

2 Pinch the victim's nostrils shut with your index finger and thumb. Place your mouth over the victim's mouth, forming a seal. Give the person two full breaths. Pause between breaths to let the air flow out.

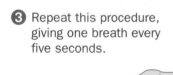

3 Repeat this procedure, giving one breath every five seconds.

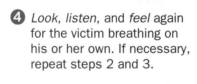

4 *Look, listen,* and *feel* again for the victim breathing on his or her own. If necessary, repeat steps 2 and 3.

When performing rescue breathing on infants and small children ages one to eight, tilt the head back just slightly. Support the head. Do not pinch the nose. Instead, place your mouth over the infant or child's nose and mouth to form a seal. Give one gentle, short breath or puff of air and count to three for infants or count to four for small children. Then give another breath. Repeat at a rate of about 20 breaths per minute for infants and 15 breaths per minute for small children.

Bleeding

If a victim has severe bleeding, it must be controlled right away. Any of the following methods can be used to stop or slow down severe bleeding:

- **Apply direct and steady pressure to the wound.** Use a clean cloth to cover the wound. Then press firmly on it. If the blood soaks through, add more clean cloth. Do not remove the first piece of cloth, however.

- **Use a combination of direct pressure and pressure to a main artery leading to the wound. Figure 9.8** shows where pressure points are found. Push on the pressure point until you feel the bone, and hold the pressure.

- **Carefully raise the bleeding body part above the level of the victim's heart.** This position slows down the movement of the blood from the heart to the body part. If the body part contains a broken bone, however, do not move it.

After the bleeding has stopped, cover the wound with a clean cloth to prevent infection.

Choking

Choking is *a condition that occurs when a person's airway becomes blocked.* As a result, air cannot get to the lungs. The victim can die in a few minutes from lack of air. The universal sign for choking—grabbing the throat between the thumb and forefinger—helps you recognize a choking victim. Other signs of choking are coughing and difficulty breathing or speaking. Choking victims may also turn reddish, then bluish.

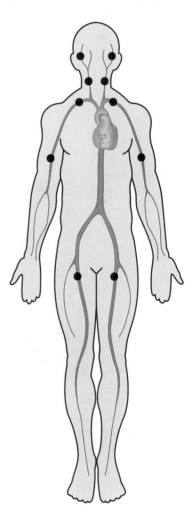

Figure 9.8
Locations of Pressure Points

By knowing where pressure points are located, you can control bleeding by applying both direct pressure and pressure to a main artery.

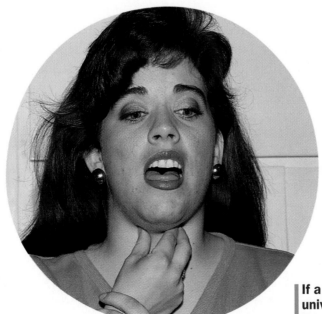

If a person gives the universal sign for choking, he or she needs help right away.

Figure 9.9
Abdominal Thrust

❶ Stand behind the victim. Wrap your arms around his or her waist. Put the thumb side of your fist against the victim's abdomen, just above the navel.

❷ Hold your fist with your other hand. Give quick upward thrusts. Repeat until the object is coughed up.

To help a person who is choking, you must remove the object that is blocking the airway. Follow the first-aid steps shown below for choking.

■ **Infants and small children.** Turn the victim on his or her side (or abdomen for infants). Give several blows with the heel of your hand between the victim's shoulder blades. This may dislodge the object. Sweep through the mouth with your finger and remove it. If this doesn't work, try the blows again. If the object is still not dislodged, turn the victim over on his or her back. Support the back of the neck and shoulders with one hand. Press two fingers into the middle of the child's breastbone. Repeat four times.

■ **Older children and adults.** First ask the person, "Are you choking?" If the person responds positively or does not answer, you can help him or her by using **abdominal thrusts.** This method uses *quick, upward pulls into the diaphragm to force out the substance blocking the airway (see* **Figure 9.9**).

■ **If you are the victim.** Use the universal sign for choking. If you are alone, use the abdominal thrust on yourself. Make a fist and thrust it quickly into your upper abdomen to force out the object you are choking on. You can also lean your upper abdomen over the arm or back of a chair for force.

Poisoning

The skull and crossbones is used to indicate poison. It may appear on containers of poisonous substances. Follow the steps in **Figure 9.10** to help someone who has swallowed poison.

Burns

Burns are identified by how much they have injured the skin. The kind of first aid that you use for burns depends on the type of burn. The three types of burns and the first aid for each are described on the next page.

Figure 9.10
First Aid for Poisoning

❶ Call 911, your doctor, or a **poison control center**—*a place that helps people deal with poisons.* You can usually find the phone number for the center on the inside front cover of the telephone book. You will be asked for your location and for information about the victim and about what happened. Listen for instructions and follow them.

❷ If an ambulance is needed, make sure that the victim is breathing

properly while you wait for it. If the person is cold, put a covering over him or her.

❸ Save the container of poison. Show it to the ambulance team, and explain what you know about what happened.

❹ Use a damp, clean cloth wrapped around your finger to remove extra bits of poison from around the victim's mouth.

A **first-degree burn** is the least harmful type of burn. It is *a burn in which only the outer layer of the skin is burned and turns red.* Examples of this kind of burn include minor sunburns and burns from touching hot water or hot objects. First-degree burns should be cooled in cold water. Keeping the burned area covered with cold water for 10 to 15 minutes keeps air away and helps relieve pain. Then the burn should be wrapped loosely in a clean, dry dressing.

A **second-degree burn** is *a more serious burn in which the burned area blisters.* This kind of burn includes severe sunburn and scalding that cause the skin to blister or peel. First aid for second-degree burns includes cooling the burn with cold water (not ice). Then wrap the burn loosely in a clean, dry dressing. Do not pop blisters or peel loose skin. Elevate the burned area.

A **third-degree burn** is *a very serious burn in which deeper layers of the skin and nerve endings are damaged.* This kind of burn is caused by fire, electricity, or chemicals. The victim of a third-degree burn needs immediate medical help. While waiting for help to arrive, you can cover the burned area with a clean, dry dressing. You can also elevate the feet and arms of the victim and have him or her sip fluids. Do not, however, apply cold water or ice to the burn or remove burned clothing.

Review

Lesson 4

Using complete sentences, answer the following questions on a separate sheet of paper.

Reviewing Terms and Facts

1. **Vocabulary**   Define the term *first aid.* Use it in an original sentence.

2. **List**   Name the four basic first-aid steps to take in an emergency.

3. **Recall**   How can you check to make sure that a victim is breathing?

4. **Identify**   Give the three methods used to control severe bleeding.

5. **Vocabulary**   What is the difference between a *first-degree burn* and a *second-degree burn?*

Thinking Critically

6. **Compare**   How is first aid for choking different if you are helping another person than if you are helping yourself?

7. **Analyze**   Why do you think it is important to save the container if someone has swallowed poison?

Applying Health Concepts

8. **Health of Others**   Work with a partner to create a first-aid handbook for baby-sitters. Include in it first aid for emergencies that may occur with young children, such as choking, bleeding, and swallowing poisons. Share your handbook with the class.

9. **Health of Others**   Illustrate the steps involved in rescue breathing for infants and small children. Next to each illustration, write a short caption describing the step. Share your drawings with the class.

Protecting Our Planet

This lesson will help you find answers to questions that teens often ask about protecting the environment. For example:

▶ **What causes pollution?**

▶ **Why is pollution dangerous?**

▶ **What can I do to prevent pollution?**

Words to Know

environment
pollution
fossil fuel
greenhouse effect
ozone
acid rain
conservation
sewage
biodegradable

The World Around Us

The **environment** (en·VY·ruhn·ment) is *you and all living and nonliving things around you.* This includes people as well as plant and animal life. It includes rivers, hills, and valleys. It also includes the schools, airports, factories, baseball fields, cars, and other things made by people. The air you breathe, the water you drink, and the land you live on also make up an important part of your environment.

Having a healthy, clean environment is important for your health. Unfortunately, the way we live often causes pollution. **Pollution** (puh·LOO·shuhn) is *the changing of the air, water, and land from clean and safe to dirty and unsafe.* Pollution affects the environment in the following ways:

■ **Air.** Pollution problems in the air include smog and acid rain.

■ **Water.** Pollution problems in the water include sewage, oil spills, chemicals, and pesticides.

■ **Land.** Pollution problems in the land include garbage that is placed in landfills and dangerous waste that has been buried underground.

Pollution can damage and destroy parts of our environment that are essential to life.

The Air We Breathe

Most air pollution is given off when we burn **fossil** (FAH·suhl) **fuels.** These are *the coal, oil, and natural gas used to power the engines of motor vehicles and factories.* Other sources of air pollution include cigarette smoke and the burning of trash.

Air Pollution

Air pollution harms people in many ways. It can cause your eyes to water, give you headaches, and make you dizzy or tired. Air pollution can also damage your lungs, causing diseases that make it difficult for you to breathe. Three different environmental conditions have been linked to air pollution.

■ Carbon dioxide is released by many kinds of human activity, including the burning of fossil fuels. When more carbon dioxide is in the air, more heat is trapped on the earth. The **greenhouse effect** is *the name for the warming of temperatures on the earth caused by greater amounts of carbon dioxide in the atmosphere.* Scientists disagree about how serious the greenhouse effect is and how it will affect life on the earth.

■ **Ozone** (OH·zohn) is *a form of oxygen found high above the earth.* A layer of ozone in the upper atmosphere helps to protect us from the sun's harmful rays. Air pollution has begun to damage this protective layer.

■ **Acid rain** is *rainfall that contains air pollution from the burning of fossil fuels.* Acid rain kills trees, plants, and fish. This environmental hazard even damages the steel and stone that are used on the outside of buildings.

Cleaner Air

A major cause of air pollution is automobile exhaust. We can all help make the air cleaner by putting fewer cars on the road. Which of these ideas can you put into effect in your life?

■ **Use cars less often.** Take public transportation such as buses, trains, or subways. Walk or ride a bicycle rather than taking a car.

■ **Ride with others.** Form car pools when you are going to work, school, or other places.

Q & A ?

Radon Risks

Q: What is radon?

A: Radon is an odorless, colorless gas produced by the decay of uranium. It occurs naturally in some soils and rocks. Exposure to radon is the second leading cause of lung cancer. In the open air radon is not dangerous, but inside some buildings radon can reach harmful levels. You can check for radon in your home with a testing kit. High levels can be reduced with simple repairs.

How are these teens helping to reduce air pollution?

Did You Know?

Lead Poisoning ACTIVITY!

A dangerous kind of water pollution is the presence of lead in drinking water. Lead can cause a number of problems, including brain and kidney damage as well as blood diseases. Lead can get into drinking water from the plumbing in a house. Call your local health department for information about testing for lead in water. Write a paragraph about your findings.

Oil spills like this one have a devastating effect on the birds, fish, and other animals that live nearby.

People can also reduce air pollution by the **conservation** (kahn·ser·VAY·shuhn) of energy. Conservation is *the saving of resources.* If less fossil fuel is burned to make energy, less pollution will be created. People can save energy at home by

■ sealing off leaks around windows.

■ keeping doors and windows closed when heat or air-conditioning is on.

■ running appliances at off-peak hours.

■ air drying dishes instead of heat drying them in a dishwasher.

To help fight air pollution, write to government leaders and join groups that work to clean up and protect the environment.

The Water We Drink

Water is important to all life on our planet. Humans, plants, and animals need water to survive. In addition, many plants and animals live in or near rivers, lakes, or oceans.

Water Pollution

Water becomes polluted in many ways. Chemicals may be dumped illegally in rivers and oceans. Large oil spills foul beaches and harm the wildlife. Fertilizers (FER·tuh·ly·zerz) from farm fields enter the water supply. The dumping of **sewage** (SOO·ij) into rivers and oceans occurs almost everywhere in the world. This includes *food, human waste, detergents, and other products that are washed down drains.*

Water filled with these wastes cannot support plant and animal life. People get sick if they eat fish that have absorbed these wastes. People may also get sick from drinking polluted water. Diseases such as cholera and typhoid, which are spread in unclean water, are major threats to humans.

Cleaner Water

You can work to keep water clean. One way to protect our water supply is to use less of it. Listed below are some specific ways you can help prevent pollution and conserve water.

- Try to use brands of detergents and cleaning supplies that are **biodegradable** (by·oh·di·GRAY·duh·buhl). These *products have chemicals that can break down in water without causing problems.* Any detergents and cleaning supplies you dump down the drain eventually end up in our water sources, including streams, rivers, lakes, and oceans.

- Get together with friends to clean litter from rivers and lakes.

- Take shorter showers.

- Have leaky faucets repaired.

- Write to government leaders about your pollution concerns.

These teens are making a difference in their community.

Review
Lesson 5

Using complete sentences, answer the following questions on a separate sheet of paper.

Reviewing Terms and Facts

1. **List** What are three major types of pollution?

2. **Vocabulary** Which of the following are harmful to the environment: *pollution, acid rain, sewage, conservation?*

3. **Restate** How does conserving energy help to reduce air pollution?

4. **Explain** Why does the dumping of sewage in waterways hurt the environment?

Thinking Critically

5. **Relate** In what way is acid rain both an air pollution problem and a water pollution problem?

6. **Predict** What do you think will happen if people do not make an effort to control air and water pollution?

7. **Compose** Create a sample letter to a government official about an air or water pollution problem in your own community.

Applying Health Concepts

8. **Health of Others** Think of a slogan that could help remind people not to pollute the air and water. Draw a poster that features your slogan, adding illustrations as needed. Place your poster along with those of your classmates in your school.

6 Reduce, Reuse, Recycle

This lesson will help you find answers to questions that teens often ask about trash disposal and the environment. For example:

▶ **Where does garbage go?**

▶ **What can I do to reduce the amount of garbage I produce each day?**

▶ **How can I reuse or recycle some of the items I would otherwise throw away?**

Words to Know

landfill
hazardous waste
nuclear waste
recycling

Mountains of Trash

Every day Americans throw out almost a billion pounds of garbage. This mountain of trash contains items as different as food, yard trimmings, discarded furniture, and industrial waste. Where does it all go? Most trash is disposed of in sanitary **landfills.** These are *places where waste is dumped and buried between layers of earth.* Landfills can't take care of all our trash, however. We are running out of space. Also, harmful substances sometimes leak into the soil and even into the water. Other trash is burned. Burning, however, can pollute the air. As a result, this method of trash disposal has been banned in many areas.

Many people feel that Americans should cut down on the trash they produce. Unfortunately, most people don't think twice about tossing out a broken item and then buying a new one. This is

HEALTH LAB

A Throwaway Society

*I*ntroduction: On the average, Americans throw away about 10 percent of the food they buy. Between 50 and 60 percent of garbage in the United States is paper.

Objective: During the next week, record the amount of trash produced at your school. Find out how much trash is thrown out per student.

Materials and Method: Ahead of time, ask the custodial staff to allow you to count the bags of trash produced by your school each day for a week. Ask the main office to report how many students and teachers are at school each day as well. Record your findings on a piece

of paper. Divide the sheet into five columns, one for each day.

Observation and Analysis: Each day, record the number of students at school and the number of bags of trash collected. At the end of the week, figure the average number of bags collected daily and the average number of students attending daily. Divide the average number of students per day into the average number of bags per day. The figure you get will tell you how much trash each student contributes, on the average, daily.

not true in countries where resources are more scarce. There people repair and reuse items instead of throwing them away. Much less trash is produced.

Hazardous Waste

Some types of waste present special problems. Plastics, paints, and chemicals used to kill insects are examples of **hazardous wastes.** These are *waste products that can cause serious illnesses or environmental damage.* **Nuclear** (NOO·klee·er) **waste** is *the radioactive waste left over from nuclear power plants and weapons factories.* Nuclear waste, like many other types of hazardous waste, has been linked to cancer. In addition, this type of hazardous waste takes thousands, sometimes millions, of years to break down naturally.

Ways to Help

One way you can help solve trash-disposal problems is to join with others who are concerned about the environment. Many different local and national organizations work to reduce waste and find ways to dispose of it safely. Just as important, however, you can take personal responsibility for your own part of the problem. You can help by doing the following:

■ Reduce the amount of trash you create.

■ Reuse items whenever possible.

■ Recycle whatever you can. **Recycling** means *recovering and changing items so they can be used for other purposes.*

Social Studies Connection

Cleaning Up Their Act   ACTIVITY!

In 1980 the U.S. government passed the Superfund Act. This act gives the Environmental Protection Agency (EPA) the power to bring lawsuits against people responsible for creating toxic waste dumps. The money recovered in the lawsuits will be used to clean up these dangerous sites. Find out more about the responsibilities of the EPA. Write a one-page report.

Use these figures to determine the volume of trash a typical student produces in a month and in a year. In addition, figure out how many bags of trash your school produces in a year. Discuss with your classmates the possible impact of your school's amount of trash. Discuss ways this amount could be reduced.

Follow-up Activity

Make a list of ways students could reduce the amount of waste they produce. Share the list with the rest of the school. Then help members of your class hold a "Trash Awareness Day." On this day, encourage students to reduce the amount of garbage they produce.

Reducing

Reducing involves thinking, before you buy, about what it will take to get rid of an item. Here are several reducing ideas:

■ Buy goods packed in materials that can be reused, refilled, or recycled, such as paper, glass, aluminum, and cardboard.

■ Avoid products that use more packaging than is needed.

■ Choose biodegradable products whenever possible.

■ Cut down on your use of disposable items.

■ Buy in large quantities. You will use less packaging.

■ Choose cans or glass rather than plastic. Even plastics that can be recycled cannot be reused as often as glass or metal.

Reusing

Another way you can help the environment is to reuse items. You may not realize how many useful items you throw away. **Figure 9.11** shows how some everyday items can be reused.

Figure 9.11
Ways to Reuse Everyday Items

A Reuse grocery bags when you go shopping.

B Turn old tires into play equipment or flower planters.

C Save and pile up yard clippings and household garbage to recycle as fertilizer.

D Use empty cans for storage.

E Save old towels or sheets to wash and dry your car.

Recycling

Recycling is becoming more and more popular in communities across the country. Following are some common recyclable items. Find out where they can be recycled in your community.

- Aluminum
- Batteries
- Cardboard
- Glass
- Oil

- Paper
- Plastic foam
- Some plastics
- Tires
- Yard trimmings and leaves

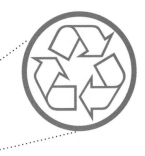

in your journal

Write down some of the excuses you think people might give for not reusing more items or recycling their trash. Choose one of the excuses. Write down a convincing argument that explains why this excuse is not a valid one.

Buy products that have the recycling symbol (see **Figure 9.12**). This symbol is found on many packages that can be recycled and packages that are made from recycled materials. A package may also include the phrase "made from recycled materials."

Figure 9.12
The Recycling Symbol

When you buy a package carrying this symbol, you are helping to reduce waste as well as pollution.

Review

Lesson **6**

Using complete sentences, answer the following questions on a separate sheet of paper.

Reviewing Terms and Facts

1. **Vocabulary** Use the term *hazardous waste* correctly in a sentence.

2. **List** Name three ways you can reduce the amount of trash you generate.

3. **Explain** Explain what it means to reuse an item.

4. **Vocabulary** What is *recycling?*

Thinking Critically

5. **Generalize** Make up a list of three "rules for shoppers" that could help

people choose products and reduce waste at the same time.

6. **Invent** Think of the kind of container that your milk comes in. How could you reuse the container?

7. **Compare** Describe the similarities and differences between reducing, reusing, and recycling.

Applying Health Concepts

8. **Consumer Health** In a small group, brainstorm some products that are overpackaged. Choose one of these products and compose a letter to the manufacturer that explains why you think the packaging is wasteful and how you would package it better. Share any replies with the class.

Chapter Summary

▶ Practicing safe behavior and avoiding unnecessary risks are important for good health. (Lesson 1)

▶ Many factors, including anger, drugs and alcohol, peer pressure, prejudice, and gun possession, contribute to the occurrence of violent acts. (Lesson 2)

▶ Communities and schools are working to keep people safe. (Lesson 2)

▶ Acting safely outdoors includes always staying with a "buddy." (Lesson 3)

▶ Being prepared and following safety rules will help you stay safe in a weather emergency. (Lesson 3)

▶ In an emergency, rescue the victim, check the victim's breathing, control severe bleeding, and get medical help. (Lesson 4)

▶ Basic first-aid techniques are valuable skills. (Lesson 4)

▶ Pollution can be found in the air we breathe, the water we drink, and the land we live on. Pollution is harmful to our health. (Lesson 5)

▶ We can all help keep the environment healthy by reducing, reusing, and recycling. (Lesson 6)

Using Health Terms

On a separate sheet of paper, write the vocabulary term that best matches each definition given below.

1. A device that makes a warning noise when it senses smoke (Lesson 1)

2. Stealing a car by threatening the driver with a weapon (Lesson 2)

3. A shooting that occurs from a moving car (Lesson 2)

4. A strong windstorm with driving rain (Lesson 3)

5. A condition that occurs when a person's airway becomes blocked (Lesson 4)

6. A form of oxygen found high above the earth (Lesson 5)

7. A place that collects and buries waste underground (Lesson 6)

Reviewing Main Ideas

Using complete sentences, answer the following questions on a separate sheet of paper.

1. What three basic safety rules help you act in a safe manner? (Lesson 1)

2. Name and define three kinds of violent crimes. (Lesson 2)

3. What are Neighborhood Watch programs? (Lesson 2)

4. Why is it important to use the buddy system when you participate in outdoor activities? (Lesson 3)

5. How should you dress to protect yourself from cold weather? (Lesson 3)

6. What is rescue breathing? (Lesson 4)

7. What are three signs that a person is choking? (Lesson 4)

8. What is pollution? (Lesson 5)

9. Name three ways that you can help prevent water pollution and conserve water. (Lesson 5)

10. What are three ways that you can help the environment? (Lesson 6)

11. Name five common recyclable items. (Lesson 6)

Thinking Critically

Using complete sentences, answer the following questions on a separate sheet of paper.

1. **Suggest** Name three ways to break this accident chain: Marla is filling the sink with water. She runs to answer the phone without turning off the water. Her sister slips and falls on the overflowed water and hurts herself. (Lesson 1)

2. **Analyze** You are walking to school and a car stops near you. The people in the car have puppies and want you to get in the car to see them. To be safe, what should you do? (Lesson 2)

3. **Explain** Why is it important to stay inside during a weather emergency? (Lesson 3)

4. **Classify** A neighbor has burned her leg with hot coffee. Her leg has blisters. What kind of burn is it and what kind of first aid is needed? (Lesson 4)

5. **Hypothesize** Why do you think pollution has become a bigger problem now than it was many years ago? (Lesson 5)

6. **Analyze** Why is it better for the environment to use rechargeable batteries than batteries that can be recycled? (Lesson 6)

Your Action Plan

There are many ways to keep yourself safe in your home, school, and community. Look back at your private journal entries for this chapter for ideas. Perhaps you want to improve your personal safety. An action plan can help you decide how to go about making changes.

Decide on a long-term goal that you want to achieve, and write it down. Next, think of a series of short-term goals you will set to achieve your long-term goal. Write these down. For example, if your long-term goal is to get certified as a lifeguard, a short-term goal might be to sign up for swim classes.

Plan a schedule for accomplishing each short-term goal. Keep checking your schedule to keep yourself on track. When you reach your long-term goal, reward yourself. Take part in an enjoyable outdoor activity with a friend or family member.

Building Your Portfolio

1. Draw a map of the area around your home and school. Use arrows to show the safest route to take from your home to school or to a place where you go often. Add this drawing to your portfolio.

2. Cut out newspaper and magazine articles about people who have careers in safety training, law enforcement, medicine, and the environment. Write down your thoughts about any of these careers that you might be interested in. Add the articles and your ideas to your portfolio.

In Your Home and Community

1. Create a safety checklist for your home, including possible hazards. Then go through each room and check the items on your list. Tell an older family member if you find anything unsafe. Then ask to post in the kitchen a list of safety checks that should be done periodically, such as testing batteries in smoke alarms.

2. Research statistics about the use of handguns in crimes or in accidents in your community. You might ask for information at the library or at the police station. Use the information to create a poster about the dangers of handguns. Ask to display your poster at school or in a local store.

Nutritive Value of Selected Foods

Nutrients in Indicated Quantity

Foods	Food energy (Calories)	Protein (Grams)	Fat (Grams)	Carbo-hydrate (Grams)	Calcium (Milli-grams)	Iron (Milli-grams)	Sodium (Milli-grams)	Vitamin A value (IU) (International units)	Thiamin (Milli-grams)	Riboflavin (Milli-grams)	Niacin (Milli-grams)	Ascorbic acid (Milli-grams)
Dairy Products												
Cheese:												
Cheddar ...1 oz	115	7	9	Tr	204	0.2	176	300	0.01	0.11	Tr	0
Cottage, lowfat ...1 cup	205	31	4	8	155	0.4	918	160	0.05	0.42	0.3	Tr
Feta ...1 oz	75	4	6	1	140	0.2	316	130	0.04	0.24	0.3	0
Mozzarella ...1 oz	80	6	6	1	147	0.1	106	220	Tr	0.07	Tr	0
Pasteurized process (American) ...1 oz	105	6	9	Tr	174	0.1	406	340	0.01	0.10	Tr	0
Milk:												
Whole ...1 cup	150	8	8	11	291	0.1	120	310	0.09	0.40	0.2	2
Lowfat (2%) ...1 cup	120	8	5	12	297	0.1	122	500	0.10	0.40	0.2	2
Nonfat (skim) ...1 cup	85	8	Tr	12	302	0.1	126	500	0.09	0.34	0.2	2
Chocolate milk (commercial) ...1 cup	210	8	8	26	280	0.6	149	300	0.09	0.41	0.3	2
Ice cream, vanilla:												
Regular ...1 cup	270	5	14	32	176	0.1	116	540	0.05	0.33	0.1	1
Soft serve (frozen custard) ...1 cup	375	7	23	38	236	0.4	153	790	0.08	0.45	0.2	1
Yogurt (made with lowfat milk):												
Fruit-flavored ...8 oz	230	10	2	43	345	0.2	133	100	0.08	0.40	0.2	1
Eggs												
Eggs, fried in margarine ...1 egg	90	6	7	1	25	0.7	162	390	0.03	0.24	Tr	0
Eggs, boiled ...1 egg	75	6	7	1	25	0.7	140	320	0.03	0.22	Tr	0
Fats and Oils												
Butter ...1 pat	35	Tr	4	Tr	1	Tr	41	150	Tr	Tr	Tr	0
Margarine ...1 tbsp	100	Tr	11	Tr	4	0.0	151	460	Tr	Tr	Tr	Tr
Oils, corn ...1 tbsp	125	0	14	0	0	0.0	0	0	0.00	0.00	0.00	0
Salad dressings (commercial)												
French:												
Regular ...1 tbsp	85	Tr	9	1	2	Tr	188	Tr	Tr	Tr	Tr	Tr
Low calorie ...1 tbsp	25	Tr	2	2	6	Tr	306	Tr	Tr	Tr	Tr	Tr
Mayonnaise:												
Regular ...1 tbsp	100	Tr	11	Tr	3	0.1	80	40	0.00	0.00	Tr	0
Salad dressing (home recipe)												
Vinegar and oil ...1 tbsp	70	0	8	Tr	0	0.0	Tr	0	0.00	0.00	0.0	0
Fish and Shellfish												
Fish sticks ...1 stick	70	6	3	4	11	0.3	53	20	0.03	0.05	0.6	0
Haddock, breaded, fried ...3 oz	175	17	9	7	34	1.0	123	70	0.06	0.10	2.9	0
Shrimp, fried ...3 oz	200	16	10	11	61	2.0	384	90	0.06	0.09	2.8	0

Nutrients in Indicated Quantity

Foods	Food energy (Calories)	Protein (Grams)	Fat (Grams)	Carbohydrate (Grams)	Calcium (Milligrams)	Iron (Milligrams)	Sodium (Milligrams)	Vitamin A value (IU) (International units)	Thiamin (Milligrams)	Riboflavin (Milligrams)	Niacin (Milligrams)	Ascorbic acid (Milligrams)
Tuna, canned, drained solids:												
Oil pack, chunk light ... 3 oz	165	24	7	0	7	1.6	303	70	0.04	0.09	10.1	0
Water pack, solid white ... 3 oz	135	30	1	0	17	0.6	468	110	0.03	0.10	13.4	0
Fruits and Fruit Juices												
Apples, raw unpeeled ... 1 apple	80	Tr	Tr	21	10	0.2	Tr	70	0.02	0.02	0.1	8
Apple juice ... 1 cup	115	Tr	Tr	29	17	0.9	7	Tr	0.05	0.04	0.2	2
Applesauce:												
Sweetened ... 1 cup	195	Tr	Tr	51	10	0.9	8	30	0.03	0.07	0.5	4
Unsweetened ... 1 cup	105	Tr	Tr	28	7	0.3	5	70	0.03	0.06	0.5	3
Bananas ... 1 banana	105	1	1	27	7	0.4	1	90	0.05	0.11	0.6	10
Cranberry juice cocktail ... 1 cup	145	Tr	Tr	38	8	0.4	10	10	0.01	0.04	0.1	108
Grapefruit ... ½ grapefruit	40	1	Tr	10	14	0.1	Tr	10	0.04	0.02	0.3	41
Grapes, green seedless ... 10 grapes	35	Tr	Tr	9	6	0.1	1	40	0.05	0.03	0.2	5
Lemonade (from concentrate) ... 6 oz	80	Tr	Tr	21	2	0.1	Tr	10	0.01	0.02	0.2	13
Oranges ... 1 orange	60	1	Tr	15	52	0.1	Tr	270	0.11	0.05	0.4	70
Orange juice (from concentrate) ... 1 cup	110	2	Tr	27	22	0.2	2	190	0.20	0.04	0.5	97
Peaches:												
Fresh ... 1 peach	35	1	Tr	10	4	0.1	Tr	470	0.01	0.04	0.9	6
Canned, in syrup ... 1 cup	190	1	Tr	51	8	0.7	15	850	0.03	0.06	1.6	7
Pears:												
Fresh ... 1 pear	100	1	1	25	18	0.4	Tr	30	0.03	0.07	0.2	7
Canned, in syrup ... 1 cup	190	1	Tr	49	13	0.6	13	10	0.03	0.06	0.6	3
Raisins, snack pack ...	40	Tr	Tr	11	7	0.3	2.0	Tr	0.02	0.01	0.10	Tr
Strawberries:												
Raw, whole ... 1 cup	45	1	Tr	10	21	0.6	1	40	0.03	0.10	0.3	84
Frozen, sweetened, sliced ... 1 cup	245	1	Tr	66	28	1.5	8	60	0.04	0.13	1.0	106
Grain Products												
Bagels ... 1 bagel	200	7	2	38	29	1.8	245	0	0.26	0.20	2.4	0
Biscuits, from mix ... 1 biscuit	95	2	3	14	58	0.7	262	20	0.12	0.11	0.8	Tr
Breads:												
Pita bread, 6½ in diam ... 1 pita	165	6	1	33	49	1.4	339	0	0.27	0.12	2.2	0
Rye bread ... 1 slice	65	2	1	12	20	0.7	175	0	0.10	0.08	0.8	0
White bread ... 1 slice	65	2	1	12	32	0.7	129	Tr	0.12	0.08	0.9	Tr
Whole-wheat bread ... 1 slice	70	3	1	13	20	1.0	180	Tr	0.10	0.06	1.1	Tr

Notes: *Tr* indicates presence of nutrients in trace amounts. All fruits and vegetables are fresh unless noted. Vegetables are fresh cooked unless noted.

Nutritive Value of Selected Foods (continued)

Nutrients in Indicated Quantity

Foods	Food energy Calories	Protein Grams	Fat Grams	Carbo-hydrate Grams	Calcium Milli-grams	Iron Milli-grams	Sodium Milli-grams	Vitamin A value Interna-tional units	Thiamin Milli-grams	Riboflavin Milli-grams	Niacin Milli-grams	Ascorbic acid Milli-grams
Breakfast cereals:												
Oatmeal . . . . .1 cup	145	6	2	25	19	1.6	2	40	0.26	0.05	0.3	0
Cornflakes . . . . .1¼ cups . . .	110	2	Tr	24	1	1.8	351	1,250	0.37	0.43	5.0	15
Crackers, snack-type . . . .1 cracker . .	15	Tr	1	2	3	0.1	30	Tr	0.01	0.01	0.1	0
French toast (home recipe) . .1 slice . .	155	6	7	17	72	1.3	257	110	0.12	0.16	1.0	Tr
Macaroni . . . . .1 cup	190	7	1	39	14	2.1	1	0	0.23	0.13	1.8	0
Pancakes, 4-in diam. . . .1 pancake	60	2	2	8	36	0.7	160	30	0.09	0.12	0.8	Tr
Popcorn:												
Air-popped, unsalted . . . .1 cup	30	1	Tr	6	1	0.2	Tr	10	0.03	0.01	0.2	0
Popped in vegetable oil, salted . . .1 cup	55	1	3	6	3	0.3	86	20	0.01	0.02	0.1	0
Rice, white, cooked . . . .1 cup	225	4	Tr	50	21	1.8	0	0	0.23	0.02	2.1	0
Tortillas, corn . . . . .1 tortilla	65	2	1	13	42	0.6	1	80	0.05	0.03	0.4	0
Legumes, Nuts, and Seeds												
Beans, dry:												
Cooked, drained, black . .1 cup	225	15	1	41	47	2.9	1	Tr	0.43	0.05	0.9	0
Peanuts, roasted and salted . . .1 oz	165	8	14	5	24	0.5	122	0	0.08	0.03	4.2	0
Peanut butter . . . . .1 tbsp . . .	95	5	8	3	5	0.3	75	0	0.02	0.02	2.2	0
Refried beans, canned . .1 cup	295	18	3	51	141	5.1	1,228	0	0.14	0.16	1.4	17
Soy products:												
Miso . . . . .1 cup	470	29	13	65	188	4.7	8,142	110	0.17	0.28	0.8	0
Tofu (2½ by 2¾ by 1 in.) . .1 piece . .	85	9	5	3	108	2.3	8	0	0.07	0.04	0.1	0
Sunflower seeds . . . . . .1 oz	160	6	14	5	33	1.9	1	10	0.65	0.07	1.3	Tr
Meat and Meat Products												
Bacon . . . . .3 slices . .	110	6	9	Tr	2	0.3	303	0	0.13	0.05	1.4	6
Frankfurter, cooked . . . .1 frankfurter	145	5	13	1	5	0.5	504	0	0.09	0.05	1.2	12
Ground beef, broiled . . . .3 oz	245	20	18	0	9	2.1	70	Tr	0.03	0.16	4.9	0
Ham, cooked . . . . .2 slices . .	105	10	6	2	4	0.6	751	0	0.49	0.14	3.0	16
Poultry and Poultry Products												
Chicken:												
Fried . . . . .3.5 oz	220	31	9	2	16	1.2	74	50	0.08	0.13	13.5	0
Roasted . . . . .3.0 oz	140	27	3	0	13	0.9	64	20	0.06	0.10	11.8	0
Vegetables												
Broccoli, cooked . . . . . . .1 spear . . .	50	5	1	10	82	2.1	20	2,540	0.15	0.37	1.4	113
Carrots:												
Raw . . . . .1 carrot	30	1	Tr	7	19	0.4	25	20,250	0.07	0.04	0.7	7

Nutritive Value of Selected Foods

Nutrients in Indicated Quantity

Foods	Food energy (Calories)	Protein (Grams)	Fat (Grams)	Carbohydrate (Grams)	Calcium (Milligrams)	Iron (Milligrams)	Sodium (Milligrams)	Vitamin A value (IU) (International units)	Thiamin (Milligrams)	Riboflavin (Milligrams)	Niacin (Milligrams)	Ascorbic acid (Milligrams)
Cooked, sliced, drained ....1 cup	70	2	Tr	16	48	1.0	103	38,300	0.05	0.09	0.8	4
Celery, raw ....1 stalk	5	Tr	Tr	1	14	0.2	35	50	0.01	0.01	0.1	3
Collards, cooked, drained ....1 cup	25	2	Tr	5	148	0.8	36	4,220	0.03	0.08	0.4	19
Corn, sweet:												
Cooked ....1 ear	85	3	1	19	2	0.5	13	170	0.17	0.06	1.2	5
Canned (cream style) ....1 cup	185	4	1	46	8	1.0	730	250	0.06	0.14	2.5	12
Lettuce, raw:												
Iceberg, pieces ....1 cup	5	1	Tr	1	10	0.3	5	180	0.03	0.02	0.1	2
Leaf, pieces ....1 cup	10	1	Tr	2	38	0.8	5	1,060	0.03	0.04	0.2	10
Onions, cooked, drained ....1 cup	60	2	Tr	13	57	0.4	17	0	0.09	0.02	0.2	12
Peas, edible pod, cooked, drained ....1 cup	65	5	Tr	11	67	3.2	6	210	0.20	0.12	0.9	77
Potatoes, baked ....1 potato	220	5	Tr	51	20	2.7	16	0	0.22	0.07	3.3	26
Spinach, cooked, drained ....1 cup	40	5	Tr	7	245	6.4	126	14,740	0.17	0.42	0.9	18
Tomatoes:												
Raw ....1 tomato	25	1	Tr	5	9	0.6	10	1,390	0.07	0.06	0.7	22
Canned, solids and liquid ....1 cup	50	2	1	10	62	1.5	391	1,450	0.11	0.07	1.8	36
Other												
Cookies:												
Brownies (home recipe) ....1 brownie	95	1	6	11	9	0.4	51	20	0.05	0.05	0.3	Tr
Chocolate chip ....4 cookies	180	2	9	28	13	0.8	140	50	0.10	0.23	1.0	Tr
Sandwich type ....4 cookies	195	2	8	29	12	1.4	189	0	0.09	0.07	0.8	0
Corn chips ....1 oz	155	2	9	16	35	0.5	233	110	0.04	0.05	0.4	1
Doughnuts, cake type ....1 doughnut	210	3	12	24	22	1.0	192	20	0.12	0.12	1.1	Tr
French fries ....10 pieces	110	2	4	17	5	0.7	16	0	0.06	0.02	1.2	5
Gelatin dessert ....½ cup	70	2	0	17	2	Tr	55	0	0.00	0.00	0.0	0
Jam and preserves ....1 tbsp	55	Tr	Tr	14	4	0.2	2	Tr	Tr	0.01	Tr	Tr
Pizza, cheese ....1 slice	290	15	9	39	220	1.6	699	750	0.34	0.29	4.2	2
Potato chips ....10 chips	105	1	7	10	5	0.2	94	0	0.03	Tr	0.8	8
Puddings:												
Chocolate, canned ....5 oz can	205	3	11	30	74	1.2	285	100	0.04	0.17	0.6	Tr
Chocolate, dry mix ....½ cup	155	4	4	27	130	0.3	440	130	0.04	0.18	0.1	1
Syrup, maple ....2 tbsp	122	0	0	32	19	Tr	19	0	0.00	0.00	0.0	0
Taco ....1 taco	195	9	11	15	109	1.2	456	420	0.09	0.07	1.4	1

Notes: *Tr* indicates presence of nutrients in trace amounts. All fruits and vegetables are fresh unless noted. Vegetables are fresh cooked unless noted.

Glossary

The Glossary contains all the important terms used throughout the text. It includes the **boldfaced** terms listed in the "Words to Know" lists at the beginning of each lesson and that appear in text, captions, and features.

The Glossary lists the term, the pronunciation (in the case of difficult terms), the definition, and the page on which the term is defined. The pronunciations here and in the text follow the system outlined below. The column headed "Symbol" shows the spelling used in this book to represent the appropriate method.

Pronunciation Key

Sound	As in	Symbol	Example
ă	hat, map	a	abscess (AB·sess)
ā	age, face	ay	atrium (AY·tree·uhm)
a	care, their	ehr	capillaries (KAP·uh·lehr·eez)
ä, ŏ	father, hot	ah	biopsy (BY·ahp·see)
ar	far	ar	cardiac (KAR·dee·ak)
ch	child, much	ch	barbiturate (bar·BI·chuh·ruht)
ĕ	let, best	e	vessel (VE·suhl)
ē	beat, see, city	ee	acne (AK·nee)
er	term, stir, purr	er	nuclear (NOO·klee·er)
g	grow	g	malignant (muh·LIG·nuhnt)
ĭ	it, hymn	i	bacteria (bak·TIR·ee·uh)
ī	ice, five	y	benign (bi·NYN)
		eye	iris (EYE·ris)
j	page, fungi	j	cartilage (KAR·tuhl·ij)
k	coat, look, chorus	k	defect (DEE·fekt)
ō	open, coat, grow	oh	aerobic (e·ROH·bik)
ô	order	or	organ (OR·guhn)
ȯ	flaw, all	aw	palsy (PAWL·zee)
oi	voice	oy	goiter (GOY·ter)
ou	out	ow	fountain (FOWN·tuhn)
s	say, rice	s	dermis (DER·mis)
sh	she, attention	sh	conservation (kahn·ser·VAY·shuhn)
ŭ	cup, flood	uh	bunion (BUHN·yuhn)
u	put, wood, could	u	pulmonary (PUL·muh·nehr·ee)
ü	rule, move, you	oo	attitudes (AT·i·toodz)
w	win	w	warranty (WAWR·uhn·tee)
y	your	yu	urethritis (yur·i·THRY·tuhs)
z	says	z	hormones (HOR·mohnz)
zh	pleasure	zh	transfusion (trans·FYOO·zhuhn)
ə	about, collide	uh	asthma (AZ·muh)

Abdominal thrust A quick, upward pull into the diaphragm of a choking person to force out the substance that is blocking the airway. (page 276)

Abstinence The avoidance of an activity such as sexual contact or the use of drugs or alcohol. (page 205)

Abuse (uh·BYOOS) A pattern of physical, emotional, or sexual mistreatment of one person by another; using drugs in ways that are unhealthy or illegal. (pages 74, 225)

Accident chain The five interrelated steps that bring about, and result from, an accident. (page 257)

Acid rain Rain that contains pollution from the burning of fossil fuels. (page 279)

Acne (AK·nee) A skin condition in which overly active oil glands cause pimples and other blemishes to develop. (page 40)

Addiction (uh·DIK·shuhn) The body's physical or mental need for a drug or other substance. (page 238)

Adolescence (a·duhl·E·suhns) The period of great growth and change between childhood to adulthood. (page 146)

Adrenaline (uh·DRE·nuhl·in) A hormone released by the body in response to stress, causing heartbeat and breathing rate to increase. (page 85)

Advertising Public messages about a product or service, used to influence people to buy. (page 51)

Aerobic exercise Continuous and vigorous activity, such as running or cycling, that builds the endurance of the heart and lungs. (page 120)

AIDS (acquired immunodeficiency syndrome) A deadly disease caused by the HIV virus. (page 206)

Alcohol (AL·kuh·hawl) A depressant drug that is produced by a chemical reaction in some foods. (page 232)

Alcoholism A disease caused by the physical and mental need for alcohol. (page 243)

Alternative (ahl·TER·nuh·tiv) A choice available to a person about how to think or act. (page 251)

Alveoli (al·vee·OH·ly) Tiny air sacs in the lungs. (page 176)

Amphetamine (am·FE·tuh·meen) A highly addictive stimulant drug. Amphetamines may be prescribed to treat attention disorders in children and obesity. (page 239)

Anabolic steroid (a·nuh·BAH·lik STIR·oyd) A drug based on the male hormone testosterone. When used illegally to increase body weight and strength, steroids can cause serious damage to the body and mind. (page 241)

Antibiotic (an·ti·by·AH·tik) A medicine that kills or stops the growth of bacteria. (page 221)

Antibody A chemical produced by white cells to destroy disease-causing germs. (page 200)

Artery A blood vessel that carries oxygen-rich blood away from the heart. (page 169)

Asthma (AZ·muh) A chronic lung disease in which airways narrow and breathing becomes difficult. (page 214)

Astigmatism (uh·STIG·muh·tiz·uhm) Condition of the eye in which objects appear distorted or wavy because of the irregular shape of the cornea or lens. (page 43)

Behavior How a person acts in situations in life. (page 141)

Biodegradable (by·oh·di·GRAY·duh·buhl) Being made of chemicals that break down in water without polluting the water. (page 281)

Blended family A family formed when two people marry and one or both people have children from a previous marriage. Blended family members not related by birth have a "step" relationship (for example, stepmother). (page 71)

Blood alcohol level (BAL) The amount of alcohol in a person's blood, stated as a percent. (page 235)

Blood pressure The force of blood against the inner walls of the blood vessels. (page 170)

Blood vessel A tube or channel that carries blood throughout the body. (page 167)

Body system A group of organs that work together to help the body perform a major function such as breathing. (page 158)

Brain The organ that is the nervous system's command center, controlling senses, thoughts, and actions. (page 162)

Bronchi (BRAHN·ky) The two tubes branching from the trachea that lead into the lungs. (page 174)

Caffeine (ka·FEEN) A chemical, found in tea, coffee, chocolate, and many cola drinks, that speeds up body processes. (page 115)

Calorie (KA·luh·ree) A unit of heat that measures the energy available in food. (page 116)

Cancer A noncommunicable disease in which abnormal cells grow in an uncontrolled way. (pages 212, 226)

Capillary Any of the tiny branches of arteries and veins that carry blood directly to cells. (page 169)

Carbohydrate A type of nutrient, including sugars and starches, that gives the body its main source of energy. (page 102)

Carbon monoxide (KAR·buhn muh·NAHK·syd) A poisonous gas released when tobacco burns. (page 226)

Carjacking Theft of a vehicle by a person who threatens the driver, often with a weapon. (page 262)

Cartilage (KAR·tuhl·ij) Connecting tissue that covers the ends of bones, cushions bones, and supports soft tissue. (page 181)

Cavity A hole that forms in a tooth, caused by acid. (page 35)

Cell The basic unit, or building block, of all living matter. (page 134)

Central nervous system (CNS) The part of the nervous system made up of the brain and spinal cord. (page 164)

Chemotherapy (kee·moh·THEHR·uh·pee) A treatment for cancer in which strong chemicals are used to destroy cancer cells. (page 213)

Choking A condition that occurs when a person's airway is blocked by food or some other object. (page 275)

Cholesterol (kuh·LES·tuh·rawl) A substance produced in the body and found in animal fats and oils; needed by the body in small amounts. (page 114)

Chromosome (KROH·muh·sohm) Any of the threadlike pieces of matter within a cell that carry the codes for inherited traits. (page 136)

Chronic (KRAH·nik) A disease that lasts a long time. (page 210)

Circulatory system The organs that transport nutrients and other materials in blood throughout the body. (page 167)

Cirrhosis (suh·ROH·sis) A disease in which liver tissue is damaged and scarred. (page 233)

Cocaine (koh·KAYN) A highly addictive stimulant drug that has dangerous, unpredictable effects. (page 239)

Colon (KOH·luhn) The large intestine. This organ collects solid waste. (page 186)

Communicable (kuh·MYOO·ni·kuh·buhl) **disease** An illness that can be spread from one person to another. (page 196)

Communication The exchange of thoughts, feelings, and ideas between people. (page 79)

Compromise (KAHM·pruh·myz) An agreement in which each person gives up some demands in order to reach a solution that satisfies each person. (page 91)

Conflict Disagreement between people with opposing viewpoints. (page 88)

Consequence A result or outcome. (page 19)

Conservation (kahn·ser·VAY·shuhn) The process of saving and protecting the earth's resources. (page 280)

Consumer A person who buys goods and services. (page 50)

Cooling down Slowing one's movements to prepare the body to stop exercising, allowing the heart rate to decrease slowly. (page 127)

Couple family A family consisting of two adults who do not have any children. (page 70)

Coupon (KOO·pahn) A piece of paper, offered by stores or manufacturers, that can be turned in for a reduced price on an item. (page 54)

Dandruff White flakes of dead skin that are shed from the scalp. (page 41)

Decibel A unit for measuring the loudness of sound waves. (page 46)

Decision A choice a person makes about what action to take. (page 16)

Depressant (di·PRE·suhnt) A drug that slows down body functions, including breathing and brain activity. (page 239)

Dermatologist (DER·muh·TAHL·uh·jist) A doctor who specializes in treating skin disorders. (page 40)

Dermis (DER·mis) Inner layer of the skin that includes blood vessels, nerve endings, and hair roots. (page 37)

Diabetes (dy·uh·BEE·teez) A chronic disease in which the body cannot use the starches and sugars in food for energy because of problems with insulin. (page 215)

Diaphragm (DY·uh·fram) A muscle that separates the chest from the abdomen. (page 176)

Diet The food and drink a person usually eats. (page 101)

Digestion (dy·JES·chuhn) The process by which food is broken down into a form the body can use. (page 186)

Digestive (dy·JES·tiv) **system** Organs that turn food into energy for the body. (page 185)

Discount store A store that sells products at a lower price than regular retail stores, but which has fewer services and salespeople. (page 54)

Disease Illness of the body or mind that interferes with a person's ability to function normally. (page 196)

Distress Stress that results in a negative reaction. Distress may cause feelings of anger, disappointment, or frustration. (page 84)

Drive-by shooting Firing a weapon from a moving car, often endangering innocent bystanders. (page 262)

Drug A chemical substance that changes the structure or function of the body or mind. (page 220)

Earthquake Movement of the earth's surface caused by a disturbance within the earth's structure. (page 271)

Egg cell The reproductive cell in the female's body. (page 132)

Emotion A feeling such as joy, anger, or fear. (page 78)

Emphysema (em·fuh·SEE·muh) A chronic disease that injures and destroys the tiny air sacs in the lungs, weakening lung function. (page 228)

Endurance (en·DER·uhns) The ability of a muscle group to perform over a period of time without getting overly tired. (page 120)

Environment (en·VY·ruhn·ment) All the living and nonliving things that surround a person. (pages 139, 278)

Epidermis (e·puh·DER·mis) Outermost layer of the skin that makes new skin cells. (page 37)

Excretion (ek·SKREE·shuhn) The process of removing liquid waste material from the body. (page 188)

Excretory (EK·skruh·tohr·ee) **system** The organs that control water balance in the body and get rid of waste. (page 185)

Extended family A family that includes one or two parents and their children as well as other relatives, such as grandparents, aunts, uncles, or cousins. (page 71)

Family The basic unit of society, in which people related by blood, marriage, or adoption meet each other's needs. (page 70)

Farsightedness Condition of the eye in which a person can see faraway objects clearly, but close objects are blurry. (page 43)

Fat A type of nutrient that provides the body with a source of energy. (page 103)

Fatigue (fuh·TEEG) Extreme tiredness of the body or mind. (page 86)

Fertilization (fer·til·i·ZAY·shuhn) The union of two reproductive cells—an egg cell from the mother and a sperm cell from the father. (page 132)

Fetal (FEE·tuhl) **alcohol syndrome** (SIN·drohm) **(FAS)** A group of physical and mental birth defects caused by an unborn baby's exposure to alcohol taken by the mother during pregnancy. (page 234)

Fiber The indigestible part of raw fruits and vegetables and wheat and other grains that helps the digestive system get rid of waste. (page 113)

First aid Care given to an injured or ill person in an emergency until regular medical care can be supplied. (page 273)

First-degree burn A burn that affects only the outermost layer of skin. (page 277)

Fitness The ability to handle day-to-day events in a healthy way. (page 118)

Flashback The experience of feeling the effects from a drug after it is no longer used. (page 240)

Flexibility (flek·suh·BI·li·tee) The body's ability to bend and move. (page 121)

Fluoride (FLAWR·eyed) A chemical substance in toothpaste that helps prevent tooth decay. (page 36)

Food Guide Pyramid A guideline to help people choose what and how much to eat from each of the five basic food groups in order to get needed nutrients. (page 105)

Fossil (FAH·suhl) **fuel** An energy source, such as coal, oil, or natural gas, that is formed from plant and animal matter within the earth. (page 279)

Friendship A relationship between people who like each other and who have similar interests and values. (page 65)

Gene (jeen) A section of a chromosome that is the basic unit of heredity; carries codes for individual traits such as eye color. (page 138)

Generic (juh·NEHR·ik) Type of product that is less expensive than the brand name version of the same product because of plain packaging and little advertising. (page 54)

Goal An aim that a person tries to reach. (page 24)

Greenhouse effect A warming of the earth's temperature caused by an increase in carbon dioxide in the atmosphere. (page 279)

Hallucinogen (huh·LOO·suhn·uh·jen) An illegal drug that distorts reality and causes the user to form images of things that are not real. (page 240)

Hate crime An act of violence against people because they belong to a certain group. (page 263)

Hazard (HAZ·erd) An object or condition that is potentially harmful or dangerous. (page 258)

Hazardous waste Waste material that poses a risk to people or the environment. (page 283)

Head lice Tiny insects that live in the hair, causing itching. (page 41)

Health A state of well-being involving a person's body, mind, and relationships with others. (page 4)

Health insurance (in·SHUR·uhns) A contract or agreement in which a person pays a certain fee to an insurance company, which in turn pays for part or most of that person's medical care. (page 57)

Health maintenance (MAYN·tuh·nuhns) **organization** A group of doctors who give care to member patients. Members pay a

yearly or monthly fee instead of paying for each treatment. (page 57)

Heart The muscle that pumps blood through the body. (page 167)

Heart and lung endurance The ability of the heart and lungs to accommodate the body's need for oxygen during exercise and their ability to return to a normal state after exercise. (page 120)

Heredity (huh·RED·i·tee) The passage of traits or characteristics from parent to child. (page 136)

HIV (human immunodeficiency virus) The virus that causes AIDS. (page 206)

Hormone (HOR·mohn) A chemical that regulates certain body functions, such as growth. (pages 78, 146)

Hurricane (HER·uh·kayn) A storm, usually near a coastline, with strong winds and heavy rains. (page 272)

Hypothermia (hy·poh·THER·mee·uh) A rapid decrease in body temperature. (page 269)

Immune (i·MYOON) **system** The cells, tissues, and organs that fight germs and that remember how to destroy those germs if they enter the body again. (page 199)

Immunity The body's ability to resist infection. (page 200)

Infancy The period of life from birth to one year. (page 144)

Infection Condition caused when germs enter the body, multiply, and harm the body's cells. (page 196)

Inhalant (in·HAY·luhnt) A substance whose fumes produce the effect of a hallucinogen when breathed in. (page 240)

Initiative (i·NI·shuh·tiv) The ability to take action without being asked. (page 151)

Insulin A hormone, made by the pancreas, that regulates the level of sugar in the bloodstream. (page 215)

Interrelated Having a close, dependent relationship in order to do a job. (page 159)

Joint The point of contact between bones. (page 181)

Kidney One of two bean-shaped organs that filter wastes from the blood. (page 188)

Landfill A site where trash is buried in the ground between layers of earth. (page 282)

Ligament (LI·guh·ment) Connecting tissue that holds bones in place at the joints. (page 181)

Liver A gland with many digestive functions, including the breakdown of fat. (page 186)

Long-term goal An aim that a person tries to reach over an extended period of time. (page 24)

Lung One of the two main organs of respiration, where oxygen and carbon dioxide are exchanged. (page 174)

Lymphocyte (LIM·fuh·syt) A white blood cell that helps the body attack germs. (page 199)

Marijuana (mehr·uh·WAHN·uh) An illegal drug from the hemp plant that increases heartbeat and pulse rate. (page 241)

Medicine A drug used to control or treat disease. (page 220)

Melanin (MEL·uh·nin) The cells in the skin's outer layer that give the skin its color. (page 38)

Mineral A type of nutrient, such as calcium or phosphorus, that the body needs to work properly. (page 103)

Misuse Failing to follow a doctor's instructions or label directions about how and when to take a medicine. (page 225)

Muscular system The body system, made up of muscle tissue, that allows the body to move. (page 179)

Narcotic (nar·KAH·tic) A highly addictive drug that is prescribed to relieve pain. (page 240)

Nearsightedness Condition of the eye in which a person can see close objects clearly, but faraway objects appear blurry. (page 43)

Neglect The failure of a parent to give a child basic care, including love, affection, food, clothing, and shelter. (page 74)

Neighborhood Watch program A program in which citizens look out for each other's safety and property. (page 265)

Nervous system The brain, spinal cord, and nerves that together serve as the body's control and communication system. (page 162)

Neuron (NOO·rahn) Any of the long, stringy cells that make up the nervous system. (page 163)

Neutral Not favoring one side over the other in a conflict. (page 92)

Nicotine (NI·kuh·teen) An addictive stimulant drug in tobacco that increases the heartbeat. (page 226)

Noncommunicable disease An illness that is present at birth, brought on by lifestyle, or caused by hazards in the environment. This type of disease cannot be spread from person to person. (page 196)

Nuclear family A family consisting of two parents and their children. (page 70)

Nuclear (NOO·klee·er) **waste** Hazardous waste consisting of the radioactive material left over from nuclear power plants and weapons factories. (page 283)

Nutrient (NOO·tree·ent) A substance in food that is important for the body's growth and maintenance. (page 101)

Nutrition The process by which a living thing takes in and makes use of food; the science that studies how the body uses food. (page 100)

Organ A body part, such as the heart or brain, that is made up of different kinds of tissues that do a specific job. (page 134)

Over-the-counter (OTC) medicine A medicine that is considered safe enough to be taken without a doctor's prescription. (page 220)

Ozone (OH·zohn) A layer of oxygen high above the earth that protects people from the harmful rays of the sun. (page 279)

Pedestrian (puh·DES·tree·uhn) A person who travels on foot. (page 260)

Peer One of a group of people of about the same age who usually share common interests. (page 66)

Peer mediation A process in which specially trained students help other students find a solution to a problem. (page 92)

Peer pressure The influence a person feels to go along with what others in his or her age group are doing or thinking. (page 66)

Penicillin (pen·uh·SI·luhn) A commonly used antibiotic that fights infection. (page 221)

Peripheral nervous system (PNS) The part of the nervous system consisting of nerves branching from the central nervous system to the rest of the body. (page 164)

Personality The sum total of a person's thoughts, feelings, behavior, and habits. (page 139)

Physical dependence A type of addiction where the body needs a substance in order to function. (page 242)

Plaque (PLAK) Sticky material that forms on teeth and contributes to tooth decay. (page 35)

Poison control center A place that provides information about poisons and about what to do if poisoning occurs. (page 276)

Pollution (puh·LOO·shuhn) Any changes to the land, water, and air that make them unclean and unsafe. (page 278)

Prejudice (PRE·juh·dis) An opinion about people that is formed without having facts about or knowledge of those people. (page 263)

Preschooler A child between the ages of three and five. (page 145)

Prescription medicine A drug that can be sold only with a doctor's written order. (page 220)

Prevention Taking steps to stop something unhealthy from happening. (page 8)

Protein A type of nutrient, made of amino acids, that is important for the growth and repair of the body. (page 102)

Psychological dependence A type of addiction where a person believes he or she needs a substance to feel good. (page 242)

Puberty (PYOO·ber·tee) The stage in life when a young person begins to develop the physical traits of an adult of his or her sex. (page 146)

Quackery The practice of selling worthless medical products or services. (page 51)

Radiation (ray·dee·AY·shuhn) A treatment for some cancers in which tumors are destroyed by X-rays and other rays. (page 213)

Recommended (re·kuh·MEN·ded) **Dietary** (DY·uh·tehr·ee) **Allowance** A guideline for the amount of each nutrient the body needs each day; based on age, gender, and activity level. (page 104)

Recycling Recovering material from a product and using it again for another purpose. (page 283)

Reinforce To make something stronger. (page 11)

Relationship (ri·LAY·shuhn·ship) A connection one person has with another. (page 64)

Reliable Dependable; able to be trusted to follow through on a promise. (page 66)

Rescue breathing Emergency method in which someone breathes air into the lungs of a person who cannot breathe on his or her own. (page 274)

Respiratory (RES·puh·ruh·tohr·ee) **system** The organs that bring oxygen into the body and rid it of carbon dioxide. (page 174)

Responsibility The ability to make choices and to accept the consequences of those choices. (page 149)

Risk A chance that may be harmful or dangerous. (pages 19, 256)

Saturated fat Fat found in animal products such as milk and meat as well as in coconut and palm oils. (page 114)

Second-degree burn A serious burn in which blisters form. (page 277)

Secondhand smoke Smoke from burning tobacco that is involuntarily inhaled by nonsmokers. (page 230)

Self-concept The thoughts or ideas people have about themselves; self-image. (page 10)

Self-esteem Belief in one's own worth; self-respect. (page 12)

Sewage (SOO·ij) Substance containing human waste, food, detergents, and other products that are disposed of in drains. (page 280)

Sexual abuse Any sexual activity between anyone and a child. (page 74)

Sexually transmitted disease (STD) A communicable disease that is passed from one person to another by sexual contact. (page 205)

Short-term goal An aim that a person tries to reach within a short period of time. (page 24)

Side effect Any reaction to a medicine that is not expected or desired. (page 221)

Single-parent family A family unit in which the child or children live with only one parent. (page 70)

Skeletal system The bones and adjoining tissues that give the body its structure. (page 179)

Small intestine The organ, resembling a long coiled tube, where most digestion takes place. (page 186)

Smoke alarm A fire safety device in a building that makes noise in the presence of smoke. (page 259)

Snuff Finely ground tobacco that is placed in the mouth instead of smoked. (page 231)

Sodium A mineral in salt that helps control the amount of fluid in the body. (page 114)

Sound wave A vibration in the air that is caused by movement. (page 45)

Specialist (SPE·she·list) A doctor who is trained to diagnose and treat one part of the body or one disease. (page 55)

Sperm cell The reproductive cell in the male's body. (page 132)

Spinal cord A long bundle of nerve cells that runs down the spine and sends messages between the brain and the rest of the body. (page 164)

Starch A complex carbohydrate, found in plant foods such as bread, rice, and beans, that gives the body energy. (page 113)

Stimulant (STIM·yuh·luhnt) A drug that causes an increase in body functions such as heartbeat and breathing. (page 239)

Strength In muscles, the most work the muscles can do at any given time. (page 120)

Stress The body's reaction to changes around it. Stress can be positive or negative. (page 83)

Stressor Anything that causes stress. (page 85)

Sympathetic (sim·puh·THE·tik) Being aware of and understanding another person's feelings. (page 66)

System A group of organs that work together to help the body perform one or more major functions. (page 134)

Tar The dark, thick liquid produced from burning tobacco. (page 226)

Target pulse rate The number of heartbeats per minute at which the heart and lungs get the most benefit from exercise. (page 126)

Tartar (TAR·ter) Hardened plaque on the teeth that threatens gum health. (page 35)

Tendon Connecting tissue that moves bones when muscles contract. (page 181)

Third-degree burn A very serious burn in which the deep skin layers and nerve endings are damaged. (page 277)

Tissue A group of similar cells that work together to perform a similar function. (page 134)

Toddler A child between the ages of one and three. (page 145)

Tolerance (TAHL·er·ence) The ability to accept people as they are; a state in which the body becomes used to the effects of a medicine, requiring greater amounts to get the same effect. (pages 89, 221)

Tornado (tor·NAY·doh) A funnel-shaped column of wind that drops from the sky to the ground. (page 272)

Tornado warning An announcement from the National Weather Service that a tornado has been sighted and that people in that area should take shelter immediately. (page 272)

Tornado watch A message from the National Weather Service that a tornado could develop in a certain area. People in that area should prepare to take shelter. (page 272)

Trachea (TRAY·kee·uh) The windpipe. (page 174)

Tumor A mass of abnormal cells in the body. (page 212)

Umbilical (uhm·BIL·i·kuhl) **cord** A tube through which food and oxygen are carried to a developing baby from the lining of the mother's uterus. (page 133)

Uterus (YOO·tuh·ruhs) The female organ in which a baby grows and develops before birth. (page 133)

Vaccine (vak·SEEN) A substance containing dead or weakened germs that is put into the body to help it develop an immunity to a disease. (pages 202, 220)

Value A belief about right and wrong and about what is important, which guides the way a person lives. (pages 20, 139)

Vein A blood vessel that carries oxygen-poor blood toward the heart. (page 169)

Violence The use of physical force used with the intention of hurting someone. (page 262)

Vitamin A type of nutrient that helps regulate body functions. (page 103)

Warming up Doing movements and activities before exercise to stretch the muscles and slowly increase the pulse rate. (page 126)

Warranty The promise a seller makes to a buyer that a refund will be given or a product will be repaired if it does not work as claimed. (page 52)

Wellness The achievement of a high level of overall health. (page 8)

Withdrawal (with·DRAW·uhl) The physical and mental symptoms felt by a person who is dependent on a drug when he or she stops taking that drug. (page 242)

Glosario

Abdominal thrust/presión abdominal Presión rápida y hacia arriba, que se hace sobre el diafragma, para forzar la salida de algo que esté bloqueando la traquea de una persona ahogada.

Abstinence/abstinencia El evitar una actividad, como el contacto sexual o el uso de drogas o alcohol.

Abuse/abuso Maltrato físico, emocional, o sexual que una persona da a otra; el uso de drogas de una forma que va contra la salud o es ilegal.

Accident chain/cadena de accidentes Los cinco pasos interrelacionados que ocasionan un accidente y que son el resultado de un accidente.

Acid rain/lluvia ácida Lluvia que está contaminada, debido a la quema de combustibles carbónicos.

Acne/acné Una enfermedad de la piel en la que se presentan granos y otros defectos, debido al exceso de actividad de las glándulas cebáseas.

Addiction/adicción Necesidad física o mental de drogas u otras substancias.

Adolescence/adolescencia El período de gran crecimiento y cambio, entre la niñez y la edad adulta.

Adrenaline/adrenalina La hormona que el cuerpo produce en respuesta al estrés y que causa un aumento en los latidos del corazón y la respiración.

Advertising/propaganda Mensajes públicos sobre un producto o servicio y que son utilizados para influenciar al público en sus compras.

Aerobic exercise/ejercicio aeróbico Actividad vigorosa y continua, como correr o montar bicicleta, que aumenta la fortaleza del corazón y los pulmones.

AIDS (acquired immunodeficiency syndrome)/SIDA (síndrome de inmunodeficiencia adquirida) Enfermedad mortal causada por el virus VIH.

Alcohol/alcohol Droga depresora que es producida a través de una reacción química en algunos alimentos.

Alcoholism/alcoholismo Enfermedad causada por la necesidad física y mental de consumir alcohol.

Alternative/alternativa Posibilidad de elección de una persona, en relación a como pensar o actuar.

Alveoli/alvéolo Pequeños sacos de aire ubicados en los pulmones.

Amphetamine/anfetamina Droga estimulante y altamente adictiva. Las anfetaminas pueden ser recetadas para tratar problemas de la atención en los niños y para la obesidad.

Anabolic steroid/esteroide anabólico Droga basada en la hormona masculina, testosterona. Esta droga puede causar graves daños al cuerpo y a la mente, cuando se usa de manera ilegal para aumentar el peso y la resistencia del cuerpo.

Antibiotic/antibiótico Medicina que mata o para el crecimiento de bacterias.

Antibody/anticuerpo El químico producido por los glóbulos blancos, para destruir gérmenes causantes de enfermedades.

Artery/arteria Vaso capilar que transporta la sangre llena de oxígeno, desde el corazón.

Asthma/asma Enfermedad crónica de los pulmones, que causa un estrechamiento de las vías respiratorias y dificultad en la respiración.

Astigmatism/astigmatismo Condición del ojo en la que los objetos se presentan distorcionados u ondulados, debido a la forma irregular de la córnea o los lentes del ojo.

Behavior/conducta La forma en que una persona actúa frente a situaciones de la vida.

Biodegradable/biodegradable Objetos hechos de químicos que se pueden desintegrar en el agua, sin que el agua se contamine.

Blended family/familia incorporada La familia que se forma cuando dos personas se casan y uno de ellos o ambos, tienen hijos de matrimonios anteriores. Las palabras que identifican a los miembros de esta familia, cuando no tienen parentesco de sangre, llevan el sufijo "astro/a" (como por ejemplo, madrastra).

Blood alcohol level/nivel de alcohol en la sangre La cantidad o porcentaje de alcohol, contenido en la sangre de una persona.

Blood pressure/presión arterial La fuerza de la sangre contra las paredes de los vasos sanguíneos.

Blood vessel/vaso sanguíneo Tubo o canal que transporta la sangre a través del cuerpo.

Body system/sistema corporal Un grupo de órganos que trabajan juntos, para ayudar al cuerpo a ejecutar una función como, por ejemplo, la de respirar.

Brain/cerebro El órgano que constituye el centro de comando del sistema nervioso y que controla los sentidos, los pensamientos y las acciones.

Bronchi/bronquios Los dos tubos que se ramifican desde la tráquea y que van hasta adentro de los pulmones.

Caffeine/cafeína Un químico que se encuentra en el café, el té, el chocolate, y muchos refrescos y que acelera las funciones del cuerpo.

Calorie/caloría Unidad de energía que mide la energía contenida en los alimentos.

Cancer/cáncer Una enfermedad no contagiosa que se caracteriza por el crecimiento incontrolado de células anormales.

Capillary/capilar Las pequeñas ramificaciones de las arterias y las venas que transportan la sangre, directamente, hasta las células.

Carbohydrate/carbohidrato Tipo de nutriente, incluidos los azúcares y las harinas, que son la fuente principal de energía del cuerpo.

Carbon monoxide/monóxido de carbono Gas venenoso que se produce al quemar tabaco.

Carjacking/robo de carros El robo de un auto por una persona que amenaza al chofer, a menudo con un arma.

Cartilage/cartílago Tejido contactante que cubre las terminaciones de los huesos, acolchona los huesos y soporta los tejidos suaves.

Cavity/cavidad Hueco que se forma en los dientes y que es causado por un ácido.

Cell/célula La unidad básica de la vida que conforma la estructura de los seres vivientes.

Central nervous system (CNS)/sistema nervioso central La parte del sistema nervioso conformada por el cerebro y la espina dorsal.

Chemotherapy/quimioterapia Tratamiento para el cáncer en el cual se usan químicos muy fuertes, para destruir las células cancerosas.

Choking/ahogo La situación que ocurre cuando el paso de aire de una persona es bloqueado por comida o algún otro objeto.

Cholesterol/colesterol Substancia que se produce en el cuerpo y que se encuentra en las grasas animales y vegetales; esta substancia es necesaria al cuerpo, pero solo en pequeñas cantidades.

Chromosome/cromosoma Las estructuras filiformes parecidas a un hilo, que se encuentran en el núcleo de las células y que contienen los códigos genéticos de las características hereditarias.

Chronic/crónica Enfermedad que dura un largo período de tiempo.

Circulatory system/sistema circulatorio Los órganos que transportan nutrientes y otras materias de la sangre, a través del cuerpo.

Cirrhosis/cirrosis Una enfermedad en la cual el tejido del hígado presenta cicatrices y está dañado.

Cocaine/cocaína Una droga estimulante altamente adictiva y que tiene efectos dañinos e impredecibles.

Colon/colon El intestino grueso. Este órgano colecta los desechos sólidos del cuerpo.

Communicable disease/enfermedad contagiosa Enfermedad que puede ser transmitida de una persona a otra.

Communication/comunicación El intercambio de pensamientos, sentimientos, e ideas, entre la gente.

Compromise/transigir Acuerdo mediante el cual cada persona renuncia a algunas de sus exigencias, con el fin de llegar a una solución que satisfaga a cada una de las otras personas.

Conflict/conflicto Desacuerdo entre personas que tienen puntos de vista opuestos.

Consequence/consecuencia El resultado de algo.

Conservation/conservación El proceso de ahorro y protección de los recursos naturales.

Consumer/consumidor La persona que compra productos y servicios.

Cooling down/enfriamiento Disminución progresiva de los movimientos, con el fin de preparar al cuerpo para la terminación del ejercicio y así permitir que los latidos del corazón disminuyan lentamente.

Couple family/pareja sin hijos La familia que consiste en dos adultos que no tienen hijos.

Coupon/cupón Un papel que ofrecen las tiendas o fabricantes y que se puede intercambiar por un descuento en un determinado producto.

Dandruff/caspa Escamas de piel muerta que se forman en el cuero cabelludo.

Decibel/decibel Unidad de medida, del volumen de las ondas del sonido.

Decision/decisión La selección que hace una persona, acerca de cuál acción tomar.

Depressant/depresor Droga que disminuye las funciones del cuerpo, incluida la actividad del cerebro y de la respiración.

Dermatologist/dermatólogo El médico que se especializa en tratar enfermedades de la piel.

Dermis/dermis La capa profunda de la piel que incluye los vasos sanguíneos, terminaciones de los nervios, y raíces del vello.

Diabetes/diábetes Enfermedad crónica en la cual el cuerpo no puede utilizar las harinas y azúcares de los alimentos y convertirlos en energía, debido a problemas con la insulina.

Diaphragm/diafragma El músculo que separa el pecho del abdomen.

Diet/dieta Los alimentos y bebidas que una persona, usualmente, consume.

Digestion/digestión El proceso mediante el cual los alimentos son transformados a una forma que el cuerpo pueda usar.

Digestive system/sistema digestivo Los órganos que transforman los alimentos en energía para el cuerpo.

Discount store/tienda de descuento Tienda que vende productos a precios más bajos que los vendidos por las tiendas regulares, pero que tiene menos servicios y vendedores.

Disease/enfermedad Enfermedad del cuerpo o de la mente que interfiere con la habilidad de una persona de funcionar normalmente.

Distress/angustia Estrés que resulta en una reacción negativa. La angustia puede causar sentimientos de ira, descontento, o frustración.

Drive-by shooting/tiroteo desde un carro Cuando se dispara un arma desde un carro en movimiento, poniendo en peligro a peatones inocentes.

Drug/droga Substancia química que cambia la estructura o funcionamiento del cuerpo o de la mente.

Earthquake/terremoto Movimiento de la superficie terrestre causado por cambios dentro de la estructura terrestre.

Egg cell/óvulo La célula reproductiva del cuerpo femenino.

Emotion/emoción Sentimientos tales como la alegría, la ira, o el miedo.

Emphysema/enfisema Enfermedad crónica que daña y destruye los pequeños sacos de aire en los pulmones y que debilita el funcionamiento de los pulmones.

Endurance/resistencia La habilidad de un grupo de músculos de funcionar durante un período de tiempo, sin cansarse demasiado.

Environment/medio ambiente Las criaturas vivientes y los objetos inanimados que rodean a una persona.

Epidermis/epidermis La capa más externa de la piel, que produce las células de la piel.

Excretion/excreción El proceso de remoción de los desechos líquidos del cuerpo.

Excretory system/sistema excretorio Los órganos que controlan el balance del agua en el cuerpo y que expulsan los desechos del cuerpo.

Extended family/familia extendida Una familia que incluye uno o dos de los padres y sus hijos y además otros parientes como los abuelos, tíos, tías, o primos.

Family/familia La unidad básica de la sociedad, en la cual personas relacionadas por parentesco sanguíneo, matrimonio o adopción, satisfacen sus necesidades entre sí.

Farsightedness/hipermetropía Condición del ojo en la cual una persona puede ver claramente los objetos a distancia, pero los objetos cercanos se le aparecen borrosos.

Fat/grasa Un tipo de nutriente que proporciona al cuerpo una fuente de energía.

Fatigue/fatiga Extremo cansancio del cuerpo o de la mente.

Fertilization/fertilización La unión de dos células reproductivas, el óvulo de la madre y el espermatozoide del padre.

Fetal alcohol syndrome/síndrome de alcoholismo fetal Grupo de defectos de nacimiento, físicos y mentales, causados por la exposición del feto a los efectos del alcohol consumido por la madre, durante el embarazo.

Fiber/fibra La parte no digerible de las frutas y vegetales crudos, el trigo y otros granos, y que ayuda al sistema digestivo a liberarse de los desechos.

First aid/primeros auxilios Cuidados que se dan a una persona herida o enferma, durante una emergencia y hasta tanto se obtiene ayuda médica regular.

First-degree burn/quemadura de primer grado Quemadura que afecta solo la capa externa de la piel.

Fitness/buena salud La habilidad de manejar eventos de la vida diaria, de una manera saludable.

Flashback/experiencia retrospectiva La experiencia de sentir los efectos de una droga, después que ya no se consume.

Flexibility/flexibilidad La habilidad del cuerpo de doblarse y moverse.

Fluoride/fluoruro Substancia química en la crema dental que ayuda a prevenir las caries dentales.

Food Guide Pyramid/Pirámide de Alimentos Una guía que ayuda a la gente a elegir sus alimentos y a decidir cuanto comer, de cada uno de los cinco grupos básicos de alimentos, con el fin de obtener los nutrientes necesarios.

Fossil fuel/combustible fósil Una fuente de energía, como el carbón, el petróleo, o el gas natural, que se forma de materia animal o vegetal, dentro de la tierra.

Friendship/amistad La relación entre personas que se gustan y que tienen intereses y valores similares.

Gene/gen La sección de un cromosoma que es la unidad básica de la herencia; los genes contienen los códigos de las características individuales, como el color de los ojos.

Generic/genérico Tipo de producto que es menos caro que las versiones similares de marca del mismo producto, debido a que su empaque es simple y tiene poca propaganda.

Goal/meta Un objetivo que una persona trata de alcanzar.

Greenhouse effect/efecto de invernadero El calentamiento de la temperatura de la tierra, causado por el aumento del dióxido de carbono en la atmósfera.

Hallucinogen/alucinógeno Droga ilegal que distorciona la realidad y que causa a la persona que la usa, la formación de imágenes irreales de las cosas.

Hate crime/crimen por odio Un acto violento contra una persona, debido a que pertenece a un grupo determinado.

Hazard/peligro Un objeto o condición que es potencialmente dañino o peligroso.

Hazardous waste/desperdicios peligrosos Material de desechos que presentan un peligro para la gente o el medio ambiente.

Head lice/piojos Insectos muy pequeños que viven en el pelo y causan picazón.

Health/salud Estado de bienestar que incluye el cuerpo y la mente de una persona y sus relaciones con los demás.

Health insurance/seguro de salud Contrato o acuerdo mediante el cual una persona paga una determinada cantidad de dinero a una compañía de seguros, a cambio del pago por esta compañía, de parte o la mayor parte de los gastos médicos de esa persona.

Health maintenance organization/ organización para el mantenimiento de la salud Un grupo de médicos que proporcionan cuidados médicos a los pacientes miembros. Por su parte los miembros pagan una cantidad mensual o anual, en lugar de pagar por cada tratamiento.

Heart/corazón El músculo que bombea la sangre a través del cuerpo.

Heart and lung endurance/resistencia del corazón y los pulmones La habilidad del corazón y los pulmones de satisfacer la necesidad de oxígeno del cuerpo, durante el ejercicio y la habilidad de volver al estado normal después del ejercicio.

Heredity/herencia La transferencia de características de padres a hijos.

HIV (human immunodeficiency virus)/ VIH (virus de inmunodeficiencia humana) El virus que causa el SIDA.

Hormone/hormona El químico que regula ciertas funciones del cuerpo, como el crecimiento.

Hurricane/huracán Tormenta, generalmente cerca de la costa, con fuertes vientos y lluvias.

Hypothermia/hipotermia Disminución rápida de la temperatura del cuerpo.

Immune system/sistema de inmunización Las células, tejidos, y órganos que combaten los gérmenes y que recuerdan como destruir esos gérmenes si estos invaden el cuerpo nuevamente.

Immunity/inmunidad La habilidad del cuerpo de combatir las infecciones.

Infancy/infancia El período de vida desde el nacimiento hasta el primer año.

Infection/infección Situación que se causa, cuando gérmenes invaden el organismo, se multiplican, y causan daño a las células del cuerpo.

Inhalant/inhalante Una substancia que produce el efecto de un alucinógeno, cuando se aspiran sus humos.

Initiative/iniciativa La habilidad de una persona de actuar, sin que se le haya solicitado que lo haga.

Insulin/insulina Una hormona producida por el páncreas, que regula el nivel del azúcar en la corriente sanguínea.

Interrelated/interrelacionado Cuando se tiene una relación cercana y dependiente, con el fin de ejecutar un trabajo.

Joint/articulación El punto de contacto entre los huesos.

Kidney/riñón Uno de los dos órganos, con forma de frijol, que filtran los desechos provenientes de la sangre.

Landfill/relleno sanitario El lugar, en el suelo, donde se entierra la basura, entre capas de tierra.

Ligament/ligamento Tejido conector que mantiene los huesos en su sitio, en el lugar donde están las articulaciones.

Liver/hígado Una glándula con muchas funciones digestivas, incluida la disolución de la grasa.

Long-term goal/meta a largo plazo Un objetivo que una persona trata de alcanzar durante un largo período de tiempo.

Lung/pulmón Uno de los dos órganos principales de la respiración, donde el oxígeno y el dióxido de carbono se intercambian.

Lymphocyte/linfocito Una célula blanca en la sangre, que ayuda al cuerpo a atacar los gérmenes.

Marijuana/marihuana Una droga ilegal proveniente de la planta de cáñamo y que aumenta los latidos del corazón y las pulsaciones.

Medicine/medicina Una droga que se usa para controlar o tratar una enfermedad.

Melanin/melanina Las células en la capa externa de la piel, que le dan a la piel su color.

Mineral/mineral Un tipo de nutriente, como el calcio y el fósforo, que el cuerpo necesita para trabajar de forma apropiada.

Misuse/mal uso Cuando no se siguen las intrucciones del médico o las indicaciones de uso, acerca de cómo y cuándo tomar una medicina.

Muscular system/sistema muscular El sistema del cuerpo formado del tejido muscular y que permite al cuerpo su movimiento.

Narcotic/narcótico Una droga altamente adictiva que se receta para aliviar el dolor.

Nearsightedness/miopía Condición del ojo en la cual la persona puede ver claramente los objetos cercanos, pero los objetos lejanos se le aparecen borrosos.

Neglect/negligente El padre o madre que no proporciona a sus hijos los cuidados básicos debidos, como amor, afecto, alimentación, ropa y techo.

Neighborhood Watch program/ programa de vigilancia del vecindario Un programa en el cual los vecinos vigilan entre ellos mismos, la propiedad y la seguridad de todos.

Nervous system/sistema nervioso El cerebro, la espina dorsal, y los nervios que, conjuntamente, sirven como sistema de control y comunicación del cuerpo.

Neuron/neurona Las células largas y fibrosas que constituyen el sistema nervioso.

Neutral/neutral Cuando no se favorece ninguna de las partes, en un conflicto.

Nicotine/nicotina Droga estimulante y adictiva contenida en el tabaco y que acelera los latidos del corazón.

Noncommunicable disease/ enfermedad no contagiosa Enfermedad que se presenta al nacimiento, o es causada por el estilo de vida, o por los peligros en el medio ambiente. Este tipo de enfermedad no puede ser transmitida de persona a persona.

Nuclear family/familia nuclear La familia consistente en los dos padres y sus hijos.

Nuclear waste/desecho nuclear Desechos que consisten en material radioactivo producido por plantas nucleares y fábricas de armas.

Nutrient/nutriente Una substancia en los alimentos que es de importancia para el crecimiento y mantenimiento del cuerpo.

Nutrition/nutrición El procedimiento mediante el cual un organismo viviente ingiere alimentos y hace uso de ellos; la ciencia que estudia como el cuerpo utiliza los alimentos.

Organ/órgano Una parte del cuerpo, como el corazón o el cerebro, formada por diferentes clases de tejidos y que ejecuta una función específica.

Over-the-counter medicine/medicamento sin receta Una medicina que es considerada lo suficientemente segura como para poder ser tomada sin la receta de un médico.

Ozone/ozono Capa de oxígeno situada mucho más arriba de la tierra y que proteje a la gente de los rayos solares dañinos.

Pedestrian/peatón Una persona que se moviliza a pie.

Peer/contemporáneo Una persona perteneciente a un grupo de gente de la misma edad y que generalmente comparte intereses comunes.

Peer mediation/mediación de contemporáneos El proceso mediante el cual estudiantes especialmente entrenados, ayudan a otros estudiantes a encontrar soluciones a un problema.

Peer pressure/presión de contemporáneos La influencia que una persona siente, de tener que seguir las acciones o el pensamiento de los miembros del grupo de su misma edad.

Penicillin/penicilina Antibiótico común que se usa para combatir infecciones.

Peripheral nervous system (PNS)/ sistema nervioso periférico La parte del sistema nervioso consistente en las ramificaciones nerviosas del sistema central y que van al resto del cuerpo.

Personality/personalidad La suma total de los pensamientos, sentimientos, conducta, y hábitos de una persona.

Physical dependence/dependencia física Un tipo de adicción, en la cual el cuerpo necesita una substancia específica para poder funcionar.

Plaque/placa El material pegajoso que se forma entre los dientes y que contribuye a la formación de caries en los dientes.

Poison control center/centro para el control de venenos Un lugar que da información sobre los venenos y sobre que hacer en casos de envenenamiento.

Pollution/polución Cualquier cambio en la tierra, agua, y aire, que los ensucie o los convierta en dañinos.

Prejudice/prejuicio Una opinión sobre la gente que es formada sin que se tengan los hechos o la debida información sobre tal gente.

Preschooler/preescolar Niño o niña entre las edades de tres a cinco años.

Prescription medicine/medicamento con receta Una droga que solo puede ser vendida con la receta escrita de un médico.

Prevention/prevención Pasos que se toman para prevenir que ocurra algo no saludable.

Protein/proteína Tipo de nutriente hecho de aminoácidos, que es importante para el crecimiento y mantenimiento del cuerpo.

Psychological dependence/dependencia sicológica Tipo de adicción, en la cual una persona cree que necesita una substancia para sentirse bien.

Puberty/pubertad Etapa de la vida, en la cual una persona joven comienza a desarrollar las características físicas propias de su sexo.

Quackery/curanderismo La práctica de vender productos o servicios médicos que no tienen ningún valor.

Radiation/radiación Tratamiento para algunos tipos de cáncer en el que los tumores son destruidos por rayos-X y otros rayos.

Recommended Dietary Allowance/ Raciones Dietéticas Recomendadas Guía que recomienda la cantidad de cada nutriente que el cuerpo necesita diariamente y que toma como base la edad, el sexo y el nivel de actividad de una persona.

Recycling/reciclaje La recuperación del material de un producto y su nueva utilización para otro propósito.

Reinforce/refuerzo Hacer algo más fuerte.

Relationship/relación La conexión que una persona tiene con otra.

Reliable/seguro De confianza; persona en la que se puede confiar en que cumple sus promesas.

Rescue breathing/respiración de rescate Método de emergencia mediante el cual una persona exhala aire dentro de los pulmones de una persona que no puede respirar por sí misma.

Respiratory system/sistema respiratorio Los órganos que proporcionan oxígeno al cuerpo y que lo liberan del dióxido de carbono.

Responsibility/responsabilidad La habilidad de decidirse por una opción y aceptar las consecuencias de esa decisión.

Risk/riesgo Una posibilidad que puede ser dañina o peligrosa.

Saturated fat/grasa saturada Grasa que se encuentra en los productos animales como la leche y la carne y en los aceites de coco y palma.

Second-degree burn/quemadura de segundo grado Quemadura seria en la que se forman ampollas.

Secondhand smoke/humo indirecto El humo del tabaco que se quema y que es involuntariamente inhalado por personas que no fuman.

Self-concept/autoimagen Los pensamientos o ideas que la gente se forma sobre sí misma.

Self-esteem/autoestima El creer en el propio valor de uno como persona; respeto hacia uno mismo.

Sewage/aguas residuales Substancia que contiene desechos humanos, comida, detergentes y otros productos y que es eliminada a través de desagues.

Sexual abuse/abuso sexual Cualquier actividad sexual entre cualquier persona y un niño o niña.

Sexually transmitted disease (STD)/ enfermedad transmitida sexualmente Enfermedad transmisible que se pasa de una persona a otra, a través de contacto sexual.

Short-term goal/meta a corto plazo Un objetivo que una persona trata de alcanzar, dentro de un corto período de tiempo.

Side effect/efecto secundario Una reacción a una medicina, que no se espera o que no es deseada.

Single-parent family/familia con sólo la madre o el padre Una unidad familiar en donde uno o varios hijos viven, únicamente, con uno de los padres.

Skeletal system/sistema óseo Los huesos y tejidos adyacentes que dan al cuerpo su estructura.

Small intestine/intestino delgado El órgano que se parece a un largo tubo enrollado, en donde se produce la mayor parte de la digestión.

Smoke alarm/alarma de humo Aparato contra incendio en un edificio, que hace ruido cuando detecta humo.

Snuff/rapé Tabaco finamente molido que se coloca en la boca, en lugar de fumarlo.

Sodium/sodio Un mineral en la sal que ayuda a controlar la cantidad de fluidos en el cuerpo.

Sound wave/onda de sonido Una vibración en el aire que es causada por movimiento.

Specialist/especialista El médico que está entrenado para diagnosticar y tratar una parte del cuerpo o una enfermedad.

Sperm cell/espermatozoide La célula reproductiva en el cuerpo masculino.

Spinal cord/espina dorsal Un largo manojo de células nerviosas que va a través de toda la médula espinal y que envía mensajes entre el cerebro y el resto del cuerpo.

Starch/fécula Un carbohidrato complejo que se encuentra en los alimentos provenientes de productos vegetales, como el pan, el arroz y las habichuelas y que dan energía al cuerpo.

Stimulant/estimulante Droga que causa aumento en las funciones del cuerpo, como los latidos del corazón y la respiración.

Strength/resistencia El mayor trabajo que pueden efectuar los músculos, durante un determinado período de tiempo.

Stress/estrés La reacción del cuerpo a los cambios que se producen a su alrededor. El estrés puede ser positivo o negativo.

Stressor/estresante Cualquier cosa que cause estrés.

Sympathetic/compasivo Estar consciente de los sentimientos de otra persona y poder entenderlos.

System/sistema Un grupo de órganos que trabajan conjuntamente con el fin de ayudar al cuerpo a ejecutar una o más de sus funciones principales.

Tar/alquitrán La substancia obscura y pegajosa que se forma cuando se quema tabaco.

Target pulse rate/velocidad deseada del pulso El número de latidos del corazón, por minuto, en el cual el corazón y los pulmones obtienen el mayor beneficio, durante el ejercicio.

Tartar/sarro La placa endurecida que se forma en el diente y que es una amenaza para la salud de la encía.

Tendon/tendón Tejido conector que mueve los huesos cuando los músculos se contraen.

Third-degree burn/quemadura de tercer grado Quemadura muy seria que daña las capas más profundas de la piel y las terminaciones nerviosas.

Tissue/tejido Un grupo de células similares que trabajan juntas, en la ejecución de una función similar.

Toddler/niño pequeño Niño o niña entre las edades de uno a tres años.

Tolerance/tolerancia La habilidad de aceptar a la gente como es. El estado en el cual el cuerpo se acostumbra tanto a los efectos de una medicina, que necesita mayores cantidades para que la medicina produzca los mismos efectos.

Tornado/tornado Tormenta de fuertes vientos, en forma de torbellino, que gira en grandes círculos y que cae del cielo a la tierra.

Tornado warning/alerta de tornado Un anuncio del Servicio Nacional de Meteorología, de que un tornado está a la vista y que la gente debe refugiarse bajo techo, inmediatamente.

Tornado watch/aviso de tornado Un mensaje del Servicio Nacional de Meteorología que indica que un tornado se puede desarrollar en un área determinada. La gente de esa zona debe prepararse para refugiarse en un lugar.

Trachea/tráquea El conducto del aire, del cuerpo.

Tumor/tumor Una masa de células anormales en el cuerpo.

Umbilical cord/cordón umbilical Un tubo a través del cual los alimentos y el oxígeno son transportados hasta el feto, desde el revestimiento del útero de la madre.

Uterus/útero El órgano femenino en donde el futuro bebé se desarrolla y crece hasta el nacimiento.

Vaccine/vacuna Una substancia que contiene gérmenes muertos o débiles y que se coloca dentro del cuerpo, para ayudarlo a desarrollar su inmunidad frente a una enfermedad.

Value/valor Creencias acerca de lo que es bueno o malo y de lo que es o no importante y que guía a una persona en su forma de vivir.

Vein/vena Un vaso capilar que lleva sangre escasa de oxígeno, hasta el corazón.

Violence/violencia El uso de fuerza física con la intención de causarle daño a alguien.

Vitamin/vitamina Un tipo de nutriente que ayuda a regular las funciones del cuerpo.

Warming up/calentamiento Los movimientos y las actividades que se hacen antes del ejercicio, con el fin de estirar los músculos y aumentar, lentamente, el pulso.

Warranty/garantía La promesa que hace un vendedor a un comprador, de que se le hará un reembolso o que el producto será reparado, en caso de que el producto no funcione de la manera prometida.

Wellness/bienestar La obtención de un alto nivel de salud total.

Withdrawal/retirada Los síntomas físicos o mentales que siente una persona que es dependiente de una droga, cuando deja de tomar esa droga.

Index

Note: Page numbers in *italics* refer to art and marginal features.

Power, conflict over struggle for, *88*
Practicing decision making, 22
Pregnancy
  alcohol's effect during, 234
  care during, 135
  development during, 132–35
Prejudice, 263
Preschoolers, 145
Prescription medicines, 220, *223*
Pressure points, location of, *275*
Prevention of illness, 8
Price, 52
Priorities, setting, 87
Product labels, 53
Products
  buying personal, 50–54
  generic, 54, *223*
Professionals, health, 55–59, 127, 142
Proteins, 102–3, *107*
Protozoa, *197*
Psychological dependence, 242
Puberty, 146. *See also* Adolescence
Pulp of tooth, *34*
Pupil, *42, 45*
  effect of light on size of, *165*

Quackery, 51
Quadrathlon sports event, 15

Rabies, *198*
Radiation, 213
Radon, *279*
Recessive genes, *138*
Recipes, family, *101*
Recommended Dietary Allowances (RDA), 104, 110
Recycling, 283, 285
Red blood cells, 170
Reducing trash, 266, 284
Refusal skills, 248–49
Reinforcement of self-concept, 11, 12–13
Relationships
  during adolescence, 148
  defined, 64
  with family, 70–75
  with friends, 64–69
  importance of, 65–66
Relaxation, 87, 121
Reliability
  of friend, 66
  and responsibility, 152
Reputation of brand product, 52
Rescue breathing, 274
Respect, 23, 153

Respiratory system, *158, 159,* 174–78, *175,* 187
Responsibility, 143, 149–53
Retina, *42*
Return policies, store, 52
Reusing items, 284
Reward for reaching goal, 28
Rh factor, 170
Risks, 19, 256
Roles, conflict over changing, *88*
Root canal, *34*
Root of tooth, *34*
Rubella, *202*
Rural areas, living in, 141

Safety, 256–72
  building safe habits, 256–57
  in community, 262–65
  electrical, 258
  fire, 259
  gun, 258–59, 260
  highway, 260
  in home, 258–60
  medicine, 223–24
  outdoors, 268–70
  in school, 263–64
  with strangers, 264
  on the streets, 265
  in weather emergencies, 271–72
  on wheels, 261
Safety belts, 166, 267
Safety rules, 166
Sales, 52
Sales staff, 52
Saliva, 186, *187,* 199
Salivary glands, *186*
Salmonella, *198*
Salt, 114
Saturated fats, 114
Saving money, 54
Saying no
  to peer pressure, 68–69, *140*
  to substance abuse, 250
Scalp problems, 41
School
  friendship based on, 65
  safety in, 263–64
School counselor, 14
Sclera, *42*
Seat belts, 15. *See also* Safety belts
Second-degree burn, 277
Secondhand smoke, 230
Self-concept, 10–13, 23
Self-esteem, 12, 23
Self-help groups for victims of abuse, 75
Semicircular canals, *45*
Services, buying health, 50–53

Serving sizes of food, *108*
Sewage, 280
Sexual abuse, 74
Sexual activity, and HIV infection, 207
Sexually transmitted diseases (STDs), 205–7
Shampoo, 41
Shelters, 75
Shoes
  for exercise, 126
  for hiking and camping, 270
Shooting, drive-by, 262
Shopping, smart, 52–54
Short-term goals, 24
Shoulder stretch, 184
Side effects, 221, 239
Side stretch, 184
Side vision, measuring, 45
Single-parent family, *70, 72*
Sitting toe touches, 184
Skateboard safety, *261*
Skeletal muscle, 182, 183
Skeletal system, *158, 159,* 179, *180,* 180–81
Skin, 37–40, *38,* 199, *222, 228*
Skin cancer, 38, *39,* 212
Skin cells, *134*
Sleep, benefits of, 39, 165
Small intestine, *186, 187, 222*
Smoke, tobacco
  secondhand, 230
  substances in, 226
Smoke alarm, 259
Smokeless tobacco, 231
Smoking, 226–30
  avoiding, *9*
  death by, *229*
  and eating, *228*
  and fitness, *124*
  harmful effects on body of, 171, 178, 211, *228–29*
  reasons young people smoke, 227
  in workplace, banning, *230*
Smooth muscle, 182
Sneeze, *177*
Snuff, 231
Social health, 4, *5,* 6, *64*
  and exercise, 119
  and expressing emotions, *79*
  and family, 70–75
  and friends, 64–69
Sodium, 114
Solid waste, 187, 188
Sound waves, *45,* 46
Specialists, 55–56
Sperm cells, 132, 137

Credits

PHOTOGRAPHS

Cover photo: Design Office/Curt Fisher.

Action Sports: Robert Matthews, page 185.

Allsport: Tony Duffy, page 111; Rich Stewart, page 77 (left).

Arnold & Brown: page 20.

Jim Ballard: page 22.

The Bettmann Archive: page 72 (left).

© Comstock Inc. 1995: Mike and Carol Werner, page 24 (left).

David Crow: pages xii (top), 194–95, 199, 203, 205, 209.

Duomo Photography Inc.: William R. Sallaz, page 142 (right).

Environmental Protection Agency: page 58.

© FPG International: E. Alan McGee, page 124; Vladimir Pcholkin, page 171.

Gamma Liaison: Sheila Beougher, page 272; L. Van Derstockt, page 280; Charlie Westerman, page 245 (right).

Ann Garvin: page 102 (left).

Richard Hutchings: pages ii–iii, viii, xii (bottom), 2–3, 4, 5 (all), 7, 10, 14 (both), 15 (left), 18, 19 (both), 21, 25, 27, 28 (both), 149, 218–19, 221, 230, 232, 236 (right), 237 (left), 243, 244 (both), 245 (left), 248 (both), 249 (left), 250, 251.

Ken Lax: pages 98–99, 100, 101, 102 (middle, right), 103 (all), 104, 105, 110, 113, 116, 118 (all), 125, 126 (all), 127, 156–57.

Medical Images, Inc.: Howard Sochurek, pages 196, 212.

Cliff Moore: pages 160, 161, 170, 172, 173 (both), 174 (all), 178, 189.

Navajo Nation Museum: James Bosch, page 208 (right).

John Neubauer: page 278.

Peerless Photography: pages 106–8 (all).

© Photo Researchers Inc.: Biophoto Associates, page 165 (both); Junebug Clark, page 249 (right); Peter Miller, page 140 (right).

PhotoEdit: Robert Brenner, page 283; Michelle Bridwell, pages 48, 49 (left), 50, 55, 147; Jose Carillo, pages xvi–1; Mary Kate Denny, pages ix (top), xiii (bottom), 32–33, 47, 57, 89, 150, 246, 263, 264; Amy Etra, page 144 (right); Tony Freeman, pages xi, 37, 43, 44, 49 (bottom right), 73, 130–31, 135, 136, 140 (left), 145 (both), 148, 213, 267 (top), 275; Michael Newman, pages xiii (top), 49 (top right), 76 (right), 267 (bottom), 271, 279; Jonathan Nourok, page 142 (left); Merritt A. Vincent, pages 96–97; David Young-Wolff, pages 39, 40, 137 (both), 139, 143, 144 (left), 152, 192–93, 254–55, 266, 281.

Photri Inc.: David Friend, page 64 (right).

Kathy Sloane: pages 62–63, 64 (left), 66, 72 (right), 75, 76 (left), 77 (right), 82, 83, 90, 91, 93.

Smoke Free Class of 2000: American Cancer Society/American Heart Association/ American Lung Association, page 236 (left).

SportsChrome East/West: Ron Wyatt, page 86.

Sports Illustrated: Rich Clarkson, page 237 (right).

Stock Boston: Bob Daemmrich, page 208 (left); Joseph Nettis, page 24 (right).

SuperStock Inc.: pages ix (bottom), 67; Tom Rosenthal, pages 65, 270.

Volvo Cars of North America, Inc.: page 15 (right).

Terry Wild Studio: page 151.

ILLUSTRATIONS

Ron Boisvert: pages 159, 162, 163, 182, 183, 188, 229.

Max Crandall: pages 13, 16, 17, 56, 69, 79, 92, 101, 119, 179, 198, 256–57, 260.

Hilda Muinos: pages 34, 35, 38, 164 (both), 168, 169, 175, 180, 186, 187.

Network Graphics: pages 6 (all), 36, 40 (all), 42, 45 (all), 51, 53, 80, 84, 85, 88, 100, 114 (all), 115 (all), 123, 124, 132–33, 134, 137, 146, 150, 167, 176–77, 184 (all), 196, 197, 200, 206, 214, 220, 222, 233, 234 (left), 241, 259, 261, 269, 274, 275, 276 (left), 284.

Parrot Graphics: pages 9, 46, 52, 59, 81, 109, 117, 120, 121, 122, 210, 223, 224, 227, 234 (bottom), 238, 240, 247, 276 (bottom), 285.

Precision Graphics: page 181.

Kay Salem: pages 70–71.

Bill Smith Studio: pages 8, 106, 107, 108.

Lou Vaccaro: pages 11, 26, 78, 112, 125 (all), 138.